INTIMATE JAPAN

INTIMATE JAPAN

❖ ❖ ❖

Ethnographies of Closeness and Conflict

EDITED BY ALLISON ALEXY
AND EMMA E. COOK

University of Hawai'i Press

HONOLULU

Printed in the United States of America

24   23   22   21   20   19   6   5   4   3   2   1

Library of Congress Cataloging-in-Publication Data

Names: Alexy, Allison, editor. | Cook, Emma E., editor.
Title: Intimate Japan : ethnographies of closeness and conflict / edited by
    Allison Alexy and Emma E. Cook.
Description: Honolulu : University of Hawai'i Press, [2019] | Includes
    bibliographical references and index.
Identifiers: LCCN 2018003982 | ISBN 9780824876685 (cloth : alk. paper)
Subjects: LCSH: Intimacy (Psychology)—Social aspects—Japan. | Social
    change—Japan.
Classification: LCC HQ682 .I58 2019 | DDC 303.4—dc23
LC record available at https://lccn.loc.gov/2018003982

ISBN 978-0-8248-7335-6 (pbk.)

Cover photo by Photographer Hal. Reproduced with permission.

For Reggie and Kohei

Contents

Acknowledgments

❖ ❖ ❖

As for any ethnographic work, we want to begin by expressing our thanks and appreciation to all the people who were so generous to share their time, ideas, and experiences with the researchers in this volume. We are deeply indebted to everyone who worked with us and thank them for their willingness to share intimate parts of their lives.

Putting together this volume has been a pleasure, with a wonderful group of thoughtful interlocutors. The editors thank the contributors for their hard work and careful thought. Years ago, when this project began, Katrina Moore was also involved. Unfortunately, she wasn't able to participate in this final version, but we acknowledge her many contributions, excellent scholarship, and continued support. Likewise, we thank Nana Okura Gagné for her early involvement and collaboration. We extend our thanks to Glenda Roberts, one of the editorial reviewers, for reading the manuscript with tremendous precision. The volume is stronger because of her suggestions. William W. Kelly generously permitted us to include his reflections in Yukari Kawahara's chapter and helped us as we reframed part of her work. He also gave extensive suggestions to improve the introductory chapter. Stephanie Chun at the University of Hawai'i Press has been supportive throughout this process, and we appreciate the work she did to strengthen the volume as it came to fruition. In the final stages of preparation, Madeline Kahl provided invaluable editorial assistance. We are grateful for Keiko Yokota-Carter's help with licenses and permissions. Finally, we thank Haruhiko Kawaguchi, working as Photographer Hal, for permitting us to use his image on the book's cover. We hope his evocative image conveys both the care and struggle involved in intimate relationships.

The editors dedicate this volume to our partners, in acknowledgment and appreciation of all the support they have given us. We can't imagine dedicating this, of all books, to anyone else.

INTIMATE JAPAN

CHAPTER 1

Introduction

The Stakes of Intimacy in Contemporary Japan

ALLISON ALEXY

In 2009, the *New York Times* ran a story about a Japanese man who was in love with a pillow (Katayama 2009a). More specifically, the article describes a man calling himself Nisan who is in love with a large body pillow printed with an image of Nemu, a teenaged character originally from a video game. The author, Lisa Katayama, narrates time she spent with Nisan and the ways he treats his pillow girlfriend: carefully putting her in a car and restaurant booth while talking to and about her as if she were a real person. Although the article focuses primarily on this one man, it claims such behaviors tell us something about Japan more generally, including a multitude of problems surrounding romance and intimacy. Using terminology that labels a human's relationship with an imaginary character "2-D love," Katayama makes macro claims that "the rise of 2-D love can be attributed in part to the difficulty many young Japanese have in navigating modern romantic life" (2009a).[1] Citing national statistics about the high percentage of virgins and low numbers of people dating, Katayama presents a problematic but recognizable image of Japan that meshes well with similarly distorted representations frequently used by American news media.

In such depictions, Japan and Japanese people are presented as the extremes of humanity: group-oriented but unable to form real attachments, dysfunctional but entertaining, and almost certainly harmless to the point of impotence. Such a profile describes a population fascinated by sex but not actually having any, fetishistically attached to both schoolgirls and inanimate objects, and thwarted by those very same preferences in any attempt to build real loving relationships. The tone of Katayama's article parallels Nisan's earnest care of his pillow and employs an uncritical cultural relativism to suggest that while Nisan might be a bit extreme, his behaviors and preferences accurately reflect more general trends in Japan. Like problematic coverage in the same newspaper in years before (Zipangu 1998) and while purporting to share some true facts about Japanese culture, this article merely repackages long-standing stereotypes. Bringing a new twist to the "culture of contradictions" thesis first popularized through Ruth Benedict's work (1946) and as a possible apotheosis of clickbait, this article resituates orientalism and exoticism by focusing on Japanese intimacies.[2] In fact, Katayama was simply wrong about her source; she either failed to understand or failed to report that Nisan is something of a performance artist intentionally presenting an overwrought extreme (James 2009).[3] Moreover, before the article was corrected, it included survey data that Katayama had radically misrepresented to support her hyperbolic claims.[4] The substantial inaccuracies within this article exacerbate popular misperceptions about intimate Japan.

Japanese intimacies command a surprising amount of attention, both within and beyond Japan. The *New York Times'* focus on so-called 2-D love is only one example of non-Japanese media coverage on Japanese intimacies. Indeed, in recent years, a broad range of fluffy news pieces have centered on particular aspects of Japanese intimacies: Japanese divorce ceremonies, the "new phenomenon" of single Japanese women throwing themselves a wedding with no groom, Japanese men literally yelling confessions of love for their wives in order to save their marriages, Japan's low rate of sexual activity but supposedly high rates of extramarital affairs, and the reverberations as other media outlets picked up Katayama's 2-D love story as if it were accurate.[5] Much of this media coverage presents Japanese people as what I label "hypersexual virgins," people who are unduly focused on sex but not actually able to convince anyone to sleep with them. This theme—unusual sexual preferences so strange as to render actual sex nearly impossible—functions as a Trojan horse enabling English-language news media to surprise readers with stories about sex that don't include much sexual activity. Depending on the reader, perhaps this type of story allows titillation combined with a sense of superiority, evidence that once powerful Japanese businessmen are so impotent now as to be a threat in neither sexual nor financial markets, making Japanese women both more grateful and more available to lovers who don't have these sexual proclivities. This certainly wouldn't be the first time that discourse about, and attention to, intimate practices has figured into geopolitical power struggles (Lowe 2015; Povinelli 2006; Stoler 2002).

ATTENTION TO INTIMACY WITHIN JAPAN

Within Japan, popular media also pay attention to intimacies, but coverage takes a very different tone, and discourse regularly represents contemporary intimate practices as a key measure of the strength of the Japanese nation. Even more than the risks from earthquakes or tsunami, in recent decades the most severe threats have come from the simultaneous problems of a rapidly falling fertility rate and an aging population. First brought to public awareness in 1989, when the national fertility rate dropped to a mere 1.57, the low birthrate issue (*shōshika mondai*) has remained a staple of popular and political attention. As people have fewer children and wait longer to have them, politicians, academics, and policymakers have been attempting to figure out why people are less inclined or able to have children and what incentives might be used to change their minds.[6] With fewer children, Japan's demographic pyramid is quickly becoming top-heavy, and the aging workforce's pension benefits and health care costs will soon be too much for younger workers and taxpayers to sustain (Traphagan and Knight 2003). Why, exactly, Japanese people are having fewer children remains an open question, but such intimate choices are both reflecting and contributing to major social shifts.

Beyond the falling birthrate, profound and ongoing social shifts occurring in recent decades have prompted both personal and public questioning about what used to be basic social norms. Although the diverse Japanese population never moved in lockstep, throughout much of the postwar period there was a strong sense of mainstream, unmarked social norms that located people in particular forms of families, school, and work: a heterosexual, middle-class couple, including a breadwinner husband and stay-at-home wife, children deeply involved in the educational system, within an extended family network shaped by gendered roles defined through the stem family system (*ie seido*). For instance, for much of the postwar period, a responsible and loving father might demonstrate his feelings by working so hard as to remove himself from a family's daily life (Allison 1994; Hidaka 2010). Love, care, and intimacy were demonstrated through behaviors that might, at first, seem to include none of those feelings. The realities of labor patterns—that only a minority of men ever held "ideal" white-collar jobs and that most mothers worked part-time jobs—did little to shift the sense of what was normal or what kinds of relationships and behaviors required no explanation (*atarimae*).

Starting in the early 1990s, these very norms have been called into question, challenged, or rendered impossible. The falling birthrate is matched by a rising age at marriage and shifting divorce ideologies (Alexy 2011; Jolivet 1997; Rosenberger 2013). Many men and women are not content with marital lives like those of their parents and are trying to negotiate new standards for intimacy within and beyond marriage.[7] Gay, lesbian, and queer people still face substantial discrimination but have been working to increase their visibility, decrease stigma, and legally formalize their relationships.[8] The "lifetime" careers previously imagined as ideal are perceived to be evaporating, and potential employees are more likely to be offered contract or part-time positions, reflecting both labor market restructuring and governmental policies.[9] People are increasingly likely to live alone, especially in old age (Hirayama and Ronald 2006), and older people are negotiating their changing sexual relationships (K. Moore 2010).

These new patterns are taking place within popular rhetoric that describes Japan as a society newly lacking "connections" (muen shakai; literally, bondless or disconnected society), where people who were once tied to extended families, paternalistic employers, or an intense education system might now float in relative isolation.[10] A more positive interpretation of these trends can be found in the popular buzzwords "independence" (jiritsu), "self-responsibility" (jiko sekinin), and "being true to oneself" (jibunrashisa), which are commonly suggested as attributes necessary for success and happiness in the contemporary moment (Fukushima 2001; Hook and Takeda 2007; Takeda 2008). Indeed, to be freed from restrictions or requirements can be both positive and negative, releasing people from rigid social norms but removing structures of support, allowing new possibilities but disrupting the social safety net.

In light of these shifting social norms, intimacy stands at the center of personal, public, and political debates about how best to conceptualize and construct relationships between selves and others. How should one build meaningful, loving, or supportive relationships if older models for behavior are no longer deemed appropriate or seem possible? What styles of intimacy create relationships that are good for the people involved in them? How can people create a sense of themselves (jibunrashisa) and feel a sense of independence (jiritsu) without becoming utterly or problematically disconnected (muen)? Rather than providing categorical answers to these questions, this volume argues that intimacy is a key platform through which people negotiate shifting social norms, balancing personal preferences and desires with what might be possible or acceptable. Through careful ethnographic analysis we challenge the two most dominant images of intimacy in Japan, arguing that intimate practices are neither the exoticized freak show represented in English-language media nor evidence of the decline of the Japanese nation-state as suggested by domestic moral panics. Instead we suggest the broad scope of intimacy represents a focus of ontological debate, if not crisis, in the contemporary moment. By focusing on intimacy, we trace how social change is becoming manifest through deeply personal choices.

DEFINING INTIMACY

Before framing this volume's contributions, we first contextualize and define our key term. The diversity of scholarship locating "intimacy" across cultural contexts demonstrates the concept's centrality but muddies definitional waters. To cite some recent research framed through this key word, is the intimacy desired when a male tech worker hires a "temporary girlfriend" for a liaison (Bernstein 2010) at all congruent with the intimacy leveraged by state violence within the Peruvian civil war (Theidon 2012) or the expectations of an American liberal arts education (Abelmann 2009)? While plausible to use the same term in English for each of these contexts, do we find productive personal, social, or phenomenological resonances among the parallel terminologies? What do we gain or lose, analytically, by joining diverse instances of intimacy within the same term? To situate our answers, I engage some of the most commonly cited definitions of intimacy and delineate this volume's use of the term and its relationship to the broad body of research.

Although a popular dictionary (*Merriam-Webster* 2015) defines "intimacy" as "a state marked by emotional closeness [and] something that is very personal or private," academic definitions challenge and complicate this simplistic equation of intimacy with closeness. An intimate relationship, Viviana Zelitzer argues, is not merely close, but also clearly marked as such; it is close in demonstrable, recognizable ways with "particularized knowledge received and attention provided" (2010, 268). She labels two types of connected and overlapping intimacy—first, the transfer of personal information and, second, wide-ranging long-term relations, both of which can contain different "kinds" of intimacy: "physical, informational, emotional" (2005, 16). Boris and Parreñas similarly suggest that intimacy might come from either "bodily or emotional closeness or personal familiarity" or "close observation of another and knowledge of personal information," factors that need not be simultaneous (2010, 2). Berlant (2000) convincingly argues that intimacy is never only as private as it might feel. Political and popular attention, not to mention moral panics, regularly focuses on intimate lives and practices, from same-sex marriage to abortion rights or citizenship acquired through family membership. Despite its feeling, intimacy is never *only* private and operates "intertwined with material social relations and public fantasies" (Frank 2002, xxviii).[11] Therefore although intimacy is often assumed to be only private, in practice it exists at the center of public consciousness (Faier 2009, 14; McGlotten 2013; Ryang 2006). Emphasizing the actions involved in intimacy, Plummer writes that "intimacy exists in the doing of sex and love, obviously, but also in the doing of families, marriages, and friendship, in child bearing and child rearing, and in caring for others" (2003, 13).

Building from these careful phrasings, in this volume we define intimate relationships to be those (1) marked by particular emotional, physical, or informational closeness or aspirations for such; (2) taking place within realms commonly understood to be "private," although we recognize the constructed nature of such a category; (3) often, though not always, framed through bonds of love and/or sexual desire and contact. We use our ethnographic attention to focus on the *doing* of intimacy—actions, practices, and patterns that are always shaped by imagination, fantasies, and various mediations.

In Japanese discourse and scholarship, intimacy stands within a cluster of terms, and the most direct translations from English are not necessarily the terms at the center of contemporary Japanese discussions. For instance, *bekkon* (別懇), *shinai* (親愛), and *shitashimi* (親しみ) all gloss the idea of intimacy. They describe relationships that are particularly close or familiar, and they can be used to describe a range of intimate relationships from friendships to parent-child bonds to sexual partnerships. In the contemporary moment there is a similar range of vocabulary used to talk about romantic love, including *ren'ai* (恋愛), *ai* (愛), *daisuki* (大好き), and *rabu* (ラブ). There is regular debate about which terms are best used to describe different forms and styles of love, and people regularly switch among these terms when they're discussing intimacy. In many confessions or expressions of love, for instance, people are more likely to use *daisuki* ("I really like you"), such that *ren'ai* or *ai* can, at times, sound a bit more formal or conservative.[12]

When people discuss or debate tensions between people who have or might want particularly close relationships, they regularly refer to a catch-all term, *ningen kankei* (人間関係), which literally means "human relationships." Often used to discuss relationality, this term represents a category broader than the intimate but has come to symbolize both a central aspiration and conundrum of the contemporary moment. Citing Shinmura (1998), Prough describes *ningen kankei* as "1) person-to-person association or interaction within society; 2) relations between individuals including a correspondence of emotions; 3) the number one workplace complaint" (2010, 2; see also Van Bremen and Martinez 1995; Rohlen 1974). As suggested by

Prough's third point, figuring out how to relate to other people—what forms of relationships might be ideal, pleasurable, or possible—not only takes energy, but can cause significant stress and has become a discursively common complaint. Navigating the particularities of intimate relationships is a small subset of this broader category of human relationships, but contemporary Japanese discourse about the former firmly situates them in the latter. Working from this shared definition, the chapters in this volume carefully trace differences in the terminology people use to describe their intimate relationships.

THEORIZING INTIMACY

In recent decades, scholarly attention to "intimacy" has boomed, particularly in the social sciences and humanities. Referring to a wide range of beliefs and practices, "intimacy" stands at the center of an amorphous but growing body of academic attention.[13] The analysis within this volume links this extensive theorization of intimacy to the myriad questions surrounding intimacy, its stakes and significance, in contemporary Japan, and in this section I provide a brief overview of this scholarship to better situate Japanese trends.

Although within anthropological literature intimacy has been explored through a myriad of themes—for example, sex, sex work, kin and friendships, violence, transnationalism, migration, citizenship and nation, and as mediated through technology—it is often linked with configurations, practices, and experiences of romantic love.[14] Although the particulars of what counts as romance are frequently shifting and remain under debate in various cultural contexts, scholars have positioned romance as a key platform through which to understand intimacy. In particular, scholarship in various cultural contexts has focused on the rising popularity of companionate marriage, also called love marriage, which Hirsch characterizes as a "new form of marriage focused on the affective elements of the relationship" (2003, 9). Rather than being founded on family obligations, reproduction, or a sense of duty, these relationships are based on a sense of "partnership" (Smith 2009, 163) or emotional intimacy, as well as "friendship and sexual satisfaction" (Simmons 1979, 54).

Across cultural contexts, anthropologists have found companionate romance represented as "the epitome of progressive individualism" (Masquelier 2009, 226), and people frequently link their love marriages with self-consciously modern sensibilities (Collier 1997; Smith 2008, 232). Thomas and Cole suggest that "claims to love are also claims to modernity" (2009, 5), and Gregg describes companionate marriages as "a core idcology of modernity" (2006, 158). For instance, some Mexican men and women insist that, compared with relationships in their parents' generation, contemporary relationships are "better—supposedly freer from constraint, more pleasurable and satisfying, perhaps even in some way more prestigious" (Hirsch 2003, 13; see also Schaeffer 2013, 17). Wardlow and Hirsch acknowledge popular assertions that certain forms of intimacy are more modern, but they make clear that contrary to such representations, companionate ideals bring "gains and losses, both for men and for women" (2006, 14). Although local interlocutors often suggest a fundamental break between older, traditional styles of intimacy and newer, modern styles, scholars instead find that even in so-called modern marriages, "ties to kin and community remain strong" (Smith 2009, 163), suggesting that discursive shifts might not be matched in practice or, more important, that the struggle to be and feel modern in an intimate relationship brings potential risks to one's identity, community standing, or physical health (Collier 1997; Hirsch 2003; Smith 2006). Thus scholarship on romance traces popular belief in particular intimate forms and practices as instantiations of modern identities at the same time that it critically positions such intimacies in structures of power and inequality.

In English and Japanese, intimacy is euphemistically linked to sexuality, and "being intimate" can be code for having sex. Giddens situates sexual desire as a fundamental characteristic of what he labels the "pure relationship" idealized and normalized in the contemporary moment (1992, 58). Akin to companionate marriages mentioned above, such relationships include sexual desire as a key manifestation of closeness—what Giddens calls "plastic sexuality"—so much so that relationships lacking regular sexual contact are likely to be judged problematic (1992, 2; Jankowiak 2008). Such a tight link between intimacy and sexuality is visible in people's choices to use (or not use) condoms or other birth control mechanisms in pursuit of "more intimate" sex (Plummer 2003, 3, quoting Becker 2000; see also Hirsch et al. 2010). Dean argues that intimacy is created not merely through lust or unprotected sex, but also "signals the emotional experiences that accompany sex" (2009, 45). Jankowiak (2008) suggests that in popular understandings, sexual desire brings ideological risk to intimate relationships by necessarily putting passion, romance, and togetherness in conflict with each other. Other scholarly engagements with risk, particularly approaches in medical anthropology and epidemiology, highlight how sexual practices, self-consciously modern identities, configurations of intimacy, and structural inequalities have tremendous ramifications on public health, especially through sexually transmitted illnesses (Hirsch et al. 2010; Mackenzie 2013). Recent work has problematized patterns in earlier scholarship that focused on sexuality or sexual practices in isolation, failing to contextualize them within structures of emotion and exchange. While arguing for more attention to the broad range of African intimacies, Thomas and Cole argue that "[much] social scientific and historical scholarship has reduced African intimacy to sex" (2009, 3; see also Spronk 2012). These efforts to refute such a reductive analysis are paralleled by those of other scholars working to situate sexuality as a key platform for expression within intimate relationships while not privileging sexuality as the only means for intimacy.[15] The chapters in this volume build on these various theorizations of intimacy to analyze contemporary Japanese practices and beliefs.

INTIMACIES IN JAPAN

In Japan, intimacy and issues broadly related to it are at the heart of contemporary questions about what it means to be a good or successful person, how to balance personal desires with responsibilities, and the future of the nation. In this section, I give an overview of key themes within intimacy in Japan to better situate the chapters in this volume, each of which explicitly engages at least one of these topics. Extant scholarship on Japan makes clear the ways in which seemingly personal and private decisions about intimate needs and wants link with larger political, social, and economic issues.

Families in a Family Nation

As a "family nation" (*kazoku kokka*), Japanese ideologies have long linked family membership with nation and citizenship. Since the Meiji reconfiguration of all citizens as children of the emperor, starting in 1868, the stem family system (*ie*) and household registry system (*koseki*) linked actual families with the ideological and ideational "Family" (Gluck 1985). Although the system is no longer a legal requirement, many scholars have argued that it continues to play a tremendously powerful role, shaping people's expectations of how families should be organized (Ueno 2009). For instance, familial roles such as "oldest son" (*chōnan*) or "daughter-in-law" (*yome*, literally bride) continue to have substantial social resonance, conveying the image of a man entrusted to take care of his entire family or a put-upon young woman struggling to learn the preferences of her affinal kin (Harris and Long 1993; Lebra 1984). Such common social tropes of family roles continue to impact Japanese people today, even as families are reshaped in light of the falling birthrate, aging population, later marriages, and changing patterns of divorce. Not only is the aging population of baby boomers stretching social services like the pension and health-care systems, but also younger people are waiting longer to have children, having fewer children overall, and are increasingly likely to forgo having children. On a national scale, these private decisions manifest in a failing social safety net because the Japanese government has long relied on families to provide support that is, in other countries, conveyed through governmental welfare systems (Goodman 2002). Much contemporary scholarship, including work in this volume, explores how changing family norms, personal preferences, and governmental policies intersect to shape the lives of individual people within families.[16]

Heteronormative Marriages

Japan's postwar economic recovery—described as miraculous until the 1990s Heisei recessions burst that bubble—was substantially structured through intimate relationships. Although academic and public attention was frequently directed at white-collar male *salaryman* and other male laborers as agents of the economic miracle, in practice these workers were facilitated through structures of intimacy (Dasgupta 2013; McLelland 2012; Plath 1980; Vogel 2013). Because salarymen and other male workers were required to work very long hours, stay out late building working relationships, and generally be available to their employers, their lives and work habits were made possible only through domestic labor and assistance (Allison 1994; Brinton 1993; Kurotani 2005). Within middle- and upper-class families, men could not work without wives taking care of basic needs like preparing food, cleaning clothes, and paying bills. At the same time, precisely because companies were offering so-called "lifetime employment" to a minority of male workers, other categories of workers were needed to be easily laid off. Especially between the 1960s and early 1990s, female workers often filled this role, acting as part-time or dispensable laborers who enabled employers to spend financial resources on other workers (Brinton 1993). Such patterns of gendered employment are visible in the M-curve graph, so named because it shows how female labor force participation changes over the course of a woman's life: typically women work before marriage or children, at which point many drop out of paid work before returning after children get older (ibid.). Writing in the 1980s, Edwards described the interconnections between labor and domestic realms as the "complementary incompetence" of each spouse, suggesting that men and women were each socialized to fulfill only half of their own needs (1989). These labor structures were often combined with patterns of same-sex socializing that meant husbands and wives rarely spent leisure time together (Imamura 1987;

Ishii-Kuntz and Maryanski 2003; Lebra 1984). During Japan's economic miracle, many scholars described social intimacies built in workplaces, such as work teams and junior/senior (*kohai/sempai*) relationships, that were used to make workers feel like part of the corporate "family" (Kondo 1993; Nakane 1967; Plath 1980).

These patterns—male laborers disconnected from the daily realities of their family lives, women serving as both domestic support and a stopgap labor force, and employers using particular social forms to build intimacies and loyalties among co-workers—have been shifting to reflect new intimate ideals and the restructured employment system. As many full-time jobs are replaced with part-time, flexible, or contract labor, young men and women especially are facing a brave new world of employment possibilities.[17] At the same time, as discussed throughout this volume, many people are questioning the intimate norms that were acceptable a generation before, finding them no longer as attractive or beneficial (Borovoy 2005; Miura 2009; Occhi, SturtzSreetharan, and Shibato-Smith 2010). Moreover, queer intimacies are increasingly visible and are challenging the heteronormative focus of marriage.

Queer, Lesbian, Gay, Trans, and Bi Intimacies

Scholarship across disciplines documents same-sex, queer, lesbian, and gay intimacies in Japan throughout history and in the current moment (Ihara 1990; Pflugfelder 1999; Tanamura and Nakagawa 2016). Much of this work complicates the terms used to label these relationships, suggesting not just troubles caused by translation to and from English, but also the deeply embedded cultural nuances that shift over time and context.[18] When scholars describe the range of experiences, connections, and desires within queer intimacies, many highlight the complicated conflicts between discourse and practices, between popular perceptions and extant discrimination toward queer people. For instance, Maree identifies both academic and mainstream misperceptions that Japan is unusually tolerant of same-sex issues: because "Japan has no laws criminalizing homosexuality or sexual acts between persons of the same sex. . . . Japan is often positioned as being queerer earlier than so-called western nations" (2014, 187). However, as Maree goes on to explain, the family registration system designs all families to be fundamentally heteronormative, a labeling that presents many problems for same-sex partners who want to start legal families together or receive any of the myriad benefits that come through family membership (ibid.; see also Ninomiya 2006). In other contexts as well, Japan's long history of same-sex loving relationships represented in art or literature, which continues through the present day, does not bring substantial relief to overt and implicit discrimination faced by queer people on a daily basis (Chalmers 2014; McLelland, Suganuma, and Welker 2007; Summerhawk, McMahill, and McDonald 1998). For instance, the strong social norms surrounding heterosexual marriage can put substantial pressure on people to enter into "paper" marriages to seem normal (Chalmers 2014; Lunsing 1995). Gay salarymen report that not having a wife presents a serious threat to career advancement—even more, potentially, than not being straight (Dasgupta 2005; McLelland 2005).[19] Within this context of continuing structural, legal, political, and social discrimination against queer people, the popularity of fiction centered on loving relationships between two men remains important to consider. These stories, often manga, include a genre labeled "Boys' Love" or *yaoi*, a shortened version of the phrase "no climax, no point, no meaning," which derogatively describes the slow place of the archetypal narratives (McLelland et al. 2015). Boys' Love comics tell (and show) stories of men falling in love with each other but are typically created and consumed by straight women (Galbraith 2015; McLelland 2000; McLelland et al. 2015). Although there is some scholarship that challenges the common gendered patterns around *yaoi* manga, much of this pop cultural attention to gay men involves few actual gay men (Hester 2015; Nagaike 2015). Paradoxically popular attention prioritizes, if not exoticizes, gay men but only or mostly within fantasy realms, a dynamic parallel to trans celebrities presented as caricatures on mainstream Japanese television (Dale, this volume).

International Marriages

Relationships between Japanese and non-Japanese people have long been a subject of both media and academic attention. Within popular consciousness, the most common pairings involving Japanese people and foreigners are typically imagined as relationships between Japanese women and foreign men (Leupp 2003, ix). In practice, however, the international marriages Japanese people enter into reflect structures of power, desire, and attraction, and in the current moment, they involve far more Japanese men married to non-Japanese women. Reflecting intersections of geopolitical power and desire, as well as class, race, citizenship, and gender, the range and types of international relationships cannot be easily grouped together (Imamura 1990; Suzuki 2000, 2005). Yamamoto, for instance, highlights substantial differences between foreign women who travel to Japan as "marriage migrants" and Japanese women who seek foreign partners in their process of "life-style migration" (2010, 3). When analyzing popular media (in Japan and elsewhere) about Japanese women's relationships with non-Japanese men, Kelsky (2001) argues that women's desire for "the West" offers a compromised but transformative force for women already at the margins of Japanese society. For these mostly elite women, engaging the West—through intimate relationships with foreign men, among other activities—can bring at least a temporary solution to patriarchal structures they face in Japan. In contrast, relationships between Japanese men and foreign women are more likely to include women from elsewhere in Asia. Partnerships between Japanese men and Filipina women might first seem to symbolize racialized, classed, and gendered power of husbands over wives, and while those structures are very much operational, in daily life such dynamics might be far more complicated. For instance, when trying to counter deeply stigmatizing images of themselves as merely bar hostesses, women used the rhetoric of "love" to articulate "globally recognizable forms of agency and subjectivity within transnational relations of power" (Faier 2009, 149).

Parents and Children

Within the broader scholarship about family lives in contemporary Japan, social scientists have focused specifically on relationships between parents and children. Continuing social norms that delineate a male breadwinner and female caregiver mean that many children are more likely to have a primary, daily relationship with their mothers, particularly in early childhood. Ivry (2009), for example, describes how common beliefs suggest that a child who isn't raised by his or her mother in the first three years of life will go on to have problems, a notion that makes women less likely to continue work after having a baby. In this belief system, being a good mother is about being present to assist and aid one's children on a daily basis (Ivry 2009; Seaman 2011). But women continue to prefer having children as part of a married couple, partly because many believe that having a husband enables a wife to be as indulgent as she wants, and perhaps needs, to be with her children (Hertog 2009).

Within common Japanese idealizations of family lives, *skinship* plays an important role linking parents, children, and siblings. A neologism Tahhan (2014, 11) has translated as "intimacy through touch," skinship describes love and affection expressed through breast-feeding, co-sleeping, bathing together, or play (Caudill and Plath 1966). Although scholars have found that Japanese children tend to be in more frequent direct contact with their mothers, parenting norms and expectations of fathers are shifting, potentially changing gendered household dynamics and intimate practices within the family.[20]

Birth Control Practices

Japanese birth control practices throughout the postwar period lie at the intersection of governmental policies, individual choice, and family norms. In particular Japanese abortion ideologies and practices have served as a counterweight to American and European patterns. Samuel Coleman's (1983) work on birth control practices among 1970s Japanese housewives, mostly those living in apartments (*danchi*) specially built for white-collar workers and their families, found that couples limited children primarily through condom use and abortions. Throughout the postwar period abortion has been available and regularly used by married housewives who already had the children they wanted (ibid.). Scholars have linked abortion with Buddhist religious practices, tracing how beliefs might allow women to understand abortions as acceptable (LaFleur 1992) and how temples have marketed expensive religious services to women who have had abortions (Hardacre 1997). Since 1999, when the birth control pill was legalized in Japan, scholarship has focused on why the pill's approval was so long delayed and how it compares with Viagra's relatively quick approval, as well as public perceptions and use of it since then (Castro-Vázquez 2006; Norgren 2001). Norgren (2001) argues that the long delay in the pill's acceptance reflects not only the paternalism and anxieties of male politicians, but also the deeply influential national doctors' lobby, which worked to protect doctors' financial interests in lucrative abortion procedures by limiting new birth control methods. Even after it has become legally available, the pill remains largely unpopular in Japan; as Sandberg (this volume) describes, these preferences reflect understandings of intimacy.

Paid Intimacies and Sex Work

Sexual contact in exchange for money in Japan is often categorized within the broad category of *mizu shobai*. A euphemism literally meaning "water business," this term encompasses businesses offering a wide range of intimate contact; they include bars, strip clubs, host and hostess clubs, and people performing sexual acts. Because only coitus is rendered illegal by anti-prostitution laws, sex workers and the establishments where they work can freely advertise other acts (Allison 1994; Takeyama 2016). Links between the labor market and paid intimacies are particularly apparent in hostess clubs, where women are paid to be flirtatious while serving drinks and food to male customers who are often socializing with co-workers or clients. During the height of Japan's economic bubble, such spaces of groping and sexualized jokes were, at least for some large companies, vital to business, both because of the male relationships fortified via hostesses and the company's co-optation of male employees' leisure time (Allison 1994). Highlighting enduring links between female sex work and male labor, Koch (2016) found prevalent rhetoric about female care needed to "heal" male workers. Although Allison's (1994) ethnographic portrait of the elite club where she worked remains a touchstone, newer research makes clear how unusually elite that space was (Gagné 2010; Parreñas 2011). In general, women working as hostesses in Japan are likely to be foreign, making citizenship and legal status vitally important (Faier 2009; Matsui 1995). Links between paid intimacies and nationality are also explored in scholarship about what are often called Japanese "sex tours"—touristic encounters especially throughout Southeast Asia (Muroi and Sasaki 1997).

Paid intimacies are not just, however, the provision of women serving men. In recent decades, host clubs have been growing in popularity in Japan. These involve male hosts catering to female clients in patterns that are parallel to, but not simply inverted forms of, hostess clubs. Takeyama (2016) argues that male hosts are likely to understand themselves as self-responsible entrepreneurs and as the embodiments of the contemporary model for "ideal subjecthood" enacting "postindustrial consumer logic and neoliberal values" (Takeyama 2010, 232).

Intimacy Panics

Throughout the postwar period, public attention has focused on intimate practices supposedly causing harm to the social order. I label these "intimacy panics" and define them as moral panics surrounding intimate topics (Goode and Ben-Yehuda 2010). Although such public anxieties focused on intimate practices are not unique to Japan, these cases demonstrate how intimacy has been an ongoing focus of attention and can often index other concerns.

The so-called "1.57 shock" of 1989 describes the first time the national birthrate fell below replacement level and prompted people to worry about the health of the nation. National worry about this topic continues to coalesce around the low birthrate problem as an instantiation of Japan's inability to reproduce itself and therefore sustain the economic development of the postwar years (Goodman 2002). In the 1990s, worries about intimacy and youth fused around "compensated dating" practices (*enjo kōsai*), in which young women would accept luxury goods as payment to go on dates that might include sex (Leheny 2006). At the time, public awareness and media discourse about the practice suggested that it was very common and that young women were quite literally prostituting themselves for Louis Vuitton goods, an anxiety that neatly tied together fears of possible female empowerment, youth cultures, sexual intimacies, and rampant consumerism. Scholars have contextualized this discourse as largely a creation of the media (Kinsella 2014) and politicians (Leheny 2006), with statistics failing to back up the hyperbolic claims of its popularity.

The late 1990s brought the term "sexless" (sekkusuresu) to describe marriages that no longer included sexual intimacy (Moriki, Hayashi, and Matsukura 2015; Moriki 2017; Narabayashi 1997). Although family norms throughout the postwar years positioned marital sexuality as directed at reproduction (Lebra 1984), discourse about sexlessness within marriage was used to describe it as a social problem. Spouses who did not have sex (or who did not want to have sex) were suddenly described as missing a key element of necessary intimacy, and discourse about sexless marriage suggested it as a warning sign of marital discord. Scholarship on the use of "love hotels" by married couples describes such hotels as a way people try to create spaces for spousal intimacy in relation to parental responsibilities (Lin 2008).

In the same period, media attention to a newly created category of "shut-ins" (hikikomori) highlighted the risks caused by and for those lacking intimate connections. Although practices vary, this population is typically described as comprised of younger people, mostly men, who remove themselves from normal society to remain within their homes and, in more extreme cases, within their bedrooms. Horiguchi traces the rapid rise in media attention concerning people not "taking part in society" to argue that the discursive category fails to reflect the true range of such withdrawn behaviors (2012, 129), which Borovoy (2008) argues often cover a variety of mental health concerns. At root, the creation of, and attention to, such categories of experience demonstrate popular and media fascination with seemingly disordered intimacies (Arai 2016; Heinze and Thomas 2014).

In the mid-2000s, public worry focused on "later-life divorce" (jukunen rikon), the possibility that couples in their sixties or beyond might suddenly end their marriages (Alexy 2007). These anxieties were pinpointed to a legal change that would make it possible for women to claim up to half of their husbands' national pension (kokumin nenkin) after divorce, a possible stimulus that had more symbolic than financial value. Yet the idea that a generation of grandparents—indeed, the very baby boom generation who had built Japan's postwar economic recovery—might suddenly divorce called into question the norms, values, and practices that had previously been held up as a strength of the nation.

Most recently, as described in greater detail by Miles (this volume), discursive anxiety has swirled around young men who are antisocial, unattractive, and potentially so feminized as to be unable to find dates or get married. Public worries about young men's masculinity, in parallel to earlier worries about young women's sexual activity, are found in the derogatory terminology labeling men "herbivores" (as opposed to "normal" carnivores) because they enact masculinity in ways that disrupt or refuse earlier models for masculine silence, emotional distance, and patriarchal control (Cook 2016; Fujimura 2006; Morioka 2008). This label could be an insult or a new badge of pride, and it's equally possible to find people who relish the distinction from older performances of masculinity or those who identify such a "loss" of masculinity as evidence of Japan's decline.

Finally, contemporary Japanese popular and academic discourse positions the potential relationship between intimacy and fandom using the term *moe*. *Moe* describes "a euphoric response to fantasy characters or representations of them" (Galbraith 2009, n.p.; Galbraith 2015) and can also be the longing, love, or intimacy a person feels for a fictional character, that character's visual image, or its material representations. For some people, as with the discourse about young men's decreasing masculinity, this type of relationship symbolizes Japan's ruination and the failure of "actual" human relationships. For others, the term describes common and frankly real feelings cultivated within Japan's broad commercial market for characters, pop culture, and figurines.[21] Rather than suggesting a decline, *moe* might instead be interpreted as offering new configurations of intimacy through fandom, capital, mediation, and popular culture. As suggested by the example that began this chapter, because *moe* is a native Japanese term, it has also been used to falsely assert that Japanese intimacies are fundamentally based on unreal or less real relationships.

OVERVIEW OF CHAPTERS IN THIS VOLUME

Given these social contexts and extant literature, this volume is designed to offer ethnographic analyses theorizing how intimacy is being imagined, constructed, and enacted in Japan or by Japanese people in other cultural contexts. We ask the following: To whom and in what contexts does intimacy matter? What can intimacy be used to symbolize, and what are the stakes of such symbols? Within the public, private, and political attention surrounding intimate decisions, how do people imagine and discuss changing intimate norms? How do intimacies relate to extant structures of power, particularly those intersecting with gender, sexuality, class, and race? How are mainstream norms created and transmitted? When people challenge or refuse such norms, how do they demonstrate their choices? What types of intimacy do people find appropriate, good, and viable? How does intimacy feel or sound, and what can it look like? What are the risks that come with intimacy for individuals, communities, or the nation-state? The chapters in this volume engage these questions from linked but diverse perspectives, building thematically in relation to each other.

In chapter 2, Yukari Kawahara analyzes an influential but largely hidden context for intimacy: the high school classroom. Focused on sexual education classes that took place in the 1990s, Kawahara's work sheds light on how men and women now in their thirties and forties—a generation experiencing changes to marriage, parenting, and labor norms—learned about, imagined, and practiced intimacy when they were still students. The in-depth case studies presented provide an ethnographic point of comparison for later chapters, giving both a sense of how things have changed and how adults today might have situated intimacy in their early lives.

Next, Shana Fruehan Sandberg explores how young, unmarried women in mid-2000s Tokyo decided what birth control to use and how such choices contributed to constructions of intimacy. Beginning from the fact that the "withdrawal" method is apparently more commonly used than previously recognized in surveys, Sandberg theorizes that women use particular birth control methods to create trust with their sexual partners. She argues that women have commonly articulated "reliability" as a necessary characteristic for intimate relationships, and birth control is a key context in which such reliability is demonstrated, challenged, and negotiated.

Laura Dales and Beverley Yamamoto extend the previous discussions of birth control to explore how women idealize and attempt to create intimacy before or beyond marriage. They argue that nuclear family ideals remain ideologically forceful, even if they are decreasingly common. Describing entangled intimacies, they find many women building relationships in the shadow of marriages or marital ideals. Focusing on women self-described as "unconventional," some of whom have had extramarital affairs, Dales and Yamamoto argue that while marriage remains discursively central to women's lives, disincentives push some women to create intimacies before or beyond marital relationships.

Allison Alexy's analysis begins from a piece of advice popularized in mid-2000s Japan: to strengthen a marriage, spouses should make sure to say "I love you" to each other. She argues that this piece of advice, and the illocutionary and perlocutionary effects being attributed to that particular phrase, reflect contemporary attempts to balance connection and independence within intimate relationships. This tip suggests that spouses should be connected through feelings of romantic love but nevertheless separate enough so as to need to verbalize those romantic feelings.

Kaoru Kuwajima explores marriage from the perspective of domestic violence. Analyzing how female victims of domestic violence understand and define intimacy, she suggests that such definitions can influence women's decisions to leave violent relationships. Although new national legislation has been designed to reduce domestic violence, this legislation requires victims to leave violent situations, something that many women are often unwilling to do. Kuwajima argues that reconsidering and redefining intimacy in these contexts is vital before a victim of domestic violence can leave a relationship and that victims' shifting definitions of, and expectations for, intimacy are often a necessary part of their recovery.

Emma E. Cook examines the ways in which intimacy is enacted by men who work in irregular jobs as *freeters* and how irregular work shapes gender roles, intimate practices, and power within relationships. Social emphasis on fulfilling particular gendered roles in intimate relationships—for example, as a male breadwinner—creates tensions when individuals find that these ideals cannot be made manifest. Cook argues that the precariousness of the irregular labor market does not easily allow men to demonstrate their ability to fulfill such expected roles to potential marriage partners, making it harder for them to create and sustain intimate relationships.

Elizabeth Miles extends the discussion of male experiences by focusing on how some men view the burdens of intimacy. The ideology and practice of "love marriage," while notable for its illusion of free choice and greater potential intimacy, contributes both to people's delaying marriage until later in life and the increase in the number of Japanese singles. Miles argues that in contemporary popular discourse, finding a potential mate now requires constant effort on the part of men, a polishing of the self and one's attributes that many men find to be onerous and in contradistinction to their idealized versions of what love is and should be.

S. P. F. Dale analyzes the lines among gender, identity, and desire in intimate acts for people who identify as "x-gender," a category neither male nor female. Akin to the English term "genderqueer," x-gender allows people to talk about their sexuality and desire in terms beyond hetero- or homosexuality. Dale argues that while this term can be used to challenge binary understandings of sexuality, it also might allow people with queer desires to avoid the stigma of being labeled homosexual. The examples presented ultimately argue that preferences in intimate acts—and the resultant negotiations in interpersonal relationships—are a central domain through which gender identity is formed.

Kathryn Goldfarb expands on the tensions inherent in familial relationships to explore a common claim that "blood ties" are central to Japanese kinship. Focusing on the incredibly low rates of child adoption, she traces a common belief that few parents would want to adopt a child not "of their own blood." Goldfarb argues that blood ties themselves are conceptualized as a type of intimacy and that discourses surrounding blood ties reflect anxieties that intimate ties without blood will fail to generate durable family bonds.

Chigusa Yamaura explores how men who have been unable to find or sustain marriages in Japan look to China for potential partners. Because most people believe that "domestic" marriages (in which both spouses are Japanese) are ideal, marriage brokers and clients work to explain their stigmatized choice to move to the international marriage market. Yamaura argues that for these Japanese men and transnational marriage brokers, perceptions of "ordinariness" are vital to construct intimate relationships. Neither love nor passion are seen as a prerequisite for intimacy but rather the ability of participants to view their relationships as socially acceptable, if not ordinary.

Diane Adis Tahhan examines tensions in international marriages between Japanese women and Australian men. Arguing that expectations for and expressions of intimacy vary between these two cultural contexts, Tahhan traces how families attempt to negotiate conflicts over how best to be intimate. Common points of tension include figuring out sleeping arrangements when parental co-sleeping is common in Japan but less so in Australia. Exploring the lived experience of intimacy through bodily practices and the conflicts caused by them, Tahhan analyzes the meanings of intimacy in these transnational relationships.

Finally, chapter 13 gathers short essays from every contributor reflecting on the methodological challenges surrounding ethnographic fieldwork about intimate topics. Because of the sensitive, private, or personal nature of many of the subjects explored in this volume, the researchers necessarily used novel and creative methods to gain access and gather data. In this final chapter, we reflect on more and less successful methodologies to provide a general overview of the practice of doing research about intimacy in Japan.

Although these chapters draw from unique ethnographic data, they are crosscut by similar themes and questions because such topics are omnipresent in contemporary Japan. Intimate relationships attract attention not only when people are invested in imagining and enacting the most ideal relationships they can, but also because intimate decisions have tremendous knock-on social effects, such as the birthrate. Paying attention to how people imagine relationships and attempt to enact those ideals, as well as the political, social, and economic antecedents to personal choices, this volume highlights the variations within the individual lives and experiences discussed. We hope that readers will identify the diversity represented within this volume, but we highlight it here to combat the pernicious stereotype of Japanese people as hive-minded automatons. There is so much debate represented in the chapters—about how to build and sustain intimate relationships, let alone how those relationships might matter in the first place—demonstrating how wrong such characterizations are. Moreover, as delineated above, because Japan is frequently represented as an "exotic" place with strange sexual practices, we hope to both engage and challenge readers who might have picked up this volume hoping either for titillation or confirmation of what they think they already know.

NOTES

1. The terminology of "2-D" contrasts feelings a person has for another person (which would presumably be in three dimensions) with those for a character in comic books, films, or television shows. In Japan, such affection for characters is often linked with "*moe*," which Galbraith (2009, n.p.) defines as a "euphoric response to fantasy characters or representations of them."

2. Although Benedict's problematic description was published half a century ago, it remains relevant because her suggestion that Japanese people are somehow more contradictory than others continues to be repeated. Benedict's book begins with a list of extreme contradictions she believes to be true of Japanese people: "The Japanese are, to the highest degree, both aggressive and unaggressive, both militaristic and aesthetic, both insolent and polite, rigid and adaptable, submissive and resentful of being pushed around, loyal and treacherous, brave and timid, conservative and hospitable to new ways" (Benedict 1946, 2). By suggesting this list was evidence of pathology—rather than normal and appropriate for any person moving through different contexts and moods—she characterized Japan as a culture of contradictions. Similar characterizations are visible in the media representations under discussion in this section.

3. This wasn't the first time that a reporter for the *New York Times* incorrectly represented an artistic project or extreme outlier as mainstream and normal. Martin Fackler (2007) incorrectly represented Tsukioka Aya's art as earnest but insane attempts to ward off imagined criminal threats by dressing as a vending machine (see also Marx 2007). Moreover, Richards (2009) suggests that Katayama might have pulled some of the Nemu story from a 2007 article published in the now defunct *WaiWai*, an online section of the English-language Mainichi newspaper that was a collection of poorly sourced, highly sexualized clickbait (M. Moore 2008).

4. In the first published version of the article, Katayama stated that according to a government survey a quarter of Japanese people were virgins, presumably evidence to support her claim that Japanese people have difficulty creating relationships with other humans. However, as visible in the correction later issued by the *New York Times*, the actual survey stated that one-quarter of *unmarried people between the ages of 30 and 34* were virgins, a population much smaller than Katayama had originally claimed (Richards 2009). According to my calculations, based on 2010 census data, her first, inaccurate claim labels about

32 million people as virgins while the survey's actual findings put that number closer to 970,000 (National Institute of Population and Social Science Research 2012). Such an inaccurate expansion—attributing the characteristics of a small segment of the population to the population as a whole—serves as a microcosmic representation of common problems English-language news media have concerning Japan.

5. On divorce ceremonies, see "Japan's 'Bizarre' Spike in Divorce Ceremonies" (2011); Demetriou (2010); Ferrari (2011); Lah (2010); Moorhead (2010); on women throwing themselves a wedding with no groom, see Aran (2014); Davis (2014); "Japan: Solo Weddings for Single Women" (2014); Kaneko (2014); McGuire (2014a, 2014b); Plautz (2014); on men yelling their love as a way to save their marriages, see BBC Radio (2015); Craft (2013); Fujita (2013); "Video" (2013); on low rates of sexual activity, see BBC Two (2013); Chavez (2011); Haworth (2013); Hoffman (2013); Kageyama (2014); Keating (2013); Waldman (2013); on Japan as a culture of extramarital affairs, see Adelstein (2013); Dehart (2014); Kageyama (2014); on reverberations of Katayama's 2-D love article, see Frucci (2009); Katayama (2009b); Mancuso (2010). Overall in this chapter, I have placed longer lists of references here in the endnotes so they are available to interested readers but won't distract from the points being discussed.

6. For more on the "low birthrate problem" and political responses to it, see L. Coleman (2008); Gelb (2003); Goodman (2002); Ogawa and Retherford (1993); Schoppa (2006); Takeda (2004).

7. Considerable scholarship analyzes the wide variety of family decisions being made in Japan, particularly in comparison with earlier generations, including the following: Aoyama, Dales, and Dasgupta (2014); Hashimoto and Traphagan (2009); Kawano, Roberts, and Long (2014); White (2002).

8. English-language scholarship explores same-sex intimacies, activism, communities, and representations; sources include Chalmers (2014); Mackintosh (2010); McLelland (2005); McLelland and Dasgupta (2005); and McLelland, Suganuma, and Welker (2007).

9. Shifting hiring and employment patterns, as well as their impacts on younger generations, are explored in greater depth in Blind and Von Mandach (2014); Brinton (2010); Cook (2016); and Takeda (2008).

10. Scholars have explored discourse about and practical responses to "disconnected society"; for instance, Andō (2013) and Rowe (2011) examine changing funeral rituals; Brinton (2010), Miyamoto (2012), and Toivonen (2013) analyze labor instability; and Allison 2013 focuses on media discourse about this as a problem.

11. To be clear, in this quote Frank does not use the term "intimacy" but is describing the materiality and communal fantasies that intertwine around the "personal erotics" she observed while doing fieldwork in American strip clubs. I use her words here because I find them to be a helpful articulation of the dynamics surrounding intimacy.

12. Hallman (2011), for instance, traces how young Japanese people build and negotiate intimacy through linguistic utterances.

13. As one measure of this increase, consider the increasing frequency with which articles archived within JSTOR's 120 English-language journals categorized as anthropology include the word "intimacy" in their titles. The first article appeared in 1972 (Barrett 1972) and was one of only two published in the 1970s. Three articles were published in the 1980s and none in the 1990s. Nine articles were published in the 2000s, and sixteen have been published from 2010 to 2015. These articles occur in conjunction with the large number of books including "intimacy" in their titles or subtitles, some of which are cited in this chapter.

14. On the intimacy of sex work, see Bernstein (2010); Frank (2002); Parreñas (2011); on the intimacy of family relationships, see Yan (2003); on the intimacy of friendship, see Bell and Coleman (1999); Desai and Killick (2010); on intimate violence, see Lancaster (1992); Lazarus-Black (2007); on how transnationalism and migration impact intimacy, see Constable (2005);

Hirsch (2003); Kelsky (2001); Suzuki (2005); Yamaura (2015); on the relationship between intimacy and citizenship, see Freeman (2011); Friedman (2006, 2015); Frühstück (2003); Lowe (2015); Plummer (2003); on intimacy and technology, see Boyle (2010); Gershon (2011); Schaeffer (2013).

15. Agustín (2007), Kulick (1998), and Reddy (2006), for instance, make it a point to emphasize how sex workers create and maintain intimate relationships beyond their work, precisely because popular representations often reduce their capacity for intimacy not just to sexuality, but also to transactional sex.

16. The centrality of family—both as a key symbol and lived relationships—is reflected in the extensive scholarship on the topic, including three recent edited collections in English: Aoyama, Dales, and Dasgupta (2014); Hashimoto and Traphagan (2009); Ronald and Alexy (2011).

17. Brinton (2010), Cook (2016), Kosugi (2008), and Rebick (2006) offer trenchant analyses of how changing employment patterns, and fewer full-time positions for younger men, are impacting family relationships.

18. Scholars conducting historical analysis (Pflugfelder 1999), media analysis (Lunsing 2005), and projects in cultural studies (McLelland 2000, 2005) have emphasized the challenges in translating terminology like "queer" or "gay."

19. Some cities and wards in Japan have recently approved same-sex partnership certificates. As of this writing, two of Tokyo's wards (Shibuya and Setagaya) and some cities elsewhere in Japan (Naha and Takarazuka) have begun to allow citizens to request a certificate formally recognizing a same-sex relationship (Esumuraruda and Kira 2015). However, these certificates neither designate the relationship a "marriage" nor force any authority to legally recognize the relationship. Although the certificates "request" that the couples be treated as married—for instance, if one partner is hospitalized—there is no guarantee that such a request will be honored (Murai 2015).

20. For more on how masculine and paternal ideals are changing, see Ishii-Kuntz (2003); Ishii-Kuntz et al. (2004); Mathews (2003, 2014); Mitsukoshi, Kohlbacher, and Schimkowsky (2016); and Roberson and Suzuki (2003).

21. Many chapters in Kelly (2004) elaborate on how products are created for, and marketed toward, fans in contemporary Japan. Lukacs (2015) further explains how digital fandoms are engaged through commerce.

REFERENCES

Abelmann, Nancy. 2009. *The Intimate University: Korean American Students and the Problems of Segregation*. Durham, NC: Duke University Press.

Adelstein, Jake. 2013. "Equal-Opportunity Infidelity Comes to Japan." *Japan Times*, July 6. http://www.japantimes.co.jp/news/2013/07/06/national/media-national/equal-opportunity-infidelity-comes-to-japan/.

Agustín, Laura María. 2007. *Sex at the Margins: Migration, Labour Markets and the Rescue Industry*. London and New York: Zed Books.

Alexy, Allison. 2007. "Deferred Benefits, Romance, and the Specter of Later-Life Divorce." *Contemporary Japan* 19: 169–188.

———. 2011. "Intimate Dependence and Its Risks in Neoliberal Japan." *Anthropological Quarterly* 84 (4): 895–917.

Allison, Anne. 1994. *Nightwork: Sexuality, Pleasure, and Corporate Masculinity in a Tokyo Hostess Club*. Chicago: University of Chicago Press.

———. 2013. *Precarious Japan*. Durham, NC: Duke University Press.

Andō Kiyomi. 2013. *Gendai kazoku ni okeru bosei to sōsō: Sono kōzō to mentariti no hen'yō* [Tombs and Funerals in Contemporary Families: Structures and Transforming Ideologies]. Tokyo: Gakujutsu shuppankai.

Aoyama, Tomoko, Laura Dales, and Romit Dasgupta, eds. 2014. *Configurations of Family in Contemporary Japan*. London: Routledge.

Arai, Andrea. 2016. *The Strange Child: Education and the Psychology of Patriotism in Recessionary Japan*. Stanford: Stanford University Press.

Aran, Isha. 2014. "Japanese Travel Agency Now Offering 'Solo Weddings' for Single Women." Jezebel.com, December 22. http://jezebel.com/japanese-travel-agency-now -offering-solo-weddings-for-1674037157.

Barrett, Richard A. 1972. "Social Hierarchy and Intimacy in a Spanish Town." *Ethnology* 11 (4): 386–398.

BBC Two. 2013. "No Sex Please, We're Japanese." John Holdsworth, director. *This World*, October 24. Available at http://www.dailymotion.com/video/x1voex5_no-sex-please -we-re-japanese-documentary-youtube_tech.

BBC Radio 2015. "Love Your Wife Day." Available at http://www.bbc.co.uk/programmes /p02h8y5c.

Becker, Gay. 2000. *The Elusive Embryo: How Women and Men Approach New Reproductive Technologies*. Berkeley: University of California Press.

Bell, Sandra, and Simon Coleman, eds. 1999. *The Anthropology of Friendship*. Oxford: Berg.

Benedict, Ruth. 1946. *The Chrysanthemum and the Sword: Patterns of Japanese Culture*. Boston: Houghton Mifflin.

Berlant, Lauren, ed. 2000. *Intimacy*. Chicago: University of Chicago Press.

Bernstein, Elizabeth. 2010. *Temporarily Yours: Intimacy, Authenticity, and the Commerce of Sex*. Chicago: University of Chicago Press.

Blind, Georg D., and Stefania Lottani Von Mandach. 2014. "Decades Not Lost, but Won: Increased Employment, Higher Wages, and More Equal Opportunities in the Japanese Labour Market." *Social Science Japan Journal* 18 (1): 63–88.

Boris, Eileen, and Rhacel Salazar Parreñas, eds. 2010. *Intimate Labors: Cultures, Technologies, and the Politics of Care*. Stanford: Stanford University Press.

Borovoy, Amy. 2005. *The Too-Good Wife: Alcohol, Codependency, and the Politics of Nurturance in Postwar Japan*. Berkeley: University of California Press.

———. 2008. "Japan's Hidden Youths: Mainstreaming the Emotionally Distressed in Japan." *Culture, Medicine, and Psychiatry* 32 (4): 552–576.

Boyle, Karen. 2010. *Everyday Pornography*. London: Routledge.

Brinton, Mary C. 1993. *Women and the Economic Miracle: Gender and Work in Postwar Japan*. Berkeley: University of California Press.

———. 2010. *Lost in Transition: Youth, Work, and Instability in Postindustrial Japan*. Cambridge: Cambridge University Press.

Castro-Vázquez, Genaro. 2006. "The Politics of Viagra: Gender, Dysfunction and Reproduction in Japan." *Body and Society* 12 (2): 109–129.

Caudill, William, and David Plath. 1966. "Who Sleeps by Whom? Parent-Child Involvement in Urban Japanese Families." *Psychiatry* 29 (4): 344–366.

Chalmers, Sharon. 2014. *Emerging Lesbian Voices from Japan*. London: Routledge.

Chavez, Amy. 2011. "Herbivorous Men, Where's the Beef?" *Japan Times*. December 17. http://www.japantimes.co.jp/community/2011/12/17/our-lives/herbivorous-men -wheres-the-beef/.

Cole, Jennifer, and Lynne M. Thomas, eds. 2009. *Love in Africa*. Chicago: University of Chicago Press.

Coleman, Liv. 2008. "Family Policy: Framework and Challenges." In *The Demographic Challenge: A Handbook about Japan*, edited by Florian Coulmas, Harald Conrad, Annette Schad-Seifert, and Gabriele Vogt, 749–764. Leiden: Brill.

Coleman, Samuel. 1983. *Family Planning in Japanese Society: Traditional Birth Control in a Modern Urban Culture*. Princeton, NJ: Princeton University Press.

Collier, Jane. 1997. *From Duty to Desire: Remaking Families in a Spanish Village*. Princeton, NJ: Princeton University Press.

Constable, Nicole, ed. 2005. *Cross-Border Marriages: Gender and Mobility in Transnational Asia*. Philadelphia: University of Pennsylvania Press.

Cook, Emma E. 2016. *Reconstructing Adult Masculinities: Part-Time Work in Contemporary Japan*. London: Routledge.

Craft, Lucy. 2013. "How Do I Love Thee? Japanese Husbands Shout the Ways." National Public Radio, NPR.org. February 13. http://www.npr.org/2013/02/13/171920006/how-do-i-love-thee-japanese-husbands-shout-the-ways.

Dasgupta, Romit. 2005. "Salarymen Doing Straight: Heterosexual Men and the Dynamics of Gender Conformity." In McLelland and Dasgupta, eds., *Genders, Transgenders and Sexualities in Japan*, 168–182.

———. 2013. *Re-Reading the Salaryman in Japan: Crafting Masculinities*. London: Routledge.

Davis, Allison. 2014. "Hot New Travel Trend: Marry Yourself!" *The Cut*. December 23. http://nymag.com/thecut/2014/12/hot-new-travel-trend-marry-yourself.html.

Dean, Tim. 2009. *Unlimited Intimacy: Reflections on the Subculture of Barebacking*. Chicago: University of Chicago Press.

Dehart, Jonathan. 2014. "How Ashley Madison Pulled Back the Curtain on Japan's 'Infidelity Economy.'" *Motherboard*, June 16. http://motherboard.vice.com/read/how-ashley-madison-pulled-back-the-curtain-on-japans-infidelity-economy.

Demetriou, Danielle. 2010. "Tokyo Sees Rise in 'Divorce Ceremonies.'" *The Telegraph*, June 13. http://www.telegraph.co.uk/news/worldnews/asia/japan/7822356/Tokyo-sees-rise-in-divorce-ceremonies.html.

Desai, Amit, and Evan Killick, eds. 2010. *The Ways of Friendship: Anthropological Perspectives*. New York: Berghahn Books.

Edwards, Walter. 1989. *Modern Japan through Its Weddings: Gender, Person, and Society in Ritual Portrayal*. Stanford: Stanford University Press.

Esumuraruda and Kira. 2015. *Dōsei pātonāshippu shōmei hajimarimashita: Shibuyaku setagayaku no seiritsu monogatari to tetsuzuki no hōhō* [The Beginning of Same-Sex Partnership Registration: Shibuya and Setagaya Wards' Procedures and Methods]. Tokyo: Potto shuppan.

Fackler, Martin. 2007. "Fearing Crime, Japanese Wear the Hiding Place." *New York Times*, October 20. http://www.nytimes.com/2007/10/20/world/asia/20japan.html.

Faier, Lieba. 2009. *Intimate Encounters: Filipina Women and the Remaking of Rural Japan*. Berkeley: University of California Press.

Ferrari, Paige. 2011. "Untying the Knot in Japan." *New York Times Magazine*, September 9. http://www.nytimes.com/2011/09/11/magazine/divorce-ceremonies-are-big-in-japan.html.

Frank, Katherine. 2002. *G-Strings and Sympathy: Strip Club Regulars and Male Desire*. Durham, NC: Duke University Press.

Freeman, Caren. 2011. *Making and Faking Kinship: Marriage and Labor Migration between China and South Korea*. Ithaca, NY: Cornell University Press.

Friedman, Sara L. 2006. *Intimate Politics: Marriage, the Market, and State Power in Southeastern China*. Cambridge, MA: Harvard University Asia Center.

———. 2015. *Exceptional States: Chinese Immigrants and Taiwanese Sovereignty*. Berkeley: University of California Press.

Frucci, Adam. 2009. "Japan's 2-D Lovers: Falling In Love with a Body Pillow." *Gizmodo*, July 23. http://gizmodo.com/5321350/japans-2-d-lovers-falling-in-love-with-a-body-pillow.

Frühstück, Sabine. 2003. *Colonizing Sex: Sexology and Social Control in Modern Japan*. Berkeley: University of California Press.

Fujimura, Masayuki. 2006. "Wakamono sedai no 'otokorashisa' to sono mirai" [The Young Generation's 'Masculinity' and Its Future]. In *'Otokorashisa' no gendaishi* [A Modern History of Masculinity], edited by Tsunehisa Abe, Sumio Obinata, and Masako Amano, 191–226. Tokyo: Nihon keizai hyōronsha.

Fujita, Akiko. 2013. "Husbands Shout Their Love on 'Beloved Wife Day.'" *ABC News*, January 30. http://abcnews.go.com/blogs/headlines/2013/01/husbands-shout-their-love-on-beloved-wife-day/.

Fukushima Mizuho, ed. 2001. *Aremo kazoku koremo kazoku: Ko o daiji ni suru shakai* [This Is a Family, That Is a Family: Toward a Society That Values Individuals]. Tokyo: Iwanami shoten.

Gagné, Nana Okura. 2010. "The Business of Leisure, the Leisure of Business: Rethinking Hegemonic Masculinity through Gendered Service in Tokyo Hostess Clubs." *Asian Anthropology* 9 (1): 29–55.

Galbraith, Patrick W. 2009. "Moe: Exploring Virtual Potential in Post-Millennial Japan." *Electronic Journal of Contemporary Japanese Studies* 9 (3). http://www.japanesestudies.org.uk/articles/2009/Galbraith.html.

———. 2015. "*Moe* Talk: Affective Communication among Female Fans of *Yaoi* in Japan." In McLelland, Nagaike, Suganuma, and Welker, eds., *Boys Love Manga and Beyond*, 153–168.

Gelb, Joyce. 2003. *Gender Policies in Japan and the United States: Comparing Women's Movements, Rights, and Politics*. New York: Palgrave Macmillan.

Gershon, Ilana. 2011. *The Breakup 2.0: Disconnecting over New Media*. Ithaca, NY: Cornell University Press.

Giddens, Anthony. 1992. *The Transformation of Intimacy: Sexuality, Love and Eroticism in Modern Societies*. Stanford: Stanford University Press.

Gluck, Carol. 1985. *Japan's Modern Myths: Ideology in the Late Meiji Period*. Princeton, NJ: Princeton University Press.

Goode, Erich, and Nachman Ben-Yehuda. 2010. *Moral Panics: The Social Construction of Deviance*, 2nd ed. West Sussex: Wiley-Blackwell.

Goodman, Roger, ed. 2002. *Family and Social Policy in Japan: Anthropological Approaches*. Cambridge: Cambridge University Press.

Gregg, Jessica. 2006. "'He Can Be Sad Like That': *Liberdade* and the Absence of Romantic Love in a Brazilian Shantytown." In Hirsch and Wardlow, eds., *Modern Loves*, 157–173.

Hardacre, Helen. 1997. *Marketing the Menacing Fetus in Japan*. Berkeley: University of California Press.

Harris, Phyllis Braudy, and Susan O. Long. 1993. "Daughter-in-Law's Burden: Family Caregiving and Social Change in Japan." *Journal of Cross-Cultural Gerontology* 8 (2): 97–118.

Hashimoto, Akiko, and John W. Traphagan, eds. 2009. *Imagined Families, Lived Families: Culture and Kinship in Contemporary Japan*. Albany: State University of New York Press.

Haworth, Abigail. 2013. "Why Have Young People in Japan Stopped Having Sex?" *The Guardian*, October 20. http://www.theguardian.com/world/2013/oct/20/young -people-japan-stopped-having-sex.

Heinze, Ulrich, and Penelope Thomas. 2014. "Self and Salvation: Visions of *hikikomori* in Japanese Manga." *Contemporary Japan* 1: 151–169.

Hertog, Ekaterina. 2009. *Tough Choices: Bearing an Illegitimate Child in Japan*. Stanford: Stanford University Press.

Hester, Jeffry T. 2015 "*Fujoshi* Emergent: Shifting Popular Representations of *Yaoi*/BL Fandom in Japan." In McLelland, Nagaike, Suganuma, and Welker, eds., *Boys Love Manga and Beyond*, 169–188.

Hidaka, Tomoko. 2010. *Salaryman Masculinity: The Continuity of and Change in the Hegemonic Masculinity in Japan*. Leiden and Boston: Brill.

Hirayama, Yosuke, and Richard Ronald, eds. 2006. *Housing and Social Transition in Japan*. London: Routledge.

Hirsch, Jennifer S. 2003. *A Courtship after Marriage: Sexuality and Love in Mexican Transnational Families*. Berkeley: University of California Press.

Hirsch, Jennifer S., and Holly Wardlow, eds. 2006. *Modern Loves: The Anthropology of Romantic Courtship and Companionate Marriage*. Ann Arbor: University of Michigan Press.

Hirsch, Jennifer S., Daniel Jordan Smith, Constance A. Nathanson, and Harriet M. Phinney. 2010. *The Secret: Love, Marriage, and HIV*. Nashville: Vanderbilt University Press.

Hoffman, Michael. 2013. "Married or Single, Japan Is a Desolate Country." *Japan Times Online*, August 31. http://www.japantimes.co.jp/news/2013/08/31/national/media -national/married-or-single-japan-is-a-desolate-country/.

Hook, Glenn D. and Takeda Hiroko. 2007. "'Self-Responsibility' and the Nature of the Postwar Japanese State: Risk through the Looking Glass." *Journal of Japanese Studies* 33 (1): 93–123.

Horiguchi, Sachiko. 2012. "Hikikomori: How Private Isolation Caught the Public Eye." In A *Sociology of Japanese Youth: From Returnees to NEETs*, edited by Roger Goodman, Yuki Imoto, and Tuukka Toivonen, 122–138. London: Routledge.

Ihara, Saikaku. 1990. *The Great Mirror of Male Love*. Trans. Paul Gordon Schalow. Stanford: Stanford University Press.

Imamura, Anne E. 1987. *Urban Japanese Housewives: At Home and in the Community*. Honolulu: University of Hawai'i Press.

———. 1990. "Strangers in a Strange Land: Coping with Marginality in International Marriage." *Journal of Comparative Family Studies*, 171–191.

Ishii-Kuntz, Masako. 2003. "Balancing Fatherhood and Work: Emergence of Diverse Masculinities in Contemporary Japan." In Roberson and Suzuki, eds., *Men and Masculinities in Contemporary Japan*, 198–216.

Ishii-Kuntz, Masako, and Alexandra R. Maryanski. 2003. "Conjugal Roles and Social Networks in Japanese Families." *Journal of Family Issues* 24 (3): 352–380.

Ishii-Kuntz, Masako, Katsuko Makino, Kuniko Kato, and Michiko Tsuchiya. 2004. "Japanese Fathers of Preschoolers and Their Involvement in Child Care." *Journal of Marriage and Family* 66 (3): 779–791.

Ivry, Tsipy. 2009. *Embodying Culture: Pregnancy in Japan and Israel*. New Brunswick: Rutgers University Press.

James. 2009. "Problems with New York Times Report on 2-D Love in Japan." *Japan Probe.* http://www.japanprobe.com/2009/07/27/problems-with-new-york-times -report-on-2-d-love-in-japan/.

Jankowiak, William R., ed. 2008. *Intimacies: Love and Sex across Cultures.* New York: Columbia University Press.

"Japan's 'Bizarre' Spike in Divorce Ceremonies." 2011. *The Week,* July 7. http://theweek .com/articles/483512/japans-bizarre-spike-divorce-ceremonies.

"Japan: Solo Weddings for Single Women." 2014. BBC.com, December 22. http://www .bbc.com/news/blogs-news-from-elsewhere-30574801.

Jolivet, Muriel. 1997. *Japan: The Childless Society? The Crisis of Motherhood.* London: Routledge.

Kageyama, Yuri. 2014. "Infidelity Dating Site Ashley Madison Is Scoring Big in Japan." *Huffington Post,* April 2. http://www.huffingtonpost.com/2014/04/02/adultery-site -big-in-japa_0_n_5078470.html.

Kaneko, Maya. 2014. "Single, Sad? Solo Weddings Pamper Both Wives and Unmarried Ladies." *Japan Times Online,* December 25. http://www.japantimes.co.jp/news/2014 /12/25/national/single-sad-solo-weddings-pamper-both-wives-and-unmarried -ladies/.

Katayama, Lisa. 2009a. "Love in 2-D." *New York Times Magazine,* July 21. http://www .nytimes.com/2009/07/26/magazine/26FOB-2DLove-t.html.

———. 2009b. "Love in 2-D." *Boing Boing.* http://boingboing.net/2009/07/23/love-in -2d.html.

Kawano, Satsuki, Glenda S Roberts, and Susan Orpett Long, eds. 2014. *Capturing Contemporary Japan.* Honolulu: University of Hawai'i Press.

Keating, Joshua. 2013. "No, Japanese People Haven't Given Up on Sex." *Slate,* October 23. http://www.slate.com/blogs/the_world_/2013/10/23/are_japanese_people _really_having_less_sex_than_anyone_else.html.

Kelly, William W., ed. 2004. *Fanning the Flames: Fans and Consumer Culture in Contemporary Japan.* Albany: State University of New York Press.

Kelsky, Karen. 2001. *Women on the Verge: Japanese Women, Western Dreams.* Durham, NC: Duke University Press.

Kinsella, Sharon. 2014. *Schoolgirls, Money and Rebellion in Japan.* London: Routledge.

Koch, Gabriele. 2016. "Producing *iyashi*: Healing and Labor in Tokyo's Sex Industry." *American Ethnologist* 43 (4):704–716.

Kondo, Dorinne. 1993. "Uchi no kaisha: Company as Family?" In *Situated Meaning,* edited by Jane Bachnik and Charles Quinn, 169–191. Ithaca, NY: Cornell University Press.

Kosugi, Reiko. 2008. *Escape from Work: Freelancing Youth and the Challenge to Corporate Japan.* Melbourne: Trans Pacific Press.

Kulick, Don. 1998. *Travesti: Sex, Gender, and Culture among Brazilian Transgendered Prostitutes.* Chicago: University of Chicago Press.

Kumagai, Fumie. 2008. *Families in Japan: Changes, Continuities, and Regional Variations.* Lanham, MD: University Press of America.

Kurotani, Sawa. 2005. *Home Away from Home: Japanese Corporate Wives in the United States.* Durham, NC: Duke University Press.

LaFleur, William R. 1992. *Liquid Life: Abortion and Buddhism in Japan.* Princeton, NJ: Princeton University Press.

Lah, Kyung. 2010. "Divorce Ceremonies Give Japanese Couples a New Way to Untie the

Knot." CNN.com, September 7. http://www.cnn.com/2010/WORLD/asiapcf/09/07/japan.divorce.ceremonies/

Lancaster, Roger N. 1992. *Life Is Hard: Machismo, Danger, and the Intimacy of Power in Nicaragua.* Berkeley: University of California Press.

Lazarus-Black, Mindie. 2007. *Everyday Harm: Domestic Violence, Court Rites, and Cultures of Reconciliation.* Urbana: University of Illinois Press.

Lebra, Takie Sugiyama. 1984. *Japanese Women: Constraint and Fulfillment.* Honolulu: University of Hawai'i Press.

Leheny, David Richard. 2006. *Think Global, Fear Local: Sex, Violence, and Anxiety in Contemporary Japan.* Ithaca, NY: Cornell University Press.

Leupp, Gary P. 2003. *Interracial Intimacy in Japan: Western Men and Japanese Women, 1543–1900.* London and New York: Continuum.

Lin, Ho Swee. 2008. "Private Love in Public Space: Love Hotels and the Transformation of Intimacy in Contemporary Japan." *Asian Studies Review* 32 (1): 31–56.

Lowe, Lisa. 2015. *The Intimacies of Four Continents.* Durham, NC: Duke University Press Books.

Lukacs, Gabriella. 2015. "The Labor of Cute: Net Idols, Cute Culture, and the Digital Economy in Contemporary Japan." *positions* 23 (3): 487–513.

Lunsing, Wim. 1995. "Japanese Gay Magazines and Marriage Advertisements." *Journal of Gay and Lesbian Social Services* 3 (3): 71–88.

———. 2005. "The Politics of Okama and Onabe: Uses and Abuses of Terminology Regarding Homosexuality and Transgender." In McLelland and Dasgupta, eds., *Genders, Transgenders and Sexualities in Japan*, 81–95.

Mackenzie, Sonja. 2013. *Structural Intimacies: Sexual Stories in the Black AIDS Epidemic.* New Brunswick, NJ: Rutgers University Press.

Mackintosh, Jonathan D. 2010. *Homosexuality and Manliness in Postwar Japan.* London: Routledge.

Mancuso, Gail. 2010. "Klaus and Greta." *30 Rock*, Season 4, Episode 10.

Maree, Claire. 2014. "Sexual Citizenship at the Intersections of Patriarchy and Heteronormativity: Same-Sex Partnerships and the Koseki." In *Japan's Household Registration System and Citizenship: Koseki, Identification and Documentation*, edited by David Chapman and Karl Jakob Krogness, 187–202. London: Routledge.

Marx, W. David. 2007. "Vending Machine Couture as Nation." *Néojaponisme.* http://neojaponisme.com/2007/10/22/vending-machine-couture-as-nation/.

Masquelier, Adeline. 2009. "Lessons from *Rubí*: Love, Poverty, and the Educational Value of Dramas in Niger." In Cole and Thomas, eds., *Love in Africa*, 204–228.

Mathews, Gordon. 2003. "Can A 'Real Man' Live for His Family? *Ikigai* and Masculinity in Today's Japan." In Roberson and Suzuki, eds., *Men and Masculinities in Contemporary Japan*, 109–125.

———. 2014. "Being a Man in Straitened Japan: The View from Twenty Years Later." In Kawano, Roberts, and Long, eds., *Capturing Contemporary Japan*, 60–80.

Matsui, Yayori. 1995. "The Plight of Asian Migrant Women Working in Japan's Sex Industry." In *Japanese Women: New Feminist Perspectives on the Past, Present, and Future*, edited by Kumiko Fujimura-Fanselow and Atsuko Kameda, 309–319. New York: Feminist Press.

McGlotten, Shaka. 2013. *Virtual Intimacies: Media, Affect, and Queer Sociality.* Albany: State University of New York Press.

McGuire, Caroline. 2014a. "Company Sells 'Solo Weddings' Where Girls Get Married

without a Man." *Mail Online*, October 24. http://www.dailymail.co.uk/femail/article
-2811347/Want-hitched-don-t-man-Head-Japan-company-sells-solo-weddings
helping-girls-experience-thrills-getting-married-without-husband.html.
———. 2011b. "Want to Get Hitched But Don't Have a Man? Head to Japan Where a
Company Sells 'Solo Weddings,' Helping Girls Experience the Thrills of Getting
Married without a Husband." *DailyMail*.com, December 28. http://www.dailymail
.co.uk/femail/article-2811347/Want-hitched-don-t-man-Head-Japan-company
-sells-solo-weddings-helping-girls-experience-thrills-getting-married-without
-husband.html.

McLelland, Mark J. 2000. *Male Homosexuality in Modern Japan: Cultural Myths and Social Realities*. London: Routledge.

———. 2005. *Queer Japan from the Pacific War to the Internet Age*. Lanham, MD: Rowman and Littlefield.

———. 2012 *Love, Sex, and Democracy in Japan during the American Occupation*. New York: Palgrave Macmillan.

McLelland, Mark, and Romit Dasgupta, eds. 2005. *Genders, Transgenders and Sexualities in Japan*. London: Routledge.

McLelland, Mark, Katsuhiko Suganuma, and James Welker. 2007. *Queer Voices from Japan: First Person Narratives from Japan's Sexual Minorities*. Lanham, MD: Lexington Books.

McLelland, Mark, Kazumi Nagaike, Katsuhiko Suganuma, and James Welker, eds. 2015. *Boys Love Manga and Beyond: History, Culture, and Community in Japan*. Jackson: University Press of Mississippi.

Merriam-Webster. 2015. Accessed online: http://www.merriam-webster.com.

Mitsukoshi, Kozuke, Florian Kohlbacher, and Christoph Schimkowsky. 2016. "Japan's *Ikumen* Discourse: Macro and Micro Perspectives on Modern Fatherhood." *Japan Forum* 28 (2): 212–232.

Miura, Seiichirō. 2009. *"Kawatteshimatta onna" to "kawaritakunai otoko": Danjo kyōdō sankaku nōto* ["Women Who Have Changed" and "Men Who Refuse to Change": Notes on Gender Equality]. Tokyo: Gakubunsha.

Miyamoto, Michiko. 2012. *Wakamono ga muenkasuru: Shigoto fukushi komyuniti de tsunagu* [Young People without Ties: Connecting Work, Welfare, and Community]. Tokyo: Chikumashobō.

Moore, Katrina L. 2010. "Sexuality and Sense of Self in Later Life: Japanese Men's and Women's Reflections on Sex and Aging." *Journal of Cross-Cultural Gerontology* 25 (2): 149–163.

Moore, Matthew. 2008. "Japanese Newspaper Admits Infamous Sex Column Was Untrue." July 22. http://www.telegraph.co.uk/news/newstopics/howaboutthat /2443937/Japanese-newspaper-admits-infamous-sex-column-was-untrue.html.

Moorhead, Laurel. 2010. "Japanese Couples Say 'I Do'—in Divorce Ceremonies." *Reuters*, June 21. http://www.reuters.com/article/2010/06/21/us-divorce-ceremony -idUSTRE65K3YV20100621.

Moriki, Yoshie. 2017. "Physical Intimacy and Happiness in Japan: Sexless Marriages and Parent Co-sleeping." In *Happiness and the Good Life in Japan*, edited by Wolfram Manzenreiter and Barbara Holthus, 41–52. London: Routledge.

Moriki, Yoshie, Kenji Hayashi, and Rikiya Matsukura. 2015. "Sexless Marriages in Japan: Prevalence and Reasons." In *Low Fertility and Reproductive Health in East Asia*, edited by Haohiro Ogawa and Iqbal Shah, 161–185. New York: Springer.

Morioka, Masahiro. 2008. *Sōshokukei danshi no ren'aigaku* [Studies of Herbivore Men's Love Lives]. Tokyo: Media fakutorī.

Murai, Shunsuke. 2015. "Tokyo's Shibuya and Setagaya Wards Issue First Same-Sex Partnership Papers." *Japan Times*, November 5. Available at http://www.japantimes.co.jp/news/2015/11/05/national/social-issues/shibuya-set-issue-first-certificates-recognizing-sex-couples/#.V4vK1dbWoaj.

Muroi, Hisae, and Naoko Sasaki. 1997. "Tourism and Prostitution in Japan." In *Gender, Work and Tourism*, edited by M. Thea Sinclair, 180–199. London: Routledge.

Nagaike, Kazumi. 2015. "Do Heterosexual Men Dream of Homosexual Men? BL Fudanshi and Discourse on Male Feminization." In McLelland, Nagaike, Suganuma, and Welker, eds., *Boys Love Manga and Beyond*, 189–209.

Nakane, Chie. 1967. *Kinship and Economic Organization in Rural Japan*. New York: Humanities Press.

Narabayashi Yasushi. 1997. *Sekkusuresu kappuru: Jidai ga umidashita yamai* [Sexless Couples: A Disease of the Era]. Tokyo: Ayumi shuppan.

National Institute of Population and Social Science Research. 2012. *Population Statistics of Japan*. http://www.ipss.go.jp/p-info/e/psj2012/PSJ2012.asp.

Ninomiya Shūhei. 2006. *Koseki to jinken* [The Family Register and Human Rights]. Osaka: Buraku kaihōjinken kenkyūjo.

Norgren, Tiana 2001. *Abortion before Birth Control: The Politics of Reproduction in Postwar Japan*. Princeton, NJ: Princeton University Press.

Occhi, Debra J., Cindi L. SturtzSreetharan, and Janet S. Shibato-Smith. 2010. "Finding Mr. Right: New Looks at Gendered Modernity in Japanese Televised Romance." In *Language in Public Spaces in Japan*, edited by Nanette Gottlieb, 87–104. London: Routledge.

Ogawa, Naohiro, and Robert D. Retherford. 1993. "The Resumption of Fertility Decline in Japan: 1973–92." *Population and Development Review* 19 (4): 703–741.

Parreñas, Rhacel. 2011. *Illicit Flirtations: Labor, Migration, and Sex Trafficking in Tokyo*. Stanford: Stanford University Press.

Pflugfelder, Gregory M. 1999. *Cartographies of Desire: Male-Male Sexuality in Japanese Discourse, 1600–1950*. Berkeley: University of California Press.

Plath, David W. 1980. *Long Engagements: Maturity in Modern Japan*. Stanford: Stanford University Press.

Plautz, Jessica. 2014. "Solo Weddings in Japan: All of the Glamour, None of the Relationship." *Mashable*, December 23. http://mashable.com/2014/12/23/solo-weddings-japan/.

Plummer, Ken. 2003. *Intimate Citizenship: Private Decisions and Public Dialogues*. Seattle: University of Washington Press.

Povinelli, Elizabeth A. 2006. *The Empire of Love: Toward a Theory of Intimacy, Genealogy, and Carnality*. Durham, NC: Duke University Press.

Prough, Jennifer S. 2010. *Straight from the Heart: Gender, Intimacy, and the Cultural Production of Shojo Manga*. Honolulu: University of Hawai'i Press.

Rebick, Marcus. 2006. "Changes in the Workplace and Their Impact on the Family." In *The Changing Japanese Family*, edited by Marcus Rebick and Ayumi Takenaka, 75–93. New York: Routledge.

Reddy, Gayatri. 2006. "The Bonds of Love: Companionate Marriage and the Desire for Intimacy among Hijras in Hyderabad, India." In Hirsch and Wardlow, eds., *Modern Loves*, 174–192.

Richards, Adam. 2009. "Nemutan's Revenge—Some Fact-Checking and Reaction to the NYT Story on Anime Fetishists." *Mutantfrog Travelogue*. http://www.mutantfrog .com/2009/07/27/nemutans-revenge-some-fact-checking-and-reaction-to-the-nyt -story on anime-fetishists/.

Roberson, James E., and Nobue Suzuki, eds. 2003. *Men and Masculinities in Contemporary Japan: Dislocating the Salaryman Doxa*. London: Routledge.

Rohlen, Thomas P. 1974. *For Harmony and Strength: Japanese White-Collar Organization in Anthropological Perspective*. Berkeley: University of California Press.

Ronald, Richard, and Allison Alexy. 2011. "Continuity and Change in Japanese Homes and Families." In *Home and Family in Japan: Continuity and Transformation*, edited by Richard Ronald and Allison Alexy, 1–24. New York: Routledge.

Rosenberger, Nancy. 2013. *Dilemmas of Adulthood: Japanese Women and the Nuances of Long-Term Resistance*. Honolulu: University of Hawai'i Press.

Rowe, Mark Michael. 2011. *Bonds of the Dead: Temples, Burial, and the Transformation of Contemporary Japanese Buddhism*. Chicago: University of Chicago Press.

Ryang, Sonia. 2006. *Love in Modern Japan: Its Estrangement from Self, Sex and Society*. London: Routledge.

Schaeffer, Felicity Amaya. 2013. *Love and Empire: Cybermarriage and Citizenship across the Americas*. New York: New York University Press.

Schoppa, Leonard J. 2006. *Race for the Exits: The Unraveling of Japan's System of Social Protection*. Ithaca, NY: Cornell University Press.

Seaman, Amanda C. 2011. "Making and Marketing Mothers: Guides to Pregnancy in Modern Japan." In *Manners and Mischief: Gender, Power, and Etiquette in Japan*, edited by Jan Bardsley and Laura Miller, 156–177. Berkeley : University of California Press.

Shinmura, Izuru. 1998. *Kojien* [Dictionary], 5th ed. Tokyo: Iwanami shoten.

Simmons, Christina. 1979. "Companionate Marriage and the Lesbian Threat." *Frontiers: A Journal of Women Studies* 4 (3): 54–59.

Smith, Daniel Jordan. 2006. "Love and the Risk of HIV: Courtship, Marriage, Infidelity in Southeastern Nigeria." In Hirsch and Wardlow, eds., *Modern Loves*, 135–156.

———. 2008. "Intimacy, Infidelity, and Masculinity in Southeastern Nigeria." In Jankowiak, ed., *Intimacies*, 224–244.

———. 2009. "Managing Men, Marriage, and Modern Love: Women's Perspectives on Intimacy and Male Infidelity in Southeastern Nigeria." In Cole and Thomas, eds., *Love in Africa*, 157–80.

Spronk, Rachel. 2012. *Ambiguous Pleasures: Sexuality and Middle Class Self-Perceptions in Nairobi*. New York: Berghahn Books.

Stoler, Ann Laura. 2002. *Carnal Knowledge and Imperial Power: Race and the Intimate in Colonial Rule*. Berkeley: University of California Press.

Summerhawk, Barbara, Cheiron McMahill, and Darren McDonald, eds. 1998. *Queer Japan: Personal Stories of Japanese Lesbians, Gays, Transsexuals, and Bisexuals*. Norwich, VT: New Victoria Publishers.

Suzuki, Nobue. 2000. "Women Imagined, Women Imaging: Re/presentations of Filipinas in Japan since the 1980s." *US-Japan Women's Journal* 19: 142–175.

———. 2003. "Transgressing 'Victims': Reading Narratives of 'Filipina Brides' in Japan." *Critical Asian Studies* 35 (3): 399–420.

———. 2005. "Filipina Modern: 'Bad' Filipino Women in Japan." In *Bad Girls of Japan*, edited by Jan Bardsley and Laura Miller, 159–174. New York: Palgrave Macmillan.

Tahhan, Diana Adis. 2014. *The Japanese Family: Touch, Intimacy and Feeling*. London: Routledge.

Takeda, Hiroko. 2004. *The Political Economy of Reproduction in Japan*. London: Routledge.
———. 2008. "Structural Reform of the Family and the Neoliberalisation of Everyday Life in Japan." *New Political Economy* 13 (2): 153–172.
Takeyama, Akiko. 2010. "Intimacy for Sale: Masculinity, Entrepreneurship, and Commodity Self in Japan's Neoliberal Situation." *Japanese Studies* 30 (2): 231–246.
———. 2016. *Staged Seductions: Selling Dreams in a Tokyo Host Club*. Stanford: Stanford University Press.
Tanamura, Masayuki, and Shigenori Nakagawa, eds. 2016. *Dosei pātonāshippu seido: Sekai no doko nihon no jichitai ni okeru donyu no jissai to tenbo* [Same-Sex Partnership: Implementation Systems in Japan and the World]. Tokyo: Nihon kajo shuppan.
Theidon, Kimberly. 2012. *Intimate Enemies: Violence and Reconciliation in Peru*. Philadelphia: University of Pennsylvania Press.
Thomas, Lynne M. and Jennifer Cole. 2009. "Thinking through Love in Africa." In Cole and Thomas, eds., *Love in Africa*, 1–30.
Toivonen, Tuukka. 2013. *Japan's Emerging Youth Policy: Getting Young Adults Back to Work*. London: Routledge.
Tomita, Takeshi, and Jonfa Ryi, eds. 2006. *Kazoku no hen'yō to jendā: Shōshi kōreika to gurōbaruka no naka de* [Gender and Family Transformations: An Aging Society within Globalization]. Tokyo: Nihonhyōronsha.
Traphagan, John W., and John Knight, eds. 2003. *Demographic Change and the Family in Japan's Aging Society*. Albany: State University of New York Press.
Treat, John. 1999. *Great Mirrors Shattered: Homosexuality, Orientalism, and Japan*. Oxford: Oxford University Press.
Ueno, Chizuko. 2009. *The Modern Family in Japan: Its Rise and Fall*. Melbourne: Trans Pacific Press.
Van Bremen, Jan, and D. P. Martinez, eds. 1995. *Ceremony and Ritual in Japan: Religious Practices in an Industrialized Society*. London: Routledge.
"Video: Husbands Gather in Japan for Love Your Wife Day." 2013. *The Guardian*. Available at http://www.theguardian.com/world/video/2013/jan/29/japan-love-your-wife-day-video.
Vogel, Ezra F. 2013 [1971]. *Japan's New Middle Class*. Lanham, MD: Rowman and Littlefield.
Waldman, Katy. 2013. "Young People in Japan Have Given Up on Sex." *Slate*, October 22. http://www.slate.com/blogs/xx_factor/2013/10/22/celibacy_syndrome_in_japan_why_aren_t_young_people_interested_in_sex_or.html.
Wardlow, Holly and Jennifer S. Hirsch. 2006. "Introduction." In Hirsch and Wardlow, eds., *Modern Loves*, 1–34.
White, Merry I. 2002. *Perfectly Japanese: Making Families in an Era of Upheaval*. Berkeley: University of California Press.
Yamamoto, Beverley Anne. 2010. "International Marriage in Japan: An Exploration of Intimacy, Family and Parenthood." Paper presented at the Eighteenth Biennial Conference of the Asian Studies Association of Australia in Adelaide, July 5–8. Available at http://www.asaa.asn.au/ASAA2010/reviewed_papers/Yamamoto-_Beverley.pdf.
Yamaura, Chigusa. 2015. "From Manchukuo to Marriage: Localizing Contemporary Cross-Border Marriages between Japan and Northeast China." *Journal of Asian Studies* 74 (3): 565–588.
Yan, Yunxiang. 2003. *Private Life under Socialism: Love, Intimacy, and Family Change in a Chinese Village, 1949–1999*. Stanford: Stanford University Press.

Yano, Christine. 2004. "Letters from the Heart," In Kelly, ed., *Fanning the Flames*, 41–58.

Zelizer, Viviana A. 2005. *The Purchase of Intimacy*. Princeton, NJ: Princeton University Press

Zelizer, Viviana. 2010. "Caring Everywhere." In Boris and Parreñas, eds., *Intimate Labors*, 267–279.

Zipangu. 1998. *Japan Made in U.S.A*. New York: Zipangu.

C H A P T E R   2

Students Outside
the Classroom

Youth's Intimate Experiences in 1990s Japan

Yukari Kawahara

In the 1990s, Japanese politicians and the Japanese public faced a range of problems broadly connected to intimacy, from the rapidly falling birthrate to new threats of sexually transmitted diseases such as HIV. An article in the *Asahi Newspaper* summarized one of the debates with the headline "Teachers Confused about How to Teach about Sexual Intercourse" (Seikō no atsukai, kyōshi ni tomadoi; *Asahi Newspaper* 1992). The article reported that there was considerable anxiety among Japanese teachers about sex education teaching methods, in particular over whether or not schools should teach children in detail about sexual intercourse. The article introduced the opposing views of two prominent educators, one insisting that it was better to teach children about sexual intercourse as early as possible before they had any preconceptions about it and the other arguing that it was premature to teach children about sexual intercourse, in particular at the elementary school level. Around the same time, the mass media presented many discussions concerning when, what, and how to teach sex education in schools. This attention occurred because the Ministry of Education revised and expanded the sex education curriculum in 1989.[1] The ministry implemented the new curriculum in 1992 for elementary schools, in 1993 for junior high schools, and in 1994 for high schools. However, when I researched how sexuality was being taught in schools, I realized that the controversy about teaching sexual intercourse was only a superficial battle. The new curriculum engaged many topics critical to contemporary concerns of the Japanese state and its population— the shape of families, gender ideologies, adolescent sexuality, and the AIDS crisis. In other words, through the medium of the new curriculum, government bureaucrats, schoolteachers, educators, parents, and adolescents were contesting and negotiating norms and meanings of gender, sexuality, intimacy, and family.

Since that time, Japan has continued to experience significant social upheavals reflecting these contested questions. The educational system has undergone major institutional changes, a weak economy and unstable politics that were new conditions of the early 1990s continue to take a toll on individual lives and aggregate prosperity, and the society has been badly shaken by the triple disasters of March 2011 (Allison 2013; Brinton 2011; Eades, Goodman, and Hada 2005; Gill, Steger, and Slater 2013). Partly by choice and partly by necessity, work careers have shifted from the secure to the insecure; men and women marry later and have fewer children; divorce is rising along with the number of never-married people; women—often against structural obstacles—have longer work careers; and there is less interest in meeting official expectations of family elder care (Alexy 2010; Kawano 2010; Kelly 1993; Kelly and White 2006; Nakano 2011; Nakano and Wagatsuma 2004; Rosenberger 2013; Rosenbluth 2007; Schoppa 2008; White 2002).

Both social institutions most directly explored in my research—the family and the education system—have shifted in substantial ways, with ideological challenges to what constitutes an "ideal" and new patterns of practice, including later marriage, fewer children, and a rapidly aging population in the family sphere, as well as bullying, school refusal, and state-led restructuring in the educational sphere.[2] Of course, as demonstrated in my original research and at present, tight links between family norms and educational practices mean that these two spheres are never totally separate.[3] Both individual families and the education system offer helpful perspectives on key questions about the nature, direction, and impact of recent societal changes. Social scientists, state authorities, and media commentators sharply debate the motivations of these accumulating individual choices and their consequences for society: is Japan becoming more open and diverse in life options or more unequal and vulnerable? How do, and should, family forms reflect these ideals?

In the mid-1990s, it was not clear whether the economic difficulties and political stasis that had recently come to beset Japan would continue, but indeed they have. It was far from certain what young people would choose in seeking jobs and spouses, in valuing personal freedom or felt obligation, in aspiring to conventional careers and family roles or crafting new adult trajectories. The teenagers whom I observed in the sex education classrooms of the mid-1990s and met with outside of school are now the thirty-something adults of contemporary Japan. The choices and dilemmas they faced in their younger years, as well as the decisions they made, reveal how personal decisions both create and reflect national patterns of change.

In this chapter, I will examine how individual adolescents in the mid-1990s made sense of their own sexuality in relation to intimate and social relationships. My broad intention is to share a baseline for adolescents' ideas surrounding their intimate expectations and experiences in the 1990s and use these earlier examples to throw into new relief the life choices and life chances of people now in their thirties, some of which are examined in subsequent chapters in this volume.

For this research, conducted from April 1994 to March 1995, I situated myself at four schools in and around Tokyo. The schools represented a range of socioeconomic levels: Eiga Girls' High School was an elite private school; Nakate Junior High School and Kida High School both included middle-class students, many of whom aspired to attend university or two-year colleges; and Tomei Commercial High School, a vocational school, had mostly working-class students who did not plan to go to college.[4] I came to understand that although a school's sexual education curriculum played a role in students' perspectives, students neither passively absorbed nor completely ignored the sex education classes. As will be demonstrated in the cases below, students were influenced through peer socializing and media exposure and recognized that the messages were often contradictory. I will first share an overview of the general patterns and trends I found concerning adolescent attitudes and expectations for intimate relationships. Then I will introduce and analyze six short narratives of adolescents who had a spectrum of intimate experiences.[5]

FRIENDSHIPS

Friends (*tomadachi*) of the opposite sex played important roles in Japanese adolescents' lives. Most of the students had such friends. In the case of high school students, these friends could come from the same high school or the same cram school, but they preferred the friends who had graduated from the same junior high school (sometimes from the same elementary school) and then attended different high schools. Such distance between students and their friends allowed them to talk about confidential matters without worrying about the spread of rumors.

These friend relationships were quite common and quite intense. For example, Machiko, a girl at Kida High School, talked with a male friend on the phone every week and met him in a cafe every other week. Some others regularly went to the movies or concerts together. Japanese adolescents, however, differentiated "friends" from "lovers" (*koibito*), at least in terminology if not in practice. The line between was often obscure in actual experience. Trust and interdependence often pushed a friendship into a love relationship. These patterns stand in sharp contrast with the contemporary patterns Miles analyzes (this volume).

LANGUAGE OF LIKE AND LOVE

When adolescents expressed their love, they often used the term *suki*. Although there is another term to express one's love—*ai shiteru*—adolescents rarely used this term, and it appeared only in literature, TV dramas, and songs.[6] The verb *suki* can be interpreted in many ways, including "like," "have a crush on," or "love," depending on the intensity of a person's feeling for his or her partner. For example, Mitsuo, a boy at Kida High School, used the term as follows: "She [one of his classmates] has long hair. She's pretty and gentle. I like [*suki*] her, but I hesitate to ask her to go out on dates." In this case, Mitsuo expresses not so much his "love" but his "like" for a girl with the term *suki*. In contrast, Atsuko, a girl at Kida High School, used the term *suki* in the following way: "I had a crush on [*suki*] the boyfriend of my best female friend. I did not want to betray my friend, so I tried to stop my emotions, but it did not work." The experience of *suki* for Atsuko included emotional longing and the sense of guilt as well as passion.

CONTRACEPTION

In their talk, adolescents maintained that contraception was a male responsibility rather than a joint responsibility.[7] For example, girls said, "Every time we have sex, *he* [not we] uses a condom," or "*He* [not we] did not use a condom last time, so I am worried now [about being pregnant]." Boys also recognized this responsibility. Kunio, a boy at Tomei Commercial High School, stated, "I have not had sex because I am afraid that I might fail using it [contraception]. I don't know how to use it correctly. Because I am young, I cannot take the responsibility for it [pregnancy]."

Because the birth control pill was not approved in Japan until 1999, most adolescents in my research depended on condoms as their only means of contraception. Both boys and girls tended to assign responsibility for contraception only to boys. This did not mean, however, that boys actually used a condom when they had sex. On the contrary, many girls reported boys' unwillingness to use one. Akemi, at Tomei Commercial High School, said, "He does not like to use a condom, so I always ask him to put it on [*tsuke te morau yō tanomu*], but he always says, 'Don't worry.'" Although boys recognized their responsibility for contraception, they often ignored that responsibility. As a result, ultimately, girls shouldered the responsibility for any unwanted pregnancies by having abortions.

MARRIAGE

When adolescents talked about their plans for marriage (*kekkon*), only a few mentioned the possibility of remaining single or not having a child. However, the term "appropriate age" (*tekireiki*), a term emphasized in Japanese health education textbooks, was hardly ever used in reference to marriage. In addition, girls did not use (and did not feel pressured by) the popular term "Christmas Cake," which was then used to mock a woman who was still not married by the age of twenty-five.[8]

Although these students did not actually use the term "appropriate age," their talk of marriage still included the issue of appropriate age in terms of their life plans. For example, Koji, a boy at Kida High School, talked about his marriage plans as follows: "I want to get married in my late twenties, after graduating from university and working for several years. I think that if you get married too young, you cannot manage to live [*yatte ikenai*]. On the other hand, if I got married too late, I would feel sorry for my child since I would be an old father." Boys tended to discuss their "appropriate marriage age" as the middle or late twenties, after they expected to have gotten a good job. Girls defined "appropriate marriage age" in diverse ways, depending on their life plans. Girls at Kida High School hoped to marry in their mid-twenties, after graduating from a two-year college and working for several years. Girls at Tomei Commercial High School tended to want to marry immediately after graduating from high school or in their early twenties. On the other hand, girls at the elite Eiga Girls' High School pushed their "appropriate marriage age" until later. For example, Yoneko told me, "I am not going to get married until my late twenties, like twenty-eight or twenty-nine. I am hoping to become a lawyer, so I want to study hard and pass the law exam before I get married." Like Yoneko, many girls at Eiga Girls' High School calculated their "appropriate age" in terms of their planned career accomplishments.

Girls often used the term "housewife" (*sengyō shufu*) when they talked about whether they planned to work after marriage. For example, Yoneko, at Eiga Girls' High School (quoted above), told me, "I don't want to become a housewife like my mother. I will continue working after marriage. After marriage, I want my husband to help with housework too. I want to have one child before thirty, so I want to live near my mother and want to get help with child care from my mother." Mariko, a girl at Kida High School, talked in a different way: "I am not going to be a housewife immediately after marriage. But once a child is born, I want to quit my job and be with the child at home. I like children, so I want to have two children." On the other hand, Naomi, a girl at Tomei Commercial High School, told me, "I want to get married around twenty-one and have one boy and one girl soon. I want to become a housewife and take good care of my children if possible, but probably I will have to have a part-time job." Like Naomi, most of the girls at Tomei Commercial High School hoped to become housewives. However, these working-class girls also accepted the reality that they would have to have part-time or full-time jobs to support household expenses.

Boys' opinions about a wife's role were divided mainly into three categories of preferences: (1) A wife should stay home after marriage; (2) A wife could work outside the home after marriage, but she should stay home after children were born; (3) A wife could work outside the home, but she would have to do the housework and child rearing by herself. Only a few boys preferred the first category, and most of them were not so concerned about whether a wife was a housewife. The majority fell into one of the latter two categories. A boy's experience with his own mother strongly affected his preferences about his future wife's role. One aim of the Ministry of Education in introducing home economics for both genders has been to reform boys' gender ideology so that men can decrease women's burdens of housework and child rearing. Many boys' opinions, however, suggested that they had no intention of helping with housework and child rearing. This is precisely one reason why more and more women delay marriage in the contemporary context. The lessons from their schools' sex education or home economics did not reach boys in ways that significantly transformed their gender ideologies.

ADOLESCENTS' INTIMATE EXPERIENCES

According to a survey among high school twelfth graders in Tokyo in 1993, 50 percent of the boys and 47 percent of the girls had experienced kissing, 35 percent of the boys and 31 percent of girls had indulged in petting, and 27 percent of the boys and 22 percent of the girls had had sexual intercourse.[9] These results tell us that almost half of the adolescents had experienced kissing and a quarter had had sexual intercourse by the time of high school graduation. These quantitative data, however, say little about the motivations adolescents attached to their sexual activities. Why did they engage in sexual behavior or avoid it? Did their sexual behaviors result from feelings of romantic love or from something else? How were their sexual experiences associated with their future life plans such as marriage? In my ethnographic research, I found various interpretations of love and sexuality among adolescents, often reflecting their subject positions and situations. Moreover, conflicts and contradictions often appeared in one person. To show the divergence and complexity, I present narratives from six adolescents, selected from forty-nine adolescents I interviewed. These narratives are arranged according to the degree of romance and sexual experience. I hope they give the reader a sense of the individual differences, as well as the shared problems that adolescents face.

Yasuo, Boy, 16, Kida High School

Romantic relationships of course always involve declarations of one's feelings of love. However, Yasuo is a shy and quiet boy. He told me that he has loved a girl in his class since he entered high school almost seven months ago. He had tried to tell her of his love several times, but he could not: "We are good classmates and good friends. However, if I confess my love for her and she refuses it, we will not be able to be good friends any more. I am afraid of ruining our current relationship. I am also worried that she will tell her friends and my classmates will know about it." Yasuo was worried about not only her rejection, but also her acceptance of his love for the following reason: "If I told her and she said OK, what should I do? It would take a great deal of trouble to think about the whole process of dating. You know, I have no time for thinking about such things because I have to study for university entrance exams."

At Kida High School, I encountered many boys who liked someone and yet did not express their affection because of having to study for the university entrance exams. The effort needed to enter a good university thus became an obstacle to initiating a romance for a boy and at the same time served to justify a shy boy's reason for not declaring his love.

Yasuo sometimes felt envious of girls because of gendered expectations about work: "I was often told by my parents that I am the eldest son and that I should enter a good university. For a girl, it is not necessary that she go to a good university. She could choose a two-year college, get a job, or get married. I don't mean that I want to become a girl, but it seems to me that a girl's life is much easier and more comfortable than mine." I interviewed Yasuo after school, and after the interview, he went home in a hurry to go to cram school. Yasuo was overwhelmed by the pressure that his parents put on him to enter a good university. However, he could not resist it and made an effort to live up to their expectations. The pressure to go to a good university was extremely strong for boys like Yasuo and often circumscribed their initiation into romance and relationships.

Tomeko, Girl, 17, Eiga Girls' High School

Tomeko was a lively cheerleader with short hair. She was very busy after school with club activities and lessons on the tea ceremony or flute. She also liked to go to a karaoke club with friends and sing songs with abandon. Tomeko came from a wealthy family, and her parents did not allow her to have a part-time job. They gave her ¥30,000 ($300) a month for pocket money, a high sum compared to the ¥5,000 ($50) that was average pocket money for the high schoolers that I met. Tomeko had had a good male friend since elementary school. Even after she had a boyfriend, she still met the male friend and talked about her love life with him. When she ended that relationship, she talked about it with him, and he consoled her. I asked if there were any possibility that he would become her boyfriend. Tomeko replied, "I don't think so. He also has a girlfriend." She made a clear distinction between a friend and a lover. For Tomeko, her male friend served as a consultant for her intimate relationships.

Tomeko liked to initiate romantic relationships: "I like chasing a man rather than being chased." In her junior high school days, she declared her love twice to boys in the same junior high school. Both declarations resulted in failure. Nevertheless, she did not feel bad or embarrassed. In her thinking, a girl who initiates a love relationship also often says good-bye first and therefore has more control. Tomeko also took the initiative toward her next boyfriend. She met him in a baseball club at Eiga Boys' High School when she went to his game as a cheerleader. She fell in love with him at first sight, got his telephone number from her male friend, and called him: "I used to use the term that I like him [*suki desu*]. But recently, I asked him, 'Please go out on a date with me [*tsukiatte kudasai*].' If I had only said, 'I like you,' then nothing would have happened. So this time, I asked him, 'Would you like to go out for a date?'" They have been dating for a while, going to a karaoke bar, visiting a cultural festival, and going to an amusement park with other friends. According to Tomeko, he is extremely shy. During the six-month relationship, he has not even touched her hands.

> TOMEKO: My friend told me that he did not touch me because I am too guarded with him. But it is not true. Once I gave him an opportunity, asking him to walk me home at night. But nothing happened on the way.
>
> Q: If he asked you to make love, would you accept it?
>
> TOMEKO: No, I don't think so. Kissing is OK. But it is too early for a high schooler to have sex.
>
> Q: Why do you think so?

TOMEKO: Well, I don't know. I don't think that you have to wait for sex until marriage, but I still feel that it is too early for high schoolers to make love.

Tomeko is an aggressive girl in her love relations; however, she is not sexually active, limiting her sexual behavior only to kissing, at least during her time in high school. Like Tomeko, most of the girls at Eiga Girls' High School are not particularly sexually active, stopping at kissing and petting.

Tomeko eventually broke up with her latest boyfriend because she planned to go to university and thought she could meet a good man there. In fact, she planned to get married at around twenty-four to someone she expected to meet at university. She hoped the man would come from a rich family background like hers: "I think that we share values if we come from the same family background. I prefer a man who has stable economic resources since I want to make a family that is similar to my family." She believed that she would meet a more promising man at the university, and her future prospects made her less involved emotionally and sexually with her high school boyfriends.

Kinue, Girl, 18, Kida High School

Kinue was a cheerful, giggling girl with a baby face. She liked children, so she planned to enter a two-year college to become a kindergarten teacher. Kinue had her first boyfriend when she was a twelfth grader:

I had been asked for dates before, but I felt that it was too early to have a boyfriend, especially when I was a junior high school student. Rather than having a boyfriend, I felt comfortable having just male friends. At first, my current boyfriend, who sat next to me, was just a friend. During the first two months, we went out together as friends. But we have gradually grown to like each other, and then he asked me to become his girlfriend.

Since then, they started getting together, studying together, going to the movies, and shopping together. Kinue's sexual experimentation stopped on the verge of sex:

Q: How far have you gone with him?
KINUE: Well [chuckling to herself]: It was above the waist [*uemade desu*].
Q: So you have not had sex with him, have you?
KINUE: No. He seemed to want it, but I told him that he couldn't go below my waist [*shita wa dame yo*].
Q: Where did you do it? In your room or his room?

KINUE: My mother and his mother stay home since they are not working outside the house, so we cannot do it in our rooms. We do it at school.

Q: School? Where at school?

KINUE: On the stairs below the rooftops when nobody was there after school.

Q: Didn't you feel that someone might find you?

KINUE: I always felt it. So whenever I heard a footstep, I told him, "Stop." Actually, I felt anxious [*ki ga kidewa nai*] whenever we did it.

To find a place for sex was a difficult task for Japanese adolescents.[10] There was another crucial reason for Kinue, however:

Q: Why did you tell him not to have sex?

KINUE: [In a small voice]: I was afraid.

Q: What were you scared about?

KINUE: I was scared of getting pregnant if he didn't take proper precautions. It could happen to me, you know. And a woman who has had an abortion may not have a baby in the future.

Q: Who told you that?

KINUE: In health education class, the teacher gave an example of a woman who could not bear children as a result of having had an abortion. I thought that I should care about my body. I don't want to hurt my body. It is terrible because I like children.

Kinue was very concerned about damaging her ability to reproduce. Her remarks show that, at least in the case of a serious student like Kinue, the sex education instruction at Kida High School has had some effect in preventing an unwanted pregnancy.

Kinue plans to work as a kindergarten teacher until she is twenty-five, then to quit her job and get married. She said that after she and her boyfriend had started making out, she intensified her hope to marry him and become a housewife. Her dream was to make a warm home with him and their children. In these ways, Kinue's sexual behavior intensified her commitment to her boyfriend, pushing her hopes in the direction of marriage.

Suzuko, Girl, 18, Tomei Commercial High School

Suzuko was a pretty and flashy girl. She was never a serious student, skipping school, sometimes wearing cosmetics and dyeing her hair even though it was against school rules. She was, however, very serious about her boyfriend. When she met him in school, he already had a girlfriend. However, she could not forget him and told him that she liked him. He spurned her then, saying, "I am sorry, but I have a girlfriend." Two months later, he called her and told her that he had broken up with the girlfriend. Two weeks after that, he told her that he liked her. Two months later, they made love. She said, "He was not the first man for me. I had sex first when I was in the tenth grade at high school. But the sex with him [her current boyfriend] is the best of all and very gentle for me. There are boys who insert it [the penis] without even a caress. However, he is not that type. After sex, I feel that he protects me more, and I love him more." They usually make love in his house before his father and mother come home from work. His grandfather and grandmother, however, are at his house:

> Q: Do you mind that his grandfather and grandmother are at home when you have sex?
> SUZUKO: No, I don't mind. They are on the first floor and we are on the second floor, and they are hard of hearing.
> Q: Have you ever used a love hotel?
> SUZUKO: Yes, I have. But we have to spend ¥5,000–8,000 there. We cannot go there every time we have sex.
> Q: When you go to a love hotel, who pays for it, he or you?
> SUZUKO: We both do. I have a part-time job [as a waitress at a restaurant], and he does not. When I have more money, of course, I pay. He says, "I am sorry to have to let you pay." But I don't mind.

Suzuko increased her working hours since they began going to the love hotel.

After beginning a sexual relationship, Suzuko became very possessive of her boyfriend. Whenever he talked to another girl, she felt jealous and asked him not to talk to her. She also made changes in herself according to his tastes. For example, she stopped wearing showy cosmetics and earrings. He, however, gradually got tired of her obsession with him and told her that he no longer wanted to be with her. They broke up for about six months. Suzuko said:

> After we broke up, I got a new boyfriend. I had sex with him too. But I was always comparing him to my previous boyfriend, and I felt bored with the new boyfriend. I told him good-bye. Then I called my former boyfriend and asked him if it was OK for me to just call. He accepted it, and then I continued to call him. One day, he said to me "Let's go out." I said to him, "But you told me that you don't want to go out with me any more." "Forget that," he replied. I was very glad to hear it. Then we went out together like before.

They used to use a condom when they first had sex. However, after they reestablished their relationship, they never used a condom: "He asked me to marry him after graduation in March. I am so glad because I really want to marry him. Since then, I haven't asked him to use a condom. The graduation from high school is soon [in March], so even if I got pregnant, there would be no problem."

Suzuko's words show that her sexual behavior was closely connected with marriage and reproduction. For Suzuko, sex with her boyfriend was not just for pleasure and connection with him; rather it strongly involved her future life course. Unlike the women represented in the materials from the Ministry of Education, Suzuko was not a sexually passive girl but one who was having sexual relationships with several boys and even earning money to pay for a love hotel. However, in the process of her sexual relationship with her boyfriend, she strengthened her commitment to him and began to hope for marriage and reproduction, ultimately reinforcing the government's pro-natal policy.

Kurao, Boy, 17, Tomei Commercial High School

Whereas girls' sexual behavior often involved their thoughts about marriage, most boys denied that their current sexual behaviors were associated with their future life plans. Kurao was one of the boys whose current sexual behavior had nothing to do with marriage. He was a tall, cool boy with a handsome face. He dreamed of becoming a professional musician, and after school he was busy practicing guitar and working at a part-time job (at a sushi bar) so that he could afford new musical instruments.

Kurao had a girlfriend. He usually asked girls to go out on dates, but in this case, it was she who asked him out. She was in another music club at the same school, and they met through joint band practice. She was not the first girl whom he dated, but she was the first girl with whom he made love:

Q: Why did you make love with her? Because she is the girl that you loved most?

KURAO: I don't think so. I liked my former girlfriend more than my current one. But I had the former girlfriend in junior high. I thought that it was too early for a junior high student to have sex.

Q: Why do you think that it is too early?

KURAO: Well, none of my friends had sex in junior high, although all the boys were saying, "I want to do it" [yaritai]. However, in high school, there have been an increasing number of friends who have had sex.

Q: Don't you think that your friends are just making up stories?

KURAO: First, I thought so and told them not to lie. But when I listened to their stories in detail, I got a feeling that they had really done it [yatta].

Q: Were you pressured by your friends' sexual experiences?

KURAO: Very much so. They did not pressure me in our freshman year of high school. But I felt impatient after I became a junior and my friends, in particular an immature one, began having sex.

Thus Kurao's sexual initiation was affected by peers, whom he wanted to emulate, rather than by any feelings of love he might have had.

Kurao told me that he planned to get married in his late twenties, but he had no plans to get married to his girlfriend, a stance that implied that his sexual behavior had little to do with marriage:

Q: Why will you not get married to her? Because it is too early for you to get married?

KURAO: That is one reason. You know, I want to meet many girls before marriage [laughing]. But more than that, she is not the type who is suited to be a wife.

Q: What kind of girl is suited to be a wife?

KURAO: A girl who is good at cooking or likes children, you know. I would like to have such a wife. She is not that type. She likes to go out.

Q: Then, after marriage, you don't want your wife to work outside?

KURAO: If she wants to have a job, that's fine. Actually, I prefer to have a wife who has a job because I plan to become a musician, and I cannot give her a secure life.

Q: Then will you do the housework?

KURAO: Well, I guess so, but I am not so good at cooking, so I prefer a wife who is good at cooking and doing housework.

Kurao wanted his future wife to both contribute to household expenses and do housework. While forcing a double burden on his wife, he had no intention of helping with housework in a positive way. School sex education had failed in reconstructing Kurao's gender ideology, as well as that of other boys.

Yoko, Girl, 18, Tomei Commercial High School

Yoko could not escape her sexual relations. She was a flashy girl with hair dyed brown, and she wore lots of cosmetics. She dated many boys, so her classmates call her a "whore" or a "slut" behind her back. When I interviewed her, however, I found that she had a sincere commitment to one boy. She met him when she was sixteen years old. They were in the same dance group. He was not a high school student but worked as a painter. He was three years older than she. He took her to many places in his car on dates. Yoko related her unforgettable memory of Christmas Eve with him: "We went to Yokosuka last Christmas Eve in his car. We looked for a love hotel in Yokosuka or Yokohama, but all of them were fully occupied that night, so we came back to his house and made love. He was very gentle then, and I remember that he held me tightly. I remember he called my name several times after sex."

Yoko's memories with him are not all so beautiful because he was frequently violent with her. Whenever she wore showy makeup or clothes or if she walked or talked with another boy, he beat her up to the extent that she could not go to school. He wanted to have sole possession of her, but he was unfaithful to her and had relationships with other girls. Yoko noticed this but did not complain because she was afraid of his violence.

When she was seventeen years old, Yoko realized she was pregnant. He asked her to have an abortion, saying that he would let her give birth next time. She honored his request, received money from him, and had an abortion. When she was eighteen years old, she again became pregnant:

> YOKO: I told him that if I had an abortion again, I might not be able to give birth to a child any more.
> Q: What did he say about it?
> YOKO: He did not say a word for a long time and finally said, "I am sorry, but please have an abortion again."
> Q: How did you feel about that?
> YOKO: I was sad because I was expecting that he would tell me we would get married this time. But he did not say that.
> Q: After the first abortion, have you tried contraception?
> YOKO: No, we have not.
> Q: Why not?
> YOKO: I don't want to. Rather, I hoped that I would get pregnant again so that he would decide to get married.

Yoko hoped to get pregnant again and to use pregnancy to demand marriage. Although Yoko was not successful in this attempt, there were some girls who were successful in such a strategy. Thus Japanese girls were not always coerced into unprotected sex by boys. Sometimes she acted in collusion with the pregnancy risk, making an attempt to empower herself (a strategy that is rarely successful).

In this research, I found that Japanese adolescent behavior in the 1990s did not always reflect clear divisions of romantic love, sexual passions, and plans for marriage. On the contrary, adolescent sexual behaviors were complex combinations in which adolescents constructed their own sexual experience by balancing these three drives in different ways. Moreover, the differences in their ways of combining these drives often reflect their gender, their age, their class, and the intersections of these characteristics.

In contrast to boys, girls tended to connect romantic love, sexual passions, and their hopes for marriage. For example, Suzuko at Tomei Commercial High School had a crush on a boy who already had a girlfriend. Even after he spurned her, her romantic love for him continued. When he finally came to her and they made love, she felt the greatest sexual passions and pleasures that she had ever had. Suzuko even increased her part-time job in order to earn the money to go to a love hotel with him. Her sexual passion intensified her commitment to him, and she was hoping to marry him. Thus in Suzuko's case, her initial sexual behavior resulted from her romantic love; then, as she developed her sexual relationship with her boyfriend, her sexual experience strongly connected with her hope for marriage with him.

In contrast to girls, many boys treated their sexual behavior as independent of their romantic love and their plans for marriage. For example, as noted, Kurao at Tomei Commercial High School had sex with a girl not because of his romantic love for her but rather in an effort to emulate friends who had begun to experience sex and talk about it. Moreover, he had no plans to get married to the girlfriend with whom he was having sex. For his wife, he desired a more "domestic" woman who was good at cooking and liked children. Thus Kurao's sexual experience had little to do with romantic love or his plans for marriage. It is wrong, however, to assume that all boys separated their sexual passions from romantic love. On the contrary, many boys were afraid of rejection, so they carefully considered the timing and situation to make a move to sex.

To be sure, unlike girls, boys tended not to combine their current sexual behavior with their marriage plans. In my interviews, only one boy talked about marriage to the girl with whom he was then sexually involved. There may have been a gender difference in their marriage prospects, but we must note that a student's age mediated the gender difference. Most of the boys planned to marry in their middle or late twenties, after they got a stable job. On the other hand, girls (other than the girls at the elite Eiga Girls' High School) tended to hope to marry before they turned twenty-five. In particular, some girls at Tomei Commercial High School hoped to get married immediately after graduating. For those girls, the partner with whom they were then sexually involved could have been a good candidate for a future husband. On the other hand, because they wanted to marry later, boys had almost ten years to meet new girls and therefore were unlikely to imagine their current girlfriends as future wives.

The sexual behavior of boys at Kida High School was often circumscribed by their aspirations and pressures to enter a good university. However, boys at Tomei Commercial High School rarely went to university and often got a working-class job immediately after graduation. They had no need to delay their sexual behavior and tended to start having sex earlier than boys at Kida High School. Thus the difference in aspirations between middle-class boys and working-class boys led to differences in their sexual initiation and behavior.

Girls also had different sexual behaviors, depending on their future plans and their class position. Girls at Eiga Girls' High School, for example, tended to delay their sexual experiences due to their aspirations to attend university, and they tended to have less commitment to their current boyfriends. They believed they would have chances to meet other desirable boys at university, so they had no need to become involved seriously and sexually with their current boyfriends. Because they recognized that they had multiple choices in their future, girls at Eiga Girls' High Schools were less emotionally and sexually involved with their current boyfriends.

In contrast, girls at Kida High School were more committed to their current boyfriends. For example, although Kinue hoped to become the housewife of her current boyfriend, she restricted her sexual behavior to petting only because she was afraid of getting pregnant. She planned to work as a kindergarten teacher until she was twenty-five and then quit her job and get married. Even if she got pregnant before that, she would have inevitably chosen abortion, which she feared because it might cause trouble in her future pregnancies.

Among girls at the three high schools, the girls at Tomei Commercial High School had the strongest commitment to their current boyfriends. Most had sexual relations with their boyfriends, and their sexual experience was strongly connected with their hopes for marriage. Because these girls did not plan to go to university, most intended to get married in their early twenties or immediately after graduating from high school. Therefore, they may well have considered their current boyfriends as their future husbands. Unlike Kinue of Kida High School, girls at Tomei Commercial High School were also less afraid of getting pregnant. Such girls as Yoko and Suzuko even desired pregnancy to encourage their indecisive boyfriends to propose marriage. In fact, for some girls, pregnancy could become decisive leverage enabling them to get married.

In sum, Japanese adolescents never had homogeneous sexual experiences. By combining their romantic love, their sexual passions, and their hope for marriage in different ways, Japanese adolescents constructed and experienced diverse sexual practices. The differences in their sexual experiences often reflected the differences in their aspirations and future plans, which were often mediated by their gender, class, and age.

NOTES

In 2013, Yukari Kawahara passed away at far too young an age. This chapter was prepared by William W. Kelly and Allison Alexy based on the fourth chapter of her dissertation, "Politics, Pedagogy, and Sexuality: Sex Education in Japanese Secondary Schools" (Kawahara 1996).

1. The newer curriculum emphasized that sex is for reproduction while elaborating on heteronormative marital ideals. Although it included some discussion of gender equality, the curriculum also presumed and described "natural" gender differences, such as males being attracted to physicality and women wanting emotional connections. For more see Kawahara (1996, 42–52).

2. Ethnographers have analyzed these issues within a broader context of educational and social change (Cave 2007; Damrow 2014; Decoker and Bjork 2013; Eades, Goodman, and Hada 2005; Fukuzawa and LeTendre 2001; Hallman 2011; Ishida and Slater 2009; Kawahara 2006; Kelly 2014; Lewis 1995; Okano and Tsuchiya 1999; Peak 1991; Rohlen and LeTendre 1999; Sato 2004; Tobin, Hsueh, and Karasawa 2009; Yoneyama 1999).

3. More recent research about sexual education in Japan further demonstrates the continuing political and social controversies surrounding the topic (Castro-Vázquez and Kishi 2002; Hashimoto et al. 2012; Ishiwata 2011; Tashiro, Ushitora, and Watanabe 2011). Frühstück (2003) examines the stakes surrounding bodies, sexuality, and education in Japan at a slightly earlier period.

4. These school names, as well as all names throughout this chapter, are pseudonyms.

5. I collected these stories through participant observation in classrooms and in private and group conversations with students. For longer narratives of these students, as well as those of students not included in this chapter, see Kawahara (1996, 196–230).

6. For more discussion about how these phrases for love are being used in the contemporary moment, see Alexy (this volume).

7. For more on this rhetoric and how it translates into birth control decisions, see Sandberg (this volume).

8. This term disparagingly compares unmarried women over the age of twenty-five to cakes sold for Christmas, which are therefore unwanted after December 25. The term remains recognizable in contemporary Japan, but because the average age at first marriage is now close to thirty for both men and women, it is no longer a common insult (Dales 2014, 227).

9. This survey was conducted among 674 boys and 796 girls who were in twelfth grade in Tokyo in 1993 (Sex Education Research Association of Tokyo 1993). In a 2002 survey involving students in twenty-five schools throughout Okinawa, similar results were obtained (Takakura, Wake, and Kobayashi 2007).

10. A Japanese Sex Education Association survey about where young people have sex found that 46.2 percent of boys had sex at their own homes, 25.5 percent at their girlfriends' homes, and 15.2 percent at a love hotel, which is a special hotel with hourly rates intended to create a space for sex (Japanese Sex Education Association 1994).

REFERENCES

Alexy, Allison. 2010. "The Door My Wife Closed: Houses, Families, and Divorce in Contemporary Japan." In *Home and Family in Japan: Continuity and Transformation*, edited by Richard Ronald and Allison Alexy, 236–253. London: Routledge.

Allison, Anne. 2013. *Precarious Japan*. Durham, NC: Duke University Press.

Asahi Newspaper. 1992. "Seikō no atsukai, kyōshi ni tomadoi" [Teachers Confused about How to Teach about Sexual Intercourse]. August 12.

Brinton, Mary. 2011. *Lost in Transition: Youth, Work, and Instability in Postindustrial Japan.* Cambridge: Cambridge University Press.

Castro-Vázquez, Genaro, and Izumi Kishi. 2002. "'If You Say to Them That They Have to Use Condoms, Some of Them Might Use Them. It Is like Drinking Alcohol or Smoking': An Educational Intervention with Japanese Senior High School Students." *Sex Education* 2 (2): 105–117.

Cave, Peter. 2007. *Primary School in Japan: Self, Individuality and Learning in Elementary Education.* London: Routledge.

Dales, Laura. 2014. "Ohitorisama, Singlehood and Agency in Japan." *Asian Studies Review* 38 (2): 224–242.

Damrow, Amy. 2014. "Navigating the Structures of Elementary School in the United States and Japan: An Ethnography of the Particular." *Anthropology and Education Quarterly* 45 (1): 87–104.

Decoker, Gary, and Christopher Bjork, eds. 2013. *Japanese Education in an Era of Globalization: Culture, Politics, and Equity.* New York: Teachers College Press.

Eades, Jeremy Seymour, Roger Goodman, and Yumiko Hada, eds. 2005. *The "Big Bang" in Japanese Higher Education: The 2004 Reforms and the Dynamics of Change.* Melbourne: Trans Pacific Press.

Frühstück, Sabine. 2003. *Colonizing Sex: Sexology and Social Control in Modern Japan.* Berkeley: University of California Press.

Fukuzawa, Rebecca Erwin, and Gerald K. LeTendre. 2001. *Intense Years: How Japanese Adolescents Balance School, Family and Friends.* New York: Routledge.

Gill, Tom, Brigitte Steger, and David H. Slater, eds. 2013. *Japan Copes with Calamity: Ethnographies of the Earthquake, Tsunami and Nuclear Disasters of March 2011.* Oxford: Peter Lang.

Hallman, Heather Spector. 2011. *Lure of the Intimate: Power Practices in Japanese Adolescent Friendship.* PhD dissertation, University of California, San Diego.

Hashimoto, N., H. Shinohara, M. Tashiro, S. Suzuki, H. Hirose, H. Ikeya, K. Ushitora, A. Komiya, M. Watanabe, T. Motegi, and M. Morioka. 2012. "Sexuality Education in Junior High Schools in Japan." *Sex Education* 12 (1):1–22.

Ishida, Hiroshi, and David H. Slater, eds. 2009. *Social Class in Contemporary Japan: Structures, Sorting and Strategies.* London: Routledge.

Ishiwata, Chieko. 2011. "Sexual Health Education for School Children in Japan: The Timing and Contents." *Journal of the Japan Medical Association* 54 (3): 155–160.

Japanese Sex Education Association [Nihon seikyōiku kyōkai]. 1994. *Seishōnen no seikōdō: Wagakuni no chūgakusei, kōkōsei, daigakusei ni kansuru chōsha hōkoku* [Sexual Behavior and Sexual Intercourse: Survey of Japanese Junior High School, High School, and College Students]. Tokyo: Nihon seikyōiku kyōkai.

Kawahara, Yukari. 1996. "Politics, Pedagogy, and Sexuality: Sex Education in Japanese Secondary Schools." PhD dissertation, Yale University.

———. 2000. "Diverse Strategies in Classroom Instruction: Sex Education in Japanese Secondary Schools." *Japanese Studies* 20 (3): 295–311.

———. 2006. "Local Discourses, Local Practices, and State Power." *Waseda daigaku daigakuin bungaku kenkyū-ka kiyō* [Bulletin of Waseda University, Graduate School of Literature] 51 (3): 49–67.

Kawano, Satsuki. 2010. *Nature's Embrace: Japan's Aging Urbanites and New Death Rites.* Honolulu: University of Hawai'i Press.

Kelly, William W. 1993. "Finding a Place in Metropolitan Japan: Ideologies, Institutions, and Everyday Life." In *Postwar Japan as History*, edited by Andrew Gordon, 189–238. Berkeley: University of California Press.

———. 2014. "Sex Education and the Dynamics of Contemporary Japan: An Appreciation of the Scholarship of Yukari Kawahara." *Waseda daigaku daigaku bungaku gakujutsu-in bunka jinrui-gaku nenpō* [Annual Record of Waseda University's Program in Cultural Anthropology, within the Graduate School of Literature] 8:1–4.

Kelly, William W., and Merry White. 2006. "Students, Slackers, Singles, Seniors and Strangers: Transforming a Family-Nation." In *Japan and Asia: The Dynamics of East Asian Regionalism*, edited by Peter Katzenstein and Tadashi Shiraishi, 62–83. Ithaca, NY: Cornell University Press.

Lewis, Catherine C. 1995. *Educating Hearts and Minds: Reflections on Japanese Preschool and Elementary Education*. Cambridge: Cambridge University Press.

Nakano, Lynne, and Moeko Wagatsuma. 2004. "Mothers and Their Unmarried Daughters: An Intimate Look at Generational Change." In *Japan's Changing Generations: Are Young People Creating a New Society?*, edited by Gordon Mathews and Bruce White, 137–154. London: Routledge.

Nakano, Lynne. 2011. "Working and Waiting for an 'Appropriate Person': How Single Women Support and Resist Family in Japan" In *Home and Family in Japan: Continuity and Transformation*, edited by Richard Ronald and Allison Alexy, 131–151. London: Routledge.

Okano, Kaori, and Motonori Tsuchiya. 1999. *Education in Contemporary Japan: Inequality and Diversity*. Cambridge: Cambridge University Press.

Peak, Lois. 1991. *Learning to Go to School in Japan: The Transition from Home to Preschool Life*. Berkeley: University of California Press.

Rohlen, Thomas P., and Gerald K. LeTendre, eds. 1999. *Teaching and Learning in Japan*. Cambridge: Cambridge University Press.

Rosenberger, Nancy. 2013. *Dilemmas of Adulthood: Japanese Women and the Nuances of Long-Term Resistance*. Honolulu: University of Hawai'i Press.

Rosenbluth, Frances McCall. 2007. *The Political Economy of Japan's Low Fertility*. Stanford: Stanford University Press.

Sato, Nancy. 2004. *Inside Japanese Classrooms: The Heart of Education*. New York: Routledge.

Sex Education Research Association of Tokyo for Kindergarten, Elementary, Junior High, and High Schools, ed. 1993. *Jidō seito no sei* [Students' Sexual Experiences]. Tokyo: Gakkō tosho.

Schoppa, Leonard J. 2008. *Race for the Exits: The Unraveling of Japan's System of Social Protection*. Ithaca, NY: Cornell University Press.

Takakura, Minoru, Norie Wake, and Minoru Kobayashi. 2007. "Relationship of Condom Use with Other Sexual Risk Behaviors among Selected Japanese Adolescents." *Journal of Adolescent Health* 40 (1): 85–88.

Tashiro, Mieko, Kaori Ushitora, and Daisuke Watanabe. 2011. "The Actual Situation of Sexuality Education in Japan and Its Problems: Fact-Finding for Teachers Interested in Sexuality Education." *Journal of Saitama University Faculty of Education* 60 (1): 9–22.

Tobin, Joseph, Yeh Hsueh, and Mayumi Karasawa. 2009. *Preschool in Three Cultures Revisited: China, Japan, and the United States*. Chicago: University of Chicago Press.

White, Merry I. 2002. *Perfectly Japanese: Making Families in an Era of Upheaval*. Berkeley: University of California Press.

Yoneyama, Shoko. 1999. *The Japanese High School: Silence and Resistance*. London: Routledge.

CHAPTER 3

Resisting Intervention,
(En)trusting My Partner

Unmarried Women's Narratives
about Contraceptive Use in Tokyo

SHANA FRUEHAN SANDBERG

In the late 1990s, Japanese national surveys asking women about contraceptive use changed terminology to include words that respondents were most likely to use. Rather than referring to the withdrawal method as "coitus interruptus" (*seikou chūzetsu*, a term that is easily confused with *ninshin chūzetsu*, abortion) it was newly described as "withdrawal" (*chitsugai shasei*), a term that is closer to what people use in everyday speech (Hayashi 2000). One survey's results made it clear that use of the withdrawal method was much more widespread in Japan than previously thought, and this shift demonstrates both the particular challenges surrounding research about birth control and how birth control practices are fundamentally embedded within webs of social meaning. The withdrawal method, as I will describe below, is popular precisely because many people feel it enables trust and reliability between partners.

In this chapter I examine intimate ideals and practices by analyzing narratives about contraception from young, unmarried women living in the Tokyo metropolitan area in the early 2000s. As described in this volume's introduction, while intimacy is often assumed to be private, in practice it reflects and reinforces a larger set of social ideals. In discussing their contraceptive choices, the women I interviewed touched upon many culturally salient issues, revealing a complex mix of desires—to engage in a sexual relationship while postponing childbearing; to protect both their own bodies and the national body from perceived dangers; and to enhance trust, intimacy, and pleasure in their relationships while remaining within the bounds of proper feminine behavior. By highlighting the strategies that these young women used to postpone reproduction, I contribute to the study of intimacy in contemporary Japan, demonstrating the way that their strategies—while constructed as purely private, personal decisions— actually reflect and reinforce wider social constructions of the body and what is considered "natural," as well as reveal constructions of femininity and the romantic ideals that women prioritize in their premarital sexual relationships (Ahearn 2001; Cole 2010; Hirsch 2003; Sobo 1995, 1998). I argue that women commonly articulated "reliability" as a necessary characteristic for intimate relationships, and birth control was a key context in which such reliability was demonstrated, challenged, and negotiated.

METHODOLOGICAL APPROACH

This chapter grew out of a larger research project (Sandberg 2010) designed to examine unmarried women's understandings of premarital romantic relationships, sexuality, and contraceptive use in light of recent demographic trends in Japan such as marriage postponement (*bankonka*) and the falling birthrate (*shōshika*). Because of this focus, the study targeted unmarried women between the ages of twenty and thirty who fit the demographic category most likely to "delay" marriage and childbearing—that is, urban women with post-secondary education from middle-class and upper-middle-class backgrounds (Edwards and Pasquale 2002; Retherford and Ogawa 2005). The research took place in and around Tokyo between 2002 and 2005. Tokyo was selected because it is a mecca for young women who want to further their education or pursue career opportunities; average ages at first marriage are higher and fertility rates are lower in Tokyo than in more rural areas (Gender Equality Bureau 2008). Through word of mouth and social contacts, I recruited forty women between the ages of twenty and thirty in the target population to participate in ethnographic interviews. All but three of the women I interviewed were attending or had graduated from four-year universities, and four had pursued education beyond the university level. The remaining three had graduated from two-year junior colleges or trade schools.

This study draws upon a mix of qualitative methods including ethnographic interviews, questionnaires, and participant observation. Questions covered the individual's understanding of dating and dating terms, recent relationship experience, thoughts about marriage, sources of sexual knowledge, and attitudes toward sexual behavior and contraception. The most sensitive questions about sexual experience and contraceptive use were presented in the form of a written questionnaire administered three-quarters of the way through the interview. This technique followed that of earlier researchers in Japan (e.g., Coleman 1991), allowing women to share sensitive, personal information without having to verbally utter words related to sexual behavior that they might have been unaccustomed to speaking aloud.

While living in Tokyo for twenty-one months, I also participated in everyday life as an unmarried woman. Living in a women's dormitory for the first six months of my research and with a Japanese host family for over a year provided insights into social institutions and interpersonal dynamics that I could not have gained through interview and survey data alone. For example, I learned about the strong role of dormitory curfews and parental expectations in reinforcing proper feminine behavior—as well as how my dorm-mates and friends circumvented these expectations on occasions when they wanted to stay out late. I also achieved a closer understanding of the lives of the young women I interviewed by reading the magazines and comic books and watching the movies and television shows that they brought up in conversation or referred to in their interviews. I accompanied them to shops, cafes, bars, and dance clubs when they extended invitations. Through these activities, I came to know the women I interviewed as individuals, and to place their words and actions in a broader context.[1]

FERTILITY REGULATION ACROSS JAPANESE HISTORY

Before discussing women's narratives about contraception, I will lay out a brief historical overview of political and social debates about reproductive policy in Japan. While birth control is often thought of as a modern invention, it has been practiced in various forms for centuries. As elsewhere, debates about contraception and abortion in Japan have been closely tied to debates about the family, sexuality, and the role of women in society. Understanding the way that women's roles and reproductive policy have been intertwined in the past will help shed light on what is at stake in women's discussions about contraception today.

During the Tokugawa, or Edo, period (1603–1868), historical records show that abortion, infanticide, and child abandonment were all commonly used as means of limiting family size (Hardacre 1999; Norgren 2001). In the Meiji period (1868–1912), an era of active nation-building, the development of a modern "health regime" involving various public health initiatives underscored the relationship between the health of individual bodies and the health of the Japanese nation (Frühstück 2003). In line with efforts to modernize and promote family stability, in 1873 infanticide was made punishable on the same terms as homicide, and the revised Penal Code of 1907 introduced the Criminal Abortion Law (Datai Zai), which specified maximum prison time for those who performed abortions and for women who received them (Norgren 2001). Despite the crackdown on infanticide and abortion, the use of birth control remained legal until later. Condoms were imported from abroad—primarily the Netherlands—beginning in the late Meiji period, and in 1909 a rubber goods factory introduced the first condom manufactured in Japan (Frühstück 2003). Even so, knowledge about birth control did not spread among the wider population until the latter half of the twentieth century.

During the 1910s and 1920s more women entered the workforce, leading to the popularization of the term *shokugyō fujin* (working woman), and also giving rise to a series of debates about women's roles, female sexuality, reproductive rights, and prostitution (Nagy 1991). As condoms and diaphragms were too expensive for most of the population, the methods most commonly recommended by social reformers active in Japan's growing birth control movement were temporary abstinence and coitus interruptus, also known as the withdrawal method (Frühstück 2003). Activists had to walk a fine line—although contraception itself was legal, discussion of it that strayed too far from a scientific base or attracted too much attention was punishable under corruption of public morality laws. In 1924, the Japanese physician Ogino Kyūsaku demonstrated that the fertile and infertile periods of a woman's menstrual cycle could be reliably predicted by estimating the time of ovulation based upon the start of the cycle. The "Ogino contraceptive method" (*Ogino hininhō*), as it is still sometimes called, or the "safe period method" (*anzenkihō*), provided a low-cost option available for those who were able to read about it (Frühstück 2003).

As Japan entered the wartime era (1926–1945), the government cracked down on many forms of activism, including the birth control movement. By the late 1930s, publications by the Ministry of Education and other books, essays, and poetry emphasized women as the "mothers of the nation" and promoted "motherhood in the interest of the state" (*kokkateki bosei*) (Miyake 1991, 271). In 1930, the Home Ministry banned the sale and display of contraceptive pins, rings, and other devices that were deemed dangerous to women, reflecting the ministry's decision to discourage contraceptive use in order to increase the birthrate and to pursue colonial expansion as the sole solution to problems of overpopulation (Norgren 2001; Tama 1994). Because condoms were not considered harmful and were crucial for controlling the spread of venereal disease among soldiers, they

were not included in the ban, but they had to be marketed as disease prevention devices rather than birth control (Frühstück 2003). By the late 1930s
and early 1940s, the government went further, banning the publication of
any material discussing birth control, raiding condom distributors, and
passing the National Eugenic Law, which allowed for both voluntary and
involuntary sterilization in people who had diseases thought to be heredi-
tary (Frühstück 2003; Norgren 2001).

The postwar period brought major changes in reproductive policy,
as the Japanese government shifted from the pro-natalist policies implemented during the Pacific War to new policies enacted under the Allied
occupation designed to address overpopulation and economic devastation.
After seeing rates of infant abandonment and illegal abortion increase,
in April 1948 the Diet passed a new law, and it became safe once again
to openly market contraception. IUDs were excluded, however, as they
were still deemed dangerous to women's health. Around the same time,
Taniguchi Yasaburō, an obstetrician-gynecologist and member of the
Upper House of the Diet, drafted a bill that liberalized the abortion law.
Called the Eugenic Protection Law (Yūsei Hogo Hō), it passed in 1948,
allowing abortions to be performed under certain circumstances but only
by "designated doctors" (shitei ishi) after approval by local evaluation com-
mittees. In 1949, a revision to the Eugenic Protection Law, now called the
"economic reasons" clause, made Japan the first country in the world to
allow abortion in cases where the mother could not afford to raise the child
(Norgren 2001). Between the late 1940s and the late 1950s, the ideal family
size shifted from five children per family to two children (Okazaki 1994),
and the total fertility rate in Japan dropped substantially.

At an international family planning conference held in Tokyo in 1955,
American biologist Gregory Pincus reported the success of clinical trials of
the new birth control pill (Tone 2001). In 1957, the United States approved
this compound as a prescription treatment for gynecological disorders,
and Britain followed suit in 1961.[2] In the late 1950s, drug companies in
Japan also received government approval to market the drug as a medical
treatment, and it became available in drugstores without a prescription
(Norgren 2001; Ogino 1994). However, fears about drug safety and resistance from women's groups ultimately derailed the process to approve and
market pills as a method of birth control in Japan. In 1971 the Ministry of
Health and Welfare (MHW)[3] suddenly issued regulations banning radio
and television programs about contraceptive pills and specifying that the
terms "the pill" (piru) and "oral contraceptives" (keikō hinin yaku) should not
be used on air in programs or commercials. In April 1972 the MHW designated the therapeutic pill a prescription drug, which further limited its

distribution (Norgren 2001), and in 1974 the prime minister made a statement that the government would no longer consider approving the pill for contraceptive reasons because of safety concerns.

Japanese feminist groups became increasingly active in the 1970s, but most either avoided the issue of the pill (in the case of the more mainstream women's organizations) or were against it (in the case of most women's liberation groups). Liberation groups did not support the pill because they generally believed that drug companies were conspiring with the government to reap profits from the pill at the expense of women's health. They also feared that approval of the pill would be used as justification for curtailing abortion rights—and indeed, some politicians did discuss revisions to the abortion law contingent upon approval of the pill and IUDs (Jitsukawa 1997; Norgren 2001). The one exception was the radical feminist group Chūpiren, which used aggressive tactics to express its support of the pill and opposition to attempts to revise the abortion law.[4]

Chūpiren's publicity-seeking activities, along with its leader's combative attitude toward other women's lib groups, made other feminist groups wary and some have even speculated that the group's activities did more to hurt acceptance of the pill in Japan than to help it (Ashino 1999; Norgren 2001).

Although the pill was reconsidered for approval as a contraceptive several times in the 1990s, it wasn't until the late 1990s that it finally became legal. In 1998, the impotence drug marketed as Viagra was approved in the United States. Although it was not yet approved for use in Japan, it created a lot of media attention and a large black market for the drug developed (Frühstück 2003). Relying solely on foreign clinical trial data, the MHW's Drug Council approved the drug for erectile dysfunction after only a six-month review in January 1999 (Frühstück 2003; Norgren 2001). This gross disparity in the treatment of Viagra in comparison to the birth control pill prompted an immediate outcry from Japanese feminist groups, female politicians, and the media. Bowing to pressure and unable to continue ignoring clinical tests concluding that the low-dose pill was safe, the MHW approved its use as a contraceptive in June 1999. Prescription guidelines are quite stringent, requiring pill users to undergo a pelvic examination every three months, as well as tests for sexually transmitted diseases and uterine cancer. Because it does not treat a particular illness, the low-dose pill—like pregnancy—is not covered by health insurance in Japan (Norgren 2001). More than ten years after its approval as a method of birth control, use of the pill remains very low in Japan. National surveys indicate that Japanese couples tend to rely on other methods, such as condoms and fertility calculations, to prevent conception.

CONTEMPORARY YOUNG WOMEN'S
NARRATIVES ABOUT CONTRACEPTION

The concept of contraception was quite familiar to the women I interviewed. All thirty of the sexually active women in my sample had used contraception at least once. In order of how widely used they were, the top three methods mirrored the top three methods indicated in national surveys, in the same order (Kitamura 2007). Condoms were the most widely used, having been used by each of the women in my sample at least once. The second-most widely used was the withdrawal method; nearly three-quarters had used that method at least once. Finally, approximately one-third had used either the rhythm method or the basal body temperature method. Only one woman had used the pill, and one had used a spermicidal film. No other methods were reported.

Condoms: Ubiquitous but Problematic

In addition to the fact that condoms were the most widely used method, over three-quarters of the women indicated that condoms were the method they liked the best. The most common reason they gave was that they were easy to obtain. "You can buy them anywhere, they even sell them at convenience stores," one woman wrote on her questionnaire. Condoms were also clearly the most well-understood method. Indeed, when asked why she preferred condoms, one woman wrote on the questionnaire that they were the "only method [I] know." Several other women also said that they preferred condoms because they were the "most familiar" (*ichiban mijika*) and easy to use.

Despite the condom's popularity and familiarity, none of the women I asked felt it was common for women to buy condoms themselves or carry them in their pockets or purses. "It's not really something that girls buy," explained a twenty-year-old university student. Although she personally did not see anything wrong with a woman buying condoms, she admitted that she was in fact too embarrassed to buy them herself. Another twenty-year-old university student said she did not think one should be embarrassed about buying condoms if one was old enough to have sex, but she acknowledged that many women probably did find buying them uncomfortable: "To take the condom, bring it to the register, and then if there's a male store clerk—it's embarrassing. He's probably thinking, 'This girl is about to have sex.'" Another woman said that she was the one who had to buy condoms in the past because her boyfriend was shy and got too nervous. Still, she tried to find a female cashier when possible.

Others indicated that having condoms on hand might signal promiscuity. A twenty-one-year-old university student said she felt that women should have access to condoms in order to protect themselves, but she also felt that if a woman carried condoms with her it conveyed a message that she was willing to have sex with anyone. A twenty-four-year-old preschool teacher expressed a similar sentiment: "If you have condoms, it's like [you're saying] you have an insatiable sex drive [*motteru to yaruki manman mitai na*]," she said. Even women who did not feel that it should be particularly shameful or embarrassing to buy or carry condoms still indicated that they preferred that their partners provide them. Speaking of women she knew, a twenty-one-year-old department store clerk said, "I get the feeling they like to entrust [having condoms] to their partners [*aite no makase*]." A twenty-one-year-old student felt it was appropriate that her boyfriend was the one in their relationship who procured the condoms. After all, "He's the one who wears it," she explained.

Social Meanings of Condoms

In *Taking Chances: Abortion and the Decision Not to Contracept*, sociologist Kristin Luker identified several social costs attached to obtaining and using contraception consistently among a sample of American women in California in the early 1970s. By obtaining contraception, a woman became "a woman who must take initiative, view herself as sexually aggressive, and abandon the traditional role of female passivity" (1975, 46). Condoms are one method that exemplifies a social cost because they require advanced planning and acknowledging to oneself (and sometimes others, like doctors and drugstore clerks) that one is going to engage in sexual intercourse. If they used condoms, most women in my sample preferred to rely on their partners to provide them. This allowed them to retain the "good girl" image for middle-class women promoted in families and schools that I discuss elsewhere (Sandberg 2010).

Furthermore, the fact that the women with whom I spoke often relied on their partners to provide contraception also allowed them to sustain the narrative that their partners were reliable and worthy of their trust. While Elisa J. Sobo has demonstrated a "monogamy narrative" and a "wisdom narrative" (1995, 1998) used by American women to justify unsafe sex with their partners, I propose a "reliability narrative" at work among young women in Japan. As noted, many of the women in my sample said that either they or their friends preferred to rely on their sexual partners to provide condoms for their sexual encounters. In parts of the interviews where women discussed relationship ideals, the ability to rely (*tayoru*) psychologically on one's partner emerged as a key ideal that women identified in discussing their understandings of steady dating relationships in Japan.[5]

Another closely related ideal was a partner's willingness to take his girlfriend's needs into account. Relying on one's partner for contraception, then, may serve as a means of signaling that one's boyfriend is someone who takes his girlfriend's desires into account and is worthy of such reliance. In this understanding, a romantic partner proves his reliability and commitment to the relationship by being willing to procure and wear a condom. Similar to the women studied by Sobo (1995, 1998), the women I interviewed upheld this "reliability narrative" even in the face of evidence to the contrary. Most women, including those who said they relied upon their partners for contraception, could point to instances where they did not use any (or resorted to a method they felt was less reliable) because their partners had failed to provide contraception, yet they maintained the relationship.

In addition to requiring advanced planning and their absence signaling a lack of trust, condoms also extract a cost because they require a couple to stop foreplay in order to apply the condom and thus can "wreck the mood" (mūdo kowareru), as several women commented on their questionnaires. This is especially significant given the ideology of romantic love that women drew upon to describe their ideals for premarital relationships and the significance of sexual activity within those relationships. Luker notes, "One part of the sexual ideology surrounding intercourse is that it must be romantic, an act of impulse infused with passion and noble feelings" (1975, 49). Viewed in this light, stopping to put on a condom is a rational and practical act—in other words, the antithesis of a romantic impulse infused with passion.

In sum, while condoms were clearly the most-preferred method, they were also considered problematic because they had to be obtained in advance, they had to be put on right before intercourse began, and they could change the way sexual intercourse felt for both men and women. For these reasons, many women alternated condom use with other methods such as withdrawal and fertility calculation; fewer than one-quarter of the women in my sample had used condoms exclusively.

Alternatives to Condoms: Withdrawal and Fertility Calculation Methods

While both withdrawal and fertility calculation methods require some degree of advance planning, both of these have the advantage of one's not having to purchase anything repeatedly.[6] In addition, during the infertile periods of a woman's cycle, fertility calculation methods do not require interrupting the sexual encounter to apply a contraceptive and do not change the way intercourse feels. The popularity of fertility calculation methods has received a relatively significant amount of attention in the anthropological literature on Japan (see Coleman 1991; Jitsukawa 1997). Because they work in line with the body's rhythms, they are generally considered more "natural" than medical interventions such as condoms and pills. Due to the extensive analyses provided on fertility calculation methods by earlier anthropologists, in this section I focus on the use of withdrawal, which has received significantly less attention in either the anthropological or public health literature on Japan.

Why is the use of withdrawal so popular in Japan? The primary reason seems to be that it provides some protection against pregnancy without requiring advance planning. When asked why they had used withdrawal, the largest number of women in my sample indicated that they had used it in situations when they and their partners "had not made preparations in advance, such as having condoms on hand." In other words, if women themselves felt uncomfortable buying condoms and they were relying on a partner to provide them but he did not, they were in a situation without a lot of other options. This finding is similar to findings based on research among American couples, some of whom said they used withdrawal because they felt that it was "better than doing nothing" (Jones et al. 2009, 409). Even the rhythm or basal body temperature methods involve some degree of advance planning because a woman needs to either keep track of her menstrual cycle or take her temperature daily in order to know whether it is the infertile time during her monthly cycle. An advantage of withdrawal is that it can be used without any planning in advance on any day of the month.

Beyond it being used as a method of last resort, withdrawal may have additional benefits that coincide with women's priorities in their romantic relationships and their understandings about the place of sexual behavior in those relationships. Several women indicated that they had used withdrawal because they wanted to deepen the relationship with their partner. Anthropologist Jennifer S. Hirsch (2003) has called into question the inherent "backwardness" attributed to "traditional" contraceptive methods by demonstrating that some couples in her ethnographic research in Mexico used "traditional" methods in order to reinforce more companionate marital roles, which are understood as "modern" by her interviewees. These companionate roles, which downplay financial support and adherence to gender hierarchies in favor of joint decision making, as well as both partners expressing their care and consideration for the other, are similar to the premarital relationship ideals that young women in Japan described to me in other parts of the interviews. As Hirsch notes, the use of withdrawal involves both parties in a joint decision and also requires both parties to sacrifice some pleasure for the sake of the relationship. The women she interviewed proudly described the way their husbands "took care" of them by sacrificing their own pleasure and exercising control for the sake of their family goals.

Within my sample, there was also evidence that some women viewed the use of withdrawal as a method that demonstrated care and communication. Miho,[7] a twenty-three-year-old woman working in the financial sector, described the way that she and her then boyfriend (who later became her husband) negotiated the use of withdrawal in their relationship: "He said that he didn't want to wear a condom, that he could feel a difference whether he was wearing one or not. So I felt a little sorry for him, and at first I thought, 'Well, it's okay [to have sex without a condom]. But later, I also said, 'You can't ejaculate inside me.' Just that, I said. We made a compromise." While at first Miho was willing to go along with condomless sex, she felt more comfortable once they reached a joint decision to use withdrawal. She told me that she did not think of it as a foolproof method, but she seemed to view it as a way that each of them could get their needs met—fulfilling her desire to use some form of contraception while also fulfilling her boyfriend's desire not to wear a condom.

In addition to the fact that the use of withdrawal involves a joint decision, it also requires a significant amount of trust between partners because a woman must trust her partner enough to be reasonably sure that he will withdraw in time. Thus the use of withdrawal may reinforce trust and uphold the "reliability narrative" discussed above. Reliability can be maintained even if one's partner "slips up," as long as it is not intentional. On her questionnaire, a twenty-year-old university student described a time when she and her boyfriend had agreed to practice withdrawal but he did not withdraw in time. "I could see he felt really bad about it," she wrote. "It wasn't deliberate, so it didn't ruin our relationship." In her view, the fact that it was not intentional and his subsequent regret both demonstrated that he cared about her and their relationship, and therefore he remained worthy of her trust.

The use of withdrawal may do more than enhance a sense of emotional intimacy. The fact that many women in my sample felt that withdrawal was less effective and that they were risking a pregnancy may have enhanced the erotic experience for them. A study of contraceptive use among Americans found that several interviewees (both male and female) described increased sexual arousal at the idea of risking pregnancy in explaining why they had not used contraception at certain times in past relationships (Higgins, Hirsch, and Trussell 2008). This finding also echoes the extensive research on "barebacking" among gay men; such research has found that erotic pleasure may be heightened for some by the prospect of risking a disease or sharing it with one's partner (Carballo-Dieguez and Bauermeister 2004; Díaz 1999; Junge 2002; Shernoff 2005).

The Pill: Burdensome, Unnatural, and Fostering the Wrong Dependency

Only one woman I interviewed had used the pill. Most of the others claimed to know little about it and expressed reluctance toward trying it. In explaining their reluctance to use the pill, most women in my sample drew upon one or more of the following discourses: the pill is burdensome to take every day; it is "unnatural" and dangerous to the body; its use could lead to an undesirable dependency on medication. The following excerpt is taken from my interview with Hitomi, a twenty-one-year-old student at a four-year university in Japan. Her interview incorporated each of the above themes and is representative of the way many women explained their feelings to me about the pill.

Q: Have you ever thought about using [the pill]?

HITOMI: No, I don't think I would.

Q: Why not?

HITOMI: I don't really know much about it, and you have to keep taking it, so there's that, and, well, it seems kind of constricting [sokubaku] that you have to take it every day. I don't like that.

Q: Have you heard anything about side effects or things like that?

HITOMI: Yes. It's a medicine, so there are definitely side effects; it's not a natural thing, you know [shizen mono ja nai deshō]? So it's scary [kowai]; it makes me uneasy [fuan].

Q: What kind of side effects have you heard about?

HITOMI: Well—probably—I'm not sure, but you can't really adjust it yourself, so it scares me.

Q: I understand. Well, putting aside the issue of whether you would use it or not, do you think it's a good idea for it to be legally available?

HITOMI: It was approved recently, wasn't it?

Q: What do you think of that?

HITOMI: I don't really. . . . Does it have the highest efficacy possible for a contraceptive?

Q: Yes, I believe so.

HITOMI: And the dosage [of hormones] was changed, right?

Q: Yes.

HITOMI: But you are dependent on a medicine [*kusuri ni tayotteru*], right? I think that's scary.

Q: What if many people began to use it?

HITOMI: It's something you [must] get at a clinic, right? Because you have to go to the clinic. If everyone started buying it, it would be a problem.

Q: Why?

HITOMI: People would think, "I have this, so it's okay."

Q: People would think, "It's okay to have sex anytime," you mean?

HITOMI: I don't really know, but it's like an addiction [*jōyō*]; you can't just use medicine habitually. I know a lot of women who use it to delay their period before they go on trips, but it doesn't feel natural [*shizenna kanji ja nai*], so I don't really [think it's a good idea].

Although Hitomi stated at the beginning that she "does not know very much" about the pill, through our conversation she revealed that she actually knew quite a bit about it when she mentioned the fact that it was available only through prescription at clinics, that it was highly effective in preventing pregnancy, and that the version recently legalized contained a lower dose of hormones than the pill previously available in Japan used for medical treatments. Despite the latter two potentially positive features, she continually returned to the discourse that the pill was "unnatural" and that it was "scary" to depend upon medication, even drawing a parallel to drug addiction. I specifically prompted Hitomi about side effects because fears about them continue to be the primary reason most women give on national surveys for not wanting to try the pill (Kitamura 2007). When asked for more concrete examples of side effects, however, most women had only vague ideas about them (see also Jitsukawa 1997). For example, a twenty-seven-year-old clerical worker mentioned side effects right away when explaining why she did not want to try the pill. When I asked her to elaborate, she said, "I haven't really heard anything specific, but, you know, like you might not be able to have children in the future or something. I've heard lots of different things." Fears about future infertility as a result of pill use were voiced by several women, along with more short-term side effects such as headaches, nausea, and weight gain. A twenty-one-year-old woman working in retail said that even though she had a friend on the pill who reassured her that she had not had any trouble with it, she remained skeptical. "If side effects appear, like in the next generation, when a child is really small, I don't like that." There remain strong links in some women's minds between the birth control pill and drug scandals in the 1960s and 1970s, including the Japanese version of thalidomide (Jitsukawa 1997; Norgren 2001).

Although the birth control pill delivers a standard dose of hormones daily and is therefore sometimes prescribed to correct hormonal irregularities, several women felt the pill could "destroy your hormonal balance" (*horumon baransu kowareru/kuzureru*). There may be an implicit comparison here between pharmaceuticals originally developed in North America and Europe (which are considered stronger and to have more side effects) and *kampō*, a form of Chinese herbal medicine that has a long history in Japan and continues to remain popular as an alternative to allopathic medicine. While women view the pill as disturbing the balance of their bodily hormones, the primary aim of *kampō* is to restore the natural balance inherent in the body (Ohnuki-Tierney 1984). The value of maintaining the internal balance of one's body has a long history in Japan and continues to be reflected in a variety of social and educational settings (Lock 2002), including the health section of women's magazines.

The construction of the pill as "unnatural" is also related to the discourse that it is a burden to have to take medication every day. "I am resistant to the idea of taking medicine," said Hiroko, "so I can't really see taking something every day." While taking medicine temporarily to clear up an infection or treat another medical problem was considered reasonable, the women in my sample expressed resistance to continuing to take the pill over a long period of time because it would not be used to treat a disease and would have to be taken even on days one did not need contraception. Furthermore, many women explained that they did not even like to rely on medication to treat temporary ailments like colds or headaches. They did not trust that these medicines were wholly beneficial and pointed to harmful effects on their bodies, as well as to the pill's propensity to foster a sense of dependency. This sentiment is similar to one of the arguments Japanese feminists used in a book arguing against the pill published by an Osaka women's health center in the late 1980s; one of the contributors stated, "I don't have sex every day and don't need contraception every day either. But if I have to take a pill every day, I feel my whole life will be revolving around the pill at the center" (Onna no Tame no Kurinikku Junbi Kai 1987, 113).

The fact that it is necessary to visit a medical clinic in order to obtain a prescription serves as a significant obstacle for Japanese women who otherwise might like to try the pill. Unless they experience a menstrual problem, most women in Japan do not visit gynecologists until they become pregnant, and the majority of women I interviewed had never been to visit one even though they were sexually active. Going to visit a gynecologist as an unmarried woman can raise pregnancy suspicions, and once there, few attempts are made to ensure privacy. As many gynecology clinics are quite small and crowded, it is not uncommon to overhear conversations between doctors and patients from the waiting room. Thus going to a clinic was equated with making a public statement that one was sexually active. Emiko had taken the higher-dose pill in the past as a medical treatment, but she would not consider going back on it in order to use it as birth control. "My parents would definitely be suspicious if I began going to the clinic," she explained. "They know I've stopped the treatment, so they would ask me why I need to go [so often]." The fact that it is relatively common in Japan for unmarried men and women to live in their natal households serves as an additional barrier to a woman's being able to obtain and take any medication covertly.

Several medical anthropologists have highlighted the way that debates about bodily health can reveal larger social tensions. In an essay on "The Mindful Body," Nancy Scheper-Hughes and Margaret M. Lock (1987) suggest that the physical body is symbolically equated with society so that healthy bodies represent a healthy society and diseased bodies represent a malfunctioning society. In a similar way, women talked about their resistance to the pill not only as a way to protect their own bodies from perceived risks, but also as a way to protect the Japanese national body. A major anxiety expressed by several women was that if pill use became more widespread in Japan, sexually transmitted diseases such as AIDS would become more rampant and pose a threat to the health of the population. Implicit in these concerns also seemed to be a fear that Japan would become more similar to the United States, which is associated in many minds with promiscuity and high rates of AIDS and other social problems.

Finally, the near-universal rejection of the pill also underscores many of the relational themes that appeared in discussions of other contraceptive methods. For example, many of the feminist groups in Japan who opposed the birth control pill until the late 1990s did so because they felt that the pill would expose women to physical harm while placing the burden of contraception on women and removing any sense of male responsibility for birth control (Jitsukawa 1997). Viewed in this light, women's preference that their partners take responsibility for providing condoms can be seen as a way to protect themselves from health risks and also ensure that their partners remained involved and committed to the shared goal of preventing pregnancy. Similarly, the use of withdrawal also fostered a sense of cooperation and shared commitment among the women I interviewed. The pill, which is lauded in much of the international family-planning literature because it is a "female-controlled method" and thus allows a woman to practice contraception without her partner's knowledge (or even against his wishes), does not further such goals. In fact, a twenty-five-year-old working in finance commented that the pill "seems like it would make men lose their sense of responsibility." A twenty-seven-year-old clerical worker suggested that the pill might be appropriate for women who were having relationships with a lot of different men. Along with reinforcing the association between using the pill and promiscuity, this statement suggests that pill use is appropriate if one has relationship priorities other than those of fostering long-term communication and cooperation. Finally, in saying they did not want to be "dependent" on the pill, as Hitomi did, women were essentially rejecting *physical* dependence on something they viewed as an unnatural technological intervention in favor of the ability to depend *psychologically* and *emotionally* on their romantic partners. Through their contraceptive choices, many women physically embody their commitment to the ideals of reliance, cooperation, and emotional intimacy that they prioritized in long-term relationships.

While condoms have remained in wide use in Japan over the past forty years and therefore much of the literature about family planning in Japan has focused on them (Coleman 1991), more recently family-planning surveys have found that withdrawal is more widely practiced than previously thought (Hayashi 2000). Among the young women I interviewed, condoms were the preferred and most widely used method due to their familiarity, efficacy, and the sense that "everyone uses them," but most women also found them problematic. Thus three-quarters of the women in my sample had relied on different methods at different times, and all but one of the women who had used multiple methods had used withdrawal at some point in the past. In fact, the use of withdrawal was viewed as fostering particular relationship goals—such as cooperation and trust—that had emerged elsewhere in my interviews as key components of premarital romantic relationships. In light of these findings, I have proposed that the use of both condoms and withdrawal allows women to sustain a "reliability narrative," in which they view a partner's role as one in which he demonstrates his commitment to the relationship by being the one to provide condoms or to withdraw at the appropriate time during sexual intercourse. Although most women did not personally feel that withdrawal was as effective as condoms in preventing pregnancy, some may have viewed a partner's willingness to risk a pregnancy with them as the ultimate sign of reliability and commitment to the relationship. Viewed in light of the historical perspective provided above, my research demonstrates the way that contraceptive strategies have changed as expectations about romantic relationships and women's priorities have changed among middle-class and upper-middle-class urban women. Rather than revealing either ignorance or patriarchal oppression, these women's contraceptive choices make sense in light of the particular priorities they hold for both their bodies and their romantic relationships.

NOTES

1. For more details about research methodology, including the interview questions used, please see related work (Sandberg 2010).

2. Because oral contraceptives deliver a standard dose of synthetic progesterone and estrogen at regular intervals, they can be used to treat gynecological symptoms that stem from uneven or low levels of these hormones.

3. As referenced in other chapters in this volume, this ministry's name and purview changed in 2001. At that point, the Ministry of Health and Welfare merged with the Ministry of Labor. Because I am here referring to regulations before this merger, I use the older name.

4. Chūpiren is an abbreviated version of the full name of the group, which was Chūzetsu Kinshi Hō Ni Hantai Shi Piru Kaikin o Yōkyū Suru Josei Kaihō Rengō, or the Women's Liberation Federation for Opposing the Abortion Prohibition Law and Lifting the Ban on the Pill (Norgren 2001, 66).

5. See Sandberg (2010, 172–175) for a more extensive description.

6. One fertility calculation method, the basal body temperature method, does require the purchase of a special digital thermometer that can measure body temperature down to a fraction of a degree. These thermometers are readily available in most drugstores and need to be purchased only once in order to use the method continuously.

7. All names in this chapter are pseudonyms.

REFERENCES

Ahearn, Laura M. 2001. *Invitations to Love: Literacy, Love Letters, and Social Change in Nepal.* Ann Arbor: University of Michigan Press.

Ashino, Yuriko. 1999. "Long Wait for Birth Control Pills." *Japan Quarterly*, October–December: 86–91.

Carballo-Dieguez, Alex and Jose Bauermeister. 2004. "'Barebacking': Intentional Condomless Anal Sex in HIV-Risk Contexts. Reasons for and against It." *Journal of Homosexuality* 47 (1): 1–16.

Cole, Jennifer. 2010. *Sex and Salvation: Imagining the Future in Madagascar.* Chicago: University of Chicago Press.

Coleman, Samuel. 1991. *Family Planning in Japanese Society: Traditional Birth Control in a Modern Urban Culture.* Princeton, NJ: Princeton University Press.

Díaz, Rafael M. 1999. "Trips to Fantasy Island: Contexts of Risky Sex for San Francisco Gay Men." *Sexualities* 2 (1): 89–112.

Edwards, Linda, and Margaret Pasquale. 2002. "Women's Higher Education in Japan: Family Background, Economic Factors, and the Equal Employment Opportunity

Law." *Working Paper Series 195*. New York: Columbia University Business School, Center on Japanese Economy and Business.

Frühstück, Sabine. 2003. *Colonizing Sex: Sexology and Social Control in Modern Japan*. Berkeley: University of California Press.

Gender Equality Bureau. 2008. *Gender Equality in Japan 2007*. Tokyo: Cabinet Office.

Hardacre, Helen. 1999. *Marketing the Menacing Fetus in Japan*. Berkeley: University of California Press.

Hayashi, Kenji. 2000. "The Trend of Family Planning Practice and Impact of Economic Burst on Fertility." In *The Population of Japan: An Overview of the 50 Postwar Years—Summary of the Twenty-Fifth National Survey on Family Planning*, edited by Population Problems Research Council of the Mainichi Newspapers, 157–176. Tokyo: Population Problems Research Council.

Higgins, Jenny A., Jennifer S. Hirsch, and James Trussell. 2008. "A Qualitative Analysis of Intermittent Contraceptive Use and Unintended Pregnancy." *Perspectives on Sexual and Reproductive Health* 40 (3): 130–137.

Hirsch, Jennifer S. 2003. *A Courtship After Marriage: Sexuality and Love in Mexican Transnational Families*. Berkeley: University of California Press.

Jitsukawa, Mariko. 1997. "In Accordance with Nature: What Japanese Women Mean by Being in Control." Special issue, "Anthropology and Contraception," *Anthropology and Medicine* 4 (2): 177–202.

Jones, Rachel K., Julie Fennell, Jenny A. Higgins, and Kelly Blanchard. 2009. "Better than Nothing or Savvy Risk-Reduction Practice? The Importance of Withdrawal." *Contraception* 79:407–410.

Junge, Benjamin. 2002 "Bareback Sex, Risk, and Eroticism: Anthropological Themes (Re-) Surfacing in the Post-AIDS Era." In *Out in Theory: The Emergence of Lesbian and Gay Anthropology*, edited by Ellen Lewin and William L. Leap, 186–221. Chicago: University of Illinois Press.

Kitamura, Kunio. 2007. "'Dai san kai danjo no seikatsu to ishiki ni kan suru chōsa' keika matomaru" [Summarizing the Results of the "Third Survey on Male and Female Lifestyle and Consciousness"]. *Kazoku to kenkō*. http://www.jfpa.or.jp/02-kikanshi1/637.html. Accessed June 11, 2009.

Lock, Margaret. 2002. *Twice Dead: Organ Transplants and the Reinvention of Death*. Berkeley: University of California Press.

Luker, Kristin. 1975. *Taking Chances: Abortion and the Decision Not to Contracept*. Berkeley: University of California Press.

Miyake, Yoshiko. 1991. "Doubling Expectations: Motherhood and Women's Factory Work under State Management in Japan in the 1930s and 1940s." In *Recreating Japanese Women, 1600–1945*, edited by Gail Lee Bernstein, 267–295. Berkeley: University of California Press.

Nagy, Margit. 1991. "Middle-Class Working Women during the Interwar Years." In *Recreating Japanese Women, 1600–1945*, edited by Gail Lee Bernstein, 199–216. Berkeley: University of California Press.

Norgren, Tiana. 2001. *Abortion before Birth Control: The Politics of Reproduction in Postwar Japan*. Princeton, NJ: Princeton University Press.

Ogino, Miho. 1994. "Abortion and Women's Reproductive Rights: The State of Japanese Women, 1945–1991." In *Women of Japan and Korea: Continuity and Change*, edited by Joyce Gelb and Marian Lief Palley, 69–94. Philadelphia: Temple University Press.

Ohnuki-Tierney, Emiko. 1984. *Illness and Culture in Contemporary Japan: An Anthropological View*. New York: Cambridge University Press.

Okazaki, Yoichi. 1994. "Economic Development and Population Problems in Postwar Japan." In *The Population and Society of Postwar Japan: Based on Half a Century of Surveys on Family Planning*, edited by Population Problems Research Council of the Mainichi Newspapers, 29–47. Tokyo: Mainichi Newspapers.

Onna no Tame no Kurinikku Junbi Kai. 1987. *Piru-watashitachi wa erabanai* [The Pill: We Don't Choose It]. Osaka: Onna no Tame no Kurinikku Junbi Kai.

Retherford, Robert D., and Naohiro Ogawa. 2005. "Japan's Baby Bust: Causes, Implications, and Policy Responses." *East-West Center Working Papers: Population and Health Series*, 118. http://www.eastwestcenter.org/fileadmin/stored/pdfs//POPwp118.pdf. Accessed March 18, 2008.

Sandberg, Shana Fruehan. 2010. "Embodying Intimacy: Premarital Romantic Relationships, Sexuality, and Contraceptive Use Among Young Women in Contemporary Tokyo." PhD dissertation, University of Chicago.

Scheper-Hughes, Nancy, and Margaret M. Lock. 1987. "The Mindful Body: A Prolegomenon to Future Work in Medical Anthropology." *Medical Anthropology Quarterly* 1 (1): 6–41.

Shernoff, Michael. 2005. *Without Condoms: Unprotected Sex, Gay Men, and Barebacking*. New York: Routledge.

Sobo, Elisa J. 1995. *Choosing Unsafe Sex: AIDS-Risk Denial among Disadvantaged Women*. Philadelphia: University of Pennsylvania Press.

———. 1998. "Narratives of Love and the Risk of Safer Sex." In *Romantic Love and Sexual Behavior: Perspectives from the Social Sciences*, edited by Victor C. deMunck, 203–231. Westport, CT: Praeger.

Tama, Yasuko. 1994. "The Logic of Abortion: Japanese Debates on the Legitimacy of Abortion as Seen in Post-World War II Newspapers." *U.S-Japan Women's Journal, English Supplement* 7:3–30. Translated by Scott O'Bryan.

Tone, Andrea. 2001. *Devices and Desires: A History of Contraceptives in America*. New York: Hill and Wang.

CHAPTER 4

Romantic and Sexual Intimacy
before and beyond Marriage

LAURA DALES AND
BEVERLEY ANNE YAMAMOTO

Increased longevity, coupled with a diversification in patterns of partnership and family formation, means that Japanese people are spending
less of their lives married. In the context of these demographic and social
shifts, we can expect that relationships crafted outside and beyond marriage and the family will take on new meanings and serve new functions.
While we are wary of conflating marriage and sexual intimacy, nevertheless a trend toward the delay and even rejection of marriage suggests
possibilities for romantic and sexual relationships across the life span to
acquire new meanings and expressions. These relationships may even
substitute—both positively and negatively construed—for sexual intimacy, hitherto confined to the marital relationship, at least for "respectable" heterosexual women. Thus while statistically marriage remains the
path most traveled for Japanese women and men (Kato 2011, 8), non-marital intimate relationships conducted before, during, or even outside the
context of marriage warrant closer investigation as sites of sexual expression, social connection, and personal fulfillment.

In this chapter we explore intimacy crafted by Japanese women outside
marriage. Drawing on interview data, we focus on urban single women's
perceptions, experiences, and expectations of romantic and sexual relationships before and beyond marriage. Recognizing the fluidity of the
term, in this discussion we focus on intimacy in the context of romantic connections and/or sexual practices that involve emotional and bodily
connections and expectations. These are situated within the broader context of non-romantic and non-sexual intimate relationships. In part we are
talking about the expectation or desire for a certain type of intimacy that

is not met. Thus fantasy and desire, as well as actual connections, would seem important to analyze.

Through this analysis a picture of entangled intimacies emerges where some intimate relationships may be conducted in the shadow of a marriage or nuclear family that is not one's own. For others romantic or sexual intimacy is a memory or something yearned for but inexplicably elusive. This work contributes to a growing body of literature that recognizes the complexity of contemporary emotional lives and relationship practices, by interrogating the possibilities for intimacy outside the nuclear family for Japanese women today.

THE POSITIONING OF ROMANCE AND MARRIAGE AND THE "SEXUAL IMPERATIVE"

The Western ideal of marriage that emerged in the mid-twentieth century was based on a convergence of romantic love, sexual desire, and companionship. These elements formed a heteronormative ideal where the imagined "perfect" soul mate was the harbinger of a "perfect" sex life and "perfect" marriage. This search for the perfect mate has dominated the Western imagination, and it is an ideal that we see acted out and reenacted routinely through film and other mediascapes of our late modern world (Appadurai 1990). Yet this emotional overloading of expectations of marriage results in supposedly permanent relationships being highly vulnerable to collapse (Coontz 2005, 211).

The late twentieth and early twenty-first centuries have seen a diversification in patterns of family formation and sexual intimacy, as other avenues are explored for finding a perfect mate who is up to meeting the emotional, erotic, and practical day-to-day needs constituted by contemporary Western culture. Yet desire in all three respects remains largely unsatisfied as society has been unable to resolve or pacify the "tripartite conflict of the sexual imperative, the romantic, and the companionate," with each driven by a different "logic and endocrinology" (Jankowiak and Paladino 2008, 3). While feelings of romantic and companionate love are difficult to hold on to at the same time, despite media presentations to the contrary, the "sexual imperative" is a force that may stand in opposition to intimacy rooted in romantic/companionate relationships.

The term "sexual imperative" is here used to refer to sexual desire that may or may not lead to physical sex (Jankowiak and Paladino 2008, 2). While sexual desire is popularly constructed in Western culture as driven by biological imperatives, we take the position of Foucault (1979), Weeks (1986), and Plummer (2002) that human sexualities and expressions of sexual desire are "social through and through" (Plummer 2002, 1). While constituted in society, sexual desire has a more universal presence across societies than romantic love, which appears to arise in societies where there is "frequent mobility, weak social networks, and few alternatives for finding intimacy" (Jankowiak and Paladino 2008, 9, citing Lindholm).

In the Japanese context, romantic love made a late entrance to heterosexual relationships and marital expectations. Even today, romantic love may be regarded, at best, as an added bonus, an "additional something" (*purasu arufa*), tied to particularly good fate (*un*). While companionship is something that both men and women appear to seek in a marital relationship, for many it is a companionability that is child-focused and pragmatic. Romance is certainly not regarded as a necessary condition for a happy marriage, and it might be regarded as unrealistic or even as an undesirable, destabilizing element in what should be a stable family unit (Borovoy 2005, 88–89). The absence of romance in a relationship would not usually be an impetus to seek a divorce and search for a new spouse (Jankowiak and Paladino 2008, 3).

The sexual imperative in the marital relationship has been tied in most closely with expectations of reproduction. As Amy Borovoy (2005, 88–89, 159) has argued, marriage in modern Japan was framed primarily as a social and economic contract between the prospective spouses and their respective families, where reproduction and maintenance of the family system loomed large as expectations. The recent rise in divorce may signal that in late modernity expectations of something more—companionate marriage and/or a sexually fulfilling marriage, perhaps—are gaining ascendancy and at the same time destabilizing the hitherto relatively stable modern Japanese marriage pattern (ibid., 164, 172–176; Alexy 2007).

Yet we have not seen a rise in cohabitation or children born out of wedlock on a significant level as an alternative pattern of family formation in Japan (Hertog 2009). This resistance to the diversification of patterns of family formation is particularly high among young women. In the Sixth Survey of Men's and Women's Lifestyles and Attitudes, carried out in 2012, close to three-quarters (74.7 percent) of the women aged 25–29 who were surveyed report that they were "opposed" or "somewhat opposed" to the idea of an unmarried couple having a child. The equivalent figure for other age groups was above 60 percent for women in all age groups other than those aged 30–34, where it stood at 58 percent. Men are not as conservative (Kitamura 2012, 58–59, figure 2-8-1).

Even in the early twenty-first century, marriage remains a rite of "passage into responsible adulthood" in Japan, and it is a rite that presumes pregnancy and childbirth as imminent events after the marriage is formalized (Maree 2004, 541). A premarital conception is usually carried to term only if the woman and/or her family can be assured that the birth will take place in the context of marriage (Hertog 2009, 153). With marital sexuality largely linked to reproduction, the completion of childbearing can just as quickly place the marital relationship on an asexual footing for an increasing proportion of married couples in Japan. This is a trend that has only strengthened over the twenty years of the "lost decades." In the Second Survey of Men's and Women's Lifestyles and Attitudes (in 2004), over 31.9 percent of married men and women responded that their marriages were sexless.[1] With each survey this figure has risen, reaching 41.3 percent by the sixth survey in 2012 (Kitamura 2013, 4). For many women in the study who reported being in a sexless marriage, sex was "just too much bother" (23.5 percent), or sexlessness was something they just "drifted into . . . after childbearing" (20.5 percent). An increasing number of married women are also reporting that they are "too tired from work" to want to have sex with their husbands, with the figure reaching 19.3 percent in the Sixth Survey on Men's and Women's Lifestyles and Attitudes (Kitamura 2012, 100; Kitamura 2013, 4). For men, "feeling tired after work" (28.2 percent) and "drifting into sexlessness after children were born" (17.9 percent) were the top reasons given for why sex was no longer a part of the marital relationship (Kitamura 2013, 4). Clearly, the "sexual imperative" is not a sustainable part of many Japanese marriages in the early twenty-first century.

With the expectation of sexual intimacy in marriage, at a basic level, linked to reproduction, expectations around desire or companionship are muted. The fulfillment of the unwritten marriage contract through childbearing may, therefore, free both partners from an obligation to engage in any further sexual relations with each other. As a result, it is easy to drift out of sexual intimacy. Moreover, in late modern Japan, motherhood, rather than wifehood, is the central pillar of domestic femininity (or "women's work"), and the successful performance of mothering and nurturance fulfills women's obligations within this contract (Maree 2004, 541). For the husband, his role as a responsible economic provider surpasses all other obligations or expectations in the marital relationship, and it is in this role that he will be assessed as a good husband and father.

If sexuality for "respectable" heterosexual women is tied closely to marriage and reproduction, what avenues are there for single women to seek sexual intimacy? This is a driving question in this chapter. We know from survey data such as those compiled by the Japan Association for Sex Education (JASE) that the majority of men and women experience sexual intimacy for the first time in their teen years and that the percentage of women reporting having experience of sexual intercourse in the mid- to late teens (15–18) is slightly higher than for men. We also know from the same sources that over the past two decades there has been a noted tendency toward having multiple partners, even concurrently or serially, among teen women and to a lesser degree teen men (JASE 2012, 12–13; Saotome 2010, 280).

Yet survey data also suggest that this sexual activity is severely dampened down by the time women and men reach their thirties. We know, for example, from a study carried out by the National Institute of Population and Social Security Research in 2005 that single women in their thirties and forties are more likely than their male counterparts to report having a lover or intimate friend. Among single women aged 30–34, 23.7 percent report having an intimate relationship (*aijin ga iru*), compared to 18.9 percent of their male counterparts; this figure drops to 11 and 7.4 percent respectively for those in their forties. Regardless of gender, however, not having a sexually intimate partner would appear to be more common for singles in their thirties and forties (see Kato 2011, 23).

It is clear from the same study that many single women and men in their thirties and forties are not socializing with potential intimate partners even as friends. In the same survey, the percentage answering that they had "no one that they could go out with socially" (*kōsai aite wa inai*) was also higher for men than women, with the situation again being positively impacted by age. For men, 55.5 percent of those aged 30–34, 65.3 percent of those aged 35–39, and 68.3 percent of those in their forties reported they had nobody with whom to socialize, compared with 51.2 percent of females aged 30–34, 53.3 percent of those aged 35–39, and 66.3 percent of those in their forties (Kato 2011, 23). While for Kato (2011, 23) these data indicate the negative disposition of singles in Japan today to individually seek out a marriage partner, they also point to the difficulties for singles of finding and maintaining intimate relationships once they reach an age where society deems that they should be married.

With these survey data giving us a clear descriptive overview of sexual intimacy before, within, and perhaps beyond marriage, this chapter transcends such a surface perspective to explore at the narrative level the stories of single women in their thirties and forties in relation to how they engage in, dream of, or avoid sexual intimacy. It starts by introducing the study and our informants. It explores single women's ideas about marriage before moving on to consider the practices of those with current or recent histories of romantic and sexual intimacy. This analysis will show the extent to which romantic and sexual intimacy are separated from, but exist in relation to, marriage and marital obligations.

OUR UNCONVENTIONAL WOMEN

The discussion in this chapter has grown out of a research project the authors commenced in 2009 focusing on women whose lives were unconventional in some way. Between October 2009 and June 2011 we interviewed thirty-six women between the ages of thirty and forty-nine. The interviews were semi-structured and in-depth, sometimes involving one, but more usually both, researchers. All but two were conducted in Japanese.[2]

Our definition of "unconventional" (tenkeiteki dewanai) focused on women whose life courses had diverged significantly from the stereotypical pattern of marriage and child rearing in the context of complete or nearly complete economic dependency on a wage-earning male spouse. The women who contributed to our study included never-married and divorced women, single mothers, women who cohabited, and women who married late. All identified as heterosexual. In addition to this formal means of data collection, we engaged in many informal conversations around the subject of intimacy with Japanese women and men—colleagues, friends, and strangers—as well as foreign nationals married to Japanese men and women.

We identified participants using a snowballing technique, asking those known to us to introduce us to women who had not followed the normative life course pattern of marriage and child rearing in the context of a nuclear family. We interviewed women living in cities in the Kanto, Kansai, and Kyushu regions. Given our own positions and networks, snowballing inevitably left us with an overrepresentation of highly educated women. This means that the observations and conclusions that we make here concern unconventional women who generally, but not exclusively, have been educated at least to university level. We analyzed these data thematically, with one prominent theme being intimacy. We wanted to explore how women who were single, had married late, were divorced, and/or were cohabiting conducted and imagined intimate relationships. Some women found it difficult or impossible to discuss topics related to sexual intimacy. Yet other women spoke with refreshing frankness about intimacy in general and sexual intimacy in particular. This chapter draws on accounts of the intimate given by our "unconventional" women.[3] Given the rich insights contained in the data, we have drawn here on the narratives of a few women whose stories appear particularly pertinent, allowing us to delve deeper into the topic of intimacy.

THE POSITIONING OF OUR UNCONVENTIONAL WOMEN: ROMANCE VERSUS MARRIAGE?

For unmarried women, the ambivalent relationship between romance and marriage may reflect an underlying separation of affect from lived practice or an awareness of the limitations of institutionalized human relations. Matsuda-san and Motohashi-san are friends; both are single women in their early thirties. Matsuda lives with her parents and works as a temp (dispatch) worker for a recruitment agency. Motohashi is a white-collar professional whose career involves considerable international travel. Neither woman has rejected marriage as an option, but their motivation to marry appears weak. Both report being disinclined to use marriage-partner hunting (*konkatsu*) strategies or to have meetings with potential marriage partners arranged by third parties (*omiai*). For them, marriage is not something pressing, despite the fact they are past the normative age to marry. Neither of these women frames marriage as something romantic.

Matsuda noted that she once had a strong desire to marry but that this desire has faded:

> I thought I could take it easy if I got married. I'd be supported, and I thought that was natural. If you didn't have a particular job that you wanted to do, a particular thing you wanted to specialize in, then that means you got married.
>
> I don't know if it [that feeling] disappeared; maybe it didn't. It's not that it's not there at all. I guess I do still have it, but maybe I don't. In the past I just wanted to marry for the sake of it, but when I became an adult, I lost interest in marriage. I don't think that I will be alone forever, and I do someday want to get married. But at the moment I don't really feel like I want to do *konkatsu* or go searching for someone who fits all the criteria at an *omiai* or party.

Here we see that Matsuda is reflective about her earlier construction of marriage as a means of gaining material and financial support and the extent to which this had been naturalized in her mindset. She views marriage as the default choice for women who do not aspire to a career. Even though Matsuda does not have job security and is unlikely to be a high earner, her desire to marry to gain economic security has faded.

Her words express a conflict over the value of marriage for her now as a working woman in her early thirties. On the one hand, she doesn't want to "be alone forever," but neither does she want to actively search out an ideal partner, "one who fits all the criteria." There is a sense of inertia, where the idea of marriage is not explicitly rejected, but, as noted in other studies of single women aged thirty or over, there is a weak "disposition to hunt out a partner individually" (Kato 2011, 23). Yet at the same time, there is a reluctance to use commercial agencies (such as dating agencies and websites) or more traditional community-based means to find a partner that involve an introduction by a third party (Kato 2011, 23).

Motohashi similarly takes a "wait-and-see" approach, expressing a lack of motivation to hunt out a partner. She is willing to leave things to time, with the vague sense that she will meet somebody eventually:

> I don't think I want kids, so for me too there isn't really any need to hurry up and get married. I think it will come along sometime, but I'm not making plans. [I'll] just kind of go with the flow. If I meet someone, we might get married and maybe have a baby. I guess I'll meet someone when I'm meant to meet him. I'm not going to break my neck trying.

While both Matsuda and Motohashi construe marriage as a possible destination point, neither is actively seeking a marriage partner. In their construction of marriage as a possible goal, they refer to its social, economic, and reproductive functions rather than as a relationship that could promise romantic or sexual intimacy. As Motohashi implies, the "need" to marry is driven by non-affective factors. Thus without a biological reproductive deadline, there is no hurry to marry.

Could cohabitation be an attractive alternative to these two women, given that they express no desire to seek a marriage partner for themselves while also not wanting to be alone? If cohabitation were seen as an alternative to marriage, would it also offer new possibilities for a stable pattern of intimacy? The answer to both questions is a resounding no. For Matsuda and Motohashi, rather than better facilitating intimacy or a different kind of relationship, cohabitation was viewed as an inferior version of marriage.

> MOTOHASHI: I think of cohabiting as a kind of substantive marriage. It just doesn't have the legal authority that marriage does. And I wonder why you'd bother living together if you're not married.
> MATSUDA: It's kind of like, "Why should I have to look after you when I'm not even your wife?"

MOTOHASHI: Because that's the point of being single. I'm single so that I can enjoy my life alone, so in fact while I might get married, I wouldn't want to cohabit. Maybe if we were sharing a house.

For these two women, cohabitation attenuates the benefits (freedoms) of singlehood without providing any of the benefits (security) that marriage may offer. If imagined marital relationships highlight the nurturing and caring roles that woman are supposed to play within marriage, cohabitation does not necessarily present itself as an attractive alternative. Rather, the idea of cohabiting without marriage may require duties of care without the reward of stability.

Cook suggests that some women choose to date *freeters* and other irregular workers precisely because "they don't want to marry them or that marriage [to them] would be difficult" due to their lack of economic stability (2014, 46). With ambivalence about the possibilities of marriage and cohabitation owing to familial and domestic links, some of our informants sought sexual intimacy with men who were quite definitely not looking for a wife. In other words, to satisfy the desire for sexual intimacy and romance they sought relations with men who were already married.

Sato-san is a forty-nine-year-old single woman who works in senior management in a non-government agency. Unlike many of the women we interviewed, she had not graduated from a four-year university but a two-year junior college. In her twenties and thirties she had considered marriage, had engaged in *omiai*, and had been introduced to men by colleagues, but she had not met a man who "made her heart flutter" (*hihitto kuru hito*). She recognizes that this was most likely because she had already had strong feelings for another man who was outside the marriage market: "There was a man I liked. As he was the best, I guess I knew that I wasn't going to find anyone better than him. And he was married, this guy." Despite her strong feelings for this man, there were no expectations of his getting a divorce and marrying her. Sato was quite clear about the nature of the relationship.

Q: Were you together for a long time?
SATO-SAN: I didn't want to constrain him, and I didn't want to be constrained. It wasn't really that type of relationship. It didn't go as far as [his speaking of divorce]. I didn't think of it going that far either.

Sato was open in telling us that she had other relationships with married men. In addition to the lack of constraints in such relationships, she confessed that she was also attracted to older men. Reflecting back on her twenties, Sato noted that she was drawn to such men precisely because they were supporting a family: "I suppose it is because they [older men] gave off an aura of someone supporting a household that men of my own age just weren't attractive in this way. I am just drawn to such men, and I can't help myself." This statement would suggest that in Sato's case the authority and confidence that men gain from being married and supporting a family increases their attractiveness relative to unmarried men. Yet these relationships with married men were still framed as stopgaps, with an expectation that somebody more attractive to her would come along. Sato appears to view these relationships as constant but contingent, stable and satisfying but limited to particular kinds of interactions: "Occasionally we'd go drinking. I suppose they were drinking friends, people I could talk to about any problems I had [sōdan aite]. I did think that if I had met someone else, then I'd get married. Without a doubt! And I also thought that I wanted kids." Now in her late forties, Sato continues to have relationships with married men and still admits that if she were to meet somebody more attractive to her who was available, she may well marry in the future, even if the idea is more wistful now: "There is somebody whom I have a reasonably good relationship with, but he is also married, so I have no thoughts of living with him. There has nearly always been somebody like this in my life. And I continue to indulge myself with the thought that if a better person comes along, I will get married."

A "better person" for Sato is not only one to whom she is attracted, but also one with whom she would consider living. It was clear from talking to Sato that keeping her independence, being able to continue working, and sharing some of the household chores were all part of the package in the search for a man she could live with. She "indulges" herself with the idea that this companionate and egalitarian style of marital relationship remains possible for her, but in the meantime she focuses her affective attention on already married men. Their availability as intimate partners is not diminished by their unattainability as marriage partners—if anything it is enhanced by it. For Sato, then, like for Matsuda and Motohashi, sexual intimacy exists in a different moral and relational framework, distinct from cohabitation and marriage.

Sato is a professionally accomplished woman who is financially independent and owns her own apartment. She is also past usual childbearing age. As a result, her consideration of romantic partners does not in any overt way need to prioritize the financial security that a man could offer her; she has never intended to be supported by a husband. Rather, the attraction of her romantic partners is defined by their emotional maturity and life experience and their ability to provide support and counsel in non-material ways. Nevertheless, this "aura" that Sato notes around men whom she finds alluring can be construed as the authority that men gain when they are professionally successful and thus also financially secure. Would it be possible for a man sharing the support for his family with a wife, or a man without professional success, to have the same aura? Although the meaning of any material status of eligible men may be different, it is likely to still have some weight.

The condition of men's marriageability represents one factor in the creation and maintenance of intimate romantic relationships. Cook (2013, 38; 2014) notes that financial security, defined by employment as a full-time, regular employee (*seishain*), is a primary condition of male marriageability. After a particular age—the normative age of first marriage—marriageable men by definition are more likely to be married. The attraction of these men as potential romantic partners for single women is, therefore, unsurprising.

Sato's experiences can be contrasted with Matsuda's and Motohashi's recollections of relationships with married men. Both admit easily to having had relationships with married men, and Motohashi concludes that if her partner had not been married, she probably would not have become involved with him.

> MATSUDA: I did have a relationship with a married man.
> MOTOHASHI: I had one too, come to mention it. When I was a university student. . . . He wasn't a marriage possibility. Maybe if he hadn't been married, we might not have gotten together. He hadn't been to university.

For women who delay or reject marriage, a romantic relationship with unmarriageable partners enables intimacy without the odious possibility that family or care responsibilities might encroach on this intimacy (Cook 2014).[4] However, these "liquid" relationships do not necessarily meet even unconventional women's desires for intimacy and reveal the risks of romantic entanglement (Bauman 2003):

> Q: Was it you who decided to break up?
> MATSUDA: Yes, it was me, but it was because I heard through someone else that he had tons of other women. He really was the worst kind of man. . . . I was an idiot to be taken in by him, but he was married, so I thought I couldn't be too nosy. . . . Even among his lovers I was second or third in line—he had his number one woman somewhere else. . . . Lots of people have affairs, and there are men who cheat on their wives, but even among these men, I wonder about this guy and what kind of person he is.

While relationships with married men may fulfill some intimate needs for unmarried women, the potential for these relationships to derail marriage plans or desires depends upon the tenacity of the affective and material bonds between lovers, as well as the woman's desire for children (which in Japan generally necessitates marriage). An attachment to a lover who is ultimately unavailable may resemble an attachment to an unfulfilling marriage in that both depend upon cruel optimism, "pieces of an argument about the centrality of optimistic fantasy to surviving in zones of compromised ordinariness" (Berlant 2007, 49).

TOLERANCE OF EXTRAMARITAL SEXUAL INTIMACY VERSUS INTOLERANCE OF DIVORCE

The weak positioning of romantic and sexual intimacy within marriage may support the construction of these elements in extramarital relationships as discrete from, or unrelated to, marital stability. Yet there are also material incentives to remain married, not only in the absence of sexual intimacy in one's own relationship, but also in the presence of clear marital infidelity. For many, the disincentives to divorce are not insignificant, particularly for women with children (Alexy 2007), with statistical data suggesting that the likelihood of divorce is halved for couples with children (Kato 2010, 83). In light of the material conditions of divorce, it may be that acceptance of a marriage lacking intimacy also sanctions the pursuit of intimacy outside marriage (Berlant 2007, 49). Nevertheless, this suggestion is not wholly uncontested.

At the time of interview, Fukuda was a thirty-three-year-old never-married professional, living in a large city and actively engaged in *konkatsu*.[5] While seeking to find a spouse, Fukuda came across as somewhat cynical rather than idealistically romantic.

> Japanese men . . . really think that for a man to have an affair is just normal, and there are a lot of people who speak openly about it, even around me. There are some friends of my mother's from high school days . . . five women friends from high school, all of them with daughters exactly my age. But they all got married in a bit of a hurry apparently . . . and among them there are only two whose husbands haven't had an affair. The other three husbands all did, and the wives really suffered. And of the husbands who didn't, one has already died [laughs].

In relating her cousin's experience of an extramarital affair, Fukuda suggested that an acceptance of affairs reflects the considerable social weight of marriage:

My cousin's husband had an affair, just after they had registered their marriage in the family registry [nyūseki], and they broke up, but I thought, actually, that was really amazing of her. To just decisively end it like that, it was great. They had been together for a long time, so maybe there was ... already something built up there in fact. But if it was me, to have to tell the company and others. . . . Once you've told everyone you're married, I think you can't just easily split up. So you'd think "I'll just put up with it and stay with him." You'd think about what others think of you, right?

It is noteworthy, however, that despite this cynical view of husbands and their (in)fidelity and an expressed admiration for a woman who was willing to leave an unfaithful spouse, Fukuda herself was actively engaged in seeking a marriage partner. It is also worth emphasizing that in Fukuda's narrative, her mother's generation put up with husbands' extramarital affairs, whereas her cousin, a woman of her own generation, did not. Tolerance of men's sexual infidelity may reflect generational differences, as well as class and education. Nevertheless, keeping face, ensuring the stability of the family, and avoiding economic hardship—the latter a painful reality for many single women raising children alone—can make putting up with infidelity a more palatable option than divorce for many women (Borovoy 2005).

SEX AS OPTIONAL OR ESSENTIAL TO RELATIONSHIPS

Some of the women in this study explicitly noted sexual relations as critical to a fulfilling life. For these women, sexual intimacy was sometimes central to the romantic relationship and at other times became significant in its absence. For women who had enjoyed multiple romantic and sexual relationships regularly over their adulthood, it seems that as an ideal, sexual intimacy is at least as important as affective connection in an intimate relationship.

Tanaka was a forty-six-year-old divorcee who was working full time while also completing her doctorate at the time of interview. A bubbly and energetic woman, Tanaka spoke candidly about her unusual personal history. At nineteen she cohabited with a thirty-eight-year-old man for several years, while at the same time running her own bar. After a subsequent passionate love affair with the bar's pianist ended, at twenty-seven Tanaka married a man twenty years her senior and moved to Tokyo. She told us that "for one year, the whole year I concentrated on being a good wife. It was so boring. So boring, I almost died."

Tanaka articulates her attraction to older men as related to the comfort they engender: "Kind of a father figure (is) what I really liked. . . . Yeah, and to me—I always say this—but . . . to me older guys are like a big, huge sofa. You know? Comfortable. I can relax, lay back." In contrast with her relationship with the pianist, Tanaka describes her marriage as a matter of "good conditions": in addition to her husband's having an excellent salary and no living mother (meaning no mother-in-law for Tanaka) and his being very kind, Tanaka identified the key element of her attraction toward her husband:

> Plus, that was very important to me at that time, but I didn't love him [my husband], because, as I said, I broke up with my pianist. And I was loving him so much, right? Then you know I was so jealous. I thought . . . if I have a chance to get married, then . . . I don't want to be in love. That's better. If I were in love, I'd always worry about him. I'd have to.[6]

This is very much the universal "rebound" narrative; Tanaka suggests that the experience of passionate but painful love in her relationship with the pianist formed the backdrop to her subsequent marriage. Indeed, the passionate affair with the pianist had placed the man who Tanaka was to subsequently marry in a most attractive light, at least temporarily. It was precisely the lack of sexual frisson and the large age gap that drew Tanaka to her future husband. Tanaka's husband was, by her own account, completely uninterested in sex, and this left her frustrated. She declared: "I really need to have sex. And then my ex said, you know, if you want to, you can have a boyfriend. To me, in the first place, [it seemed] like he's crazy, but he was serious. . . . I was dying for [sex]; I was dying for it." What Tanaka sought was romantic as well as sexual intimacy: "Yeah, but having sex is not the thing that I really want. The connection, right. The connection. OK, we can go to a male prostitute or something. But no connection at all. Right?" While she identifies sexual intimacy as essential, Tanaka observes that it is not in itself a sufficient grounding for romantic intimacy—rather, she seeks an emotional bond or "connection" to transform sex into an affective act.

This chapter has sketched the intersecting and divergent perceptions, experiences, and expectations of marriage and of romantic and sexual intimacy among "unconventional" single women in urban Japan. While we have sought to introduce the voices of "unconventional" women, it is important to note that the term functions more as an etic than an emic label. While the women introduced here are by no means a representative sample, their reflections offer insight into an increasing proportion of the Japanese demographic: the unmarried female adult. As the narratives of the women introduced here suggest, experiences and perceptions of extramarital romantic and sexual intimacy elucidate the meanings of marriage as much as they reflect the implications of singlehood for women's sexuality and affective connections.

Evidently, the primary functionality of marriage does not preclude the possibility of romantic and sexual intimacy but rather displaces it as a central condition. Bauman (2003) has argued that the possibility for love as fundamental is limited by the fragility of the bonds that love creates—particularly in light of the strong pull from "liquid modern" society, which values convenience, consumption, immediate satisfaction, and unfettered freedom. He suggests that in contemporary society, "Commitment to another person or persons, particularly an unconditional commitment . . . looks ever more like a trap that needs to be avoided at all costs" (2003, 90). Our interviewees who spoke of affairs with married men talked of relationships that had some level of commitment and even a degree of stability, however fleeting this might turn out to be.

While Bauman's statement implies the commitment of one individual to another, there is the further layer of commitment created in the Japanese context of familial obligations. If marriage is inextricable from these obligations, there would appear to be even less incentive for independent women to concede to marriage.

The desire to marry reflects the economic and social meanings with which marriage is imbued. Conversely, it also reflects the stigma that remains attached to singlehood as a life-long status, particularly but not exclusively for women. As Lahad observes outside the Japanese context, contemporary tropes of singlehood for women contain the tacit warning: "Being too selective can lead to self-destruction, isolation and loneliness, the ultimate social punishments" (2013, 24). Where marriage avoidance or deferral is understood as a function of choice, the responsibility for singlehood and its travails is entirely individualized. This is reflected, for example, in the subtitling of the Japanese television drama "Around Forty," a story that centers on an unmarried woman approaching forty, as a "Demanding Woman" (*yōkyū takai onna*). The age-inappropriate single woman is characterized by excess: "too self-determined, too choosy, and overly self-confident, 'they are asking for too much' and exceeding the boundaries of their ascribed place" (ibid., 24).[7]

While marriage remains discursively central to Japanese women's lives, the disincentives and obstacles to marriage are also well noted (Dales 2014;

Dalton and Dales 2016; Haruka 2000; Hinz 2004; Lahad 2013, 28; Sakai 2003). The potential for intimacy in romantic relationships before and beyond marriage is modulated by structural imperatives, including women's capacity for financial independence, the availability of good opportunities (*deai*), and the construction of women as sexually passive. These factors influence women's choices in relation to romance and shape expectations and experiences of intimacy in romantic and sexual relationships before and beyond marriage.

For many of the women in this study, particularly those with financial independence, singlehood enabled a variety of relationships that provided sources of fulfillment, including friendships, work relationships, and romantic relationships that did not lead to marriage. These relationships provided some buoyancy against the weight of familial social pressure and counter discourses of femininity as incomplete before/beyond marriage and motherhood. While they may not ultimately replace marriage as a marker of adulthood, social maturity, and the sanctioned space for reproduction, it is clear that intimate relationships before and beyond marriage represent potential sources of fulfillment, sexual expression, and meaning.

NOTES

1. "Sexlessness" was defined here according to the definition provided by the Japan Society of Sexual Science in 1994. A couple is sexless if "in the absence of any special circumstances a couple has had no consensual sexual intercourse or sexual contact (petting, oral sex, etc.) for a month or longer and this situation is likely to continue into the future" (cited in Kitamura 2013, 4, and translated by Yamamoto).

2. The authors acknowledge the Japan Society for the Promotion of Science for a postdoctoral research fellowship and a small grant-in-aid (2109751) that enabled this project. The chapter also draws on research conducted by Dales as part of an Australia Research Council Discovery Early Career Researcher Award (DE120101702).

3. The research was approved by the University of South Australia Ethics Review Committee and was conducted on the basis of informed consent. All names used in this chapter are pseudonyms. All data were transcribed and then translated into English where we had interviewed in Japanese.

4. Cook's work indicates that the association of marriage with obligation and responsibility is also strongly felt by *freeter* men, a finding that supports Nagase's study (Cook 2014, 42; Nagase 2006).

5. Less than a year after the interview, Fukuda had found a suitable partner and married.

6. Tanaka was one of two informants we interviewed in English. In order to preserve the integrity of her narrative, we transcribed her speech directly here.

7. It is interesting that the theme song for the serial, entitled "The Measure of Happiness," features the following English lines: "Count what you have now/Don't count what you don't have" (Freedman and Iwata-Weickgenannt 2011).

REFERENCES

Alexy, Allison. 2007. "Deferred Benefits, Romance, and the Specter of Later-Life Divorce." *Contemporary Japan* 19:169–188.

Appadurai, Arjun. 1990. "Disjuncture and Difference in the Global Cultural Economy." *Public Culture* 2 (2): 1–24.

Bauman, Zygmunt. 2003. *Liquid Love*. Cambridge: Polity Press.

Berlant, Lauren. 2007. "Cruel Optimism: On Marx, Loss and the Senses." *New Formations* 63 (Winter 2007/8): 33–51.

Borovoy, Amy. 2005. *The Too-Good Wife: Alcohol, Co-Dependency and the Politics of Nurturance in Postwar Japan*. Berkeley: University of California Press.

Cook, Emma E. 2013. "Expectations of Failure: Maturity and Masculinity for Freeters in Contemporary Japan." *Social Science Japan Journal* 16 (1): 29–43.

———. 2014. "Intimate Expectations and Practices: Freeter Relationships and Marriage in Contemporary Japan." *Asian Anthropology* 13 (1): 36–51.

Coontz, Stephanie. 2005. *Marriage, a History: How Love Conquered Marriage*. London: Penguin Books.

Dales, Laura. 2014. "Ohitorisama, Singlehood and Agency in Japan." *Asian Studies Review* 38 (2): 224–242.

Dalton, Emma, and Laura Dales. 2016. "Online *Konkatsu* and the Gendered Ideals of Marriage in Contemporary Japan." *Japanese Studies* 17 (1): 1–19.

Foucault, Michel. 1979. *The History of Sexuality*, vol 1: *An Introduction*. London: Penguin.

Freedman, Alisa, and Kristina Iwata-Weickgenannt. 2011. "'Count What You Have Now. Count What You Don't Have': The Japanese Television Drama around 40 and the Politics of Women's Happiness." *Asian Studies Review* 35 (3): 295–313.

Haruka, Yōko. 2000. *Kekkon shimasen* [I'm Not Getting Married]. Tokyo: Kodansha.

Hertog, Ekaterina. 2009. *Tough Choices: Bearing an Illegitimate Child in Contemporary Japan*. Stanford: Stanford University Press.

Hinz, Christienne. 2004. "Women beyond the Pale: Marital 'Misfits and Outcasts' among Japanese Women Entrepreneurs." *Women's Studies* 33 (4): 453–479.

Jankowiak, William, and Thomas Paladino. 2008. "Desiring Sex, Longing for Love: A Tripartite Conundrum." In *Intimacies: Love and Sex across Cultures*, edited by William Jankowiak, 1–36. New York: Columbia University Press.

JASE. 2012. *Seishōnen no seikōdō—waga kuni no chūgakusei, kōkōsei daigakusei ni kansuru dai 7 kai hōkoku* [The Sexual Behaviour of Youth: Report on the 7th Survey of Junior High, High School, and University Students]. Tokyo: Japan Association for Sex Education.

Kato, Akihiko. 2010. "Mechanisms Underlying Very Low Fertility in Japan: The Trend toward Later and Less Marriage, the Rising Divorce Rate and Declining Marital Fertility." In *The Changing Transition to Adulthood in Japan*, edited by National Institute of Population and Social Security Research. Tokyo: National Institute of Population and Social Security Research.

———. 2011. "Mikonka no mekanizumu" [The Mechanism Underlying the Trend toward Singlehood]. In *Shōshika no Yōin toshite no seijinki ikō no henka ni kansuru jinkōteki kenkyū* [Demographic Study Concerning Changing Transitions to Adulthood as a Factor in the Trend toward Low Fertility], edited by National Insitutute of Population and Social Security Research. Tokyo: National Insitutute of Population and Social Secuirty Research.

Kitamura, Kunio. 2012. *Dai 6-kai danjo no seikatsu to ishiki ni kansuru chōsa hōkoku* [Report on the Sixth Survey of Men's and Women's Lifestyles and Attitudes]. Tokyo: Nihon keikaku kyōkai.

—— . 2013. *Dai 6-kai danjo no seikatsu to ishiki ni kansuru chōsa: Kekka hōkoku* [Sixth Survey of Men's and Women's Lifestyles and Attitudes: Report on the Results]. Tokyo: Japan Association for Sex Education.

Lahad, Kinneret. 2013. "'Am I Asking for Too Much?' The Selective Single Woman as a New Social Problem." *Women's Studies International Forum* 40:23–32.

Maree, Claire. 2004. "Same-Sex Partnerships in Japan: Bypasses and Other Alternatives." *Women's Studies* 33 (4): 541–549.

Nagase, Nobuko. 2006. "Japanese Youth's Attitudes towards Marriage and Child Rearing." In *The Changing Japanese Family*, edited by Marcus Rebick and Ayumi Takenaka, 39–53. London: Routledge.

Plummer, Ken. 2002. "Introduction." In *Sexualities: Critical Concepts in Sociology*, vol. 1, edited by Ken Plummer. London: Routledge.

Sakai, Junko. 2003. *Makeino no tōboe* [The Howl of the Loser Dog]. Tokyo: Kodansha.

Saotome, Tomoko. 2010. *The Reality of Sexuality for Teenage Girls in Japan*. Tokyo: Japan Medical Association.

Weeks, Jeffrey. 1986. *Sexuality*, 2nd ed. London: Routledge.

CHAPTER 5

What Can Be Said?

Communicating Intimacy in Millennial Japan

ALLISON ALEXY

When Yumiko wanted to tell me about the difficulties she was having relating to her mother, she started by talking about their pet dogs. Years before I'd known her and her family, they'd had a corgi named Ma-chan, who had eventually succumbed to old age but whose pictures still filled their home. While we ate dinner together, they'd regularly mention Ma-chan and tell me stories about cute things she used to do, how she'd beg for food or visit each family member before eventually going to sleep in Yumiko's mom's bed.

A few years after Ma-chan's death, Yumiko's mother decided to get a new dog and found another corgi. They named this dog Mi-chan, a name clearly designating her a second to Ma-chan, and it was obvious that this second dog had been abused.[1] She whimpered and cowered. She hated Yumiko's older brother, who was tall and had a deep voice. It took her weeks to believe that they weren't going to hurt her. But when she finally got comfortable with Yumiko's family, she was unbelievably affectionate, especially toward Yumiko's mom. As Yumiko described it to me, Mi-chan did the equivalent of jumping up and down shouting, "I love you!" She followed Yumiko's mother around, never left her side, covered her in little corgi licks, cuddled with her, and generally made her affection incredibly obvious.

According to Yumiko, her mother didn't appreciate, and frankly distrusted, such obvious expressions of love. She thought that such professions were not performing a true affection but covering for a *lack* of affection. Mi-chan was loving too much and was too vocal (as it were) for Yumiko's mother to believe. Although Yumiko had different perspectives on the dogs and their relative behaviors, she told me about them to describe the similar gaps between her mother's and her own ways of displaying affection. Comparing herself to the second dog, Yumiko said she liked to make her love clear. She liked to use the phrase "I love you" (*aishiteru*) and to give her mom hugs and kisses. Although they have an incredibly close and loving relationship, Yumiko's mother bristles at these displays of affection and, like her reaction to Mi-chan, tends to distrust emotions made explicit. Yumiko characterized her mother's opinion as "If you have to make it obvious, it can't be real." For Yumiko, in contrast, obvious expression and real emotion were not inversely related, and she would be happy to express her feelings to her mother without making her uncomfortable. To be clear, Yumiko thinks she has a wonderful relationship with her mother and never doubts how much her mother cares about her. What is at stake, and what sometimes makes Yumiko uncomfortable or sad, is how different their styles of affection are. Though she can understand—and, indeed, articulate to me—her mother's perspective, Yumiko isn't satisfied with her affection always going unsaid. "Love like air" is not what she wants.

"Love like air" (*kūki youni*) is one standard Japanese idiom that idealizes intimate relationships as best when they are un- or understated. In this belief—common enough to be recognizable to even those who don't hold it—the best relationships are those in which partners understand the love they share for each other through actions rather than words. Within this logic, articulating love is a Catch-22: if people verbalize emotion too frequently (or maybe *at all*), that means they are overcompensating for a lacking emotion. Verbalizing an emotion automatically calls the emotion itself into question. If you really love someone, you have to demonstrate it through actions rather than merely, and quickly, stating it as a given. In its most positive understanding, "love like air" is reassuring because it is always present but not ostentatious or cloying, and it suggests a mature, secure love that does not need to be constantly reiterated. Such understandings link deeply intimate feelings with non-verbal "telepathic" communication (*ishin denshin*), which describes the ways that truly intimate people can communicate without speaking. Although these expectations are still articulated in the current moment, they are more typically associated with what is now described as "traditional" or "old-fashioned" ways of thinking about marital relationships that some people, like Yumiko, find unsatisfying. She is not the only one. The risks and possible conflicts surrounding expressions of love, affection, and intimacy become readily apparent when exploring spousal relationships in twenty-first century Japan.

In mid-2000s Japan, one prominent tip proffered to improve marriages or reduce the risk of divorce suggested that people actively work against the idea that good love should be like air. On television programs, in advice books, and in private counseling sessions or semi-public support groups, many counselors advised spouses to verbalize their love for each other—out loud and on a regular basis (Ikeuchi 2002; TBS Broadcast Staff 2006; Watanabe 2004). This tip is frequently summarized as a deceptively simple command: "Say 'I love you' to your spouse." Counselors aren't the only people engaging the possibility that new styles of communication might improve marriages. In the course of my ethnographic fieldwork exploring experiences of divorce in contemporary Japan, a range of people discussed with me how it might be a good idea to verbalize love: single, married, and divorced people; men and women; younger and older folks.[2] Even the people who didn't feel comfortable enacting the suggestion nevertheless were aware of it as an increasingly common piece of advice.

This tip became popular at a moment when intimate relationships, and especially heterosexual marriages, were increasingly under stress. For most of the postwar period, heterosexual marriage has been a powerfully normative social force marking people as responsible social adults (*shakai-jin*; literally, "social person"). The vast majority of people got married, and ethnographers have demonstrated that heterosexual marriage was used as evidence of a person's "normalcy" (Dasgupta 2005; McLelland 2005). In the current moment, however, both the centrality of heterosexual marriages and the particular forms those relationships should take are being implicitly and explicitly called into question. Japan's rising average age at first marriage and the increasing number of "never-married" people surely include both those who explicitly reject marriage and those who might very much want to get married but haven't found the right person or an acceptable situation (Miles, this volume; Nakano 2010).[3] At this time, many public debates and private conversations compare contemporary relationships with the relational ideals of older generations, describing newer practices, preferences, or recommendations in explicit comparison with what used to be done. When people repeat the tip that in good marriages spouses regularly say "I love you," they are idealizing intimate behaviors diametrically opposed to patterns popular just a generation before.

In mid-2000s Japan, the state of and ideal forms for intimate relationships were frequently discussed through metapragmatic attention to styles of communication between partners. Verbalizing affection and emotion—particularly saying "I love you"—came to be understood as a common measure for the health and strength of a marriage. This chapter's analysis begins from the premise that there are many different styles of intimacy possible for any intimate relationship and that people are constantly deciding not just *that* they want to share intimacy, but also *how* that intimacy should be performed, embodied, and experienced. In contemporary discussions about which styles of intimacy are best, language and communicative acts often index different styles of intimacy. For instance, an older model for intimacy suggested that spouses should be ideally fused into "one body" (*ittai*), making them so deeply connected as to not need language to communicate (Lebra 1984, 125). Although this model remains popularly recognizable, newer styles of intimacy suggest that spouses should instead be connected as two loving, but fundamentally separate, people. This intimacy through separation—what I label "connected independence"—finds its contemporary apotheosis in the idea that spouses should say "I love you" to each other. This tip suggests that spouses should be connected through feelings of romantic love but nevertheless separate enough so as to need to verbalize those romantic feelings. I argue that this piece of advice, and the illocutionary and perlocutionary effects being attributed to this particular phrase, reflect contemporary attempts to balance connection and independence within relationships. As people struggle to imagine the particular forms of intimacy they desire, let alone to create and sustain relationships based on those ideals, language in and about relationships indexes, facilitates, and performs intimacy in contemporary Japan.

SILENCE, INTIMACY, AND COMMUNICATION

Anthropological and linguistic research offers a rich context in which to analyze contemporary Japanese debates about how intimacy is facilitated through silence or speech. Besnier (1990, 430) frames linguistic research on affect as engaged with a central question that is similarly relevant in the contemporary Japanese context: how can you (or I) tell who is expressing a "real" emotion and who might be faking?[4] What, exactly, does real feeling sound like?[5] Citing Urban's work on socially expected wailing in Amerindian Brazil, Besnier suggests that all answers are fundamentally cultural: if certain ritualized or expected linguistic utterances are culturally defined as valid and true, they are so within that context no matter their "ritual" performance (Besnier 1990, 430; Urban 1988). Urban concludes that when Amerindian adults cry and wail in socially appropriate contexts, they are simultaneously demonstrating their (true) sadness and doing so in a culturally intelligible way that serves to bind them to other social persons: "One wishes to signal to others that one has the socially correct feelings at the socially prescribed times" (1988, 393). In the contemporary Japanese context, the socially prescribed feeling—that intimate partners should love each other—remains true even as convictions in particular forms of expression have shifted.

Research examining the cultural uses of silence often concludes that silence is fundamental to communication and can be used to convey a range of feelings that might include love. In his analysis of silence in Shakespeare's plays, Bock traces the shifting messages conveyed through silence, ranging from "deep love" to "extremes of alienation," suggesting that silence should be interpreted contextually (1976, 289). In Albert's (1972, 82) examination of speech in Burundi, silence can signal truly held respect as well as temporary placation that will be undermined as soon as the speaker is gone. Basso's (1970) typology of the uses of silence in Apache communication similarly presents silence as a mutable communicative method that can serve in different situations, from meeting strangers to children returning home to courting. In the last case, young sweethearts might spend significant time in silence, even when they are alone, because they don't know how to be with each other and are trying not to do or say something embarrassing (ibid., 218–219).[6] In opposition to common Japanese understandings of the links between silence and love, Basso describes Apache expectations that intimate partners move from silence to speech as they build a deeper intimacy. Similarly, Wright and Roloff (2009) examine American beliefs that speech indexes intimacy—or, more accurately, that speech is necessary but not sufficient for intimacy— through young people's use of "the silent treatment" to punish or signal anger to dating partners. They found that young Americans who expect their romantic partners to be able to understand them without words are likely to be *less* satisfied in their intimate relationships, a conclusion that contrasts with common perceptions in Japan (ibid., cited in Matsunaga and Imahori 2009, 24).

Like Apache people and Native Americans more generally, Japanese people are often stereotyped as especially silent, and the rich literature that has grown in response remains relevant to my analysis of metapragmatic attention to communicating intimacy. Linguistic research about Japan has labeled it a "high-context" society, meaning that speakers and listeners often expect that important information will be left unsaid and must instead be inferred through context (Hall 1976). Lebra's (1987) classic meditation on the uses of silence in Japan suggests that it can be used to convey very different messages, from truthfulness to defiance. Although Lebra (1987, 345) emphasizes the ways in which Japanese cultural uses of silence should not be read as further proof of Japan's inscrutable uniqueness, in other literature attempts to describe Japanese communication can quickly become orientalizing, exoticizing, or simplistic generalizations not based on empirical evidence (for an overview of examples, see Miller 1994a, 1994b). Many researchers have commented on positive Japanese attitudes toward silence, suggesting that knowing when and how to be quiet is a mark of social maturity (Clancy 1986; Kohn 2001; Morsbach 1973; J. S. Smith 1999; Tahhan 2014). At the same time, precisely because silence could represent a range of possible meanings, it can cause significant stress for Japanese speakers as they try to interpret a silent moment (Hasegawa and Gudykunst 1998, 681).

DISCONNECTED DEPENDENCE
AND LOVE IN THE AIR

Especially for generations of Japanese people building families in the 1970s, 1980s, and 1990s, strong social norms dictated a disconnection between gendered spheres of influence. In an archetypal family, fathers were associated with paid labor outside the home, and mothers were associated with domestic responsibilities inside the home. Moreover, many men worked long hours, augmented by obligatory late-night drinking, leaving little time for anything else. For requirements of basic living—food, clean clothes, paid bills—a man relied on his wife, who often accomplished all tasks surrounding the household and children (Dasgupta 2005, 2013; Hidaka 2010). Even though women regularly left their homes and often worked part-time at various points in their lives, older generations can still articulate a standard that women should be home as much as possible (Edwards 1989; Imamura 1987; Rosenberger 2001). Men, laboring as salarymen or otherwise, were responsible for the paid income coming into a family and were associated with outside-ness. Women, even if they worked outside the home, were still idealized as people better suited to, and more reflective of, inside-ness. These separate spheres were reflected in friendship groups and socializing practices (Inaba 2009; Ishii-Kuntz and Maryanski 2003). Within older generations, neither spouse would be inclined to socialize in mixed-gender groups. In ideology, labor realms, and patterns of socializing, spouses were largely disconnected.

Despite such practices separating spouses in the contexts of labor and socializing, in other important ways these spheres were fundamentally connected, often through particular structures of dependencies. Men who were responsible only for outside labor were dependent on their wives to provide all domestic needs, even the most basic ones. Deep connections underlie these dynamics, and each spouse was supported, in social terms, by the other's complementary set of responsibilities. Walter Edwards (1989) created an evocative phrase to capture the particularities of such relationships: complementary incompetence. Rather than describing an intellectual incompetence, this term describes the simultaneous need and separation between Japanese spouses. Because labor norms often discriminated against married women or mothers to push women out of full-time labor, the average woman was unable to find a career that enabled her to support herself. Men, on the other hand, were not taught basic domestic necessities like how to do laundry or cook nutritious meals. Even if a particular man had domestic skills or knowledge, the demands of his work schedule would likely make it impossible for him to feed and clothe himself. Thus, Edwards convincingly argues, Japanese spouses in the 1970s and 1980s were linked together partially through their complementary needs and abilities—her need for a financially viable salary and his for the domestic assistance required to earn such a salary.

Particularly compared with patterns within more contemporary intimate relationships, these older styles of marriage embody what I label *disconnected dependence*. In this term, I am trying to capture both the centrifugal and centripetal forces that were commonly exerted on Japanese marital relationships. Gendered labor policies, the demands placed on male employees, and family norms pushed men and women to be structurally dependent on each other. Judged solely by the archetypal ways married couples shared money—a husband earned money but dutifully turned his whole paycheck over to his wife, who took care of family expenses and quite likely gave her husband a small weekly allowance—Japanese spouses were fundamentally linked. And yet these strong social centripetal forces were met, in practice, with equally common disconnections between the spouses. While they might need each other, many spouses didn't want to spend too much time together. When I talk with older female friends in their seventies and eighties about their husbands, what I hear are often hilariously crafted narratives of annoyance and incompetence: husbands are punch lines and are regularly made fun of, especially if they are around "too much." Indeed the ethnographic record contains many examples of Japanese wives suggesting that a good husband is "healthy and absent" or that husbands at home are bothersome and under foot.[7] In these ways, discursively and in practice, typical marital relationships for most of the postwar era have been framed through *disconnected dependence*: spouses absolutely needed each other and fully recognized that dependence but often led social and emotional lives that were fundamentally disconnected from each other.

Although marriages built on such linkages might not seem particularly intimate to an American audience, Japanese cultural norms in the 1970s and 1980s described representations of such relationships as ideally romantic, and this romance was facilitated through air-like communication. In such historical representations, spouses who worked hard at their separate responsibilities and rarely needed or wanted to verbally communicate with each other were held up as beautiful examples of mature love. Ella (Embree) Wiswell, researching with her husband John in Suye village in the 1930s, heard a group of younger married men comparing romantic love with married love to suggest that the latter was more subtle, stable, and constant (Smith and Wiswell 1982, 179; see also De Vos and Wagatsuma 1961, 1210). In contrast to an immature or childish "puppy love," for instance, Lebra's interlocutors in the 1970s described mature love as occurring between spouses who lived largely separate lives but did so for each other's benefit. Indeed it is precisely because spouses understood themselves as fundamentally dependent on each other, as two halves of a single social unit, that their intimate communications were so subtle:

> Because husband and wife are viewed as being *ittai* (fused into one body), it would be unnecessary to display love and intimacy between them. To praise rather than denigrate one's spouse would amount to praising oneself, which would be intolerably embarrassing. In this interpretation, aloofness is not a matter of deception but *a sign of* ittai *feeling*, or an extreme form of intimacy. Many Japanese seem to convey this view when they wonder how American spouses can express their love for each other without embarrassment (Lebra 1984, 125, emphasis in original; see also Vogel with Vogel 2013, 13).

In this logic, the deep (and socially necessary) links between husbands and wives bind them such that verbal communication of affection feels saccharine and embarrassing. Compared with marital advice given in the more contemporary moment, the patterns of belief and behavior described here imply causation as much as correlation; when spouses don't need to verbally communicate with each other, that could be both a sign of the maturity of their relationship and a way to make their marriage even stronger. Less verbal communication, in these older descriptions, is held up as a measure of and tool for marital strength.

In these representations of non-verbal marital intimacy, "love like air" is often linked with telepathic communication. Glossed as "tacit communication" or "telepathy," it describes an ideal and constant communication that needs never to be clearly articulated (Befu 2001, 39). Telepathic understanding is understood as a beautiful manifestation of deep intimacy between people, a loving mind-meld that renders mere speech evidence of unmet intimate understanding. It is important that these models for intimate relationality through non-verbal communication were not limited to spouses or sexual partners. Linking with this chapter's opening example between a mother's and daughter's differing views of how best to communicate love, ethnographic research has found telepathic communication idealized among family members in other situations (Tahhan, this volume). For instance, Japanese nurses contemplating how best to provide end-of-life care describe family members communicating with each other non-verbally. Because Japanese medical professionals were long unlikely to inform a patient of a terminal prognosis, nurses imagined that patients came to understand that they were dying through telepathic communication with family members (Konishi and Davis 1999, 184).[8] Therefore telepathic communication, which was once idealized as evidence of the best kind of marriage, needs to be understood in relation to a broad cultural context that privileges non-verbal communication.

CONNECTED INDEPENDENCE
AND LOVE OUT LOUD

Although tacit or unstated affection remains a recognizable cultural form, in the contemporary moment marriage counselors are likely to emphasize "communication" (*komyunikēshyon*) as a key measure of marital quality. Compared with earlier pieces of advice, this rhetoric both emphasizes that communication is necessary for "good" marriages and regularly suggests that it should be occurring in ways that are more than tacit or telepathic. As the divorce rate has continued to rise in the past decades, "communication" has become a key idiom in which counselors and spouses find inherent risk and possible salvation. In contemporary marital guidebooks, on websites, on television shows, and in my conversations with people, creating and sustaining marital love are regularly premised on rhetorics of "communication." While tacit "love like air" can be attractive or reassuring, marital problems and impending divorces can also be demonstrated through silence. Moreover, an unkind spouse could use "telepathic communication" as an excuse to be coldly silent, unpleasant, or uncaring.

In one example of the pervasiveness of "communication" rhetoric, on a website devoted to sharing marital tips directed at middle-aged couples, "communication adviser" Uchida uses broad definitions of "communication" to frame what he describes as key ways to protect and save marriages. For him, words, actions, and hearts should all be understood as vehicles for communication; in all of these examples, communication is the key frame through which marital relationships should be understood.

言葉のコミュニケーションは、まさに会話。ご夫婦でキャッチボールは出来ていますか?ボール (パートナーにかける言葉) すら持っていない、というご夫婦もあると思います。. . . .

Communication with words is absolutely about conversations. Is a couple able to play [conversational] catch-ball?[9] I think there are certainly spouses who aren't able to have the word (or ball) to pitch at their partners. . . .

そこで、私がもっとも大切に思っているのは、心のコミュニケーション。『以心伝心』とよく言われますが、これはかなりハイレベル。「わかってると思ってた」なんて、喧嘩の種にしかなりません。

But I think that, by far, the most necessary communication is with hearts and souls. People talk a lot about "telepathic" communication, but that only happens at really high levels. There are many fights when one partner says, "I thought you had understood!"[10]

In this model, communication is clearly key, but its definition is also broad enough to include almost every action imaginable to save or protect a marriage. Moreover, Uchida specifically advises against the telepathic communication that was recommended in previous generations. The point is not that improving communication improves marriages but that, in many counselors' tips, "communication" becomes the general rubric through which marital advice is framed (Waki 2009).

A new group, the National Chauvinistic Husbands Association (Zenkoku teishu kanpaku kayokai), became a media darling in 2006, outlining the ways through which communication could save marriages. Founded in 2005, the group rose to prominence during the national reconsideration of conjugal relationships that occurred on the eve of the 2007 pension law change (Alexy 2007). As outlined on the group's website, the association members are husbands who recognize and want to change problems in their marital relationships.[11] In a play off twelve-step recovery programs but with apparent earnestness, this group enumerates a hierarchy of traits that demonstrate a husband's recovery from chauvinism. The list provides an example of common expectations that contemporary marital problems stem from male (mis)behavior, as well as a summation

of standard foci of marital risk. For our purposes, the fundamental point
is the qualitative difference in the three highest levels below the "plati-
num master level"; these highest degrees of transformation come when
men become able to speak.

初段 3年以上たって「妻を愛している」人	Level 1 A man who still loves his wife after more than three years.
二段 家事手伝いが上手な人	Level 2 A man who shares the housework.
三段 浮気をしたことがない人、ばれていない人	Level 3 A man who hasn't cheated or whose cheating hasn't been found out.
四段 レディーファーストを実践している人	Level 4 A man who puts "ladies first" principles into practice.
五段 愛妻と手をつないで散歩ができる人	Level 5 A man who hold hands with his darling wife while taking a walk.
六段 愛妻の話を真剣に聞くことができる人	Level 6 A man who can take seriously everything his darling wife says.
七段 嫁・姑問題を一夜にして解決できる人	Level 7 A man who can settle any problems between his wife [literally, bride] and mother in one night.
八段 「ありがとう」をためらわずに言える人	Level 8 A man who can say "thank you" without hesitation.
九段 「ごめんなさい」を恐れずに言える人	Level 9 A man who can say "I'm sorry" without hesitation.
十段 「愛している」を照れずに言える人	Level 10 A man who can say "I love you" without hesitation.
プラチナ・マスター段 妻にプラチナをプレゼントして「プロポーズ・アゲイン。」した人	Platinum Master level A man who gives his wife a "platinum present" by proposing again.

In this self-consciously performative example, anti-chauvinistic enlightenment comes not when men can say "thank you," "I'm sorry," or "I love you" with *true feeling*, but when they are able to say them *at all*. Conforming to a model of "love like air," in which spouses love each other but never articulate those feelings, this model for advancement never questions a man's love for his wife—seemingly, the men who don't love their wives wouldn't be interested in the group or wouldn't get past the introductory level. Instead of asking men to rediscover their love to save marriages, this chart asks men to *explicitly articulate* the feelings they are assumed to already have, suggesting that such articulations are the hardest things for men to do and the surest way to save a marriage.

The need to communicate love and affection in such explicit—and verbal—ways reflects new models for relationality between spouses. While the earlier norms suggested the best style of intimacy was for spouses to be fused into one body, thereby obviating the need for any verbal communication, the current models suggest that even if spouses feel like they shouldn't have to verbally communicate with each other, such communication is vitally necessary for a healthy relationship. Spouses who say "I love you" to each other are not just verbalizing their love, but are also simultaneously demonstrating their need to talk, thus attesting to the lack of any fusion between selves. Needing to speak suggests that spouses are fundamentally separate beings who, nevertheless, work to care for each other. In contrast to the older patterns of relationality and intimacy, this pattern of *connected independence* emphasizes the complicated web of connections and disconnections through which spouses build a relationship with each other. In this model for intimacy, spouses are ideally linked through emotional and affective ties rather than highly gendered structures of labor. Saying "I love you"—both having loving feelings and being able to share them out loud—marks relationships as aspiring to this newer kind of ideal type.[12]

Sadako, a semi-professional marriage counselor, described the work she and her husband needed to do around this specific point. In her mid-thirties and living a few hours from Tokyo, Sadako turned herself into an unpaid online marriage counselor. With a website advertising her willingness to answer questions, she estimates that she's exchanged emails with many thousands of clients over the few years she has been dispensing advice. Her training for this position was, she explained to me, the practice that came with listening to her friends, watching TV shows, and reading popular magazines.[13] Her ideas about what makes a good marriage, and therefore the advice she dispenses, frame verbal communication as an important signifier of a healthy relationship. While her husband puttered around their kitchen assembling lunch for all of us (as well as their infant daughter)—very much playing the role of an *ikumen*[14]—Sadako contrasted their current happiness with how they used to treat each other.

あの頃はあの頃で普通だなって思ったんだけど。今思うともう冷め切っていて会話もないし、毎日仕事で帰りが遅くて、子供がいなかった時。で帰ってきて、ご飯を出して、「いただきます」も言わないで食べて。終わったらそのままで、お風呂入って寝ちゃうっていう。私がもうイライラしちゃって。イライラしちゃうから強く当たっちゃうんですよ。そしたらやっぱり、そういう夫婦が多いんですよね。だからこのままじゃマズイと思って穏やかにして自分を。毎日笑顔を忘れずに「お帰り」とか「ただいま」とか、挨拶を自分から多くするようになって。で、少しづつだんなもそれに答えてくれるようになって。一杯私が話しかけるの。会話が一番大事だと思うから、夫婦にとって。

In those days, we thought we were "normal." Back before we had kids, my husband would stay at work late, and we would only talk a little. After he got home, I'd serve dinner, but he wouldn't say "Thank you for this meal" or anything, but just eat, take a bath, and go to bed. I got so irritated! It was really irritating. But there are many couples living this way, I think. I started to think about it and realized that this was really bad. We couldn't go on this way. I started to remember every day to smile, to say, "Welcome home" or "I'm happy to be home."[15] Little by little, my husband got better at responding, and we started to actually talk. Conversation is the most important thing for couples, I think.

Sadako brought up her own marriage to demonstrate how common patterns of non-communication are and how problematic they can become. Not communicating, especially if spouses assume their feelings are clear and obvious, causes trouble and increases the likelihood of divorce in her mind.

Fujita-san, a happily married man in his mid-thirties with whom I talked in 2006, shared opinions and experiences that demonstrate the potential gaps between theories and practices surrounding the stakes of intimate communication. When I asked him directly, Fujita-san articulated the idea that better, stronger relationships were those that were built on air-like relationality. He suggested that a person who was so crass as to say "I love you" was doing something that was at once unconvincing, cinematic, and potentially American.

アリー：プロポーズはしましたか？

Allison: Did you propose [to your wife]?

藤田さん：一応しましたよ。したけど、そんな「結婚してください」とかそういうんじゃなくて。でもうちの奥さんも多分全然結婚する気だったんだと思うんで。自然に。どうする？　　いつ来る？みたいな。じゃあ今度の3月でいいかなみたいな。そういうノリ ... でした。
そんなテレビとか映画のような「アイ・ラーブ・ユー」 みたいなのはなかった。自分もうちの奥さん。もよく言っているのは、2人とも空気みたいな人。

アリー：どういう意味ですか？

藤田さん：要は、なきゃ困る。空気だから、なきゃ困る。でもあっても邪魔じゃない。

Fujita-san: I did in a roundabout way. I did, but it was none of this "Will you marry me?" kind of stuff. See, I knew that she wanted to get married. Just naturally, I knew. We knew. "What are we going to do?" "When should we?" Those kinds of things were what we were talking about. Things like, "OK, so, next year in March would be good, huh?" Kinda like that. It wasn't like how it's on TV or in the movies! There was none of this "I love you" stuff. Sometimes we call each other "people like air."

Allison: What does that mean?

Fujita-san: Basically, if it wasn't there, we'd be in big trouble. It's air, so if it wasn't there, we'd be in trouble. But its existence is not intrusive.

The typed transcript fails to represent the mincing sarcasm with which Fujita-san delivered the key phrase in this quote: *I love you*. Although many Japanese people regularly use so-called English "loan words," Fujita-san rarely did (Stanlaw 2004). He does not speak English and generally described himself as an undereducated everyman who had been working in a suburban barbershop since he graduated from high school. This context, and my previous interactions with him, made his abrupt switch even more striking when he said "I love you" (pronounced *ai rābu yū*) with an English-derived pronunciation rather than the myriad ways to say a similar idea without referencing English. Although Japanese television dramas (to which he explicitly refers) could also include such outright articulations of affection, Fujita-san's switch into an English register made me think he was picturing the line being delivered by an American celebrity, a screen-sized Brad Pitt making a treacly declaration.

While Fujita-san presented himself as part of a quiet partnership demonstrated more through action than words, in practice his experience told a very different story. In introducing his marriage to me, he described his wife as a close friend with whom he shared deeply affective ties, saying, "My friend became my wife" [友達から奥さんになったって感じ]. Ten years into their marriage, with a son who is four years old, Fujita-san remained glowingly happy about his relationship. Atypically, he and his wife both live and work together; she also cuts hair in the same barber shop, so they regularly see each other for many hours of every day. Although in the quotes above Fujita-san represented their relationship as one that rested on tacit communication so strong that they did not really need to discuss their decision to marry, in practice that exact time of his life was characterized by tremendous amounts of language. Fujita-san described his decision to marry his future wife as stemming from a series of absurdly expensive phone bills:

結婚したきっかけは、やっぱり経済的なこと。自分が千葉まで車で奥さんを送迎していたけど、高速代やガソリン代がかかって。あとは電話代。今みたいに携帯も無いし、電話料金が八万円にもなった。毎日話していたから。うちの奥さんが年下だから電話代ぐらいは自分が持とうと思って、かかってくると一回切って、こっちからかけ直した。なるべくうちの奥さんに負担をかけないようにね。でも八万円を超えた時はね。だって家賃より高かったから。

I decided to marry her because of financial reasons. Every time we went out, I drove to Chiba to pick her up and drop her off. Gas fees and toll-road fees cost me a lot. But the worst was a phone bill. There were no cell phones at that time. I was once charged ¥80,000 as a monthly charge.[16] We talked on the phone every day. But I didn't want to impose a financial burden on her because she is younger than me. So when she called me, I hung up right away and called her back.[17] But over ¥80,000 was too much. That was more than my rent.

Although Fujita-san first characterized his relationship as one in which understanding occurs without speech, in practice he had an obvious measure of precisely how verbal their relationship was. In this example, we see two divergent understandings of how a marriage proposal was prompted, discussed, and settled; his first characterization of their relationship as ideally air-like is rapidly revised to include so much talking that it became financially burdensome. I interpret this seeming contradiction to reflect Fujita-san's deep happiness with his marriage. In trying to represent it to me, he employed the rhetoric of "old-fashioned romance" while describing a relationality built through constant contact and verbal communication. It is also quite possible that all the talk that ran up an ¥80,000 phone bill did not seem, to Fujita-san, to be real "communication." Sure, they were talking, but precisely because they were talking about everyday occurrences rather than big ideas or deep feelings, such talk might have seemed less substantial. Speech, talking, and communication are not necessarily the same thing, and each connotes shifting and contested intimacies in contemporary Japan.

❖ ❖ ❖

In January 2014, I received an email request from BBC Radio report-
ers asking if I'd be willing to provide context and analysis of an event
they were covering. "Love Your Wife Day," an event that began in 2008
in Tokyo, involves men yelling professions of love to their wives (Fujita
2013). Standing in a public park, in front of a powerful sound system, the
men yell as loudly as possible, suggesting a hope that sheer volume might
translate into affective efficacy. In video news coverage, the wives stand
and giggle while their husbands shout love and afterward congratulate
the embarrassed husbands for their courage and efforts ("Video" 2013).
Although I had never attended this particular event, I was aware of similar activities that asked men to loudly and publicly verbalize their love;
such activities are of a piece with the newly popular idea that verbal communication can be used to save marriages.

BBC interest in this event was not unusual, and in recent years multiple English-language news organizations have covered the relatively small
event (Craft 2013; Fujita 2013). Such foreign media attention to Japanese
intimate practices should be neither surprising nor overlooked. As discussed in this volume's introductory chapter, Japanese intimate practices
have long been an object of fascination in the English-language press.
The written introduction to this audio story makes clear its orientalizing
efforts, describing the event as "one of the stranger rituals" within "the
sometimes-bizarre standards of modern Japanese culture" (BBC Radio
2015). I interpret these media stories to simultaneously allow viewers
to feel a self-satisfied degree of cultural relativism ("I am open-minded
enough to accept strange practices as normal in Japanese culture") and
enjoy the laughable weirdness of the situation ("What a strange way to be
romantic!"). The Japanese example feels informational, if not educational,
and yet nevertheless entertaining and wacky—everything a fluffy news
piece aspires to. Although I taped a short interview with a BBC reporter in
January 2014, I was told that it wouldn't air for another year; the network
was preparing background with which to cover the same story in 2015 and
seemed untroubled by the changes that might occur between those two
disparate moments (BBC Radio 2015).

Although metapragmatic interest from foreign news media often overlaps with easy exoticism, this kind of story parallels Japanese attention to
how people communicate and what they say in contemporary intimate
relationships. As older styles of intimacy, symbolized through non-verbal "telepathic" communication, are increasingly read as representative
of unhealthy connections, people work to negotiate between what feels
good, what they think they should do, and what their partner might want.

Finding a balance between degrees of dependence and forms of connection, people use styles of communication to simultaneously enact and represent their intimate relationships. It is never easier said than done.

NOTES

This chapter is based on research that was conducted with the generous support of the Fulbright IIE Fellowship and a Japan Foundation Short Term Research Grant. I am extremely grateful to all the people who talked with me and allowed me to spend time in their lives. This chapter has been improved by suggestions from Emma Cook, Laura Miller, Katrina Moore, Hoyt Long, Yuka Suzuki, and China Scherz, as well as Niko Besnier, Oskar Verkaaik, Anneke Beerkens, the other generous workshop participants at the University of Amsterdam, and research assistance from Alison Broach.

1. "Mi" follows "ma" in the Japanese syllabary system, as Mi-chan followed Ma-chan in Yumiko's family.
2. The fieldwork on which this chapter is based occurred first from 2005 to 2006, with regular follow-up research since then. I conducted ethnographic research in various marital, family, and personal counseling centers; spent time with married, divorcing, and divorced people; and conducted interviews among the same groups, as well as with counselors, lawyers, and religious leaders. Primarily based in Tokyo, I also conducted fieldwork in Chiba (the far suburbs of Tokyo) and Matsuyama city on Shikoku Island.
3. Since 1990, the population of men and women who have never been married increased substantially. For instance, in 1990, 6.7 percent of men aged 45–49 were never married, but that increased to 22.5 percent in 2010. Comparatively, in 1990, 4.6 percent of women aged 45–49 were never married, a figure that more than doubled to 12.6 percent in 2010 (Ministry of Internal Affairs and Communication 2010). See Raymo (2003) and Ueno (2009) for more on the increasing rates of never-married men and women.
4. Although I do not have space in this section to engage it all, a large body of scholarship analyzes the intersection of emotion and language; for instance, see Levy (1984); Lutz (1988); Lutz and Abu-Lughold (1990); Ochs and Sheiffelin (1989); Palmer and Occhi (1999); Stankiewicz (1964). My ideas in this chapter draw from this rich literature.
5. Caffi and Janney use evocative phrasing to describe the risks inherent in representing emotion through language: "The complexity of the interface between language, people, and affect is implicit in the observation that: (1) we can all express feelings that we have, (2) we can all have feelings that we do not express, (3) we can all express feelings that we do not have, or feelings that we think our partners might expect or wish us to have, or feelings that simply might be felicitous to have in a given situation for particular reasons" (1994, 326).
6. Basso (1970, 219) also suggests that in the context of courting, young women especially are told to keep as silent as possible because speech might be read as a sign of wanton sexual experience.
7. One classic pattern is comparing annoying husbands to garbage (*sodai gomi*; literally, garbage so large one has to pay to get rid of it) or wet leaves (*nure ochiba*), which are clingy and hard to clean up. Taking such rhetorical patterns seriously, we also need to be aware of the ways in which these highly gendered performances of complaining might reflect the social norms of female talk about (annoying) husbands, rather than actual annoying husbands (Lebra 1984, 124; Salamon 1975). My research engages the joys and social rewards possible for men and women telling stories of marital dissatisfaction, while I also register and represent attempts to convey genuine dissatisfaction about marital relationships. The patterns of complaint and the gaps between speech that might be fun to say and speech intended to convey a real problem remain worthy of attention.

8. This practice is no longer as prevalent as it once was but was built from the premise that if a person knew he or she was dying, the experience would be even more stressful and difficult. Therefore, especially for patients with cancer, Japanese medical professionals regularly did not inform a patient of a terminal diagnosis and relied on family members to decide if the patient should be told. Although this system might seem distasteful or patronizing, it meshed with frankly paternalistic attitudes by doctors and a sense that the doctors were trained and able to bear the burden of terminal diagnoses (Annas and Miller 1994; Higuchi 1992). I thank China Scherz for pointing out that such strategic silences by doctors surrounding terminal diagnoses are not limited to Japan (Harris, Shao, and Sugarman 2003; Rothman 1992).

9. A similar idea is expressed by Waki (2009, 61).

10. The broader context for this quote, including more advice about communication, can be found on the original website: http://www.jukunen-rikon.com/2007/03/post_37.html.

11. This list was originally published on the organization's website: http://www.zenteikyou.com.

12. At the same time that the benefits of air-like relationships are being questioned in intimate relationships, a relatively new insult derides people who "can't read the air" (*kūki yomani*; often shortened to KY)—that is, those who are socially oblivious or clueless. The insult derived from this idea is not limited to intimate relationships and is instead a general term to describe a socially awkward person. While being able to "read the air" might be judged as a positive attribute, it is different from the notion that married spouses assume their feelings are so obvious as to not need verbalization. The centrality of "air" in contemporary Japanese discourse about relationality seems ripe for future theorizing. I thank Laura Miller for bringing up this point.

13. Sadako told me that she used advice from magazines to give suggestions to her online clients. For more on the ways that magazines directed at women influence public discourse about gender and intimacy, see Holthus (2010) and Sato (2003).

14. This newly popular term describes fathers who are actively involved in rearing their children.

15. Like "Thank you for this meal," an expression Sadako used above in this quote, the phrases she uses here are everyday greetings that are very typically used to demonstrate the kind of "polite speech" that should occur within healthy families. These are *aisatsu* phrases, which are commonly recognized greetings and responses. Elsewhere (Alexy 2011, 896) I have written about Japanese marital guidebooks suggesting the regular use of *aisatsu* as a way to improve one's marriage.

16. This is approximately $800.

17. In Japan, only the person placing a call is charged; someone receiving a call isn't charged at all. In this situation, Fujita-san was being generous and bearing the cost of all the phone calls between himself and his future wife, even when she was the person who initiated many calls.

REFERENCES

Albert, Ethel. 1972. "Culture Patterning of Speech Behavior in Burundi." In *Directions in Sociolinguistics: The Ethnography of Communication*, edited by John J. Gumperz and Dell Hymes, 72–105. New York: Holt, Rinehart and Winston.

Alexy, Allison. 2007. "Deferred Benefits, Romance, and the Specter of Later-Life Divorce." *Contemporary Japan* 19:169–188.

———. 2011. "Intimate Dependence and Its Risks in Neoliberal Japan." *Anthropological Quarterly* 84 (4): 895–917.

Annas, George, and Frances Miller. 1994. "The Empire of Death: How Culture and Economics Affect Informed Consent in the U.S., the U.K., and Japan." *American Journal of Law and Medicine* 20 (4): 357–394.

Basso, Keith H. 1970. "'To Give Up on Words': Silence in Western Apache Culture." *Southwestern Journal of Anthropology* 26 (3): 213–230.

BBC Radio. 2015. "Love Your Wife Day." Online at: http://www.bbc.co.uk/programmes /p02h8y5c.

Befu, Harumi. 2001. *Hegemony of Homogeneity: An Anthropological Analysis of "Nihonjinron."* Melbourne: Trans Pacific Press.

Besnier, Niko. 1990. "Language and Affect." *Annual Review of Anthropology* 19: 415–451.

Bock, Philip K. 1976. "'I Think but Dare Not Speak': Silence in Elizabethan Culture." *Journal of Anthropological Research* 32 (3): 285–294.

Caffi, Claudia, and Richard Janney. 1994. "Toward a Pragmatics of Emotive Communication." *Journal of Pragmatics* 22:325–373.

Clancy, Patricia M. 1986. "The Acquisition of Communicative Style in Japanese." In *Language Socialization across Cultures*, edited by Bambi Schieffelin and Elinor Ochs, 213–250. Cambridge: Cambridge University Press.

Craft, Lucy. 2013. "How Do I Love Thee? Japanese Husbands Shout the Ways." National Public Radio, NPR.org, February 13. http://www.npr.org/2013/02/13/171920006/how -do-i-love-thee-japanese-husbands-shout-the-ways.

Dasgupta, Romit. 2005. "Salarymen Doing Straight: Heterosexual Men and the Dynamics of Gender Conformity." In *Genders, Transgenders, and Sexualities in Japan*, edited by Mark McLelland and Romit Dasgupta, 168–182. London: Routledge.

———. 2013. *Re-Reading the Salaryman in Japan: Crafting Masculinities*. London: Routledge.

De Vos, George, and Hiroshi Wagatsuma. 1961. "Value Attitudes toward Role Behavior of Women in Two Japanese Villages." *American Anthropologist* 63 (6): 1204–1230.

Edwards, Walter. 1989. *Modern Japan through Its Weddings: Gender, Person, and Society in Ritual Portrayal*. Stanford: Stanford University Press

Fujita, Akiko. 2013. "Husbands Shout Their Love on 'Beloved Wife Day.'" *ABC News*, January 30. http://abcnews.go.com/blogs/headlines/2013/01/husbands-shout-their -love-on-beloved-wife-day/.

Hall, Edward T. 1976. *Beyond Culture*. New York: Anchor Books.

Harris, Julian, John Shao, and Jeremy Sugarman. 2003. "Disclosure of Cancer Diagnosis and Prognosis in Northern Tanzania." *Social Science and Medicine* 56 (5): 905–913.

Hasegawa, Tomohiro, and William B. Gudykunst. 1998. "Silence in Japan and the United States." *Journal of Cross-Cultural Psychology* 29 (5): 668–684.

Hidaka, Tomoko. 2010. "Masculinity and the Family System: The Ideology of the 'Salaryman' across Three Generations." In *Home and Family in Japan: Continuity and Transformation*, edited by Richard Ronald and Allison Alexy, 112–130. London: Routledge.

Higuchi, Norio. 1992. "The Patient's Right to Know of a Cancer Diagnosis: A Comparison of Japanese Paternalism and American Self-Determination." *Washburn Law Journal* 31 (3): 455–473.

Holthus, Barbara. 2010. *A Half Step Ahead: Marriage Discourses in Japanese Women's Magazines*. PhD dissertation, University of Hawai'i.

Ikeuchi, Hiromi. 2002. *Koware kake fūfu no toraburu, kaiketsu shimasu* [Couples' Troubles and Their Resolutions]. Tokyo: Magajin housu.

Imamura, Anne. 1987. *Urban Japanese Housewives: At Home and in the Community*. Honolulu: University of Hawai'i Press.

110   Allison Alexy

Inaba, Akihide. 2009. "Fūfu kankei no hyōka" [Examining Relationships between Husbands and Wives]. In *Gendai nihonjin no kazoku: NFRJ kara mita sono sugata* [Modern Japanese Families: Perspectives from NFRJ (National Family Research of Japan)], edited by Sumiko Fujimi and Michiko Nishino, 122–130. Tokyo. Yūhikaku.

Ishii-Kuntz, Masako, and Alexandra R. Maryanski. 2003. "Conjugal Roles and Social Networks in Japanese Families." *Journal of Family Issues* 24 (3): 352–380.

Kohn, Tamara. 2001. "Don't Talk—Blend: Ideas about Body and Communication in Aikido Practice." In *An Anthropology of Indirect Communication*, edited by Joy Hendry and C. W. Watson, 163–178. London: Routledge.

Konishi, Emiko, and Anne Davis. 1999. "Japanese Nurses' Perceptions about Disclosure of Information at the Patients' End of Life." *Nursing and Health Sciences* 1 (3): 179–187.

Lebra, Takie Sugiyama. 1984. *Japanese Women: Constraint and Fulfillment*. Honolulu: University of Hawai'i Press.

———. 1987. "The Cultural Significance of Silence in Japanese Communication." *Multilingua—Journal of Cross-Cultural and Interlanguage Communication* 6 (4): 343–358.

Levy, Robert I. 1984. "Emotion, Culture, and Knowing." In *Culture Theory: Essays on Mind, Self, and Emotion*, edited by Richard A. Shweder and Robert A. LeVine, 214–237. Cambridge: Cambridge University Press.

Lutz, Catherine A. 1988. *Unnatural Emotions: Everyday Sentiments on a Micronesian Atoll and Their Challenge to Western Theory*. Chicago: University of Chicago Press.

Lutz, Catherine A., and Lila Abu-Lughod, eds. 1990. *Language and the Politics of Emotion*. Cambridge: Cambridge University Press.

Matsunaga, Masaki, and Tadasu Todd Imahori. 2009. "Profiling Family Communication Standards: A U.S.-Japan Comparison." *Communication Research* 36 (1): 3–31.

McLelland, Mark. 2005. "Salarymen Doing Queer: Gay Men and the Heterosexual Public Sphere." In *Genders, Transgenders, and Sexualities in Japan*, edited by Mark McLelland and Romit Dasgupta, 96–110. London: Routledge.

Miller, Laura. 1994a. "Japanese and American Meetings and What Goes on before Them: A Case-Study of Co-Worker Misunderstanding." *Pragmatics* 4 (2): 221–238.

———. 1994b. "Japanese and American Indirectness." *Journal of Asian Pacific Communication* 5 (1–2): 37–55.

Ministry of Internal Affairs and Communications. 2010. "Marital Status." Available online at http://www.stat.go.jp/english/data/kokusei/2010/poj/pdf/2010ch03.pdf.

Morsbach, Helmut. 1973. "Aspects of Nonverbal Communication in Japan." *Journal of Nervous and Mental Disease* 157 (4): 262–277.

Nakano, Lynne. 2010. "Working and Waiting for an 'Appropriate Person': How Single Women Support and Resist Family in Japan." In *Home and Family in Japan: Continuity and Transformation*, edited by Richard Ronald and Allison Alexy, 229–267. London: Routledge.

Ochs, Elinor, and Bambi Sheiffelin. 1989. "Language Has a Heart." *Text* 9:7–25.

Palmer, Gary, and Debra J. Occhi. 1999. "Introduction: Linguistic Anthropology and Emotional Experience." In *Languages of Sentiment: Cultural Constructions of Emotional Substrates*, edited by Gary B. Palmer and Debra J. Occhi, 1–22. Amsterdam and Philadelphia: John Benjamins Publishing.

Raymo, James M. 2003. "Educational Attainment and the Transition to First Marriage among Japanese Women." *Demography* 40 (1): 83–103.

Rosenberger, Nancy. 2001. *Gambling with Virtue: Japanese Women and the Search for Self in a Changing Nation*. Honolulu: University of Hawai'i Press.

Rothman, David. 1992. *Strangers at the Bedside: A History of How Law and Bioethics Transformed Medical Decision Making.* New York: Basic Books.

Salamon, Sandra. 1975. "Male Chauvinism as a Manifestation of Love in Marriage." In *Adult Episodes in Japan*, edited by David Plath, 20–31. Leiden: Brill.

Sato, Barbara. 2003. *The New Japanese Woman: Modernity, Media, and Women in Interwar Japan.* Durham, NC: Duke University Press.

Smith, Janet Shibamoto. 1999. "From Hiren to Happī-Endo: Romantic Expression in the Japanese Love Story." In *Languages of Sentiment: Cultural Constructions of Emotional Substrates*, edited by Gary B. Palmer and Debra J. Occhi, 131–150. Amsterdam and Philadelphia: John Benjamins Publishing.

Smith, Robert, and Ella Wiswell. 1982. *The Women of Suye Mura.* Chicago: University of Chicago Press.

Stankiewicz, Edward. 1964. "Problems of Emotive Language." In *Approaches to Semiotics: Cultural Anthropology, Education, Linguistics, Psychiatry, Psychology*, edited by Thomas A. Sebeok, Alfred S. Hayes, and Mary Catherine Bateson, 239–264. The Hague: Mouton.

Stanlaw, James. 2004. *Japanese English: Language and Culture Contact.* Hong Kong: University of Hong Kong Press.

Tahhan, Diana Adis. 2014. *The Japanese Family: Touch, Intimacy and Feeling.* London: Routledge.

TBS Broadcast Staff. 2006. *Jukunen rikon 100 no riyū* [100 Reasons for Later-Life Divorce]. Tokyo: Shōnensha.

Ueno, Chizuko. 2009. *Otoko ohitorisamadō* [Men on Their Own]. Tokyo: Hōken.

Urban, Greg. 1988. "Ritual Wailing in Amerindian Brazil." *American Anthropologist* 90 (2): 385–400.

"Video: Husbands Gather in Japan for Love Your Wife Day." 2013. *The Guardian.* Available at http://www.theguardian.com/world/video/2013/jan/29/japan-love-your-wife-day-video.

Vogel, Suzanne, with Steven K. Vogel. 2013. *The Japanese Family in Transition: From the Professional Housewife Ideal to the Dilemmas of Choice.* Lanham, MD: Rowman and Littlefield.

Waki, Mitsuo. 2009. *Zero kara hajimeru kekkon nyūmon* [Introductory Handbook for Marriage]. Tokyo: Bungeisha.

Watanabe, Junichi. 2004. *Otto toiu mono* [A Thing Called a "Husband"]. Tokyo: Shueisha.

Wright, Courtney, and Michael Roloff. 2009. "Relational Commitment and the Silent Treatment." *Communication Research Reports* 26 (1): 12–21.

CHAPTER 6

❖ ❖ ❖

My Husband Is a Good Man
When He Doesn't Hit Me

*Redefining Intimacy among
Victims of Domestic Violence*

Kaoru Kuwajima

> It is not that he hits you because he doesn't love you.
> There are many men who say, "I love you" and hit you.
> —Female advocate for the rights of domestic violence victims

Many women I encounter at women's shelters wonder whether they should get a divorce. Despite experiencing brutal violence at the hands of their husbands, these women struggle to decide if they should leave permanently, a choice that is neither clear nor easy. The complexity of such a decision reflects many factors, including economic needs and resources, social norms surrounding families, and the women's own emotional attachments, as well as the ambivalent nature of intimacy itself. It is precisely the confusing link between violence and intimacy that makes it difficult for quite a few victims to end their relationships.[1] Some women eventually return to a previously violent relationship, and others ultimately choose not to. Many spend significant time trying to decide what to do and feel tremendous conflict during the process. A primary challenge faced by victims of domestic violence is to disentangle the complex linkages between intimacy and violence.

"Intimacy" is commonly defined as a state that includes closeness, emotional connection, mutual care, shared beliefs, the ability to fully open up, and a sexual relationship (in the context of romantic intimacies). Although intimacy can be a critical base for a joyful connection in the contemporary world, intimate relationships are increasingly likely to include reported violence. Japan is no exception, and, as I discuss below, the rates of reported domestic violence are increasing. For many people without personal experience, intimate-partner violence might challenge a basic definition of intimacy. In common assumptions, intimacy is more typically linked with love than violence. However, many violent acts toward intimate partners are excused with the term "love." Thus, because so few people link intimacy and violence, the main puzzle of this chapter traces how female survivors, with help from staff at support centers, are trying to figure out how violence can exist within intimacy.

Despite the generally positive connotations many people hold about intimacy, in this chapter I explore how intimacy and violence can be fundamentally intertwined in the lives of women in Japan. By examining the experiences of female victims of domestic violence and the interactions between victims and support agents (such as shelter staff and caseworkers), I trace how women reconsider and redefine intimacy with their partners. I argue that reconsidering and redefining intimacy is vital before a victim of domestic violence can leave a relationship to begin a new life and that shifting definitions of, and expectations for, intimacy are often a necessary part of recovery after a victim has experienced violence. In and of itself, disassociating intimacy and violence is not likely to decrease the violence, but this process appears to give the victims a chance to turn toward a different future.

This chapter draws from ethnographic fieldwork I conducted from 2006 to 2009 in three temporary protection shelters for female victims of domestic violence in and around major cities in Japan.[2] These shelters are operated by organizations designed to support women's rights and work in cooperation with several municipal government social welfare offices. One shelter is for emergency care and is available for only two weeks, while at the other two, women and children can stay from several months to nearly one year. During my research, I was in regular contact with women who had fled violence; because of confidentiality and safety concerns, I was not able to talk with their male partners to verify the perspectives I heard, nor was I able to contact the women after they left the shelter.[3] Therefore this chapter is based on my observations, reflections from various shelter personnel and female caseworkers, and my interactions with female victims during their temporary protection. All names are pseudonyms, and I have altered some of the details of the cases to maintain privacy.

THE EMERGENCE OF DOMESTIC VIOLENCE
AND LEGAL RESPONSES IN JAPAN

Violence by intimate partners occurs in every country in the world, and the reported prevalence of women who have experienced physical and/or sexual violence ranges widely, from 15 percent among urban populations in Japan to 69 percent in rural Peru (UNICEF 2000, 2; WHO 2005, 6). In the last fifteen years in Japan, the number of reported domestic violence cases has increased. Japanese police recorded 69,908 consultations (*sōdan*) concerning domestic violence in 2016—the highest number since the statistics started to be gathered in 2001—and they prosecuted 8,291 cases, a 242 percent increase from five years earlier (National Police Agency 2017, 5). Of the 5,117 women who received temporary protection in fiscal year 2015, 73 percent were fleeing from violence inflicted by their husbands and partners (MHLW 2016, 2). According to the Gender Equality Bureau Cabinet Office (2015), a national study on spousal violence conducted in 2014 showed that 23.7 percent of women and 16.6 percent of men in Japan have experienced either physical assault, psychological threats, sexual coercion, or economic abuse perpetrated by current or former spouses.[4] One out of five people in contemporary Japan have faced violence from their spouses.

In Japan, intimate-partner violence was virtually unaddressed before the mid-1990s (Yoshihama and Sorenson 1994, 63). When Sharman Babior, an American anthropologist, conducted fieldwork in a women's shelter in Tokyo in 1987, there was little public awareness of domestic violence among Japanese people (Babior 1996). The new public attention to this topic began for a number of reasons, including the 1995 United Nations' Fourth World Conference on Women, held in Beijing, during which the prevalence of domestic violence was discussed. After significant efforts by grassroots activists, lawyers, caseworkers, researchers, and female politicians, the Act on the Prevention of Spousal Violence and the Protection of Victims was passed in 2001.[5] This act is commonly referred to as the "DV Prevention Act" (DV Bōshihō); "DV" is a common acronym for "domestic violence." A significant part of this act is the provision that directly focuses on assisting victims. Consequently, legal and institutional support systems for victims increased. However, the act is mainly designed to help victims, mostly single mothers with children, utilize the various social welfare services already in place. One person with whom I spoke, a director of a women's rights organization, pointed out that although the act is certainly important and necessary, it can be effective only if the victim leaves the perpetrator, gets a divorce, and starts a new life. The deputy manager of a gender equality department in Chiba Prefecture explained, "If the DV female victims enter into the welfare system, everything else will flow smoothly." Thus the most important legislation attempting to ameliorate domestic violence in Japan is structured around the presupposition that all victims will necessarily leave their abusive partners, a proposition that my ethnographic fieldwork uncovers as far from true.

The DV Prevention Act delineates municipal governments as responsible for providing assistance, including temporary protection, to the victims of spousal violence.[6] The act specifically designates existing prefectural women's counseling centers (*fujinsōdanjo*) to provide counseling, information, guidance, and temporary protection.[7] In addition to these state institutions, private shelters for victims of domestic violence appeared in the late 1980s and have increased in number since then (Shelter-DV Mondai Chōsa Kenkyū-Kaigi 4 2000).[8] Some of the early shelters were started in response to the emergent needs of women from elsewhere in Asia who were the victims of human trafficking (ibid., 69). Since that time, municipal governments' responsibility for the protection and support of victims of domestic violence has grown, and cooperation with private shelters has been increasingly necessary to create a more versatile and effective support system.

WHY DO WOMEN STAY?

When love and violence coexist, the victims live in a "world where it is difficult to distinguish between a safe situation and a dangerous one, a gesture of love and a violent, uncaring gesture" (hooks 1997, 280). Not only are women confused by the cycles of violence and gentleness, but also the ambivalent nature of intimacy clouds women's perceptions of their relationship. Here, I would like to elaborate on two points demonstrating the ambivalent nature of intimacy: first, intimacy includes the potential for violence, and, second, control of one's partner can easily be mistaken for intimacy.

Drawing on the sociology of emotion, Matsushima states that intimate relationships tend to simultaneously enfold emotions of love and violence, "two states seemingly far away from each other" (2001, 76). She argues that the emotion of love, which constitutes intimacy, is not generated spontaneously but is socially constructed and thus gendered in specific ways. People in intimate relationships can feel "love" if certain kinds of expected actions are carried out (ibid., 83). Based on Matsushima's argument, within Japanese heterosexual couples, a woman's demonstration of her love is thought to occur when she takes care of a man; therefore she must express the emotion of intimacy through assuming a gendered role. At the same time, men are normatively required to assume *kaisho*, or economic responsibility, for their female partners. In this theory, the emotion of intimacy is inscribed in highly gendered ways that reinforce a power imbalance between men and women. This imbalance within intimate relationships contains "a bud of violence" (ibid., 83).

Ichiro Numazaki, a Japanese anthropologist who has explored intimate-partner violence, argues that the imbalance of care distribution between men and women is maintained and reinforced through men's dependent need (*amae*) for their female partners.[9] A man who demands interest, care, involvement, and/or help for himself without giving any of those to his partner is "imposing his dependent needs [*amae*]" on her (Numazaki 2004, 169). In this understanding, *amae* links a person's dependency with his attempts at control.[10] The perpetrator needs his wife, but he beats her; he depends on her, but he controls her. If she ever tries to refuse this *amae*, which is his dependence on and desire to control her, she faces his sanctions and retaliations. He controls her by manipulating *amae*; it is through a "politics of *amae*" that such a relationship is constructed (ibid., 168–170).[11] This tactic resonates with how feminists in other contexts define domestic violence as "gender and power" (Yllö 2005, 20).

For people within it, this kind of controlling relationship seems like an intimate one because it is exclusive, closed, and maintained and mediated by emotions. However, the intimacy that comes through violence marks this type of relationship as substantially different. Numazaki labels this a "controlling and confining sphere [*seibaku-ken*]," which emerges when domestic violence is disguised as merely an intimate sphere (2004, 166). Care itself is non-violent, but in domestic violence the demand for care can be used as an attempt to control a partner. These dynamics of dependence, care, and control are reflected in the dilemmas some women face while balancing their love for a violent partner with a desire to leave although they might lack the economic means for divorce. These two theoretical viewpoints explain the potential for violence built into an intimate relationship, as well as possible difficulties distinguishing intimacy from control and confinement. In addition to the ambivalent characteristics within intimacy, the following section presents other reasons women give for not permanently leaving an abusive relationship, including socioeconomic conditions and cultural norms.

REASONS NOT TO DIVORCE

"Why do women stay?"[12] This is a question that has long been asked of women victimized by intimate partners (Miyaji 2005, 122). The term "co-dependency" has been used to explain why battered women do not leave a relationship (Matsushima 2001, 85), though such understandings tend to pathologize and blame victims. According to medical anthropologist and psychiatrist Naoko Miyaji (2005, 122), violence often starts after women are put in a situation where it is difficult for them to leave, such as after having sex, getting married, becoming pregnant, or having a child. "It is after the situation worsens that women start seriously thinking what to do," according to Kiyoko Yoshihiro (1997, 222), a writer who interviewed victims of domestic violence. Some women mentioned problems they faced when they tried to leave a perpetrator—his crying and apologizing, their fear of a possible escalation of violence, his refusal to agree to any divorce that doesn't give him custody of their children—all of which typically result in a woman staying with her perpetrator just as he had intended (Yoshihiro 1997; Chiba-ken DV Kenkyūkai 2004).

According to a qualitative study conducted in Chiba Prefecture, women who were battered decided not to divorce for the following reasons: economic security; love for their husbands; not wanting to take their children's fathers away from them; fear of the husbands' stalking them or escalating the violence; positive changes in the husbands' attitudes and a decrease in violence; and resisting husbands' requests to divorce (Chiba-ken DV Kenkyūkai 2004, 65–72).[13] Some respondents expressed ambivalent feelings toward their partners: "Sometimes he still has good sides. I thought we would be all right" (ibid., 66). One woman said, "We loved each other and got married, and—how should I put it?—I thought I was done with him, but still a part of me respects him and wishes we could start over again" (ibid., 76). At the same time, this woman kept her medical records with her at all times so that if she suddenly decided to seek a divorce, she could prove her husband's violence. While these reasons work together in complex ways to prevent women from leaving violent relationships, those women who chose to divorce listed the following reasons: escalation of violence; no sign of an improvement in the husbands' violent attitudes; and the visible effects of violence on their bodies (ibid., 79–84).

Some women choose to stay in an abusive relationship in order to survive. Their lack of economic resources, such as employment, education, or work skills, further serves to keep them in abusive relationships (Chornesky 2000, 485). Economic reasons for not getting a divorce are an important part of these decisions, particularly in light of the tight connection between gender and labor patterns in Japan. In 2012, women made up 42.2 percent of the entire labor force, but about half of these workers were engaged in non-regular employment (MHLW 2013, 1, 14). Women make up 70 percent of workers in unstable, non-regular employment (Statistics Bureau 2013, 2), a status that often makes it difficult for them to support themselves and any dependent children. The average annual income of a female-headed household in Japan is approximately ¥2,910,000 ($29,100), as opposed to a male-headed household with ¥4,550,000 ($45,500) (MHLW 2012). About 60 percent of female-headed households have never received alimony or child support from ex-husbands after they divorced (Sugimoto 2004, 81). Without the possibility of independent economic security, women tend to stay with their abusive partners.

CULTURAL VALUES, THE STIGMA OF DIVORCE, AND ENDURANCE

Social norms and cultural values regarding gender relations also serve to keep women in intimate relationships, despite possible dangers. For example, stigma toward a divorced woman is still prevalent in Japan, though the number of divorces has been gradually increasing in recent years (Sugimoto 2004, 79). As is clear from the derogatory term *demo-dori* (literally, "leave and return"), used to describe a female divorcée, a woman with whom I spoke murmured, "People will know instantly what happened if I went back to my parents' house." In her reasonable estimation, an adult daughter returning to her natal household could easily be seen as the result of a divorce. To avoid this stigma, divorce was not an option she wanted to consider.

Cultural values about women's behaviors and dispositions in an intimate relationship also suggest that women are expected to stay. Some women I encountered at shelters recalled that they had never tried to escape from violent husbands specifically because they thought endurance (*gaman*) was a moral necessity. A seventy-three-year-old woman who came to a shelter after many years of violence told the staff that she thought "it was a virtue to endure his violence." She also thought it was natural for her to say nothing and take care of everything so that he could concentrate on his work. Such understandings of endurance were coupled with women's frequent belief that if they could just do things correctly, the violence would stop. Many women in various generations articulated some version of, "I thought the violence would stop if I did things right." This thinking becomes linked to self-blame when victims of violence blame themselves because they think (or are told) they have done something wrong.[14]

WOMEN'S DECISIONS AND SHELTER STAFF DILEMMAS

It is not simple or easy for shelters to support women who are likely to swing between deciding to leave or return to their husbands. Though shelter staff members understand these women are in difficult situations, they sometimes face dilemmas when they are asked to support women's decisions. The following cases describe how shelter staff members have tried to acknowledge women's personal preferences and desires while also advising them to minimize violence and risk in their lives.

Even after deciding to leave a violent relationship, some women who finally managed to escape nonetheless return to the perpetrators. For example, in 2007, a divorced man fired a gun, injuring his daughter and son and killing a policeman in Nagakute town, Aichi Prefecture. The man had been asking his ex-wife to get back together, and she had gone to his house when the shooting took place. At that time, she had already been granted a divorce from him and was living in a dormitory for single women, working part time. The director of a shelter where I was volunteering commented on the incident:

> Many women go and see their ex. Even though a year and a half had passed after her divorce, this woman still went to see him. For those of us who run temporary shelters, some of the most important work we do is not only preventing the perpetrators from coming to the shelter, but also not letting women go to visit their husbands. If a woman really wants to see her husband, we have to ask her to leave the shelter.

The national news occasionally includes tragic cases that end with women being killed by their husbands or ex-husbands.[15] Staff workers realize the danger of a woman's returning to the perpetrators and are concerned not only with the safety of the woman and the people around her, but also about where to draw a line in assisting the women at a shelter.

After running from an abusive relationship, many women struggle to decide if they should ask for a divorce or return to their partners. This can be further complicated when the victims are not Japanese. Maria, a Filipina woman married to a Japanese man, stayed in a shelter with her toddler and baby for about six months. During her stay, she repeatedly expressed her desire to go back to her husband's house. A shelter staff member had the following conversation with Maria when she came to talk one morning:

SHELTER STAFF MEMBER: You want to go home, don't you?

MARIA: Yes. Here, everyone helps me, but after I leave here, I will be all by myself, and I don't know what to do. I can't even read Japanese.

SHELTER STAFF MEMBER: If that is what you really want, we won't stop you. Are you thinking that you should go because of the children?

MARIA: They will hate me because I don't have money.

SHELTER STAFF MEMBER (in a gentle way): We won't stop you. But you need to know it would be more difficult and complicated if you tried to escape again because he would not let the children go next time. If that happened, I am afraid you would have to go back to the Philippines without the children. You might want to think about that. Do you think you can take whatever he might do to you?

MARIA: I love him. If he knew how much I cared for him, he would be OK. We can get through with love.

SHELTER STAFF MEMBER: He did not hit you because he does not love you. There are many men who hit women while saying "I love you."

MARIA: If he saw his children, he might change his mind and become gentle. I want to be happy.

SHELTER STAFF MEMBER: I understand, but you shouldn't expect that [he will change]. Not every woman who returns to her husband is treated badly. Some women manage. If you go back, you will be on your own and have to do whatever you can do to survive there. Can you handle that?

Maria decided to think about it overnight, and in the morning she shared her decision, saying, "I've decided not to go back. I remembered he and my mother-in-law used to tell me that I was a maid, and they treated me badly."

The staff speculated that Maria wanted to return owing to financial hardship and the difficulties of rearing children on her own. Her mother-in-law used to look after the children. If she got divorced, she would have to rely on welfare assistance until she found a job, a possibility that seemed difficult for her. Although the staff gave her a realistic assessment of her husband's future violence, she expected that her "love" for him and the children would change him. Staff members, who had seen many cases of domestic violence, were well aware that any "love" he felt would not prevent him from hitting her. In these kinds of conversations, shelter staff tries to highlight the contradictions between a husband's genuine feelings of love for his wife and his violent acts against her.

Shelter staff members start from the premises that "perpetrators are dangerous" and "violence cannot be cured." These perspectives stand in contrast with those held by many women in the shelter. For example, one woman thought domestic violence was "something like an illness," and she thought it would be cured if she gave her husband time to repair and heal himself. When she shared this opinion, the staff made it a point to correct her, saying, "Domestic violence is not an illness. That is why we handle it through law." This woman's sense of domestic violence is common, and the phrase used in this chapter's title—"My husband is a good man when he doesn't hit me"—is regularly expressed by victims of domestic violence.

Women who are victimized often say they don't like what a man has done to them, but they love the man (Hattery 2009, 146).

While firmly believing that violence cannot be cured, shelter staff also understand that some women still feel attached to their husbands. A shelter director explained this perspective to me: "They [the spouses] have shared time. She wasn't always scared of him. There were times when she was happy with him. I think she is still attached [*aichaku ga aru*] to him. It doesn't necessarily mean co-dependency." In this way, staff members recognize that violence does not always erase intimate or positive feelings that a victim holds toward a violent partner.

BUT WHAT ABOUT THE CHILDREN?

Though shelter staff members respected every woman's decision to go back, they often tried to persuade women not to return when child abuse was involved. Some of the children who come to shelters are found to be physically and sexually abused. Perpetrators are often their fathers, stepfathers, mothers' boyfriends, or, sometimes, their own mothers.[16] Child abuse is one of the most critical factors staff members take into consideration when they try to decide where a woman and children should live after leaving the shelter. When trying to make this decision, shelter staff, a caseworker from the welfare office, and the woman involved have meetings and discuss where she wants to go next—if not permanently, at least for the next couple of years. Various public facilities, including welfare assistance and homes for mothers and children (*boshiryō*), are options that women frequently choose.[17] At the homes for mothers and children, the residents can receive support and advice on how to raise children, and they are able to coordinate living situations. Shelter staff members often recommend such dormitories for at least a few years because they regularly see that women who have moved into their own apartments too quickly return to the perpetrators owing to the hardship of raising children on their own. Staff members stressed to me that they would never force a woman to stay if she wanted to go home and that the central purpose of the shelter was "to ensure the self-determination of women" (*josei no jikokettei no sonchō*). They said, however, that they felt especially disappointed to see victimized children go back to an environment where they might be abused again.[18] Staff members are constantly negotiating between potentially contradictory interests: respecting women's "self-determination" and supporting the safety of women and children.

CREATING A CHRONOLOGICAL
REPORT OF EVENTS

According to the director of a women's organization, the most critical role for temporary shelters for the victims of domestic violence is to provide a safe, secret place where women can recover both physically and psychologically and decide how they want to move forward. The shelter staff tells women that the staff encourages them to think and make their own decisions and that the shelter supports the process. The staff believes legal problems such as divorce, custody, and debt need to be resolved for the women to regain strength. The shelters I observed focused on case work rather than therapy. They supported women utilizing the various social services, such as dormitories, public housing, public assistance, and child welfare programs.

To imagine and plan for their lives after leaving a shelter, women need to figure out what kind of problems they face and decide what they want to do in a relatively short time. At one shelter, to help women sort out their thoughts, staff members recommended that a woman write down events in her life. This is a method to help women engage with their past and make plans for the future.[19] In this activity, women are asked to make a chronological report of their lives, listing the "facts" in their relationships before they decided to flee.[20] A director of the organization that runs this shelter explained why they asked women to do this:

> To write even simple sentences a woman must look back over her life. We want to look at the specific facts. She might say, "I want to move into an apartment and raise my two kids on my own." But is it really feasible? Maybe she can do that after she recovers with a little more support. Through the process of making a report, we help her to figure out the problems that might appear when she moves forward. We help her prioritize what to do while respecting what she wants to do.

Staff members know it is not possible for some women to readily show self-determination or a strong sense of how they should move forward. Therefore, they help women prioritize what should be done, believing that such prioritization will lead to self-sufficiency in the future. They regard self-determination in a longer-term perspective, something that a woman will be able to achieve some day. Making a list, the staff believes, is an effective tool that enables women to see what needs to be done.

When writing such a list, women are requested to write down what happened in chronological order up until the time they came to the shelter, intentionally excluding their own feelings in these moments. The list delineates what happened, described in short sentences. The simplicity of the sentence structure represents a partner's violent acts in a very straightforward way and often conveys the cruelty of violence even more clearly. Starting from the time when a woman met her husband, the reports often include narration of the woman becoming pregnant, getting or losing a job, having illnesses, and changes made in her lifestyle after cohabiting with her husband's or her own parents. Some women write ten to twenty pages. Reports demonstrate a husband's cycles of violence and apologies, and they calmly list the microwave oven, TV, fan, heater, windows, and doors that he broke. Various other examples of violence are also described: the woman was held at knifepoint; she was made to sit with her legs folded under her (*seiza*) all night long; she was made to write apologies to him; he held their children under water; he woke up their son and beat him through the night. Writing such a report makes some women realize how badly they and their children have been treated.

Not everyone can write such a report without hesitation. There are times when women do not want to write one or have trouble describing what happened because their emotions are too strong. Some refuse to write saying, "This is meaningless." For those who can't write or don't want to write, the staff will not force them. However, in the process of creating such a report, some women come to new insights about their lives. Junko, a mother with a teenaged daughter, had a hard time putting her report together at first. Shelter staff members were concerned because Junko seemed to care only about her own problems and not her daughter's. All she could put on the paper were her emotions and not the "facts." When Junko finally finished writing down the events of her life, she became aware that her marriage with her second husband had been empty. He had molested Junko's daughter, his stepdaughter, a fact Junko had refused to face. The report clearly showed that to protect herself and her daughter, she must cut off contact with him. Junko was furious with him and in deep shock. After writing the report, she proceeded with filing for a divorce, and her daughter began to receive counseling from a prefectural child counseling center. Staff members explained to me that it was very painful for Junko to make her report, but it was necessary for her to move on. The exercise was meant to sort out women's thoughts and prioritize issues, while at the same time it produced a platform for them to rethink their intimate relationships and reconsider their views.

In her ethnography of a shelter for battered women, Loseke (1992, 96) discussed how shelter workers believed that their support for battered women was supposed to transform clients into new, independent, self-sufficient people. Although the transformation of women is not the explicit or primary goal of the shelter I observed, some women substantially changed their views of their intimate relationships. The listed "facts" on paper enabled women to see how much violence they had gone through and reminded them of who they used to be.[21] For some women, it could be just a reconfirmation of her partner's brutal acts, but for others it could change their perceptions of the relationship and make them realize that what they had understood as love and intimacy was more likely deep control. Through the writing, focusing only on facts seems to have helped some women reduce ambiguity. For Junko, the transformation created closer ties with her daughter beyond the intimate, yet violent, relationship in which they had been caught with their abuser. Through this process, some women are able to objectify and reposition their relationship with their husbands. Chornesky notes that "[a victimized] woman who leaves an abusive relationship has a different worldview, a different sense of herself" than those who stay (2000, 497). In a sense, the process of making a chronological report can lead to transformations in how women view their intimate lives and therefore their sense of self.

TOWARD A NEW LIFE

Violence in various forms regularly occurs in supposedly intimate relationships. In this chapter, the complex linkages between intimacy and violence have been discussed by focusing on the experiences of women in Japan who have suffered domestic violence. In contrast to the legal support system's presuppositions, in which various welfare services are available to those who escaped and got divorced, there are many victims who escape briefly but return to abusive relationships, as well as those who have difficulty deciding whether or not to get a divorce even after they leave a relationship. Behind the difficulties of leaving domestic violent situations, there are complex factors, including socioeconomic conditions, cultural norms, and the ambivalent nature of intimacy.

To disentangle intimacy and violence, this chapter presented ethnographic data from emergency shelters for the victims of domestic violence. One example, the chronological report, was designed as a means for women to organize their thoughts, prioritize possible solutions to address problems in their lives, and prepare for new lives. Through the process of creating the report, they could come to face their lives with their partners and see how their relationships were filled with violence and control that could lead some women to question whether their relationships were truly based on "love." Through shelter life, spending time away from a perpetrator, interacting with shelter staff, and creating reflective documents, female victims can revise and regain their sense of self. They can realize what they had with their husbands was not based on positive intimacy but was control disguised as intimacy. This process of redefining and repositioning their intimate relationships with their partners helps some women make the decision to leave the perpetrators and move on with their lives. Providing social services and welfare support alone is not enough for the victims of domestic violence to end problematic relationships; they must also pick apart their expectations that violence and intimacy are always intertwined. From academic and policy perspectives, the intertwined nature of violence and intimacy must be taken seriously in order to create a better support system, particularly for those victims of domestic violence who can't simply escape.

NOTES

1. Though using the term "victim" (*higaisha*) risks reducing women to seem *only* to be victims, in this chapter I use the term a "victim of domestic violence" to specify the relationship between the perpetrator and the victim and the legal responsibilities of the perpetrator. My fieldwork took place in contexts directly related to legal policies around domestic violence, and the term "victim" was commonly used among my informants. I would also like to note that some advocates use the term "survivor" (*sabaibā*) to emphasize that women survive violence and hardship, while others prefer to use *"DV higai tōjisha,"* (literally, a person with direct experience of domestic violence), which describes the damaged party with less of a tone of victimhood.

2. During fieldwork I gathered data at several municipal government agencies and private women's organizations for the victims of domestic violence. I was located at the social welfare office of a local government for six months and at three private shelters for seventeen months all together. At the same time, I interviewed twenty-three social workers with local governments, nineteen public officials in public policy positions concerning domestic violence issues, two police officers, eleven women activists who ran temporary shelters, and two women who had experienced domestic violence—a total of fifty-seven interviews. I also sat in on two divorce trials initiated by the female victims of domestic violence.

3. Men are also victimized by female partners, and domestic violence among same sex couples is reported. However, this chapter is based on my fieldwork with predominantly heterosexual female victims, and thus my discussion presupposes male perpetrators and female victims.

4. The Cabinet Office conducted this national survey on spousal violence with 1,811 women and 1,733 men over the age of twenty.

5. Haigūsha Karano Bōryoku no Bōshi oyobi Higaisha no Hogotō ni kansuru Hōritsu (Act No. 31 of 2001). The act was revised in June 2013. See Goodman (2006) for more on the social policy approach to domestic violence in Japan.

6. The act applies to the victims of violence from a spouse, ex-spouse, and live-in partner.

7. The women's counseling centers, located in each prefecture and established under the authority of the Anti-Prostitution Act (first enforced in 1958), have been engaged in helping women with various needs, including those who are victims of domestic violence (Hori 2008, 107).

8. There were seventeen private shelters for domestic violence victims reported in 2000 (Shelter-DV Mondai Chōsa Kenkyū-Kaigi 4 2000). According to the Cabinet Office, the current number of private shelters is nearly one hundred throughout Japan. http://www.gender .go.jp/e-vaw/soudankıkan/05.html (accessed July 13, 2014). The DV Prevention Act requires collaboration with private organizations.

9. In scholarship, *amae* is now a contested term because of its use within *"nihonjinron,"* (literally, theory of Japanese-ness), a discourse that essentialized Japan as a mystifying and entirely unique "Other" (Stevens 2015, 26). Yet still to this day, Japanese people use *amae* to talk about various human relationships, including domestic violence. The word is often used to explain the reasons that a man commits violence against his partner. One shelter staff worker described a man as being *amae-te-ita*, meaning that he acted selfishly, thinking that whatever he did would be forgiven. It goes without saying that we must be careful in using the term so as to avoid reducing complex and diverse Japanese experiences into an oversimplified structure. It is, however, worth noting Numazaki's argument about domestic violence using the framework of *amae* because it corresponds to the ambivalent nature of intimacy: it is considered an expression of "love" when a woman takes care of her partner, but he may use his request for care within an exclusive and closed relationship to control and manipulate her.

10. Numazaki (2004) analyzes intimate-partner violence drawing on the concept of *amae* as analyzed by Hosoya (1994, 61), who defined being dependent as a form of asserting one's power.

11. Numazaki (2004, 162) defines an intimate sphere as a relationship between free subjects actively and willfully providing interest, care, engagement, and help for each other for the further freedom and empowerment of each other.

12. Asking this question could be seen as blaming the victims. However, my intent here is to highlight various forces surrounding women that might impact them and prompt them to answer this question in different ways.

13. The interviews were conducted in 2002 with sixteen Japanese women, ranging in age from their twenties to their fifties. Seven of them were still living with their partners. This report suggests that few female victims were exploring the possibility of divorce. One informant said that divorce was worse for women; she refused to get a divorce, despite violence, because she would receive a smaller pension, although she had done nothing wrong to deserve such a reduction (Chiba-ken DV Kenkyūkai 2004, 71).

14. Such thinking can also be seen among women in Euro-American societies (Chornesky 2000, 484).

15. For example, in December 2006 a woman who was living apart from her husband was stabbed to death by her husband in front of their three children. This occurred despite a restraining order against him ("DV satsujin yōgi-sha 'kodomo ni mo satsui' tantei yatoi, tenkyo-saki shiru" 2006).

16. If the state discovers child abuse serious enough for it to intervene, children will be removed and placed into a prefectural child counseling center (*jidōsōdanjo*), a state care facility.

17. *Boshiryō* (literally, dormitories for mothers and children) are one of the provisions designated in the Child Welfare Act to support children's well-being.

18. In such cases, the caseworker will contact the welfare office that has jurisdiction in the area to which the woman is moving so that the new caseworker can pay regular visits. Although child abuse has long been a critical issue in Japan, intervention has not always been successful (Goodman 2006, 155). See Goodman (2006) for discussions about what caused the failure of intervention in child abuse cases and the revisions of the Child Welfare Law in 2005.

19. Such writing projects started because, originally, shelter staff asked a woman to make a list of violent events and personal history in order to submit to a divorce lawyer when she was filing for a divorce. Shelter staff then found that making such a list was helpful

for some of the women because it helped them realize the extent of the violence they had endured and what needed to be done to move on with their lives. Thus creating a chronological report was not based on a theory or on expert opinion but was born out of shelter support practices over the years.

20. Naturally, these are the "facts" from the women's points of view, and they might not necessarily coincide with the "facts" as understood by the perpetrators or other people involved.

21. I relate the document practice at the shelter to what Foucault has called "self technology," through which "an individual acts upon himself" (1988, 19). According to Foucault, when he traced the development of self technology in historical contexts, taking notes on oneself to be reread was an important practice to take care of oneself (ibid., 27).

REFERENCES

Babior, Sharman L. 1996. *Josei eno bōryoku: Amerika no bunka jinruigakusha ga mita nihon no katei nai bōryoku to jinshin baibai* [Violence against Women: Japanese Domestic Violence and Human Trafficking Seen by an American Cultural Anthropologist]. Tokyo: Akashi shoten.

Chiba-ken DV Kenkyūkai. 2004. *Heisei 13 nendo josei eno bōryoku jittai chōsa: Mensetsu chosa hen* [2001 Study on Violence against Women: Interview Results]. Chiba: Chiba-ken DV Kenkyūkai.

Chornesky, Alice. 2000. "The Dynamics of Battering Revisited." *AFFILIA: Journal of Women and Social Work* 15 (4): 480–501.

"DV satsujin yōgi-sha 'kodomo ni mo satsui' tantei yatoi, tenkyo-saki shiru" [Domestic Violence Murder Suspect "Even Killed Children" and Hired Private Detective to Locate Victim's New Address]. 2006. *Asahi Newspaper*, December 26, p. 27.

Foucault, Michel. 1988. "Technologies of the Self." In *Technologies of the Self: A Seminar with Michel Foucault*, edited by Luther H. Martin, Huck Gutman, and Patrick H. Hutton, 16–49. Amherst: University of Massachusetts Press.

Gender Equality Bureau Cabinet Office, 2015. *Danjokan ni okeru bōryoku ni kansuru chōsa hōkokusho: Gaiyōban* [Research Report on Gender Violence: Summary]. http://www.gender.go.jp/policy/no_violence/e-vaw/chousa/pdf/h26danjokan-gaiyo.pdf. Accessed November 30, 2017.

Goodman, Roger. 2006. "Policing the Japanese Family: Child Abuse, Domestic Violence and the Changing Role of the State." In *The Changing Japanese Family*, edited by Marcus Rebick and Ayumi Takenaka, 147–160. London and New York: Routledge.

Hattery, Angela. 2009. *Intimate Partner Violence*. Lanham, MD: Rowman and Littlefield.

hooks, bell. 1997. "Violence in Intimate Relationships: A Feminist Perspective." In *Gender Violence: Interdisciplinary Perspectives*, edited by Laura L. O'Toole and Jessica R. Schiffman, 279–284. New York: New York University Press.

Hori, Chizuko. 2008. "Fujin-hogo-jigyō no genzai" [Women's Protection Programs Today]. In *"Fujin-hogo-jigyō" 50 nen* [Fifty Years of Women's Protection Programs], edited by Chiyo Hayashi, 99–159. Tokyo: Domesu shuppan.

Hosoya, Minoru. 1994. *Seibetsu chitsujo no sekai: Jendā sekushuariti to shutai* [The World of Gender Order: Gender/Sexuality and Subject]. Tokyo: Maruju-sha.

Loseke, Donileen R. 1992. *The Battered Woman and Shelters: The Social Construction of Wife Abuse*. Albany: State University of New York Press.

Matsushima, Kyō. 2001. "Shinmitsu na kankeisei ni okeru bōryokusei to jendā" [Violence in Intimate Relationships from a Gender Perspective]. *Ritsumeikan sangyō shakai ronshū* 36 (4): 75–91.

MHLW (Ministry of Health, Labor, and Welfare). 2012. *Heisei 23 nendo zenkoku boshi setai tou chōsa kekka hōkoku* [2011 National Survey of Single Mother–Headed Households]. http://www.mhlw.go.jp/seisakunitsuite/bunya/kodomo/kodomo_kosodate/boshi-katei /boshi_setai_h23/dl/h23 17.pdf. Accessed September 12, 2014.

———. 2013. *Heisei 24 nenban hataraku josei no jitsujo* [Data on Working Women in 2012]. http://www.mhlw.go.jp/bunya/koyoukintou/josei-jitsujo/dl/12b.pdf. Accessed September 12, 2014.

———. 2016. *Heisei 27 nendo fujin hogo jigyō jisshi jōkyō hōkoku no gaiyō* [Summary Report of Programs for the Protection of Women in Fiscal Year 2015]. http://www.mhlw .go.jp/file/06-Seisakujouhou-11900000-Koyoukintoujidoukateikyoku/0000065113 .pdf. Accessed November 30, 2017.

Miyaji, Naoko. 2005. "Shihai toshite no DV: Koteki ryōiki no arika" [DV as Control: Are there Individual Domains?]. *Gendai shisō* 33 (10): 121–133.

National Police Agency. 2017. *Heisei 28 nen ni okeru sutōkā jian oyobi haigūsha karano bōryoku jiantō eno taiō jōkyō ni tsuite* [Responses to Stalking and Spousal Violence Cases in 2016]. https://www.npa.go.jp/safetylife/seianki/stalker/seianki28STDVsyosai.pdf. Accessed November 30, 2017.

Numazaki, Ichiro. 2004. "Ai to bōryoku: Domesutikku baiorensu kara tou shinmitsu-ken no kankeirinri" [Love and Violence: Relationship Ethics of Intimate Spheres Probed from Domestic Violence]. In *Iwanami ōyō rinrigaku kōgi 5 sei/ai* [Iwanami Lectures of Applied Ethics, 5 Sexuality/Love], edited by Yoshiko Kanai, 160–179. Tokyo: Iwanami shoten.

Shelter-DV Mondai Chōsa Kenkyū-Kaigi 4. 2000. *Sherutā ni okeru enjo ni kansuru jittai chosa* [Study on Support Services Provided at Shelters]. Yokohama: Yokohama-shi Josei Kyōkai.

Statistics Bureau, Ministry of International Affairs and Communications. 2013. *Rōdōryoku chōsa no kekka o mirusai no pointo* [Points in Labor Force Survey], No. 16. http://www.stat.go.jp/data/roudou/pdf/point16.pdf. Accessed July 13, 2014.

Stevens, Carolyn S. 2015. "Anthropology of Modern Japan." In *The SAGE Handbook of Modern Japanese Studies*, edited by James Babb, 22–32. Los Angeles: SAGE Publications.

Sugimoto, Kiyoe. 2004. *Fukushi-shakai no jendā kōzō* [Gender Structures of Welfare Societies]. Tokyo: Keisō shobō.

UNICEF. 2000. *Innocenti Digest 6*. http://www.unicef-irc.org/publications/pdf /digest6e.pdf. Accessed July 13, 2014.

WHO. 2005. *WHO Multi-Country Study on Women's Health and Domestic Violence against Women*. http://whqlibdoc.who.int/publications/2005/9241593512_eng.pdf. Accessed July 13, 2014.

Yllö, Kersti A. 2005. "Through a Feminist Lens: Gender, Diversity, and Violence: Extending the Feminist Framework." In *Current Controversies on Family Violence*, edited by Donileen R. Loseke, Richard J. Gelles, and Mary M. Cavanaugh, 19–34. Los Angeles: Sage Publications.

Yoshihama, M., and Susan Sorenson. 1994. "Physical, Sexual, and Emotional Abuse by Male Intimates: Experience of Women in Japan." *Violence and Victims* 9 (1): 63–77.

Yoshihiro, Kiyoko. 1997. *Naguru otto nigerarenai tsuma* [Husbands Who Beat, Wives Who Can't Run Away]. Tokyo: Aoki shoten.

CHAPTER 7

Power, Intimacy, and Irregular Employment in Japan

Emma E. Cook

Shimizu, a twenty-nine-year-old man, takes a sip of his coffee and pauses. We have been talking about intimate relationships and work, and he feels sure that his unstable employment situation is making it difficult for him to create and maintain a meaningful intimate relationship: "I'm single at the moment," he says. "To be honest, I would like to be in a serious relationship. If I was working in a full-time [*seishain*] job, then I think maybe I would be. Many of my friends from high school are now marrying, but at the moment I'm not a good catch. I don't earn much, and my job isn't stable. . . . I can't offer much."

Not being able to offer much is a common concern among men in their late twenties working in irregular jobs. Although characterized as largely a female space in the postwar period, since 1990 the number of men working in the irregular employment sector has risen from 8.8 to 29.8 percent in 2013 (Abe 2008; MIAC 2013a).[1] Such employment now constitutes approximately 35.2 percent of the employment market, up from around 18 percent in 1990 (ibid.). The increase of men in this sector is having ramifications not just on life chances and future earnings, but also in the intimate sphere and on opportunities to create long-term intimate relationships.[2] Examining marriage rates of men in their twenties and thirties, a Cabinet Office (2011) survey reported that just 12.1 percent of men in part-time and temporary work were married, compared to 47.6 percent of full-time employees.[3] Research has suggested that male irregular workers are considered undesirable marital partners because of their limited earning potential and because doing such work is understood to signify a potentially weak character with a tendency to not take responsibility for oneself and others, endure difficult situations, or try one's best without quitting (Cook 2014, 2016; Honda 2002).

The difficulties of irregular workers in getting married are part of changing marriage trends in which delayed marriage is increasingly the norm. One reason given for this trend is that men and women now have different expectations of marital relationships. For example, Sandberg (2010) has argued that women's understandings of marriage in Japan have shifted from a social duty linked with adult status to a prioritization on feelings of attachment, intimacy, emotional closeness, cooperation, and mutual understanding (see also Nemoto 2008; Tokuhiro 2010). In contrast, male expectations have remained more traditional, with many men continuing to expect women to take primary responsibility for the domestic sphere (Nagase 2006).

Despite women's increased emphasis on companionate ideals, practical matters relating to the division of household labor and finances continue to factor into relationship choices and how relationships play out (Cook 2014; Tsuya and Bumpass 2004). The undesirability of marriage to a male irregular worker is linked to the structural constraints that women experience in the workplace. Japan has one of the largest gender wage gaps, almost twice the OECD average, at 25.7 percent as of 2017 (OECD 2017).[4] Given that women constitute approximately 70 percent of the irregular employment sector (MIAC 2013a), their low wages, combined with a general expectation that many women will stop working for a time to raise children, shape women's life chances, especially those who work in part-time jobs or non-career-track positions.[5] Because of these constraints on female employment and wage earning, the financial security of potential husbands remains an important measure for marriageability. Thus the general expectation that men should be (or be able to be) primary breadwinners within a household, as well as meet the emotionally intimate criteria outlined above, continues to pervade gendered understandings and possibilities of the marital contract.

These ideas not only reinforce a gendered employment sphere, but also reinforce the primacy of the heteronormative necessity for marriage to consist of specific roles that men and women expect (and are expected) to occupy. The precariousness of the irregular labor market, however, does not easily allow men to demonstrate their ability to fulfill such expected roles to potential marriage partners. Although precarity can be understood in terms of economic vulnerability, Vij (2013) has rightly argued that the condition of precarity is much more than that. She frames it as "the loss of mastery entailed by the movement of men from once secure to insecure work that mobilizes an affective-political turn under the sign of precarity" (ibid., 122). Vij's focus is primarily on precarity's emancipatory potential in Japan, specifically for feminism, and she argues that within this process of lost mastery precarity "potentially enables the undoing of attachments to gendered social identities and the emergence of nomadic subjectivities" (ibid.). While acknowledging the potential for the transformation of intimate practices and gendered identities under conditions of precarity, I argue that such a process of "undoing attachments," of letting go of structural social identities, is neither easy nor—in many cases—desired. With a loss of male mastery, precarity also engenders significant shifts in power within intimate relationships. The presence—or absence—of such a desire to let go thus significantly shapes the possibilities, practices, and experiences of intimate relationships under conditions of precariousness.

This chapter examines the ways in which intimacy is enacted within the relationships of men who work in irregular jobs and how irregular work shapes gender roles, intimate practices, and power within their relationships. The strong social emphasis on taking particular gendered roles in intimate relationships throws up tensions when individuals find that, in practice, it is not possible for these ideals to be played out.[6] Although this situation can therefore provide space in which gendered ideals and practices become transformed, as Vij (2013) envisions, this is often simultaneously jarring and deeply uncomfortable for the people involved—especially when it is not desired. Instead of embracing potential changes, individuals try to find ways to redress the (ideal, normative) balance, with ramifications for intimate relations and practices.[7] I argue that although irregular employment potentially offers the opportunity to undo attachments and create new gendered social identities and nomadic subjectivities, for many men in practice it doesn't. Instead, they have a sense of failure about their inability to live up to the marital ideals embedded in mainstream understandings of manhood (see also Cook 2013; Miles, this volume). Without a desire and commitment to transcend normative ideals of gender or to undo attachments, the effects of precarity and irregular employment on intimacy may be more conflicted and potentially damaging than liberating to intimacy and intimate practices within relationships.

In this chapter, these issues are primarily analyzed through a 2008 documentary film, *Japan: A Story of Love and Hate*, which documents, and puts at its center, an intimate heterosexual relationship within the context of irregular employment and precarity. Issues of power, masculinity, normative gender roles, and the desires and limits of intimacy emerge as key themes for exploration within the documentary. The analysis in this chapter is also informed by, and draws on, long-term ethnographic research I carried out since 2007 with men who work in jobs defined as part-time.

The data presented in this chapter focus only on men in established non-marital relationships; however, for a discussion of intimate relationships of irregular workers who are married see Cook (2014, 2016, 2017).

JAPAN: A STORY OF LOVE AND HATE (2008)

The documentary opens with the British documentary maker running along a river, panting out his frustrations that after two years he had been unable to complete a documentary about "what makes Japan tick." Originally commissioned to make a documentary about Tokyo for the NHK and BBC, he struggled to find people willing to participate. In the end, after meeting a fifty-six-year-old man named Naoki, he abandoned filming in Tokyo and moved to Yamagata to follow Naoki's life. This was his "last attempt at getting inside Japan," provided by a man who had "broken all the rules."

The documentary revolves around Naoki's work and personal life. A radical Communist and student protester in his youth, he became a successful businessman running a bar, which was just one of three family businesses. However, because of the prolonged recession since the 1990s, his successes ended with bankruptcy. He had also been married and divorced three times. In 2008, estranged from his only family left in the city, Naoki worked part time in the insurance section of Japan Post, collecting insurance premiums for ¥800 an hour.

Naoki met Yoshie, his long-term girlfriend who was half his age, when he owned the bar. After losing the business, Naoki moved in with Yoshie, and to cover their expenses she took a second job. By day she works in an office, and in the evening she works as a hostess.[8] Since she started her second job they typically have about an hour to spend together in the evening, which they usually spent napping. Yoshie wants Naoki to get a second job, and it is never expressed clearly in the documentary why he doesn't; the film leaves unexplored whether he is unable to find extra work because of his age or if it is a form of resistance to a capitalist system that he intensely dislikes.

The documentary deals with individual repercussions of prolonged recession, experiences of being working poor, the difficulties of making ends meet without access to social welfare, and the effects these conditions have on mental health and intimate relationships. Throughout the documentary it is clear that the director and Naoki have become good friends. This works in the film's favor, leading to direct conversations about the situation of the working poor in Japan and the realities of Naoki's life.

However, the director's tendency to assert his own cultural expectations—for example, with regard to workplace relations and practices and to intimacy and physical contact—often provide viewers with an overly simplistic view. Such a view reinforces stereotypes that Japanese social life is somewhat incomprehensible and that the working environment is "crazy" without exploring in depth the multiple structural-economic reasons for the current situation. Despite these limitations, it is a gritty portrayal of living on the breadline in Japan, and the conversations and interactions between Naoki and Yoshie are a rich resource for analysis. They reveal a complex interplay of power in their relationship that is clearly linked to their socioeconomic situations and understandings of normative expectations of gender roles.[9]

INTIMACY, EMPLOYMENT, AND POWER

Quietly smoking a cigarette and resolutely watching television, Naoki asks Yoshie if he can borrow ¥1,000 ($10). Yoshie grumbles quietly, gets up, finds her wallet, fishes out the money, and hands it over. Once she sits back down, she looks at the floor. "It's very dirty in here," she says. Naoki puts his cigarette down, grimaces sheepishly at the director, picks up a sticky roller, and begins to clean the rug as Yoshie looks on.

Money and housework have become hotspots for Naoki's and Yoshie's gendered power struggles. Naoki does all the housework, taking on what has typically been a female responsibility, in an attempt to make up for his low earnings.[10] Yoshie's role as the primary breadwinner, earning double Naoki's yearly wage, has affected their intimate relationship in important ways by creating a balance of power that goes against normative expectations and is—crucially—unwanted by both Yoshie and Naoki. A number of themes are apparent throughout the documentary: communication problems, powerlessness and impotency, gender role reversal, poverty, and the fear of homelessness. Throughout runs the narrative of Naoki's irregular work status.

It is pertinent here to reflect briefly on what is meant by "power" in the context of this chapter. In feminist theory there have been generally three ways of understanding the issue of power: power as domination (or subjection/oppression, understood as power over someone or something); power as a resource to be redistributed; and power as empowerment (Allen 2011). In the latter articulation, it is argued that power is an ability or a capacity. Layder, in his work on intimacy and power, expresses the sense of capacity in the following way:

In a general sense, power is an abstract *capacity*; it is not a particular kind of behaviour or an outcome of that behaviour. That is, power is about the *ability* to do things, transform circumstances or bring about change. Thus, power and control may be in the service of either benign or malign intentions, and their behavioural consequences. In this sense benign forms of power and control are essential to the capacity for love and for the caring responses that go with it. (2009, 19; emphasis in original)

While power is a capacity, an ability to do things, not all people feel they have power or the capacity to use power. They may feel significantly disempowered and powerless. The political theorist Mark Haugaard offers a helpful way to understand this. Drawing on Wittgenstein's idea of a "family resemblance," he argues that power should be understood to consist of "a cluster of concepts, each of which qualifies as 'power'" (2010, 420).[11] He points to a number of different aspects:

Episodic power refers to the exercise of power that is linked to agency. *Dispositional power* signifies the inherent capacities of an agent that the agent may have, irrespective of whether or not they exercise this capacity. *Systemic power* refers to the ways in which given social systems confer differentials of dispositional power on agents, thus structuring possibilities for action. (Ibid., 425; emphasis in original)

Haugaard also argues that power may take the following forms: power over, power to, domination, empowerment, and legitimate power. However, he doesn't argue that consequently "anything goes," but instead highlights how these different manifestations of power may be drawn upon, used, and rejected by the signifier and referent at different times and in different ways. In this chapter I build from Haugaard's conceptualization of power to explore how individuals within intimate relationships draw on different types of power as they negotiate personal values, desires, and structural conditions. Acknowledging the complex ways in which power may be present in interactions frees us from looking for the "best" definition and instead allows us to analyze the various manifestations of power that can occur within intimate relationships.

WORK, IMPOTENCE, AND POWERLESSNESS

A dominant tension that runs through Naoki and Yoshie's relationship relates to their employment situations. Yoshie appears exhausted and frustrated at Naoki's lack of earnings. Naoki, meanwhile, finds Yoshie's job at a hostess bar particularly threatening:

NAOKI: Her customers believe she is single. So every night, every day, they invite her out, propose to go on a date.

DIRECTOR: But they just want to talk, just want to eat; they don't want anything else, or do they want . . . ?

NAOKI (interrupting): Yes, they just want to talk and eat and sing a song together.

DIRECTOR: Nothing else?

NAOKI: Nothing else.

DIRECTOR: No kissing?

Yoshie shakes her head in the negative, and Naoki continues: "No kissing. Sometimes they touch." Yoshie, with lips pursed, shakes her head more vehemently, and Naoki turns to Yoshie and asks if they kiss; again she shakes her head and responds negatively. Naoki goes on, "Her boss suggests to her, like this [he mimes pressing his legs together]. This is so polite." Yoshie interjects by clapping her hands and exclaiming, "Waa, sugoi! Nandemo homenai to," and Naoki translates it into English: "You have to compliment the customer for everything," and they both laugh as if it is ridiculous.

The scene cuts to Yoshie applying makeup in preparation to go to her second job. "Are you happy?" the director asks. Yoshie responds that she is too busy to think about if she is happy or not, but she enjoys her second job more because she feels like a woman: she must praise anything men say, but in turn she is treated to meals and given attention. In her office job, however, she feels like a robot. For Yoshie, feeling like a woman is tied into ideas of emotional labor and gendered interactions with men (Hochschild and Machung 2012). It is clear throughout the documentary, however, that the energy she has to do such emotional labor is exhausted by the time she returns home. Naoki continues: "Every night, every day, it's work, work, work to get money. It's poverty, our level. Yoshie works fifteeeen [he draws the word out] . . . hours a day. . . . It's capitalism." Yoshie rejoins: "Today, I want to sleep, really. But now I have to go to work." Although she feels more "womanly" in her second job, she is tired and reluctant to go. The tension it causes in their relationship is apparent when on another occasion Yoshie says, "I have to go to the sushi shop. He says, 'I envy you,'" and she laughs quietly but incredulously and shakes her head slightly.[12] In contrast, Naoki worries about whether she will come home or if she'll meet someone else. This concern is not only because of the financial situation in which they find themselves, but also because it relates to issues they have with physical intimacy.

Since Naoki lost his bar and began working part time, he and Yoshie have struggled with the shift in dynamic in their relationship, both emotionally and physically. Naoki turns to the camera: "These days I have no sex [he shrugs]. It doesn't work. [He and Yoshie laugh slightly.] It's broken. I have depression. It doesn't work, my baby [referring to his penis and laughing sadly]." The director asks Yoshie if it is difficult for her, given her young age. Looking at Naoki, she responds: "Even if I'm young, there are times when people don't need sex." Naoki continues: "If I had a more stable life, I could have sex, maybe. She's young. But I'm afraid. She loves me, but sometimes she needs a friend who can have sex. I'm afraid. I worry about her having a new boyfriend."

Although Naoki's narrative here suggests mostly that the loss of his business and ensuing depression caused his sexual impotence, his fear that Yoshie will leave him for another man—perhaps someone she could meet at her second job, a man with the money to go to such bars—feeds his feelings of impotence. Naoki was also concerned that they were not communicating well and that she would eventually leave him. Yoshie, meanwhile, seemed unable to provide the kind of emotional support for which Naoki expressed a need:

> NAOKI: My life, when I had a wife, I talked, talked, talked. . . . Yoshie dislikes talking. She told me, "You're noisy; shut up [urusai]. . . . I love talking."
> DIRECTOR: Why is she with you, do you think?
> NAOKI: I don't know. I am sure it's not my speaking. Maybe I'm useful. Maybe she loves me. But she cannot allow me my [small] income. Every day it causes stress and struggle.
> DIRECTOR: Does she blame you?
> NAOKI: Yes, she drinks too much every day. She . . . is tired. Maybe tonight, after drinking, she will strongly express her true mind.

The scene shifts to a bar after work where Naoki and Yoshie are sitting talking. Holding some peanuts, Yoshie drunkenly tells Naoki to "open up" his mouth so she can feed him:

> NAOKI: I'm not your client.
> YOSHIE: Just open up.
> NAOKI (forcefully): I'm not your client!
> YOSHIE: No, you're not. No, you're not. My clients are easier to handle.
> NAOKI (frowning): I have no money, but I do have pride. . . .

YOSHIE: I don't have clients like you who have no money. . . . [She turns to the director.] Always, always, always the same. He has nowhere else to go. [She turns back to Naoki.] Where's your home then?

NAOKI (looking hurt and upset): Do you think it's funny to tease someone?

YOSHIE: No, but you started it.

NAOKI: You're blaming me again.

YOSHIE: No, I'm not. [She throws some peanuts around and toward Naoki's beer glass.]

NAOKI: Who's going to clear that up?

YOSHIE: You. . . . Where do you work then? What kind of job have you got then?

NAOKI: Shut up!

YOSHIE: You're so annoying. [She starts to grab his collar and pushes him. Naoki grabs her around the throat and shoves her back.]

NAOKI: Stop it. Just stop it! You're being rude!

YOSHIE: No, you're the rude one.

NAOKI: Why are you doing this?

YOSHIE: Oh, forget it. [She takes up Naoki's glasses and says:] Look what I can do. I can crush it to bits. See what I can do? I always have to pay for him. [She starts to cry.] Always, always, always, always I am paying. I'm working so hard, and I never have any money. No matter how hard I work. I give him ¥1,000 a day. [She laughs slightly through her tears.] That's the way it is.

They get home, and Naoki helps Yoshie get into bed fully dressed and covers her gently with the duvet. A few weeks later things have gotten worse. Naoki says, "I've stopped talking with Yoshie because I'm afraid she'll retaliate. She has a place to run away: her hometown. I have nowhere, just here. Or if she decides to fuck me away, I have to go. . . . On the road maybe [homeless]. I couldn't borrow. No bank, no friend, no home. So this is a way to become homeless. It's very near to my position; it's very close."

After not speaking to each other at all for nearly two weeks, Naoki appears desperate to discuss the situation. Sitting in their tiny living room, the scene begins with Yoshie.

YOSHIE: So why are we together?

NAOKI: I don't know.

YOSHIE: How can you say you don't know?

NAOKI: You think it's macho to not talk about feelings. I'm not that kind of man. I need to say how I feel. . . . People aren't human if they can't even say how they feel. In Japan, it's cool if you keep quiet; that's bullshit. I used to be like that; no one talks, people get frustrated, families break up . . . and it leads to suicide. Sean [the director] said it in a roundabout way: you're the boss here. If you get into a kind of master and slave relationship that means you could say, "Get out of my house and die on the street." If we are going to stay together, don't oppress me in that way. You can do that at work but not to me. [Yoshie begins to cry, and there is a long pause.]

YOSHIE: I didn't do anything wrong. I don't know why you blame me. I don't want to listen.

NAOKI: You've never listened in the past anyway.

YOSHIE: Do you think I like to work?

NAOKI: I know you don't like your job or having to drink to make money. You work hard, and then you drink to find yourself again. I ran a bar for eleven years. I know very well.

YOSHIE: It sounds like I enjoy my job.

NAOKI: In the past I used to blame you for coming home late. Now I just want to know that you're coming home. Because I don't want you to leave me.

YOSHIE (sighing): My face will be swollen tomorrow [from crying so much].

Living in a state of insecurity, always worried about whether Yoshie would leave him, Naoki feels powerless and impotent in a myriad ways: he is a previously successful, independent man who is now reliant on his girlfriend working two jobs to put a roof over their heads; he depends on her desire to still be with him and give him a place to live; and he resents his own job, which he hates and which doesn't pay enough for him to afford the rent on an apartment of his own. The impotence in his financial life is reflected in his sexual impotence. The dependence that his employment situation engenders significantly affects their relationship, and the picture that emerges is one of exhaustion, anger, and need. The stress caused by Naoki's financial instability and the necessity for Yoshie to be the main breadwinner clearly illustrate the strong normative ideals that continue to hold sway: men should be the primary breadwinners, and when they are not—or are not able to be—significant issues and effects on intimacy can be seen. Maciel, Van Putten, and Knudson-Martin (2009) argue that to understand gendered power we need to look beyond a couple and their personal dynamics to analyze the individuals' positions in a wider society. The importance of this argument is clear in the documentary. Naoki's and Yoshie's worries, silences, and arguments, while intimate and individual to the couple's dynamic, are also embedded in their tiredness and frustrations with their relative positions in the world.

In an attempt to redress and reclaim the earlier gender balance of their relationship Naoki expresses how it is his responsibility to stay with and protect Yoshie because of her depression. She takes an anti-depressant each night that provides a minimum of six hours sleep; however, it also causes memory loss, and she doesn't remember what happens before falling asleep. Naoki says, "We cannot get special treatment from the government. If we were European, the nation [would] give me a kind of welfare, a kind of mental support. [There are] so many types of support. First, I have to protect her. I'm afraid she has a kind of disease. So I can't separate from her. I can't leave her. Who will look after her?" Here we see the contradictions inherent in the precarious situation in which they live. Dependent on Yoshie financially and psychologically, Naoki also strives to create a narrative of protection in which he is a central needed figure crucial to Yoshie's health and well-being. This approach helps manage his anxiety and profound sense of rupture and provides him with a narrative that is inherently normative and patriarchal, even as he has lost other symbols of patriarchal power.

Through the conversations presented above we can see the complex ways in which power is enacted and drawn upon. At times Naoki suggests he has no power—he is subjected to forces outside his control (capitalism and labor) that exert a type of systemic power and provide different amounts of agential power that structure Naoki's potential to act (Haugaard 2010). At the age of fifty-six and with a failed business, he was unable to find any job except one that was part time, paying ¥800 yen an hour. Contrary to Vij's (2013) argument that precarity and large structural changes create opportunities for individuals to let go of structural social identities, Naoki's precarity, irregular employment, and age are at the heart of his impotence. He is unable to let go. Naoki feels he is at the whim of the economy, of his low-paying job, of his advancing age, and of Yoshie to keep him from homelessness. His impotence appears to be the result of feeling that he has less agential power than at any point in his life thus far. The buttresses of his identity prior to the loss of his bar—the confident, successful, self-employed businessman in control of his destiny and with the ability to conspicuously consume (and support the women in his life)—have crumbled. Therefore, instead of embracing this new situation as an opportunity to embrace new norms, Naoki and Yoshie struggle. They both feel at the mercy of systemic power—that their situation as working poor leaves them with few options to act.

Instead they engage in a power struggle within their relationship, struggling to adapt to the new conditions in which they find themselves. Naoki clearly tries to reassert his position through the exercise of episodic power, as when he tries to force Yoshie to acknowledge that she has been treating him as a slave and to stop it (a type of "power over"). Yoshie, meanwhile, also uses episodic power through her passive-aggressive accusations that Naoki's low earnings are not acceptable, as when she taunts him that her clients have money and are easier to handle or when she gives him ¥1,000 but then comments that the floor is dirty, leading to Naoki's cleaning it (both "power over" and "power to"). The ability to act (agential power) is focused *within* the relationship owing to their sense of their limitations within a structural situation that they feel powerless to act on. They therefore act where they feel they can—on each other.[13]

These power struggles, born predominantly from frustration at their economic and intimate situation, are also, however, interspersed with what Layder terms benign forms of power, which are part of "intimate strategies" as a "means of getting what they want or need" (2009, 6). We see such benign power from Naoki when he covers Yoshie gently with a duvet after she drops into bed drunk and exhausted, when he ruffles her hair affectionately as he passes her, and when they settle down to sleep in each other's arms. Thus, while the documentary portrays the ways in which their physical and emotional intimacy have been worn down and the various ways they use power over each other to try and redress the balance, the protagonists also episodically reach out through small caring gestures—what Jamieson (2011) refers to as "practices of intimacy"—as a means through which they attempt to maintain their intimate links.

IRREGULAR EMPLOYMENT, INTIMATE POSSIBILITIES, AND FUTURE PLANS

In the documentary we can see how significant Naoki's employment situation is on the internal workings of their relationship and how narratives of the future were muted; they were focused primarily on surviving day to day. For irregular workers, work and financial (in)stability often emerge as a focal point around which intimate practices and possibilities revolve, and these concerns significantly factor into future plans.

Sumiko (twenty-nine) and Masao (thirty-two) had been together for six years and living together for four, sharing a council (*danchi*) apartment with Sumiko's father.[14] Masao had years earlier worked as a full-time employee for a year but had disliked the work environment and quit. He had spent the previous ten years in the irregular employment sector. Money and work were a significant cause for concern when considering future plans:

SUMIKO: It made sense for Masao to move here. I live with my dad and look after him and the apartment. My mum died when I was younger, so he relies on me a lot. Masao and I want to get married but don't know when. But we definitely want to marry. It will make the living situation complicated, though. At the moment it's a secret that Masao is living in our apartment. We can't afford to rent privately. If the city office finds out that he has moved in, I think the rent will go up, and we can't afford that. I'm afraid they might make us move out, so that is complicated too. Also, we both have credit card debts that we are paying off each month.

MASAO: We want to marry and perhaps move out. I like Sumiko's dad, but it's not ideal. It all depends on work. Now I am searching for full-time work. . . . It's hard, really hard. I'm thirty-two, and my previous work is irregular. I've been working the whole time, but still. . . . I should get a full time [seishain] position. I have to really. I will need one if we get married; it will be my responsibility to be a breadwinner. I accept that. But I feel a lot of pressure about it. . . . I don't even know if it's possible now for me to find full-time work.

As Masao stopped talking, he looked slightly harried. He took a sip of his drink, and Sumiko took up the thread:

I want us to marry, and I really want to have kids. But I don't want to work seven days a week any more. I want to get married. I want to be a house-wife and work part time, two or three days a week. It is not my responsi-bility to keep earning all the money. That is my dream. But at the moment it's not possible for us to marry and have children yet. We can't afford it; we have no money, and we have credit card debt.

Sumiko felt that time was running out because of her age, and pressure on Masao—though not ideal—was necessary.

SUMIKO: I'm twenty-nine. I'm worried. I thought that I would be married with children by now. . . .

MASAO: I'm trying to find work. I'm searching every day and going to inter-views, but they hire other people. I think they want to hire younger people, not people like me who have changed jobs a few times. They probably think I am not going to stick at it. . . . I don't know how to per-suade them. I will keep trying, though. That's all I can do.

Despite his determination to find something, Masao gradually began to feel that finding a full-time position was not going to be possible. He increasingly looked stressed, and Sumiko worried that they would not be able to marry and achieve the family ideal that she imagined. In a later meeting Masao confessed:

We argue quite a lot these days. Sumiko knows I am trying to find work, but she is worried about her age and wants to marry and have children. Maybe she thinks I should try harder. . . . I don't know. To be honest, I know I should get a full-time job, but at the same time I don't really know if I want one. I worked that way before, and it was not good. There was a lot of pressure all the time. But at the same time, if we have children, it is better to have a stable environment. So I am trying.

The expectation for men to be or become primary breadwinners thus significantly mediates intimate possibilities and realities (Cook 2013, 2014, 2016; Silva 2013; Tichenor 1999). Sumiko appeared to feel that marriage was not a possibility until Masao had found full-time work. Moreover, like Yoshie, she was unhappy that she was working more than Masao, and she clearly articulated that she felt it wasn't her responsibility. In research on power in marital relationships in the United States, Tichenor (1999) found that 60 percent of status-reversal couples—defined as couples in which the women earned 50 percent more than their spouses—were dissatisfied with their marriages, in part because they wanted to be part of a conventional relationship. Their unhappiness was also related to how they had come to be a status-reversal couple. It is perhaps not surprising that choice was the key element in satisfaction. The spouses that had not chosen the situation—where husbands' opportunities had dwindled and those of wives hadn't—were the most dissatisfied.

Choice, and the power to make that choice a reality, were critical factors in the intimate relationships of men in irregular employment. Sumiko and Masao both talked of wanting to create a legal family unit and have children but felt unable to, in part because of limited full-time employment possibilities, but also because of their own imaginary of what the intimate sphere of family should look like. Difficulties regarding employment, cash flow, debt, and their own desires and expectations of individual roles within a family unit effectively limited the intimate possibilities to which they aspired in their relationship. Crucially, neither seemed to want to create a family outside of the roles they envisaged, and they did not seem overly willing, Sumiko particularly, to negotiate non-normative marital gender roles within a dual-income family. The tension created by balancing traditional role aspirations and the realities in which they found themselves were arguably creating a situation in which they necessarily would have to negotiate alternative gender roles if they were committed to remaining in the relationship. It is in this context that Vij (2013) argues that there is considerable scope for existing gendered attachments to become undone and in which there is much emancipatory potential. The two examples given in this chapter suggest that while this emancipatory potential exists, individuals may not view this positively nor desire such changes. Instead, these couples expended considerable energy in trying to achieve a balance based primarily on traditional gendered and intimate norms, rather than creating new ones.

In this chapter I have argued that intimacy and intimate possibilities are significantly challenged by the precarity of irregular employment. Although such precarity could potentially lead to new gender norms, this was not particularly desired by either of the couples discussed above. Rather than feeling the emancipatory potential of the situation, they felt rather helpless in terms of the reversal of gender roles it engendered.

Naoki and Yoshie sought to re-reverse their roles and the balance of power in a number of ways. For example, although their household labor roles were reversed, their communication strategies revealed the contradictions inherent in their positioning, swinging from Naoki's argument that he was in a master-slave relationship and one step away from homelessness to asserting Yoshie's need for him to protect and look after her. Throughout the documentary film, Naoki is trying to find ways in which to create a gendered balance of mutual dependency in a way that makes sense to him. Sumiko and Masao, meanwhile, were attempting to move past Masao's status as an irregular employee. His inability to make this a reality, however, was creating much strain within their relationship, and Sumiko was adamant that marriage was not possible until Masao had achieved the conventional male role of primary breadwinner. Through anchoring the possibilities of intimacy and family creation to money and financial stability, both couples appear to understand male value primarily in terms of earning ability, creating a commodified masculine selfhood (Takeyama 2010, 2016). Naoki in particular illustrates the deep psychological struggle this may entail.

Maciel, Van Putten, and Knudson-Martin have argued that "pushing the gender line"—a line they understand to demarcate the division of power and equality in an intimate relationship—is a process of adaptation that happens quietly:

> Contextual shifts . . . inform couple decisions and behavior in ways that subtly challenge the old gender structure while at the same time limiting overt disruption to the couple's existing gendered power system. This tension between stability and change involves a balancing act as alternative constructions of gender are either required in the new societal context or made possible as consciousness and opportunities. (2009, 15)

Changing employment opportunities for men and women, and the difficulties people have in achieving normative ideals of gender roles because of these employment realities, contribute to a pushing of the gender line for irregular workers in intimate relationships. However, it is important to stress that this was often not a conscious or desired pushing but a side effect of the practical realities of irregular employment in terms of finances and social status. Moreover, this is a contested process in which both men and women often seek to reassert a balance based on preexisting cultural narratives of heterosexual romantic relationships and personal expectations of what marital roles should look and be like. Therefore, while acknowledging the potentiality of Vij's (2013) argument that precarious conditions create opportunities for individuals to let go of normative gendered expectations and identities, I have argued that many couples appear to be unable to take these conditions as an opportunity to create alternatives. With a primary focus on the here and now of economic survival, individual potential to act is constrained by the structural conditions in which individuals are embedded and is focused within the relationship. Furthermore, an individual's agential power is structured through the expectations of the person with whom that individual is interacting, in this case a romantic partner. The power to act for the couples discussed above—through the use of episodic and dispositional power—thus became focused on re-reversing relationship roles rather than creating new ones. What results is a sense of stasis, an inability to move forward. The difficulties for male irregular workers in getting married are thus more complex than a lack of financial stability and are deeply embedded in heteronormative understandings of gender roles in intimate relationships. Moreover, it is not simply the case that women don't want to marry irregular workers, but also that men themselves may feel deeply uncomfortable if they are unable to embody the responsibilities they envisage of a male partner/husband. Therefore, rather than throwing out their understandings of intimate roles and creating new ones that broaden intimate possibilities, many individuals continue to hold onto normative ideas while negotiating the complexities of intimate relationships in a precarious landscape.

NOTES

1. These figures exclude students who are working in the irregular employment sector.

2. In this chapter intimacy is explored only in the context of romantic heterosexual relationships.

3. This trend is not specific to Japan but can be seen around the world, with male wage earning exhibiting a strong link with marriageability (Sweeney 2002; Tichenor 1999).

4. The gender wage gap is calculated based on the difference between the median earnings of men and women as compared to the median earnings of men (OECD 2013). Japan's gender wage gap, while the third highest among OECD countries, has gradually dropped from 32.8 percent in 2005 (OECD 2017).

5. The average gap between men's and women's monthly earnings differs in large, midsize, and small companies. In large companies of over one thousand employees, men and women start out on approximately the same salary but then diverge. Men in their thirties earn on average ¥400,000 a month, a figure that rises to approximately ¥550,000 for men in their fifties. Meanwhile, women in their thirties earn approximately ¥280,000 a month, a figure that rises to approximately ¥330,000 for women in their fifties. The same trend bears out in midsize and small companies (though with lower wages for both). These differences result from the fact that men are promoted to management positions at greater rates than women and that, as per the M-shaped curve, women are more likely than men to leave the workforce in their late twenties and early thirties after marriage and childbirth (MIAC 2013b).

6. Of course, not all men are able (or want) to live up to expectations to be the main breadwinners and patriarchal heads of household. Different spheres of masculinity and understandings of gender roles are emerging, and many people live on the margins of these norms, picking and choosing the ones that work for them, depending on their individual situations and values. However, it is important to note that these normative ideals remain strongly articulated and aspirational in individual narratives of both men and women when they discuss expectations of marriage and marital roles (see Cook 2013, 2016).

7. I follow Jamieson (2011) in understanding intimacy as being both feeling and practice. Jamieson argues that feelings of closeness are created and sustained through practices that "enable, generate and sustain a subjective sense of closeness and being attuned and special to each other" (ibid., 1). Such practices include, for example, sharing time and affection, taking care of each another, and actively knowing each other. However, they are also tightly interlaced with relations and practices of power, the subject that is the focus of this chapter.

8. Hostesses work in bars where they facilitate an enjoyable evening for (mostly male) customers. For a detailed analysis of hostess clubs, see Allison (1994) and Gagné (2010).

9. A note on language: throughout the documentary Naoki shifts between English (that is often broken) and Japanese. A translator is behind the camera most of the time but not always. In the documentary Naoki's English remains as it was spoken, but for ease of reading and meaning in this chapter I have edited some of the grammar. Most of the conversations between Naoki and Yoshie are translated from the Japanese, whereas most of the conversations between Naoki and the director were conducted in English.

10. The Statistics Bureau of Japan's basic survey of social life in 2011 (http://www.stat.go.jp/data/shakai/2011/) illustrates that on average women do significantly more hours of unpaid household chores each week than men.

11. Wittgenstein's idea of "family resemblance" denoted "concepts that overlap in usage while there is no single essence that unites all these usages" (Haugaard 2010, 424).

12. Yoshie often gets invited out for dinner by long-term customers, and she accepts such invitations in order to maintain the relationship. After the meal the customer and Yoshie make their way to the bar.

13. Various issues of power within intimacy can also be seen in the context of domestic violence and in the redefinitions of intimacy noted by Kuwajima (this volume).

14. The relationship of Sumiko and Masao is described briefly and in a condensed form in Cook (2013, 38; 2016, 120–121).

REFERENCES

Abe, Masahiro. 2008. "Hiseiki shain no kōzō henka to sono seisaku taiou" [Policy Response to the Structural Changes of Non-Regular Employees] In *Nira kenkyū hōkokusho: Shūshoku hiyōgaki sedai no kiwadosa takamaru koyō risuku ni dō taiō subeki ka?* [Nira Research Report: How Should We Support the Employment Ice-Age Generation on the Edge of High Employment Risk?], edited by Nira: Sōgō Kenkyū Kaihatsu Kikou [National Institute for Research Advancement], 25–34. http://www.nira.or.jp/pdf/0801report.pdf. Accessed November 14, 2014.

Allen, Amy. 2011. "Feminist Perspectives on Power." In *Stanford Encyclopedia of Philosophy.* http://plato.stanford.edu/entries/feminist-power/. Accessed August 5, 2014.

Allison, Anne. 1994. *Nightwork: Sexuality, Pleasure, and Corporate Masculinity in a Tokyo Hostess Club.* Chicago: University of Chicago Press.

Cabinet Office. 2011. "Kekkon, kazoku keisei ni kan suru chōsa hōkokusho" [Studies on Marriage and Family]. http://www8.cao.go.jp/shoushi/cyousa/cyousa22/marriage-family/mokuji-pdf.html. Accessed December 2, 2013.

Cook, Emma E. 2013. "Expectations of Failure: Maturity and Masculinity for Freeters in Contemporary Japan." *Social Science Japan Journal* 16 (1): 29–43.

———. 2014. "Intimate Expectations and Practices: Freeter Relationships and Marriage in Contemporary Japan." *Asian Anthropology* 13 (1): 36–51.

———. 2016. *Reconstructing Adult Masculinities: Part-Time Work in Contemporary Japan.* London: Routledge.

———. 2017. "Aspirational Labour, Performativity and Masculinities in the Making." *Intersections: Gender and Sexuality in Asia and the Pacific* 41. Available online at http://intersections.anu.edu.au/issue41/cook.html.

Gagné, Nana. O. 2010. "The Business of Leisure, the Leisure of Business: Rethinking Hegemonic Masculinity through Gendered Service in Tokyo Hostess Clubs." *Asian Anthropology* 9 (1): 29–55.

Haugaard, Mark. 2010. "Power: A 'Family Resemblance' Concept." *European Journal of Cultural Studies* 13 (4): 419–438.

Hochschild, Arlie, and Anne Machung. 2012. *The Second Shift: Working Families and the Revolution at Home.* London: Penguin Group.

Honda, Yuki. 2002. "Jenda- to iu kanten kara mita furiita-" [Gender Approach to "Freeter"]. In *Jiyū no taishō/furiita-* [The Cost of Freedom: Freeter], edited by Reiko Kosugi, 149–174. Tokyo: Nihon Rōdō Kenkyū Kikō.

Jamieson, Lynn. 2011. "Intimacy as a Concept: Explaining Social Change in the Context of Globalisation or Another Form of Ethnocentrism?" *Sociological Research Online* 16 (4): 1–13.

Layder, Derek. 2009. *Intimacy and Power: The Dynamics of Personal Relationships in Modern Society.* London: Palgrave Macmillan.

Maciel, Jose A., Zanetta Van Putten, and Carmen Knudson-Martin. 2009. "Gendered Power in Cultural Contexts: Part I. Immigrant Couples." *Family Process* 48 (1): 9–23.

MIAC (Ministry of Internal Affairs and Communications), Statistics Bureau. 2013a. "Rōdōryoku chōsa no kekka wo miru pointo No. 16: Hiseiki no yaku 7 wari ha josei ga shimeru" [Labor Force Survey Results Point 16: Women Account for Approximately 70 Percent of Irregular Workers]. http://www.stat.go.jp/data/roudou/pdf/point16.pdf. Accessed August 2, 2014.

———. 2013b. "Statistical Handbook of Japan 2013." http://www.stat.go.jp/english/data/handbook/c0117.htm. Accessed August 2, 2014.

Nagase, Nobuko. 2006. "Japanese Youth's Attitudes Towards Marriage and Child Rearing." In *The Changing Japanese Family*, edited by Marcus Rebick and Ayumi Takenaka, 39–53. London: Routledge.

Nemoto, Kumiko. 2008. "Postponed Marriage: Exploring Women's Views of Matrimony and Work in Japan." *Gender and Society* 22 (2): 219–237.

OECD. 2013. "Gender Equality: From Education to Work—Jobs and Wages." http://www.oecd-ilibrary.org/sites/factbook-2013-en/13/02/02/index.html?itemId=/content/chapter/factbook-2013-106-en. Accessed August 2, 2014.

———. 2017. "The Pursuit of Gender Equality: An Uphill Battle—How Does Japan Compare?" https://www.oecd.org/japan/Gender2017-JPN-en.pdf. Accessed November 21, 2017.

Sandberg, Shana. F. 2010. "'Marriage Delay' (*Bankonka*) and Women's Shifting Priorities in Japan." *Anthropology News* 51 (5): 39.

Silva, Jennifer. M. 2013. *Coming Up Short: Working-Class Adulthood in an Age of Uncertainty*. Oxford: Oxford University Press.

Sweeney, Megan. M. 2002. "Two Decades of Family Change: The Shifting Economic Foundations of Marriage." *American Sociological Review* 67: 132–147.

Takeyama, Akiko. 2010. "Intimacy for Sale: Masculinity, Entrepreneurship, and Commodity Self in Japan's Neoliberal Situation." *Japanese Studies* 30 (2): 231–246.

———. 2016. *Staged Seductions: Selling Dreams in a Tokyo Host Club*. Stanford: Stanford University Press.

Tichenor, Veronica J. 1999. "Status and Income as Gendered Resources: The Case of Marital Power." *Journal of Marriage and Family* 61 (3): 638–650.

Tokuhiro, Yoko. 2010. *Marriage in Contemporary Japan*. London: Routledge.

Tsuya, Noriko, and Larry Bumpass. 2004. *Marriage, Work and Family Life in Comparative Perspective: Japan, South Korea and the United States*. Honolulu: University of Hawai'i Press.

Vij, Ritu. 2013. "Affective Fields of Precarity: Gendered Antinomies in Contemporary Japan." *Alternatives: Global, Local, Political* 38 (2): 122–138.

CHAPTER 8

❖ ❖ ❖

Manhood and the
Burdens of Intimacy

Elizabeth Miles

"I have no girlfriend, and it is solely for this reason that my life has collapsed" (*Kanojo ga inai, tada no itten de jinsei hōkai*). These were some of the final words—as posted on the Internet—of the now (in)famous Katō Tomohiro. On June 8, 2008, Katō drove a truck down the crowded main shopping street of Tokyo's famous electronics district, Akihabara, closed off at that time to vehicular traffic. After crashing into several pedestrians, he then left the vehicle and proceeded to stab wildly with a knife at the crowds. Though he was quickly subdued and arrested, the total cost of his actions was seven dead and ten injured. While the Japanese and Western media primarily focused on the uncommon violence of the incident and its probable causes in Japan's neoliberal reforms, several authors and activists have claimed this act and the man himself as a potent symbolic of the "love gap" (*ren'ai kakusa*) in contemporary Japan.

A little over two weeks after what is now termed the Akihabara Incident, the news weekly *AERA* published an article profiling the possible social dynamics behind Katō's action. Entitled "The Cruelty of the Supremacy of Desirability" (Fukuda and Katō 2008), this essay describes how many Japanese men are engaging with what I label the increasing burdens of love and intimacy in postindustrial Japan. In this, I am taking up Shibuya Tomomi's conceptualization of love as an act, a deed, and not merely as a goal in and of itself. While recognizing the diversity of the meaning of the concept "love" (*ren'ai*), Shibuya defines it as the "action of building an intimate relationship with another person" (*tasha to shinmitsu na kankei wo kizukō to suru kōi*) (2009, 75). Love and intimacy are not solely emotional states brought on by, and directed toward, another individual (or several). When I have asked my male interviewees how they define love, the overwhelming response has been that it is a way of deepening feelings, creating an intimacy. Yet for many young men, even taking the first steps of love—specifically meeting women and dating—have proven to be difficult, with love experienced, and imagined, as an increasing impossibility.

Even those with only a passing familiarity with the Japanese mainstream media are cognizant of Japan's population woes. In reference to the declining birthrate (*shōshika*), the increasing number of non-working seniors (*kōreika*), or, most relevant for the purposes of my study, the swelling number of late-marrieds (*bankonka*) and even non-marrieds (*mikonka*), there is a prevailing sense of crisis within the media, the government, and among various academic specialists in Japan. A 2013 report by the Ministry of Health, Labor, and Welfare (MHLW 2013) on youth consciousness claims there is less pressure within society to get married and that marriage has become just one choice among many, though no other choices are mentioned. Nevertheless, marriage is still viewed by many as a necessary entry into adult society (Cook 2013). Heterosexual coupling, marriage, and the reproduction of children have been the ideological norm. Japan has been posited as a "marriage-based society," or *kaikon shakai* (Tokuhiro 2010), with heterosexual marriage viewed as "common sense" (Lunsing 2001).[1] As a cross-culturally recognized rite of passage, weddings, in Edwards's view, "touch on fundamental notions about society itself and the individual's place within it" (1989, 8–9). Marriage symbolizes and makes socially official one's entrance into the adult world. Within the "complementary incompetence" of Japan's gender system, heterosexual marriage is, as Edwards explains, "necessary because individuals—both men and women—are always incomplete; their deficiencies, moreover, are complementary" (1989, 123). Though Lebra claims that "marriage was a necessary way to provide proof of femininity" (1984, 91), it is equally important for men, as indicative of both their desirability and thus their (heterosexual) manhood. However, despite this prevailing view on marriage, a 2013 Ministry White Paper states that as of 2012, 19.3 percent of men fifty years of age and older were unmarried and thus considered to be life-long unmarrieds (*shōgai mikon*). The report claims that around 60 percent of unmarried men between the ages of eighteen and thirty-nine are neither dating a woman nor have any female friends. When asked why they did not want a partner, 52.6 percent of male respondents claimed that "love is burdensome" (*ren'ai ga mendō*). Moreover, 14.6 percent claimed that "engaging with the opposite sex is frightening" (*isei to kōsai suru no ga kowai*) (MHLW 2013, 76). These concerns are reflected in postwar marriage rates, which have exhibited gradual decline throughout this period, reaching a new postwar low in 2014 (approximately 640,000 couples, with 80 percent first marriages) (MHLW 2016, 66).

The shift in feelings toward both dating and marriage, as well as the statistical shifts in marriage rates, have prompted many in Japan to examine the changing nature of such intimate relationships throughout the postwar period. McLelland (2012), writing on the Occupation-era shift in norms around dating and couplehood, argues that the introduction of romance and "free choice" had profound effects on the interaction between the sexes. Yet it has been the demographic and ideological shift from so-called "arranged" (omiai) marriages to those based on love (ren'ai) that has prompted the most critical attention surrounding the marriage "woes" of young Japanese singles. In the 1930s, for instance, about 70 percent of marriages were "arranged"; in the 1960s this began to change (Katō 2004, 74). Today, approximately 90 percent of all marriages are "love marriages (ren'ai kekkon) (MHLW 2013). Two of the most outspoken critics of this shift are Yamada Masahiro and Shirakawa Tōko. Writing about the "marriage hunting" (konkatsu) boom that began in the late 2000s, the authors claim that Japan has entered, for both men and women, "the age of wanting to get married but being unable to" (kekkon shitakutemo dekinai jidai) (2009, 24–25). Watanabe Shin, head of the All-Japan Virgin League (Nihon Zenkoku Dōtei Rengō) and self-proclaimed as the "most famous virgin in Japan," has responded to "imaginary critics" who claim that "anyone can do love" by arguing that this is all ideology, a product of this shift from "arranged marriages"—what some saw as a lack of choice—to love matches (2007, 20). For Yamada, Shirakawa, and Watanabe, the ideology and practice of "love marriage," while notable for its illusion of free choice and therefore greater potential intimacy, contributes both to the delay of marriage until later in life and the increase in the number of Japanese singles.[2] In his attempt to understand the issue, Miura Atsushi, a marketing analyst and author of *Unpopular Men! The Age of Male Suffering*, claims that "love today is a competitive free market" with social Darwinist implications for Japanese men and society as a whole (2009, 60). Despite various fundamental differences in their approach to the issue, these and other authors agree that being in love today is a competitive arena, wherein love is neither easily attained nor guaranteed. Such acknowledgements and criticisms point to larger discourses on how love in contemporary Japan functions not only as a form of work, but, moreover, as a form of social recognition comparable to one's occupational and company status, that many see as unavailable to an increasing number of young women and, especially, men.

Through the following ethnographic vignettes, I present two contrasting depictions of how young men are engaging with, and often defying, contemporary demands on men in the "marriage/love market." While they may seem wildly disparate and therefore incommensurate, I argue that there are linkages among them and with broader society-wide discourses on "doing love" and intimacy—and their burdens—among single men. The burdens of intimacy, as I see them, are twofold. On the one hand, contemporary popular discourse describes finding a potential mate as now requiring constant effort on the part of men, a consistent polishing of the self and one's attributes that many men find to be onerous and in contradistinction to their idealized versions of what love is and should be. Furthermore, many men find the pecuniary expectations of women—a high male income that translates into spending power—to be particularly onerous and untenable. On the other hand, love and marriage function as signs of desirability (*moteru*), and this desirability is, in turn, symbolic of one's humanity (*ningenrashisa*). These burdens are part and parcel of what Itō, Kimura, and Kuninobu term the "age of love pressure (*gendai shakai ha, ren'ai kyōhakushō no jidai*) (2011, 116). In the following, I share two fieldwork encounters in order to illustrate the increasing burden on young men in today's "marriage market" and how some are choosing to respond. The first is a series of demonstrations against the three major "love" holidays in Japan; the second, a dating event in Tokyo. Both encounters took place between the fall of 2013 and the spring of 2014 as part of my doctoral research on youth masculinity in contemporary Japan.

BURDEN AND RESISTANCE: *KAKUHIDŌ* AND THE POLITICS OF *HIMOTE*

One of the unharmed bystanders in Akihabara on the day of Katō's attack was Furusawa Katsuhiro, the former head of the Kakumeiteki Himote Dōmei (Unpopular Men's Alliance; Kakuhidō for short). Influenced by the student activism he saw on campus when he was a student at Hosei University, as well as by Marxism, Furusawa founded the group in 2006 (Furusawa and Sekiguchi 2009, 58). Now headed by Mark Water (this Japanese gentleman's *nom de guerre*), Kakuhidō bills itself as trying to make "a bright future for *himote*" (*himote no akarui mirai o sōzō suru*). *Himote*, or unpopular man/men, derives from the Japanese terms *hi*, meaning negative or un-, and *mote* from *moteru*, meaning popular. In his *Otaku Encyclopedia*, Patrick Galbraith defines *himote* as follows:

> Unpopular, especially with females. *Himote* guys believe that the status of women is built on the backs of men, who must slave to earn money and win female attention. In some cases, *himote* have a political bent and

gather to boycott Christmas, Valentine's, and White Day, when men are expected to make extravagant "offerings" in the name of romance. They spend a lot of time online, and it's a chicken-or-egg question as to whether they are unpopular because of the theory, or created the theory because they are unpopular. (2009, 100)

From my own research, I find this definition to be an exaggeration, but it also speaks to some "truths" about self-proclaimed *himote*. For instance, Furusawa seems to view *himote* as akin to other sexual minorities, and in an interview with the journal *Sexuality*, he explicitly compared the "love system" in Japan to that of capitalism, in which people are classified and hierarchized.

Having learned about this group, I emailed the head of the group, Mark Water, to request an interview. Perhaps questioning my interest, he instead invited me to the Christmas Smashing (*kurisumasu funsai*) demonstration in Shibuya.[3] Consequently, in late December I met up with the group in Miyashita Park in central Shibuya about thirty minutes before the scheduled demonstration was to begin. I saw a group of about five men in the northern part of the park, some with bullhorns, some wearing masks. I shyly headed toward them, feeling out of place owing to my gender and my flashy sartorial choices. Wearing a pink net shopping bag over his face, topped with sunglasses and a helmet, Mark Water approached me, and we introduced ourselves. After he introduced me to Hatoya-san, a journalist and Communist, we exchanged business cards (*meishi*) and hung around, discussing the group and its aims. They explained some of the basic tenets of the protest; the most important point was that they saw a discriminatory structure (*sabetsu kōzō*) in the way single people are treated in comparison with those in couples. Water-san mentioned the pressure (*atsuryoku*) to be in a pair. At this point, other participants, mostly men but a few women, arrived; while about twenty-five people had gathered in total, only fifteen (thirteen men, two women) participated in the march. The new arrivals brought with them the group's flag, reading "Smash Christmas!" which was held up at the front of the protest line. We were led by police officers and orderly arranged ourselves into three lines. At this point, we made our way through one of the busiest sections of Shibuya, taking a tour around the park and through the major shopping area in front of the JR station. Water-san led us in shouting "Smash Christmas!" (*kurisumasu funsai!*). A young man wearing a blue Japan Aviation Association jacket was yelling into a bullhorn, urging couples to break up (*kappuru wakareyo!*). He was eventually told by police to calm down, but otherwise the protest proceeded peacefully. As we made our way back to the park, past large crowds of shoppers, people were staring. At one point, two young men in their late teens or early twenties raised their hands and cheered in support. Most pedestrians stared and/or took pictures. In total, the protest took only about thirty minutes. When we returned to the park, Water-san declared the protest over and had people pose for final photographs.

After the Christmas demonstration, I attended the other two *funsai* (smashing, pulverizing) events for Valentine's Day and White Day. Neither of these holidays is strictly a celebration of "love," though that element exists as well. On Valentine's Day women are expected to give chocolates to the men in their lives—regardless of romantic intent—including their work colleagues. This custom is then repeated, with the genders reversed, a month later, on White Day, when men are expected to make a return offering of chocolates (see Ogasawara 1998). All three "smashing" events have as their aim, other than ultimately building that "bright future," of destroying the "love capital system" (*ren'ai shihon shugi*).

At the Valentine's demonstration, I felt an even greater sense of anger among those gathered, quite possibly because social norms surrounding this holiday allow for a highly gendered, and typically public, evaluation of a man's popularity. The demonstrators' anger was not directed at women in particular but at the love-capital system itself. Prior to the actual demonstration, approximately twelve minutes of speeches were made by those gathered. Many of the speeches focused on the giving of chocolates on Valentine's Day, when men are expected only to receive, not give, them as gifts. As vividly described by Ogasawara (1998), this practice means that a man who receives few or no gifts of chocolate is right to understand the message that he is disliked and unattractive. The speakers correctly assumed they were speaking to a group of men who were unlikely to receive chocolates and deeply felt the sting of that rejection. Water-san began with the impassioned claim that "This Valentine's day thing, every year we try to smash it, but it grows up like mushrooms after the rain." Referring specifically to the custom of giving chocolates, he claimed that it is a bad custom promoting and fostering inequality among people (*kakusa wo jochōsuru hidoi shūkan*) because some men are inevitably given more or fewer chocolates. Next, a man who appeared to be in his late thirties or early forties stepped up to the microphone and stated, "We are living in an age when men's value is determined by how many chocolates they receive. This must be ended!" He concluded his speech by telling the assembled crowd that even though they may not receive chocolates, they are still great (*Choko wo desu ne, mattaku morawaranai hito demo jinkaku ga sugureta desu ne*). He was followed by writer and consultant Tsunemi Yōhei, who declared that a society (such as Japan's) that evaluates one's humanity (*ningen*) based on the number of chocolates received is not a good one (*chokorēto no maisū de ningen no kachi wo kimeru shakai ha yokunai*). The next speaker was a freshman at Keiō University in Tokyo who would be celebrating his first Valentine's Day as a college student. However, he lamented that he would be spending it working all day at his part-time job and did not expect to receive anything on the appointed day. The final speaker, who remained anonymous, closed out the speechmaking by declaring, "Love is a tool of exploitation of workers by capitalists" (*Ren'ai ha shihonshugi no shihonkatachi ga rōdōsha wo sakushu suru tame no dōgu de arimasu*). Earlier he compared the customs of Valentine's and White Day to prostitution, a comparison that was met with laughs and a rousing "Yes, indeed!" (*Sō da!*). Despite laying much of the blame at the feet of the government and capitalism, he ended with the claim that "There are women who expect a man to make more than ¥6 million per year.[4] But according to statistics, no such men of marriageable age exist!" These claims, which may strike some as odd amid the overall critique of a chocolate-based evaluation of one's humanity, lie at the heart of much of what Shibuya Tomomi (2009) calls the "external" (*gaihatsu ha*) *himote* movement. As opposed to their "internal" (*naihatsu*) brethren, *gaihatsu ha* critique the "love capital system," which they see as the primary love system, as a whole.[5]

Kakuhidō is just one part of a larger "movement" seeking to publicize the increasing difficulties that men (in particular) face in an increasingly competitive, and burdensome, love/marriage market. One of the more outspoken critics of love in contemporary Japan is Denpa Otoko ("Radio-Wave Man"), Honda Tōru. Published in 2005, Honda's manifesto, *Denpa otoko*, is a critique of the "love-capital system" and a call for young people to embrace "two-dimensional love." The anonymous Kakuhidō protester's prostitution comparison implicitly draws on Honda's work and is a common refrain within the *himote* discourse. The primary critique is that men feel they are expected to make large cash outlays, in the form of presents, dinners, and travel, in order to both find and keep a girlfriend. Rather than being accepted ostensibly for who they are, regardless of clothing choices and career aspirations (and the attendant income), men are converted into another commodity owing to the linkages between love and capitalism in contemporary Japan (see Cook, this volume). These men are not necessarily rejecting love per se but rather its commodity-like fetishism. Like Furusawa, Kakuhidō, and others, Honda borrows from Marxist critiques of capitalism, questioning Japan's "new religion of love" and its firm entrenchment with capitalism. For Honda, this system divides men—and he is specifically talking about men—into "haves" (*moteru*) and "have nots" (*motenai*).[6] The latter are branded as "social losers" and in effect cast out of society, in what he also deems a system of "sexual apartheid." Calling for men to withdraw from this unfair system, Honda argues that it is only in the two-dimensional world—for instance, video games, figurines of characters and/or idols—that one can experience love free from capitalist exploitation and its attendant burdens.

However, love within the virtual world is not without its various burdens. Despite being held up by some as being free from the disappointments of "real love" (*jissai no ren'ai*),[7] even "love simulation games" (*ren'ai shimyurēshon gēmu*) are enmeshed in a dating culture that requires time and effort on the part of the player. Within the simulated reality world of the highly popular, and perhaps most well-known dating game for men, Konami's LovePlus, love and intimacy require work.[8] The character ("you") changes his schedule in order to cultivate certain skills that then result in unlocking the heart of one of the three female characters.[9] To increase one's "boyfriend power" (*kareshi no chikara*), you must increase your intelligence, charm, physical training, and sensitivity through various school and extracurricular activities. LovePlus tacitly acknowledges that love is not given freely but is a form of work. However, separating it from reality is the lack of both rivals for a young woman's affection and a relative lack of risk. Thus the game separates the player from the reality that a desired partner could find someone better.

Viewing themselves as having been denied access to love and intimacy, men such as Honda, Furusawa, and those in Kakuhidō, have chosen to drop out of the competitive arena. They experience the freedom of the love market not as the beginning of new opportunities—for love but also for the self—but as the foreclosure of intimate possibilities. Intimacy, for them, should be free from the demands of the market—that is, not dependent on one's income and spending power. But in the typical meat market, intimacy entails onerous burdens, both financial and emotional. While their critique is aimed particularly at the pecuniary expectations on potential (male) lovers, their palpable anger, coupled with moments of light-hearted comic bantering, speaks to the larger burdens felt by many young men in Japan who are attempting to find love. For those in Kakuhidō and others, the non-receipt of chocolates on Valentine's Day represents a lack in themselves, a sign of their non-desirability, which in turn signifies a certain social deficiency on their part. Securing love—as exemplified not just by having a girlfriend or wife, but also by being recognized as a potential mate—thus is a burden in and of itself, one that bears the weight of granting men access to the realm of social recognition and normality.

ON THE MEET (MEAT) MARKET

While the men of Kakuhidō and others choose to resist what they view as the increasingly burdensome norms of love in contemporary Japan, there are many others who endure. In particular, events self-consciously designed for people to find a marriage partner, clustered under the term "marriage hunting" (*konkatsu*), have become popular in recent decades. Taking part in *konkatsu* events, they still seek to find love and intimacy. One popular form of *konkatsu* is the *machikon*, which suggests a local setting or gathering for people looking for relationships, as opposed to a more Western "blind date." Usually arranged by a commercial outfit, such as Machicon Japan, these events allow male and female participants to intermingle in a restaurant or bar. Food and drinks are included in the set price, with men typically paying twice as much as women.[10] The usual setup for a *machikon* is that one is assigned to arrive at a restaurant or bar at the appointed time. When one checks in, he or she is given a map pointing out the other available restaurants nearby. Staff members encourage participants to remain at the first venue for about an hour, then recommend checking out the other spaces and meeting new potential mates. Such a procedure allows participants to meet more single persons than at a typical *gōkon* or group date.[11]

Attending various *machikon*, I was able to observe firsthand the skills necessary for finding love. At my first *machikon*, in September 2013 in Ebisu, I was keenly aware of the palpable sense of nervousness among the attendees, as it was a mirror of my own. The first to arrive at the small Italian restaurant to which I was first assigned, I was given a map and instructions and told to sit at a table in the back of the room. I was soon followed in by a young man in a white button-down shirt and blue jeans. Surveying the room, he sat down at a table two tables down from mine; though we politely nodded at each other, no words were exchanged, and he, like I, was visibly nervous. By the appointed start time more attendees had arrived; the organizers announced the opening of the bar, and we toasted (*kampai!*) to the evening and the potential matches that could be made. I introduced myself to the young woman sitting to my left, complimenting her on her fashion. We exchanged simple conversation and were eventually drawn into a larger group discussion with the other men and women at our table. However, that initial young man spent most of the time sipping his tea and staring at the table, until he was asked to join our table.

This young man was certainly struggling. A full-time postal worker (a fact that he shared after much prompting), he was eventually aided in his attempts by two men in their early thirties who had made themselves his unofficial coaches. They urged him to ask questions of the women at the table, but he was very hesitant to do so. When both men and women prompted him with questions, he never made any eye contact, choosing instead to look at the table and mumble his replies. At one point he refused to even sit at the table with us, choosing instead to skulk near the exit of the room. It is possible to imagine that this young man, had he come of age two decades earlier, would have married with relative ease. Because he possessed a stable (though not particularly glamorous) job, his parents would have engaged the services of marriage brokers or those of a coworker acting as a go-between (*nakōdo*) in order to find a bride for him. Yet here he struggled to even engage in the most basic of conversations with both the men and the women.

In this "new" marriage market, the ability to communicate has become both a necessity and a potential burden for young men. A publication from Men's Center Japan tells (male) readers that "in regard to building a good relationship, it is necessary to have good communication with your female partner. You may think this is burdensome or problematic [*mendōkusai*], but it is very important" (2000, 16; see also Alexy, chapter 5 in this volume).[12] In response to what many see as the inability of today's young men to communicate with women or to attract them by other means, there has been a growth in specialty services and *moteru* guides. As Yamada claims, finding love (via *konkatsu*) is not just about seeking a partner, but also entails improving oneself (2010, 27). Within the *moteru* boom, these guides advise young men to polish (*migaku*) themselves in order to find love. A recent comic, *Moteru manga* (Yū and Sō 2013) aims, through comedy, to instruct stereotypical "social losers" in how to navigate the contemporary dating scene. The protagonist, Tadano-san, laments his lack of a girlfriend; however, when confronted by the "lady killer" Onnada Kō (literally, "Many Women Luck"), who was brought in by his boss to help his male employees, he claims that if he is just himself, women will find him desirable, and therefore he is okay just as he is (ibid., 19). Onnada intensely disagrees, telling him that being as he is now is like showing up to a job interview in pajamas or taking a university entrance exam without having studied— that is, wholly unacceptable and guaranteed to fail (ibid., 21). Onnada and others urge their targets (presumably undesirable men) to think of love as a market and themselves in terms of goods to be sold. Fujita Satoshi (2009, 62), founder of the Cram School for Undesirable Men (Himote Nanpa Juku) and author of various dating guides, compares men to cars, with women being the customers, and urges the polishing of the self in order to be the best on the market.[13]

Like the ideas expressed by Honda Tōru, these works acknowledge how the means of, and the preferred attributes for, finding intimacy— the work of love—are shifting, comparing the process and the field of competition itself to a capitalist market. However, while Honda urges readers to withdraw from the market in full, Fujita, Yamada, and others recognize the necessity of change—on the part of men. The young postal worker I met at the Ebisu *machikon* reminds me of one of Fujita's pupils as described in a 2008 *AERA* essay. Fujita recalls how his student ran up to a woman, asked her to marry him, and promptly ran away at the young woman's disgusted look (cited in Fukada and Katō 2008, 26). Lacking even the ability to look a woman in the face, such young men represent not only the potential failures in the new system, but also the new burdens on young men. Yamada claims, "When *omiai* marriages were still fairly common, men who thought that they weren't desirable could still hope that they could get married. But since the bursting of the bubble, there has been a widening of economic disparity, and women have increasingly entered society. Undesirable men now have no hope" (2010, 27).[14] Works such as *Mote baiburu* and *Moteru manga* aim to give young men hope for finding love and intimacy; however, they also make clear the increasing burdens that love now entails.

To some, men such as the young postal worker and Fujita's pupils are pitiable or, even worse, symbolic of new forms of misogyny in contemporary Japan. Feminist scholar Ueno Chizuko (2010, 57) criticizes *himote* as merely angry young men who objectify (*mono suru*) women as a means toward fulfillment of their masculine identity. She goes on to claim that they hold a grudge (*ensa*) against the changing marriage market and thus are desirous for a return to the previous marriage system, wherein almost anyone could get married with little effort. In my work, building intimacy does not necessarily stem from a long-term relationship with an individual, developed over multiple meetings and deep discussions. Rather, intimacy can be a process of sharing stories of vulnerability and finding a connection, a potential common cause, even common humanity, with my informants, owing in part to the fact that their worldview is both challenging to and in agreement with my own. Watching young men attempt to meet women at *machikon* or laying bare their "undesirability" has made me (often painfully) aware of my own situation as a researcher in Japan. When I have talked about these young men, several of my interviewees and colleagues have scoffed at their protestations, seeing in them, as Ueno does, a nostalgia for the "good old days," a desire to return to a more masculinist system of matchmaking. However, through empathy, in their struggles I see my own reflected. The process of fieldwork bears striking similarities to a search for love in that it is often a fight to be perceived as desirable (or in my case, as respectable) on one's own terms, regardless of income, looks, status, and communication skills. Regardless of whether or not anyone loves these men, they deserve to be recognized as fellow humans and citizens, not as social outcasts.

Reflecting on the goal of anthropology and the ethnographer, Nancy Rosenberger argues the following:

> [The anthropologist's] main aim is to give voice to these people's stories and experiences through a process of listening closely and thinking about them in relation to almost everything else she reads and does. The final result is her tale of these stories, for in their retelling the anthropologist also recounts a tale of herself, of her encounter with these people, and of the meaning that she understands in these encounters. (2013, 1)

In this chapter I have demonstrated how intimacy in contemporary Japan is experienced, and responded to, as a burden for young Japanese men. Alone, my *konkatsu* and Kakuhidō encounters might seem extraordinary; however, when placed within the wider discourse—on marriage hunting, *moteru*, and the "love gap"—such stories take on a recognizable cast and become symbolic of broader social issues in post-mainstream, postindustrial Japan. While the men of Kakuhidō may embrace their undesirability—in the process questioning the very foundation of such a phenomenon—and men such as the postal worker continue to "compete" despite their undesirability, these two oppositional responses nevertheless highlight both the competitiveness of the love market and its work-like burdens on young men. Their reactions point to feelings of inadequacy and frustration at their inability not only to just get married (*kekkon dekinai*), but also to not "do" love. Love in Japan now comes with new risks, as well as a new sense of importance for the self and one's social standing. While Itō, Kimura, and Kuninobu (2011) claim that love is an issue of adulthood (*ichininmae*), I claim that being "desirable" (*mote*) goes beyond issues of adult norms to that of social recognition.

After months of fieldwork, I met with masculinity studies scholar Tanaka Toshiyuki to discuss varying issues regarding contemporary Japanese masculinity. Tanaka-san's most recent research focuses on men and the issue of "work-life balance"; as we discussed varying issues regarding contemporary Japanese masculinity, he recognized that though for young men work may be their primary concern, love and desirability were a close second. Both function as forms of social recognition (*shōmei*) and are thus a burden on the self. Following his theorization, I understand love and marriage to index a certain normalcy, but one to which many young men feel they no longer have access owing to shifting partner norms. In a recent essay on the changing demands on men, anthropologist Gordon Mathews makes the claim that "Being a man in a changing Japan is harder than ever, it seems" (2014, 78). While the decline in career and work opportunities—the primary markers of Japanese masculinity in the postwar era—has garnered the most critical attention in the past decade, the burdens evoked by Mathews extend beyond this "traditional" sphere into what I see as the new arena of work: love and intimacy.

NOTES

This research was conducted with the generous support of a Fulbright Japan grant. I am deeply appreciative of all the men and women who have allowed me to do fieldwork with them. I would also like to thank my adviser, Karen Nakamura, for her constant support, both in the field and outside it. Special thanks are due to the two editors of this volume, Allison Alexy and Emma Cook, both for their encouragement during this trying fieldwork period, and for their insightful and always helpful comments on this chapter.

1. The persuasive force of this "common sense" extends to homosexual men and women as well. Describing marriage vis-à-vis gay men and women as "a system that does not fit their needs and on the other hand does not leave them untouched either," Lunsing (2001, 120) highlights the tactic used by some (primarily) queer men of engaging in "camouflage marriages" (*gisō kekkon*). By entering into a heterosexual marriage, lesbians and gay men feel more able to ensure their adulthood and fulfill natal family obligations.

2. The idea that "love match marriages" allow for greater intimacy between spouses is predicated on the belief that the long(er)-term evolution of the relationship—from initial meeting to the confession of romantic feelings (*kokuhaku*) and ultimately up to and through marriage—necessarily involves learning more about the respective partner, thus deepening interpersonal communication and understanding. Furthermore, it is also expected for couples to have experienced sexual intimacy prior to marriage, thus ensuring carnal compatibility.

3. Lest one think that demonstrating against Christmas marks these men as particularly grinchy, it is necessary to give a brief explanation of this holiday in twenty-first-century Japan. Writing in 1963 and 1982 respectively, David Plath and Walter Edwards described Christmas as a family holiday, marked off from more adult (that is, sake-filled) end-of-year celebrations. However, this unofficial holiday—it is not a day off from work, and from my own recent experience, life functions as normal—is now neither a celebration of the birth of Christ nor even a time for the family to gather; Christmas today is a couples' holiday. Kawahara notes that this "domesticated" holiday offers "a 'romantic' stage for the young to develop their sexual relationships" (1996, 182). Beginning in late November, colorful imagery in the subways, department stores, and magazines across Japan advertises the love aspects—couples packages to hot springs (*onsen*), special dinners, romantic walks through one of Tokyo's various illumination events. During one of my many jaunts throughout Tokyo I even came across a flier for a *machikon* aimed at finding a special someone in time for the Christmas holiday. In this way it is very much akin to Valentine's Day celebrations and expectations in the United States. For example, Kawahara (this volume) narrates romantic expectations for Christmas in the case of Yoko.

4. Approximately US$60,000.

5. The internal *himote*, per Shibuya, believe that their undesirability is an individual/personal problem. Unlike the external *himote*, they have few problems with the "love-capital system" (2009, 89–90).

6. This is actually a play on words, not uncommon in the Japanese language. *Moteru* (being desirable) and *motsu* (to have; *motteiru*) sound similar.

7. Dobashi, Katsuya, and Tsuji refer to this as *kitai hazurenonai anshin*, or "the sense of security that comes when one's expectations are not thwarted" (2011, 72).

8. Not long after LovePlus's initial release, an anonymous user posted a chart on Ni-channeru (Channel Two, a popular message board) outlining the difference between the game and "three-dimensional love." With LovePlus the outcome is "heaven" (*tengoku*). However, love in the "real world" holds the potential for disappointment (one's being denied love) or eventual marriage. Regardless, both outcomes are labeled as being "a living hell" (*ikijigoku*), as they leave men often feeling frustrated (Dobashi, Katsuya, and Tsuji 2011, 73).

9. The gender of the player, both in the real and simulated realities, is marked as male. While a player is not required to enter a gender (*seibetsu*) when creating a profile, the player's character is male, as evinced by vocal cues, dress, etc. When I discussed such games (though not particularly LovePlus) with one informant, he conceded that women could play them but that they were designed for men.

10. For instance, at a *machikon* event I attended in Akihabara, the cost for a single female attendee was ¥3,200 (approximately $34) and ¥6,800 yen ($70) for a single male attendee. At the time of my reservation, about a week and a half prior to the event, all the men's slots (single, couple, and group) had sold out. However, on the day of the event there seemed to be an equal ratio of men to women in attendance.

11. At a typical *gōkon* party, participants are usually selected from among one's friends and acquaintances and limited in the number of participants, usually about ten individuals all together (five women, five men).

12. Men's Center Japan is the first, and one of the few remaining, men's rights organizations in Japan.

13. For the Cram School for Undesirable Men, see http://www.fujitakikaku.com/nanpa/.

14. Here, Yamada is referencing women's increasing participation in long-term career track employment, which provides them with a high degree of economic independence. This financial independence has translated into what anthropologist Lynne Nakano views as "higher expectations of [the women's] potential mates" (2014, 173). These include being able to communicate with a partner and his active engagement in household tasks.

REFERENCES

Ambaras, David Richard. 2006. *Bad Youth: Juvenile Delinquency and the Politics of Everyday Life in Modern Japan*. Berkeley: University of California Press.

Cook, Emma E. 2013. "Expectations of Failure: Maturity and Masculinity for Freeters in Contemporary Japan." *Social Science Japan Journal* 16 (1): 29–43.

Dobashi, Shingo, Minamida Katsuya, and Izumi Tsuji, eds. 2011. *Dijitaru media no shakaigaku: Mondai wo hakken shi, kanōsei wo saguru* [Sociology of Digital Media: Discovering Problems, Searching for Possibilities]. Tokyo: Hokuju shuppan.

Edwards, Walter D. 1982. "Something Borrowed: Wedding Cakes as Symbols of Modern Japan." *American Ethnologist* 9 (4): 699–711.

———. 1989. *Modern Japan through Its Weddings: Gender, Person, and Society in Ritual Portrayal* Stanford: Stanford University Press.

Fujita, Satoshi. 2009. *Mote baiburu* [Bible of Desirability]. Tokyo: Chūkei shuppan.

Fukuda, Akihiro, and Yūsuke Katō. 2008. "Mote shijō shugi no zankoku" [The Cruelty of the Supremacy of Desirability]. *AERA*, October 6, 25–27.

Furusawa, Katsuhiro, and Hisashi Sekiguchi. 2009. "Hinkon jidai no wakai dansei no genjitsu: Kakumeitoki himote dōmei ni kiku" [The Reality of Young People in the Age of Poverty: Listening to the Revolutionary Unpopular Men's Alliance]. *Sekushuaritī* [Sexuality] 39: 58–65.

Galbraith, Patrick W. 2009. *The Otaku Encyclopedia*. Tokyo: Kodansha.

Honda, Tōru. 2005. *Denpa otoko* [Radio-Wave Man]. Tokyo: Sansai Books.

Itō, Kimio, Minori Kimura, and Junko Kuninobu. 2011. *Joseigaku/danseigaku: Jendāron nyūmon* [Women's Studies/Men's Studies: An Introduction to Gender Studies]. Tokyo: Yūhikaku.

Katō, Shūichi. 2004. *Ren'ai kekkon ha nani wo motarashitaka? Seidōtoku to yūseishisō no hyakunenkan* [What Has Love Marriage Wrought? One Hundred Years of Sexual Morality and Eugenic Thought]. Tokyo: Chikuma shobō.

Kawahara, Yukari. 1996. "Politics, Pedagogy, and Sexuality: Sex Education in Japanese Secondary Schools." PhD dissertation, Yale University.

Lebra, Takie Sugiyama. 1984. *Japanese Women: Constraint and Fulfillment*. Honolulu: University of Hawai'i Press.

Lunsing, Wim. 2001. *Beyond Common Sense: Sexuality and Gender in Contemporary Japan*. London: Kegan Paul.

Mathews, Gordon. 2014. "Being a Man in a Straitened Japan: The View from Twenty Years Later." In *Capturing Contemporary Japan: Differentiation and Uncertainty*, edited by Satsuki Kawano, Glenda S. Roberts, and Susan Orpett Long, 60–80. Honolulu: University of Hawai'i Press.

McLelland, Mark. 2012. *Love, Sex, and Democracy in Japan during the American Occupation*. New York: Palgrave Macmillan.

Men's Center Japan, ed. 2000. *Otoko no hito no sei no hon: Samazamana sekushariti* [Book of Male Sex: Various Sexualities]. Osaka: Kaihō shuppansha.

MHLW (Ministry of Health, Labor, and Welfare). 2013. *Ministry of Health, Labor, and Welfare White Paper: Searching for Youth Consciousness*. Tokyo.

———. 2016. *Ministry of Health, Labor, and Welfare White Paper: Thinking about the Shrinking-Population Society*. Tokyo.

Miura, Atsushi. 2009. *Himote! Dansei junan no jidai* [Unpopular Men! The Age of Male Suffering]. Tokyo: Bunshun shinsho.

Miyadai, Shinji. 2013. *Zetsubō no gendai no kibō no ren'aigaku* [A Study of the Hope of Love in a Hopeless Age]. Tokyo: Chūkei shuppan.

Nakano, Lynne Y. 2014. "Single Women in Marriage and Employment Markets in Japan." In *Capturing Contemporary Japan: Differentiation and Uncertainty*, edited by Satsuki Kawano, Glenda S. Roberts, and Susan Orpett Long, 163–182. Honolulu: University of Hawai'i Press.

Ogasawara, Yuko. 1998. *Office Ladies and Salaried Men: Power, Gender, and Work in Japanese Companies*. Berkeley: University of California Press.

Plath, David W. 1963. "The Japanese Popular Christmas: Coping with Modernity." *Journal of American Folklore* 76 (3): 309–317.

Rosenberger, Nancy. 2013. *Dilemmas of Adulthood: Japanese Women and the Nuances of Long-Term Resistance*. Honolulu: University of Hawai'i Press.

Shibuya, Tomomi. 2009. *Heisei otoko juku: Nayameru danshi no tame no zenrokushō* [Cram School on Heisei Men: Six Chapters for Worried Men]. Tokyo: Chikuma shobō.

Tokuhiro, Yoko. 2010. *Marriage in Contemporary Japan*. New York: Routledge.

Ueno, Chizuko. 2010. *Onnagirai: Nippon no misojinī* [Women Hating: Japanese Misogyny]. Tokyo: Kinokuniya shoten.

Watanabe, Shin. 2007. *Chūnen dōtei: Shōshika jidai no ren'aikakusa* [Middle-Aged Male Virgins: The Love Gap in the Age of the Declining Birthrate]. Tokyo: Fusōsha.

Yamada, Masahiro. 2010. *Konkatsu genshō no shakaigaku: Nihon no haigūsha sentaku no ima* [The Sociology of the Marriage-Hunting Phenomenon: Japanese Spousal Selection Today]. Tokyo: Tōyō keizai shinpōsha.

Yamada, Masahiro, and Tōko Shirakawa. 2008. *Konkatsu jidai* [Age of Marriage Hunting]. Tokyo: Discover Twentyone.

———. 2009. *Umaku iku! Otoko no [konkatsu] senryaku: Nanimoshinai to kekkon dekinai!* [Get Great! Marriage Hunting Strategies for Men: If You Do Nothing, You Can't Get Married!]. Tokyo: PHP Kenkyūjo.

Yū and Sō. 2013. *Moteru manga* [Being Desirable Comic]. Tokyo: Shōnen gahōsha.

Gender Identity, Desire, and Intimacy

Sexual Scripts and X-Gender

S. P. F. DALE

In the paper "Is K 'trans'?" ("K-san wa 'toransu' ka"), the sociologist Sugiura Ikuko (1999) tries to unravel the gender/sexual identity of her informant, K. Sugiura contacted K as part of research on the lives of females who love females—that is, women who identify as lesbian or bisexual. As such, when Sugiura asked K about their sexuality, she was expecting the response to be an emphatic "lesbian."[1] However, K replied that they do not identify as lesbian but rather as "either transsexual or transgender." When Sugiura further probed K about their gender identity, K made it clear that they do not like their female body and that they consider themselves masculine, or rather manlike, in various ways, yet they also acknowledge themselves as "female" when asked about their sex (*seibetsu*).[2] Although K made statements such as "If only I were a man" (*otoko ni naretara naa*) and said that they might be transgender, Sugiura was reluctant to recognize them as transgender, or rather "trans" (*toransu*). Sugiura attributes her hesitance to certain inconsistencies in K's narrative, such as the fact that K refrained from forthrightly identifying as male and was unsure of what the term "sexuality" (*sekushuaritei*) meant. Sugiura defines "trans" as having "discomfort with one's body" and "discomfort with one's sex/gender"—in other words that one's biological sex and gender identity do not match—a definition that she does not see K as straightforwardly complying with (ibid., 70). Sugiura reaches the conclusion that K is "a manly girl who likes girls and is thinking about becoming a man" (ibid., 69). Through exploring K's narrative, Sugiura seeks to bring forth the ambiguity that may exist in acts of classification, both by researchers and their subjects. However, in order to render her subject legible she ends up overriding K's understanding of themselves and privileging her own understandings of terms rather than K's.

As cases such as this demonstrate, there often exists a discord when it comes to the relationship between sexuality and gender identity. This discord occurs not only between a researcher and informant over particular terms, but also as a more general discord surrounding ideas about how sexuality and gender form identity and the ways either of these characteristics can be privileged over the other. This case also exposes the difficulties a researcher experiences in clarifying the identity—in this case, gender and sexuality—of informants. In this chapter, I examine the lines drawn among gender, identity, and preferences in intimate acts. "Preferences" here refer to the type of individual to whom one is attracted, the desired roles, and how one wishes to be recognized in a relationship—for example, as a man or as a woman. Rather than drawing a neat line between gender and sexuality as Sugiura does, I explore the messy lines drawn across and between gender and sexuality to tease out the complexities that exist in how individuals understand their identity, gender, and intimacy. I base my analysis on interviews I conducted with individuals who identify as "x-gender" (*x-jendā*). X-gender is an emergent gender identity in Japan and refers to a person's identifying as neither female nor male, although how the term is understood and used is highly contingent (Dale 2012, 2014). X-gender can be likened to the term "genderqueer," which has emerged in Western Anglophone contexts, given that both terms emerged in the 1990s and have been influenced by developments in lesbian, gay, bisexual, and transgender politics. There is no recognition of x-gender as an official gender category in Japan.

In this chapter, "intimacy" is understood as "democratized" (Giddens 1993), as not relegated to the sphere of reproduction, but rather as that which covers the field of intimate individual acts, relationships, and desires. As Berlant writes, intimacy "involves an aspiration for a narrative about something shared, a story about both oneself and others that will turn out a particular way" (2000, 1). Using the concept of sexual scripting (Gagnon and Simon 1973; Simon 1996) and focusing on romantic and sexual relationships and desires, I analyze the stories that x-gender individuals articulate about their intimate desires and the wider social stories on which they rely and pull forth. As I will show, in people's understandings of themselves and their intimate desires, there is no clear-cut line demarcating gender from sexuality, but rather the two intercross and interweave, and each is implicit in the construction of the other. Individuals make use of different cultural scenarios when articulating their desires, and gender is used as a means to articulate specific desires and means of desiring.[3]

In this chapter I utilize pronouns of choice, and "they" is employed as a singular gender-neutral pronoun. In Japan, acronyms are often used in talking about transgender identities—namely, FTM (female to male); MTF (male to female); and, in the case of x-gender, FTX (female to X), MTX (male to X), and XTX (used in the case of intersex individuals or individuals who say that they have never identified as female or male and refuse to recognize a point of time when they were F or M). The transition here refers to one from assigned gender—the gender that an individual is assigned upon birth—to gender of identity, or transition in terms of official gender. "Official gender" refers to an individual's implied gender on the family registry (*koseki*), and it is possible to change one's official gender in Japan if one has Sex Reassignment Surgery (SRS) and thus meets the superficial physical requirements of what it means to be "female" or "male" (that is, have what is judged to be a "female" or "male" body).[4] How each individual understands x-gender identity, as well as personal transition, is a highly contingent matter, and the specifics of individual cases will be described below. None of the individuals examined in this chapter have changed their legal gender, although one (Honda) has modified their body and passes as male although they remain officially female.

SEXUAL SCRIPTS AND X-GENDER

Sexual scripts can be roughly divided into three types: (1) cultural scenarios; (2) interpersonal scripting; and (3) intrapsychic scripting. The first type refers to cultural contexts and expectations, and I would also include here institutional discourses, such as that of heterosexual and monogamous marriage and legitimatized sexual stories (Plummer 1995). The second type refers to interpersonal relationships and is also the means for individuals to negotiate their sexual fantasies into reality, be it with other individuals or on their own—for example, with toys or through masturbation. The third type is that of fantasy—what individuals desire but not necessarily what they experience or can necessarily attain. Although Gagnon and Simon (1973) distinguish these three levels, the types are not necessarily distinct, and they blend and play into each other. Intrapsychic and interpersonal scripting bleeds together, and cultural scenarios are forged through and with interpersonal relations and fantasies. Individuals may desire a specific sexual scenario precisely because they understand it as a "fantasy" that is not translatable into reality. Take, for example, the case of emotional attachment to fictional characters. One informant, whose case will not be examined in this chapter, said that they felt attracted to manga characters and visual-*kei* singers.[5] They understood that physical relationships with these characters and individuals were unattainable and enjoyed the dynamics of these one-sided relationships precisely because they were not reciprocal. Cultural scenarios also set the limits of what an individual is socially permitted to desire, as well as how one may go about making fantasies into reality—for example, understanding that it is legal to look at animated child pornography in Japan but not actual photographs of nude children in sexually suggestive poses. Certain cultural scenarios are especially pertinent in the accounts that will be looked at in this chapter—namely, Gender Identity Disorder (GID), discourses of gender expectations (what it means to be a "woman" or "man"), and homosexuality.

Transgender identities are not a recent phenomenon in Japan (Mitsuhashi 2008), but much of the current discourse on transgender has been shaped by the legislation of GID.[6] GID became medically recognized in Japan in 1998 and was officially translated/recognized as *sei dōitsu sei shōgai*—literally, "gender identity disability." Shortly after, in 2002, the popular television drama *Teacher Kinpachi from Class 3B* (*San nen B gumi no Kinpachi sensei*) featured a female-assigned high school student who identified as being transgender male. Since then, transgender issues are often covered on variety shows and news programs in a sympathetic manner, but almost always using the terminology of GID. Consequently, GID has become socially recognized at various levels, to the extent that now a range of non-gender-normative or non-heteronormative identities has been subsumed by it. For example, if a story pertaining to transgender or gender variance were to be taken up by a news source in Japan, the term most likely to be used would be GID.

The prevalence of GID discourse initiated in the late 1990s has affected not only the framing of transgender identities, but sexuality as well. Although GID gives individuals the possibility to "change" gender, it does so by enforcing a strictly male/female gender dichotomy. In order to change gender officially an individual must conform to the social expectations of that gender physically (by undergoing surgery), mentally (by "feeling" like a "man" or "woman"), and, most important, visibly (to be judged "male" or "female" by the doctor).

Halberstam has written that "the invention of transsexuality as a medical category has partly drained gender variance out of the category of homosexuality and located gender variance very specifically within the category of transsexuality" (1998, 143–144). Given the dominance of the GID discourse in Japan, I found that most individuals with whom I conducted research, and who identified as x-gender, framed their identity as an aspect of GID or transgender and very rarely associated it with

S. P. F. Dale

homosexuality. One may postulate, however, that prior to the rise of popular discourse about GID, similar ways of being may have been framed differently, and Stein (2010) has made similar conjectures in her research on changing lesbian identities in the United States. GID has become more socially recognized than homosexuality in Japan, and this has shaped personal formulations of sexuality and identity pertaining to gender.

As non-normative gender presentations have become increasingly associated with transgender identities, homosexuality has become increasingly associated with gender normativity. Moriyama (2012) has written about how gay publications in Japan tend to support a specific image of a masculine, gender-normative gay man, thus leading to the exclusion of individuals who do not fit this model. More generally, homosexual relationships also tend to be considered as a desire for sameness and equality—individuals with a similar appearance, having the same desires, and desiring to be treated the same way. The issue of sameness and supposed desire for sameness is one that has long plagued discourses of homosexuality, and although it has been shown to be untrue (Dunne 1999), it continues to persevere.

In contrast to the image of gender normativity outlined above, homosexuality as presented in popular media is often in the form of a flamboyant, cross-dressing queen, the most prominent example being Matsuko Derakkusu, a *josōka* who is regularly on television.[7] Television personalities such as Matsuko Derakkusu, Haruna Ai, and Ikko are collectively known as *onē kyara*, a broad category that encompasses transgender women (individuals assigned male who identify as female), drag queens, and gay men who use queen's speech.[8] These personalities often appear on light-hearted variety shows and in some cases are treated as the butt of jokes. Haruna Ai, for example, is often called out for being a "man," although she identifies as female and is officially female given that she has had SRS and legally changed her gender. Distinctions are not often made among the individuals who fall into the category of *onē kyara*, thus confusing public understandings of transgender and homosexuality. Such confusion creates and sustains the idea of only two polarizing types of male homosexuality—the gender normative, often hyper-masculine male presented in gay magazines and spaces and the flamboyant, hyper-feminine drag queen. Female homosexuality, on the other hand, is hardly presented on television and remains largely invisible in the public sphere. Mitsuhashi (2003) describes a transgender boom that occurred in the 1980s, before the recognition of GID, including extensive coverage of what was then termed "Mr. Lady" (male assigned, feminine presentation) and "Miss Dandy" (female-assigned, masculine presentation) individuals. When I spoke with people now in their forties, many remembered these shows and described them as eye opening. Despite the Miss Dandy characters of the 1980s, in the current moment lesbian desire remains largely hidden from the public gaze, although it is present in the sphere of manga.

Same-sex sexuality and romantic liaisons have become a popular topic for manga and a recognized genre in themselves. Manga featuring female-female intimate relations are known as girls' love (GL) or *yuri* comics. More than GL, however, it is boys' love (BL; also known as *yaoi* or *shōnen ai*) manga that have really taken off. Most bookstores have a marked section for BL manga, and there is a plethora of titles, as well as fan-produced amateur manga (*dōjinshi*), often featuring male-male couplings from popular manga. Although BL and GL manga depict same-sex relationships, there have been criticisms that GL manga are created for the heterosexual male readership and BL manga for a heterosexual female audience. Hori (2013) and Welker (2011) point out that BL manga in particular have been criticized by gay men for painting unrealistic portraits of their lives and objectifying them for the consumption of heterosexual women. No matter how realistic GL or BL manga may be or who the intended readership may be, these manga have shaped how individuals of various genders and sexualities have come to imagine intimate relations, as well as understand their own desires.

X-gender has emerged in tandem with these discourses. What it means to identify as x-gender depends on how individuals came into contact with the term, as well as their situationality (age, gender, social context) and the cultural scenarios of which they are aware and privy to. Although the individuals examined in this chapter all identify as x-gender, this identity means different things for each individual. Gagnon and Simon (1973) emphasize the importance of individual situationality with regard to sexuality, and as Simon writes, "Persons can share a nearly identical portfolio of roles without sharing similar commitments or coming to them from similar origins" (1996, 6).

The fieldwork and interviews on which this chapter is based were part of a larger research project that examines how x-gender identity is constructed and understood (Dale 2014). Interviews were conducted with a total of twenty-five individuals who self-identified as x-gender; interviews were conducted in the Kanto and Kansai regions, as well as Nagoya and Kita-Kyushu. Most of my informants were found through the Internet, where I made use of websites such as Mixi and Twitter to talk about my research and also ran a blog with information about my work.[9] Some informants were also found through snowball references. All interviews were conducted in Japanese, and repeat interviews were conducted a year to two years following the first interview. I continue to maintain contact with most of my informants and meet up with some of them in social contexts as well. In this chapter I will focus on five individuals. These individuals were chosen not because they are representative of x-gender overall, but rather for how they demonstrate the differences that exist in how individuals understand their identity and sexuality. They were also chosen for the similarities that run through them: all of these individuals are attracted to what may be termed the "same sex" in terms of assigned gender or gender identity. This chapter therefore should not be taken as representative of the sexuality of x-gender individuals, but rather as a case study and examination of how gender, intimacy, and identity can intersect as desire and identity are articulated. It should also be noted that intimacy and desire are not the only factors that lead an individual to identify as x-gender. Other aspects such as the body and social environment are relevant but will not be explicitly examined in this chapter.

GIRLS' LOVE, BOYS' LOVE

Yamazaki is in their late thirties, female-assigned, and female-bodied. They identify as FTMTX (female to male to X). In their case this refers to identifying as male but not desiring to physically change their body. Because it is not possible to change one's official gender without undergoing SRS in Japan, their official gender will remain female but their identity is male. They recognize themselves as x-gender given the incongruence between their official female gender and male identity, an incongruence that they believe distinguishes them from FTM, transgender men. Although not all transgender men desire to undergo SRS and change their official gender, at the time of our first interview Yamazaki believed that identifying as specifically FTM indicated a desire to eventually undergo SRS. Suffixing FTX to FTM was a means for them to assert that they did not desire bodily modification.[10]

For Yamazaki, the key to thinking about their gender identity came through their interest in BL comics. Yamazaki started reading BL comics in high school and was also an avid reader when they entered university during the period of the "gay boom" in the 1990s. This led them to read well-known gay writer Fushimi Noriaki's book *Queer Paradise* (*Kuia paradaisu*), which was displayed prominently in a bookstore. At the time, Yamazaki did not question their identity as a woman and to some extent regarded themselves as *okoge*—literally, "burnt rice," but slang referring to a woman who enjoys the company of gay men, although in their case this affiliation was primarily fictional and obtained through reading manga.

However, Yamazaki also says that they felt a certain discomfort with the category of "woman" and that something felt "unnatural" (*fushizen*) about being recognized as a woman. Through Fushimi's text, Yamazaki learned about the concept of transgender through an interview with Torai Masae, a famous FTM writer who also served as the model for the transgender student in the television program *Teacher Kinpachi from Class 3B*. Torai's account instantly resonated with them, and from that point on Yamazaki began to identify as FTM (and later FTX) and, given their romantic and sexual interest in men, as gay.

It was through reading these BL manga that Yamazaki eventually came to the realization that they desired what was depicted in the comics—that is, male-male romance. As such, although attracted to men and physically being on the female spectrum, Yamazaki does not consider themselves heterosexual but gay. However, they have as yet had no experience with romantic and sexual relationships and also describe difficulty that they have been having with regard to finding an appropriate partner:

> I realized that I was FTM and gay around the time I was about to graduate from university. During that period there was a man I liked, and we got along well as friends. I told this person about myself, and he accepted me, but he said, "I like women so that means I can't be attracted to you." After that, the people I've come to like all tend to be straight, so it's impossible, or rather, if there was a chance that I went out with someone, that person would probably like women, so I'd have to go out with him as a hetero-sexual woman. However, for me the feeling would be of going out with the same sex, so it'd be incredibly difficult. Because of the shape of my body, if I were to become more male, it'd be different, but with my body female as it is. . . . A heterosexual relationship would not be favorable, but I only fall for heterosexual individuals, so it would be doomed to become a heterosexual relationship. I just can't get over this hurdle.

Yamazaki experiences a discordance among the object of their desire (straight men), their sexuality (gay), and their body (female)—all of which make it difficult for them to find an appropriate partner. To an extent it seems that Yamazaki has given up on finding a partner, and they also note that although they would not consider themselves asexual, they have a low sex drive and as such do not feel any urgent need to get into a relationship.

Despite being female-bodied and attracted primarily to heterosexual men, Yamazaki identifies as gay because of the imagined dynamics of a same-sex relationship that they have idealized through reading manga. For them, the possibility of actualizing their ideal relationship is one they regard as being close to nil, but they do not see the need to actualize their desires. For them, there is a distinct difference between being treated as a man and being treated as a woman in a relationship, and it is for this reason that they desire to be treated as a man by prospective partners. Being recognized as a woman would call forth the social expectations that come with being a woman in a heterosexual relationship—expectations pertaining to gender roles, performance, and how one's body is handled and treated in intimate acts.

Welker has written about how lesbian desires can be articulated through BL manga. Male homosexuality in these cases serves as an imaginary tool to help women imagine "unliveable desires" (2011, 222). For Yamazaki, the situation certainly seems very similar, although in their case they rule out the fulfillment of this intimate desire not only because they are not male-bodied, but also because they tend to desire straight men.

For Yamazaki, manga served as a means of identification and provided them with a cultural scenario to latch onto and aspire toward. For other people, it is not only BL manga that serve as a cultural scenario, but GL manga as well. Nishimura, who is male-assigned, has been in a long-term relationship with a female-assigned and female-bodied individual. They say that the dynamics of their relationship are not what one would call "heterosexual," although they may appear that way given that they are a male-female couple. Rather, Nishimura describes their relationship as one where gender roles are not felt and also as resembling a lesbian relationship. For them, gender roles refer to expectations about what a woman or man should do in a relationship. Responsibilities in their relationship were not dependent upon gender but rather negotiated with their partner, akin to the negotiated equality in lesbian relationships that Dunne (1999) describes. Nishimura is also an avid manga reader and especially fond of GL manga. They say that they find themselves identifying with the relationships depicted in these manga and that they have sex with their partner "like lesbians." They describe their partner as the more aggressive one during sex and say that the sex that they have is not the same as heterosexual, penetrative sex.

For both Yamazaki and Nishimura, "heterosexual" and "homosexual" specify not only sexual orientation—the gender of the individual to whom one is attracted—but also a specific relationship dynamic. Given their assigned gender, as well as that of the individuals to whom they are attracted, one may be tempted to label them "heterosexual." However, the scenarios provided them by GL and BL manga have given them a means to reimagine their intimate relationships and desires, as well as their own identity. They can evade, or perhaps overcome, the discourse of heterosexuality and its implied social expectations and articulate their sexuality and desires in terms that go against the expectations of their assigned gender. Manga have provided them with modes of desiring and desires that would otherwise be unavailable to them.

NOT "GAY"

Kojima is in their mid-twenties, is male-assigned and male-bodied, and identifies as MTX. Kojima says that although they recognize themselves as belonging to the social category of "male," they have never identified as a specific gender. After thinking they had GID from middle school until high school, they began thinking they might be gay but felt somehow different from the masculine images and discourses of gay men with which they were familiar. They say that although they could identify with gay men in online discussions of sexuality, there was some aspect of gay identity with which they just could not identify, that did not match their "heart" or who they were (*jibun no kokoro ja nai*).

Kojima regularly turns to the Internet for information and found out about x-gender through browsing various websites. It was a term that they gradually got hooked onto, and they find it apt for describing themselves—not quite male, not quite female, and *chūsei* (loosely translatable as "androgynous"). Kojima says that although they do not identify as male, they feel no specific discomfort toward their body and thus distinguish themselves from individuals who identify as having GID.

Although attracted to men, Kojima does not think of themselves as "gay." Owing to their male body and their attraction to males, they find it necessary to distinguish themselves from the gay male—an identity that would otherwise be automatically bestowed upon them. Kojima says that they have always been aware of a femininity (*joseisei*) about themselves that distinguishes them from men. However, they are also aware that because of their appearance, they are likely to be judged as gay by others around them, and this is something that they say they intensely dislike—to be taken as a stereotype. In our most recent conversation, Kojima said that following "heterosexuality," the category of "gay" has become the most socially recognized category, and because of this it is rife with preconceptions. They do not desire to be taken as or judged as a gay stereotype. Although they have not yet engaged in a sexual or committed relationship, in an ideal relationship they desire gender roles and want to be treated "as a woman." As they say, "When it comes to love, I want to have the role of the woman; I want to be dated as a woman" (*renai ni kan-shite wa josei no yakuwari wo shitai, josei to shite tsukiatte hoshī*). When asked what it means to be a woman in this context, Kojima referenced having clear gender roles in a relationship—as man and woman—whereby the woman is taken care of and coddled. This image of what it means to be a woman in a (presumably heterosexual) relationship is one that might seem antiquated and off-putting but also one that runs strong in popular discourses, especially where the ideal male is expected to act as a "gentleman" and the woman is treated as the "weaker sex" in need of protection. It is this desire of Kojima's that differentiates them from "gay men," whom they presume desire as, and want to be treated as, "men." Kojima desires gender difference in their relationship, and for them homosexuality is associated with sameness. Identifying as x-gender is therefore a means for them to articulate their desires and differentiate themselves from their image of male homosexuality. It is a means for them to articulate an aspiratory narrative, not just of anticipation, but also of rejection—a desire for gender roles and a negation of homosexual sameness.

For Kojima, it is the juxtaposition among their assigned gender (male), whom they desire (men), and how they desire to be treated in intimate relationships (as a woman) that leads to the formulation of their x-gender identity. This identity helps them to distinguish their desires from what they understand to be homosexuality, as well as to describe their identity in terms of being transgender and heterosexual rather than homosexual. Unlike the United States and Europe, where transgender rights are lagging behind lesbian and gay rights, in Japan it may be said that the opposite is the case, and there is greater recognition of transgender individuals (albeit through the pathological discourse of GID) and efforts to present such individuals in a sympathetic manner. Kojima also seems conscious of this greater recognition in their conversations with me, and at one point stated that they may be "homophobic" (*homofobia*). An approach such as Sugiura's, outlined at the start of this chapter, might argue that Kojima is "actually" gay. However, this is not the point I wish to make. Rather, the emergence of different cultural scenarios to talk about intimacy and gender has made it possible for Kojima to describe their identity and sexuality without resorting to the discourse of homosexuality. The possibility and discourse of x-gender identity has given them a way to frame their desire without being "gay." Although their desires dislodge them from the category of heterosexual male, they can still cling to the category of heterosexuality through claiming identity as x-gender, hence also avoiding the stigma of being gay.

WITH THE EYES OF A MAN

Honda is in their mid-forties. They are female-assigned and started taking testosterone close to fifteen years ago, when they were in their late twenties. They pass and get read as male in most social contexts and acknowledge that they are unable to access certain female spaces—for example, female toilets. Honda has not had any surgical modifications, and other than the influence of testosterone injections, their body remains physically female. They describe their clothed physical appearance as being masculine but their nude self as undeniably possessing a female body.

Honda has been intimately involved with women since they were in high school, an environment where they were immersed in relationships with fellow female students. Honda's teachers even knew about their relationships and were fully supportive. Honda presently lives with their female partner and their partner's children from a previous relationship.

Honda distinguishes themselves from lesbians as well as heterosexual men in how they feel toward and treat their partner: "When I look at women, it's because I'm not a woman. It's not that I want to be male-gendered, but rather that I desire with male-gendered emotions." Since starting on testosterone, Honda says that the changes in their body have affected not only their physical appearance, but also their confidence and comfort toward their body. They say that prior to taking testosterone, they were cautious of their body and hesitant about how it was seen and handled. After starting testosterone, they say that they have become uninhibited with their partner during sex and enjoy touching as well as being touched. They also say that once they started testosterone, they experienced a surge in their sex drive and in fact are pleased when their partner desires to sexually satisfy them. This confidence was spurred by the security they now feel in their identity—afforded through hormones—a confidence that they were not a woman, and even if they used their "female" body parts in intimate acts, this would not make them a woman either. They distinguish themselves from women through the act of "looking" at women—not as a woman but as a man. Yet they are not a man because they do not desire to become one. As such, they emphasize their gender identity through their sexuality: gender is in the (sexual) gaze.

Hara is around the same age as Honda and is also female-assigned. Up until the present they have been in only one relationship, albeit one that lasted for ten years. It was during high school that they first realized that they were attracted to women, and their first girlfriend was a classmate of theirs. Hara says that during this period, when the discourses of GID and transgender were not yet prevalent, they had not thought much about their specific gender identity but did not consider themselves to be a "woman." When engaging in sexual activity with their girlfriend, they never disrobed, and only their girlfriend would be nude. As Hara says, they do not like being touched, and in their sexual relationship with their partner they took on an exclusively active role. It is also in this regard that they distinguish themselves from being lesbian: "When I think of lesbians, I think of two naked women embracing each other, taking turns pleasuring as well as being pleasured by each other. I don't want my body to be seen, to be touched; I just don't like it. That's why I'm different from lesbians [rezu]."

Hara also says that it is because of this discomfort with their body that they are envious of FTM individuals who have had their breasts removed: they are able to embrace their partners without a shirt on and while nude themselves. For Hara, revealing their body to their partner is unfathomable. Like Honda, Hara also defines their gender identity through their sexual preferences, in their case distinguishing themselves from lesbians because of their desire to not be touched and not be nude (with a female body) with their partner. For Hara being lesbian equates to an image of two naked female bodies—both touching and being touched. Their disaffiliation with this image also prevents them from latching onto a lesbian identity.

For both Honda and Hara, being a lesbian signifies a specific mode of desiring—that is, as a "woman" and desiring to be treated in such a way. They possessed certain expectations as to how a lesbian woman desires others and desires to be touched, and their inability to abide by these expectations prevents them from affiliating with this identity. Unlike Yamazaki and Nishimura, who aspire toward and identify with lesbian and gay relations, for Honda, Hara, and Kojima the issue is one of negating and rejecting the homosexual identities that would otherwise be automatically bestowed upon them given their assigned gender and preferences.

GENDER, DESIRE, AND INTIMACY

The accounts explored here all deal with preference for one specific gender, and although in some cases individuals are attracted to the same gender, they describe their desire in different ways. The individuals presented also grew up in different generations, different regions, and different situations, and thus the cultural scenarios with which they found themselves grappling are various. Kojima, for example, was in high school as the concept of GID became known at a popular level and has described themselves as having a period of identifying as GID prior to taking on an x-gender identity. For them the concept of homosexuality came secondary to that of gender identity. At the same time, owing to their lack of contact with queer communities, they have also relied on Internet stories to forge their opinion of what transgender, as well as homosexuality, means.

Cultural scenarios pertaining to GID, homosexuality, and gender expectations have been conveyed to individuals through media such as television, manga, and the Internet, as well as through interactions with people around them. As Simon (1996) has emphasized, in this "postmodern age," as he terms it, there is an increasing amount of choice that an individual has with regard to identity, and this goes for one's sexuality as well. Although individuals may not necessarily view their sexuality as a choice, it is nevertheless something that they shape through their interactions with others, as well as with the materials and discourses around them.

The influence of cultural scenarios on intrapsychic scripting can be seen in how individuals who have not yet had sexual experience (with others) have set ideas of their ideal relationship, as well as specific fantasies and desires. Yamazaki and Kojima, for example, were very specific about what they wanted in a relationship, although neither of them had had any relationship or sexual experience. Their desires were to some extent shaped by ideals gained from reading manga, as well as from the cultural expectations of gender roles. Cultural scenarios not only influenced personal sexual desires, but also shaped how the individual interpreted those desires.

The desire for a specific (gendered) relationship dynamic plays a large role in how all of these individuals conceive of themselves—being "a woman" in a relationship, liking a woman "as a man," having sex "like lesbians." Same-sex relationships are often conceived as involving a sense of equality or sameness in terms of roles, and desiring or not desiring such roles serves to orientate individuals toward or away from the terms that denote them. The desire for difference in sexual roles is understood as "heterosexual," or at least as differing from "homosexual" desire. For these individuals, it is clear that being "gay" or "lesbian" is more than a matter of sexual orientation or preferences. Being "gay" or "lesbian" is understood as a specific mode of intimate desiring and of being desired. Desires are very much gendered, in terms not only of the gender to which one is attracted, but also how one experiences these desires and desires to be treated. These accounts also demonstrate a reinforcement of stereotypical gender roles and sexuality and reveal the assumptions behind what it means to desire as and be treated as a specific gender or a person with a specific sexual identity. X-gender provides individuals a discourse and a means to override the expectations associated with their assigned gender or the sexuality that would otherwise be bestowed upon them. Through identifying as x-gender, individuals are, in a sense, free to desire, largely because x-gender is a relatively new concept and not currently burdened by any expectations, although my recent research (Dale 2014) shows that this is changing. They are, however, also restricted in the fulfillment of these desires given the limitations imposed upon them by their bodies or the impossibility of living up to a cultural scenario given their identity and desires.

Gender identity is not formed in personal isolation but rather through negotiation—through interpersonal relationships and how each individual desires to be recognized in intimate relations with others. Intimacy and interpersonal relationships are intrinsic to how individuals understand themselves, be this in the cultural scenarios of intimacy provided by manga or intimate relations and how one desires to be treated. Preferences in intimate relationships play into how individuals understand themselves, and their gender.

At the start of this chapter I briefly discussed Sugiura's attempt to neatly assuage and classify the gender identity and sexuality of her informant, K. My chapter has taken a different approach from hers, and rather than delineating, I have sought to mess up—to explore the complexities that exist in sexuality, gender, and the formation of identity. This effort has also involved an examination of the sexual scripts—both social and personal—that individuals use in articulating their intimate desires and identity. Cultural scenarios are not fixed constructs but rather change through time and context, as do identities. In the construction of identity, individuals "select images to emulate or reject" (Stein 2007), and through this selection articulate a desire that is, one may say, on one's own terms.

NOTES

1. As will be explained below, "their," "they," and "themselves" refer not to multiple people but serve as gender-neutral pronouns to describe K.

2. Sugiura uses the term *seibetsu*, which is translatable as "sex" or "gender." There is no distinction between the biological and social for this term as there is for the English sex/gender.

3. There are, of course, other methods of examining desire as well, such as through storytelling (Plummer 1995) or as fields (Green 2014). Sexual scripting is used in order to examine an individual's desire in connection with the larger social context in which it takes place and with recourse to social discourses pertaining to sexuality and gender.

4. The family registry does not directly state sex, but rather gendered relationships—wife, father, daughter, and so on.

5. Visual-*kei* refers to a genre of music that has an emphasis on visual display and often includes elements of cross-dressing and androgyny. For more, see McLeod (2013).

6. It should be noted that the medicalization of transgender identities and bodies is not unique to Japan but rather common in most postindustrial countries, such as the United States.

7. *Josō* refers to dressing as a woman, and *josōka* usually refers to a male dressing as a woman, although it may also refer to a woman doing so.

8. Queen's speech refers to *onē kotoba* (literally, big sister's speech). Although the language used is similar to what is known as women's speech, queen's speech is differentiated in how it is used. Rather than embodying politeness (an attribute for which women's speech is known), queen's speech is scathing and sarcastic. For more, see Maree (2013).

9. In most cases informants contacted me to be interviewed after reading my posts on Mixi and Twitter, as well as my blog.

10. During our second interview, held a year and a half after we first met, Yamazaki said that they no longer use FTX to refer to themselves, as the term had taken on a different connotation from when they first started using it. They now use only FTM. This shift demonstrates the broader fluidity of these terms and their use.

REFERENCES

Berlant, Lauren. 2000. "Intimacy: A Special Issue." In *Intimacy*, edited by Lauren Berlant, 1–8. Chicago: University of Chicago Press.

Dale, S. P. F. 2012. "An Introduction to X-Jendā." *Intersections: Gender and Sexuality in Asia and the Pacific* 31. http://intersections.anu.edu.au/issue31/dale.htm.

———. 2014. "Mapping X: The Micropolitics of Gender and Identity in a Japanese Context." PhD dissertation, Sophia University.

Dunne, Gillian A. 1999. "A Passion for 'Sameness'? Sexuality and Gender Accountability." In *The New Family?*, edited by Elizabeth B. Silva and Carol Smart, 66–82. London: Sage.

Gagnon, John H., and William Simon. 1973. *Sexual Conduct: The Social Sources of Human Sexuality*. Chicago: Aldine Publishing.

Giddens, Anthony. 1993. *The Transformation of Intimacy: Sexuality, Love and Eroticism in Modern Societies*. Cambridge: Polity Press.

Green, Adam Isaiah, ed. 2014. *Sexual Fields: Toward a Sociology of Collective Sexual Life*. Chicago: University of Chicago Press.

Halberstam, Judith. 1998. *Female Masculinity*. Durham, NC: Duke University Press.

Hori, Akiko. 2013. "On the Response (or Lack Thereof) of Japanese Fans to Criticism That *yaoi* Is Antigay Discrimination." *Transformative Works and Culture* 12. doi: 10.3983/twc.2013.0463.

Maree, Claire. 2013. *Onē kotoba ron* [Theories of Queen's Speech]. Tokyo: Seidosha.

McLeod, Ken. 2013. "Visual Kei: Hybridity and Gender in Japanese Popular Culture." *Young* 21 (4): 309–325.

Mitsuhashi, Junko. 2003. "Nihon toransujendā ryakushi (sono 2): Sengo no shintenkan" [A Brief History of Transgender in Japan (Part 2): Developments after the War]. In *Toransujendarizumu sengen* [Declaration of Transgenderism], edited by Izumi Yonezawa, 104–118. Tokyo: Shakai hihyō sha.

———. 2008. *Josō to nihonjin* [Female Crossdressing and the Japanese]. Tokyo: Kodansha.

Moriyama, Noritaka. 2012. *"Gei komyunitei" no shakaigaku* [Sociology of "Gay Communities"]. Tokyo: Keisoshobo.

Plummer, Kenneth. 1995. *Telling Sexual Stories: Power, Change, and Social Worlds*. London: Routledge.

Simon, William. 1996. *Postmodern Sexualities*. London: Routledge.

Stein, Arlein. 2007. "Shapes of Desire." In *The Sexual Self: The Construction of Sexual Scripts*, edited by Michael Kimmel, 93–104. Nashville, TN: Vanderbilt University Press.

———. 2010. "The Incredible Shrinking Lesbian World and Other Queer Conundra." *Sexualities* 13 (1): 21–32.

Sugiura, Ikuko. 1999. "K san ha 'toransu' ka—seiteki aidenteitei no rikai kanōsei. [Is K "Trans"?—Understanding Sexual Identity]. *Kaihōshakai kenkyū* 13 (March): 53–73.

Welker, James. 2011. "Flower Tribes and Female Desire: Complicating Early Female Consumption of Male Homosexuality in Shōjo Manga." *Mechademia* 6:211–228.

CHAPTER 10

Beyond Blood Ties

Intimate Kinships in Japanese
Foster and Adoptive Care

KATHRYN E. GOLDFARB

In a television broadcast from 2010 featuring a family with six unrelated foster children, the narrator notes the bonds of the heart or spirit (*kokoro no kizuna*) among these family members (NNN News 2010). The foster father tells the camera, "Eating together, sleeping together, you become parent and child; you become siblings. I always say even if your last names are different, you're still siblings. It's interesting; it's fun, that transformation." The narrator closes dramatically: "Even without a blood tie (*chi no tsunagari nakutemo*), this big foster family is energetic!" The dramatic tension of the broadcast hinges on the assumption that at first glance, this foster family looks like a "normal" large and lively family, while the surprising revelation is that the children are not related to each other or to their foster parents by blood. Kinship connections have emerged over time through shared food and contact. The viewer is left impressed with possibilities for alternative intimacies.

Intimacy has become the prevailing trope for public discourses surrounding foster care and adoption in Japan, focused particularly on the ways that caregiving and mundane everyday practices—like eating, sleeping, and bathing together—can create kinship ties where there were previously none. This focus on intimately created kinship is itself a modern rhetoric for understanding relatedness that articulates with twentieth- and twenty-first-century ideals of the nuclear family bound by love (McKinnon and Cannell 2013). But intimacy can also be a measure of exclusion: in Japan, non-blood-related children are sometimes seen as irredeemably "other," a type of difference articulated by references to "the child of a stranger" (*tanin no ko*) who is impossible to love. A stigma surrounds children who become wards of the state when their own intimate biological kinship relationships are seen to have failed them.

In contemporary Japan, people often claim that "blood ties" are central to Japanese kinship. In this chapter, I argue that the very notion of blood ties cannot be understood outside of culturally and historically specific understandings of intimacy. Rather than indicating exclusively biogenetic relatedness, discourses surrounding blood ties in Japan point to culturally legible ways of articulating intimate connections. These discourses are part of broader conceptual frameworks through which people understand what it takes to be considered "family." Claims that Japanese people value blood ties in families reflect a relatively recent and historically specific narrowing of family ideologies, which focus increasingly on genetic relatedness. These transformations also speak to broader concerns regarding kinship practices among people who are not socially recognized as "family," possibilities for intimacy with unrelated children, and stigma against children of unknown origin. While I argue, on the one hand, that blood ties themselves are conceptualized as a type of intimacy, in this chapter I also show how discourses surrounding blood ties reflect anxieties that intimate ties will fail to generate durable family bonds.

This analysis is based on ethnographic research in Japan from 2008 through the present. Seeking to understand the interactions among Japanese family ideologies, kinship practices, child welfare systems, and well-being, from 2009 to 2010 I conducted participant observation at a child welfare institution (a "children's home") and a self-help organization for young people who had grown up in child welfare institutions (both located in the Kanto region) and with members of a similar self-help group in the Kansai region.[1] I spent extensive time with foster families in both areas and interviewed foster parents, adoptive parents, and people who had undertaken infertility treatments in order to conceive. My objective was to understand how people conceptualized their own family desires and practices vis-à-vis what they framed as "normal" Japanese family ideals, and I explored how ideologies about "Japaneseness" were mobilized to explain contemporary welfare systems and practices.

JAPANESE CHILD WELFARE AND ITS "CULTURAL" UNDERPINNING?

As of 2016 of the 45,000 children who were wards of the Japanese state because their parents could not—for some reason or another—take care of them, over 30,000 were cared for in child welfare institutions, which range in size; the smaller institutions house around 30 children, and the largest around 150 children.[2] Additionally, almost 3,000 newborns, infants, and toddlers were cared for in child welfare institutions for babies (*nyūjiin*).[3] In contrast to large-scale welfare institutions, family-based or small-scale care serves a minority of children; a Japanese government report records 4,973 children placed in family foster care (11 percent of children in state care), with 1,261 more children living in "family homes," houses with a maximum of 6 foster children that are run either by registered foster parents and a hired staff member or by child welfare institution staff members (MHLW 2017, 1). Many children spend a large portion of their young lives in institutions; the average stay for children in state care is almost five years (MHLW 2014). Under increasing international pressure from the United Nations, the Japanese Ministry of Health, Labor, and Welfare has stated an objective to increase its rate of foster care placements to 30 percent by the year 2029 (MHLW 2010; UNCRC 2010).[4] The family foster care placement rate in Japan remains significantly lower than in many other "developed" nations, with Korea registering around 44 percent; Germany and Italy, around 50 percent; England, the United States, and Hong Kong, above 70 percent; and Australia, over 93 percent (MHLW 2014, 23).

Although the Japanese government is working to increase family-based child welfare provisioning, it has not promoted adoption as a possible child welfare intervention. However, prospective foster parents have the option to register with the intent to adopt, a possibility if the child's birth parents relinquish parental rights. Japan's child guidance center employees generally do not pressure birth parents to relinquish their rights, so it is common in Japan for people hoping to adopt to register, instead, as *foster parents caring for children* unavailable for adoption and who then stay in foster care long-term (Goldfarb 2013; Bamba and Haight 2011). Although the legal frameworks are entirely different, adoption and fostering are often spoken of as similar for this reason; foster parents often enter the process resolved to fully incorporate an unrelated child into their family.

People in Japan tend to cite Japanese cultural preferences for blood ties as an explanation for why fostering and the adoption of an unrelated child are still relatively uncommon. I have argued elsewhere that these cultural explanations are insufficient, rooted as they are in ahistorical and timeless qualities of Japanese culture; they fail to recognize that cultural trends are historical products and that Japanese family ideologies have changed over time. Cultural explanations tend to neglect the capacity of policies and practices to shift and instead conflate current child welfare practice on the ground with an intransigent notion of timeless culture as a barrier to change (Goldfarb 2012, 2013).

Certainly, systemic transformation is possible, and changes due to the efforts of local actors are in clear evidence; some areas in Japan with dedicated local government intervention in child welfare practices have seen significant increases in foster care placements, most strikingly Shizuoka City, where foster care rates increased from 14.9 percent in 2005 to 46.9 percent in 2015 (MHLW 2017, 16). It is also worth noting that many more households are registered as foster parents than are currently caring for a foster child; across Japan in 2016, 8,445 households were registered as foster parents without the intent to adopt, with only 3,043 households actually caring for a child; 3,450 households registered with the intent to adopt, with only 233 households currently caring for a child (MHLW 2017, 1). There are thus many more people who hope to foster and adopt than have the opportunity to do so, a situation that is due in large part to systemic privileging of biological parents' rights, on the level of both social work practice and family court decisions (Tsuzaki 2009).

Rather than focusing naively on Japanese culture as an explanation for child welfare practices, I attend here to the notion of "blood ties" as a culturally and historically specific idiom for expressing the possibilities for connection, ties that simultaneously mark boundaries of exclusion and stigma. Contemporary use of the concept of "blood ties" must be understood in historical perspective, alongside social policy transformations and in conversation with common discourses about what makes "family." It is necessary to attend to daily intimate practices that are understood, in Japan, to constitute family—regardless of biogenetic relatedness.

WHY "BLOOD TIES" HAVE COME TO MATTER IN JAPAN

Despite ubiquitous public discourses regarding the importance of "blood ties" to Japanese culture, the valorization of blood ties within Japanese families is relatively recent. Before the Meiji Restoration of 1868 and the creation of the *koseki* system of family registration, family practices across Japan were extremely diverse. Even after the Meiji Restoration, when the extended family form of the *ie* became the basic, legally recognized unit of society, scholars of Japanese family practices have long noted the "flexible" ways families incorporated outsiders as a strategy to perpetuate the *ie*.[5] While kinship practices in China and Korea are often described as focused on maintaining the patriline, the *ie* system in Japan is not historically oriented around upholding a literal male bloodline. Indeed, "blood ties" have not historically been a significant metric for accounting for membership in a Japanese *ie*. Although primogeniture (inheritance passing to the eldest male child) is one characteristic of historical *ie* ideology, in practice, inheritors might be younger sons, a daughter, a daughter's husband, the child of an extended family member, an unrelated couple, employees, or even (in the past) servants or slaves. Adoption of such people has long been a central characteristic of Japanese *ie* maintenance (Bachnik 1983; Hozumi 2004; Nakane 1967; Norbeck and Befu 1958).

The degree to which *ie*-oriented mentality persists today is a topic for debate, although my own research accords with the view that the *ie*—at least the inherited family name and the need to care for ancestral graves—remains important to many people, particularly but not only in rural areas of Japan. This is in spite of the post–World War II American occupation's reframing of the Japanese constitution, in which the *ie* system's legal grounding was abolished and individuals, not families, were made the basic social unit (Paulson 1984).[6] The type of adoption long associated with *ie* maintenance ("regular adoption," or *futsū yōshi engumi*) remains widespread; in such adoptions children or adults are incorporated into a family registry without cutting legal ties with the family of origin.[7] However, the adoption of young children who are unaffiliated with the family is much less common. Only in 1988 was a legal system created to adopt children "for the sake of the child," rather than for the sake of family continuity; in such an adoption the child's ties are legally cut with the family of origin, and he or she is entered into the family registry as the "actual child" (*jisshi*) of the adoptive parents (Hayes and Habu 2006).[8] This type of adoption, called "special adoption" (*tokubetsu yōshi engumi*), is marked as non-normative in its very legal designation.

At their base, "regular" and "special" adoptions are entirely different practices. Adopting a known adult or a relative's child might make sense to ensure family continuity. However, the practice of making a young child from an unknown family into kin strikes many Japanese people as strange. People tend to consider it risky—given that the child's family history is often unknown—and pathetic (*kawaisō*), both because the adopting couple is perceived as desperate to raise a child and because the child has been abandoned by his or her family of origin. An old adage, "You don't know from which horse the bone comes" (*Doko no uma no hone ka wakaranai*), is known to many of my interlocutors and is sometimes cited in order to explain distaste for the adoption of a child from an unknown family.[9] Most centrally, my research subjects—many of them adoptive parents themselves—told me time and again that the incorporation of non-kin into families is fundamentally an unfamiliar practice to Japanese people, who value blood ties in families.

When and how, specifically, did blood ties become commonly cited as the basis for Japanese kinship? Research on the transformations of Japanese family practices often points to spatial regimes that have emerged since the mid-1800s, most particularly in the twentieth century with the increase of nuclear families. These include the decline of multi-generation households, housing structures with units divided from the surrounding community and further divided into private bedrooms, and a gendered division of labor and availability of household appliances that, for middle-class households, ended the use of outside domestic laborers in the private space of the home (Ochiai 1997; Ronald and Alexy 2011; Sand 2003). In his exploration of the emergence of modern "myths of Japaneseness," Oguma (2002) argues for the mutual influence of family ideologies and national policies of inclusion and exclusion. Oguma links Japanese openness to non-blood-related *ie* members with Japanese expansionist rhetoric about incorporating non-Japanese others into the national body. However, after World War II, Japanese myths of self were reoriented not as inclusive, containing heterogeneous and diverse peoples, but were reframed as homogeneous, exclusive, and "mono-ethnic" (ibid.; Dale 1986; Harootunian 1989; Lie 2001; Robertson 2002). These national discourses of self, focused on narrow conceptions of Japanese bloodlines, have likely played a role in shaping contemporary perceptions of Japanese selves as valuing blood ties within families. Further, as Japan's birthrate has declined, there are fewer "undesired" children in families. While a childless couple might have in the past adopted a child of a sibling or a cousin, decreasing family size makes this practice less pragmatic.

These processes have contributed to changing family ideals, in which the concept of "blood ties" has new ideological salience—even as blood ties are often understood as pointing to something beyond biological relatedness. Ochiai (1997, 76–77) describes the ideal type of contemporary Japanese households as those in which families are intimate and by their very intimacy, also exclusive, with their boundaries narrowing to encircle a (generally) nuclear family separated from public spheres; in such a family emotion binds members, and kin are separated from non-kin. Scholars of infertility treatment in Japan have further argued that the availability of advanced reproductive technology enabling couples to have their own biological children means that the standard of having a biologically related child has become a coercive norm (Shirai 2010, 2013; Tsuge 1999). Family in Japan has been progressively medicalized and biologized, such that "blood ties" have increasingly come to refer to narrow concepts of genetic relatedness, even as "blood" often simultaneously points to the expansive or "symbolic" interconnectedness that anthropologists of kinship have long examined (Carsten 2004; Schneider 1984). These transformations have, I suggest, contributed to the contemporary centrality of blood ties in discourses of Japanese family. While blood ties are often described as a characteristic of Japanese national-cultural family values, we should see this as an "invented tradition" (Vlastos 1998).

LOVING THE CHILD OF A STRANGER

In the accounts of my interlocutors, it is evident that the meaning of "blood ties" exceeds conventional understandings of biogenetic relatedness. Blood ties mark membership in an intimate, known sphere, in contrast to those who are experienced as different, embodying the alterity of an unknown family, and imagined as potentially unlovable. Blood ties are thus discursively engaged to summon a sense of intimate proximity or distance.

Yamaguchi Akihiro and his wife had pursued infertility treatment for many years before conceiving and giving birth to their son.[10] From the start of our interview, Yamaguchi described how difficult it was for his wife to undergo many attempts at artificial insemination and finally *in vitro* fertilization before becoming pregnant. When I asked him whether they had ever considered adoption, he said they had not, and even if his wife had never conceived, they would probably still not have thought of adoption. Referring to one of my earlier questions about the ways blood relationships are perceived in families, Yamaguchi explained:

> Maybe one can say that Japanese people value blood ties? For me too, as expected [*yappari*], I wanted my own child, but what about a child that a stranger has given birth to [*tanin no unda kodomo*]? A child that is not blood related to me, the question of whether or not I could love that child [*aiseru ka dō ka*]—that's really something I don't know. That's not to say that after five or ten years, if we still couldn't have a child—maybe then I could accept adopting; maybe at that time my feelings would be different. Maybe I could love that child. But we never had to go that far, so I don't know the answer.

Yamaguchi implies that desperation and the passage of time might widen the range of lovable children. A lack of blood ties is not a categorical quality prohibiting the feasibility of adoption but one that shifts with circumstances. At the same time, the articulations of love and blood ties indicate the centrality of affect in Yamaguchi's understanding of "blood."

Takano Saki, a woman who had been pursuing infertility treatment for over eight years, cited the same logic when she described a conversation with her husband about the possibility of adopting. Her husband had one basic fear: whether he could love another person's child [*hito no ko, aiseru ka dō ka wakaranai*]. She had that concern for herself as well, but she had heard enough accounts from foster and adoptive parents that she was reasonably sure she could come to love the child of a stranger. She wasn't sure about her husband.

> The ability to come to love the child, well, that's obviously the best, isn't it? But not being able to love. . . . Like, what about when there is trouble, or when the kid is rebelling, the sort of thing that happens with one's own child anyway—the idea of thinking, despite oneself, "It's because the child was adopted." In order to adopt . . . you have to be *absolutely* certain you won't do that.

Takano's inability to ensure both her and her husband's capacity to unconditionally love the child of a stranger was ultimately a central factor in their decision not to pursue fostering or adoption.

This lack of confidence in being able to love the child of a stranger appeared many times in my interviews, particularly in cases where people did not have regular contact with unrelated children. The narrowing confines of the family—in which members have limited contact with non-kin and child rearing is increasingly an isolated project—have likely contributed to this uncertainty. One's *own* child might seem "lovable," but why would the child of a stranger be in any way appealing? Concerns with lovability were prevalent enough in the extensive surveys and interviews conducted by sociologist Shirai Chiaki that she used it as a category of analysis: "I don't have the confidence that I will be able to love a child that is not my own" (*Watashi no kodomo de nakereba aiseru ka jishin ga nai*) (2013, 73). Shirai places this sentiment under the category of "social and psychological distance," arguing that people tend to perceive their own kin as having qualities of intimacy (*shitashimi*), friendship, and camaraderie (*nakama kankei*) (ibid., 79), in opposition to the child of a stranger that one is not sure one can love. A preference for blood ties is, then, related in an important way to rather narrowly circumscribed groups of people who are perceived as lovable by virtue of their intimate proximity.

STIGMA OF ORIGINS

In addition to concerns driven by intimate proximity, the issue of origin looms large for many foster and adoptive parents. In line with the adage quoted above—"You don't know from which horse the bone comes"—children who have been for some reason abandoned by their families are often thought to have "bad" or "dirty" blood (*ketsuen ga kitanai*) (Goodman 2000; Nishida 2011).[11] Children who are not cared for by kin are often considered "pathetic" specifically because they exist outside of and excluded from networks of care that are understood as normative and proper.

In an extended joint interview, two foster mothers, Hara Kazuko and Funabashi Tomomi, elucidated different aspects of lingering stigma against children from state care, specifically surrounding exclusion from proper kinship. Hara and her husband had two foster sons, and while they had told their family about the children, they represented the boys to their neighbors as the children of kin. "If the neighbors looked at the children and thought, 'Ah, they are *that* kind of kid,' it would just be pathetic [*kawaisō*]," Hara said. "Is there less prejudice toward children of kin, then?" I asked. Hara considered. "It's just that people would think, 'Those kids were raised in a child welfare institution'; . . . it's that—there is no one to take them in [*ukeire ga nai*]. It's that kind of situation. It's different, having people think, 'What *kind* of child is that, I wonder [*dōiu ko nano ka na tte*]?' versus thinking, 'This is the child of kin [*shinseki no ko tte*].'" Hara's contrast between pathetic children with no one to take them in and children living within an extended kinship network enacts starkly divergent models of family solidarity and care. By Hara's representing her foster children as children of kin, the children are socially converted from "pathetic" and abandoned with mysterious and unsavory pasts, to cared for and socially legible members of a known family. Otherwise, the question of the *kind* of children they are remains underdetermined, a source of speculation and suspicion.

Funabashi Tomomi, the other foster mother participating in this interview, had herself worked in a child welfare institution and did not feel negatively about children in state care. However, experiences with neighbors and friends had made her aware that her children were perceived negatively. She learned shortly after taking in her first foster son that rumors surrounding the family had been circulating within their housing complex. She had brought the eighteen-month-old boy to play in a nearby park. The little boy was running around the park and picked up a twig and threw it. A woman Funabashi had never met but who lived in the same complex was watching her own child play in the park. Observing Funabashi's son throw the twig, she commented to Funabashi, "Just as one might expect [*yappari*], children raised in that kind of place are violent [*ranbō*], aren't they?" Dismayed by this attitude and now aware of rumors, Funabashi and her husband decided to move. It wasn't good, she said, for a child so young to be subjected to that kind of stigma.

Later on, Funabashi happened to meet a woman who lived in her old housing complex. The woman, referring to Funabashi's foster children, commented, "Wow, in your household you're raising them properly [*chanto sodateteru*], aren't you?" Funabashi, who is a soft-spoken woman, made clear her indignation. "It's as if she *wanted* to say, 'Wow, you're not hitting and kicking your children, are you!'" Referring to Hara's account, Funabashi said she understood why it might be preferable to present one's foster children as the children of kin. Indeed, she and her husband had decided not to tell anyone—including the children themselves—that they were not biologically related.

These logics about "bad blood" and a "pathetic" background constitute what Goffman has called a "stigma theory," an "ideology to explain [a person's] inferiority and account for the danger he represents" (1963, 5). One who experiences stigma, Goffman writes, "is likely to feel that the usual scheme of interpretation for everyday events has been undermined. His minor accomplishments, he feels, may be assessed as signs of remarkable and noteworthy capacities in the circumstances" (ibid., 14). Despite Funabashi's children's supposed dark pasts; despite the strangeness of the act of fostering and the ascription of that strangeness to the foster parents themselves; despite prevalent myths that non-related parents are more likely to abuse children than biologically related parents—she was "properly" raising her boys.[12] The mere ordinariness of her care for the children provoked wonder and surprise.

Having listened to Funabashi's account, Hara elaborated her own perspective about prejudice (*henken*). "It's about the conditions that caused a child to need to go to a welfare institution in the first place, right? You find out about the children's backgrounds, and they're not normal situations; that's why they're in the institution." Hara argued that making family relationships better would obviate the need for state care. For her, socioeconomic distress, illness, and broader social constraints—like Japanese laws prohibiting dual custody, which make caring for children difficult for a single parent—seemed to be less significant than poor kinship relationships.[13] The very presence of a child needing state care draws a discriminatory gaze because the child illuminates something dark and flawed within the family that does not accord with contemporary notions of intimacy and affection. In Hara's account, intimacy itself takes on a normative and transformative power. Hara continued:

> As a result, there's the sense that because it's *these* children [from "bad" families], one assumes that the child will do something bad. It's totally normal to think that, isn't it? Sorry, but it's just normal [*Moshiwakenai kedo, futsū de*]. . . . The idea of doing a certain thing. . . . Well, for example, the type of family line that ends up with love triangles or something. . . . In

the end, you have this sort of situation, and that's why you have these sorts of children.[14] . . . I guess you could call it prejudice, but normally when one thinks about it, I mean you're not supposed to put it in words, but in the end there it is. Sorry, sorry [*gomennasai, gomennasai ne*].

Hara ended her statement laughing rather bashfully, after having articulated that which should not properly be confessed: her sense that prejudice and bias toward children from child welfare institutions is entirely normal, rooted in conventional notions of improperly intimate families whose pedigree marks children as problematic. For Hara, these children are understandably stigmatized because they represent a particular "danger" (Goffman 1963, 5), the danger of broken family ties that necessitate state intervention.

SECRECY AND CONFESSION

Concern with a child's origins is often articulated along with a pathos that both characterizes these children and attaches to the people who would consider taking them as their own. Although these worries are often articulated as a lack of "blood ties," the meanings behind "blood" center on emotion, specifically the sorrow of loss and abandonment. Despite the fact that foster and adoptive parents believed that care, intimacy, and physical proximity contributed to children and caregivers becoming "family," this original disconnection and loss—a child's abandonment by his or her birth parents and a couple's inability to conceive—contributed toward insecurity regarding the child's status in the family and the ways the family would be viewed by outsiders.

This pathos haunted the account of an adoptive mother, Hamabata Toshiko, who had not "confessed" to her teenage son that he had been adopted. Hamabata's narrative elaborates the ways that similarities (in shared habits, behaviors, and blood type) mitigate the perceived otherness of her son, while differences (physical appearance and the traces in bureaucratic records) highlight an otherness that is visibly evident and eventually impossible to conceal. In Hamabata's quandary, we can better understand the importance for many Japanese families of *visually* embodying a "normal" household. Material markers of otherness problematize the hope of many foster or adoptive parents that intimate proximity will seamlessly transform difference into sameness (Yngvesson 2010; Goldfarb 2016).

Hamabata told me that it took her and her husband a long time to consider adoption. "It just has a very . . . dark feeling [*kurai kanji*], doesn't it? Doesn't it make you feel a little unpleasant [*iwakan*]?" she asked with a slight laugh. "I've heard people say that," I answered. "It's not the sort of thing you could say easily in public," Hamabata went on, "but . . . it's like, 'pitiable, pathetic' [*kawaisō*]." When she and her husband finally decided to adopt a small boy from a child welfare institution, she described her surprise at the joy with which the children's home staff sent him off. Later, I realized her surprise was rooted in her sense that adoption was fundamentally a dark, pathetic practice, connected to the dark past and pathetic experiences of the children in question and the pathos of the adopters like the Hamabatas, whose inability to conceive led them to welcome [*mukaeru*] unknown children from unknown families.

A common concern of Japanese foster or adoptive parents is that their non-normative family practices would be, in some way, evident to all. I interviewed Hamabata at a cafe in the town where she lived, a decision I quickly regretted. After peeking into two cafes near the train station, both of which were full, we ended up at a coffee shop where, Hamabata told me in a whisper, the mother of one of her son's schoolmates worked. We conducted our interview in awkward *sotto voce*, Hamabata pointing to the word "adoption" (*yōshi engumi*) on my list of interview questions rather than speaking it out loud. While Hamabata engaged in social welfare volunteer work and had a long-term foster care relationship with a young woman who was now living independently, Hamabata had not told her son that he himself had been adopted through the foster care system, and she and her husband kept this fact a secret from non-foster parent friends and neighbors. When the boy first came to their house, they had traveled to a distant hospital to care for him when he got sick, hoping not to run into anyone they knew. After they formally adopted him and changed his name, they switched schools.

With some concern in her voice, Hamabata told me that as her son grows older, he looks more and more dissimilar to her and her husband. But, she said, his mannerisms (*kuse*) are the same, and his voice on the phone sounds like her husband's. Hamabata noted that this happens with married couples that start to look alike (*niteiru fūfu*)—a natural result, she said, of eating the same food and living together. Troubling physical dissimilarities were thus balanced by slightly less tangible similarities, signs of long affiliation. In addition, Hamabata told me, both her son's and her husband's blood types are B, while she is an O. Since her husband is B, and it was thus biologically possible for their son to also be a B, it's all okay (*daijyōbu*); otherwise, she said, they would certainly have had to confess the truth (*kokuchi suru*) to their son by now.[15]

But this secrecy lived on borrowed time. Irrefutable proof of the Hamabatas' son's origins lay in his household registry, which documented all the addresses where he had lived during his life: a baby home, a foster home, another children's welfare institution, and finally the Hamabata household. He had recently taken his household registry with him to apply for his driver's license, and when he returned from that errand, he left the registry unfolded on the dining room table. Hamabata knew that he understood the implications of the registry, just as she was aware that he surely remembered something of the time before he came to their household as a five-year-old. ("Do *you* remember anything from when you were five?" she asked me.) Yet she was sure he could not bring himself to ask her about it, and she could not make herself broach the subject with him. His registry remained open on the family table, the site of eating and care that had made him come to resemble the Hamabatas to begin with, untouchable proof of that which could not be said.[16]

Although Hamabata articulated her relationship with her son as one of increasing intimacy and similarity as time went by, she could not imagine "confessing" the truth of originary disconnection, a stance that surely contributed to the pathos she ascribed to their situation. While Hamabata was aware that her silence was at odds with contemporary understandings of a child's "right" to know his or her own background—and while she knew that her son knew the truth, making his status a "public secret" in their household—she was unable to articulate this reality. Another foster parent mused, in an interview, that what makes it so hard to confess a lack of blood ties is the knowledge that the child *wants* to believe he or she is the parents' biological child. A failure to confess thus might express a desire to protect the child from presumed deep disappointment.

Recall the example with which this chapter begins: the "big foster family" in which parent-child relationships emerge and unrelated foster children become siblings over time. Neither biogenetic connections (this foster family contains six unrelated children) nor legal ties (their names are different) are necessary to transform these children and caregivers into family, as long as there exist the bonds of heart or spirit (*kokoro no kizuna*) (see Schneider 1980). According to this account, although these family members were initially unconnected, through the intimate practices of daily life they became family, and from an outside gaze, they came to look like any large household. They were recognizable as "family" precisely because of the bonds that connected them (Goldfarb 2016).

Many of the public narratives surrounding alternative kinships in Japan hinge on the idea that intimacy bridges differences to constitute family. Indeed, awareness that the intimacy of family living can *make* a child into the kin of foster or adoptive parents is precisely the reason why many Japanese child welfare officers hesitate to place children in family-based care in cases when the child's biological parents are unable to care for the child. Child welfare officers themselves often fear that new intimate ties will replace a child's tenuous bonds to biological kin, proving problematic if the biological parents ask for the return of custody (Goldfarb 2012; Omori 2016).

While kinship in Japan is often currently framed in terms of the presence or absence of "blood ties," this chapter has illustrated how blood ties themselves signify much more than a biogenetic relationship. The concept incorporates shifting intimate boundaries, which have transformed historically through demographic transitions, changes in housing styles, and along "modern" notions of love and affection as characterizing kinship. While blood ties are often invoked to speak to the social legibility—or illegibility—of family forms, blood ties themselves powerfully point to current idealizations of intimacy and emotion within families. An insufficient degree of intimacy made my interlocutors concerned that they would not be able to love the child of a stranger. Similarly, the pathos of unknown origins and original disconnection shaped the perception that children from state care—as well as their foster and adoptive caregivers—were "pathetic" or justifiably perceived in a negative light. Intimacy is thus a shifting measure of inclusion and exclusion in contemporary Japan, both delimiting kinship to those who are known, proximate, and lovable, and expanding these boundaries through caregiving and daily household routines that create new kinships where there were none before. Blood ties in contemporary Japan are social constructs through which people attempt to assure themselves of intimate connection, all the while knowing the impossibility of such certainty.

NOTES

I gratefully express thanks for research funding from Fulbright IIE and the Wenner-Gren Foundation; dissertation-writing fellowships from the International Chapter PEO Sisterhood and the University of Chicago's Center for East Asian Studies; and support for research and writing from Harvard University's Program on U.S.-Japan Relations.

1. Kanto describes the plain that includes Tokyo and surrounding prefectures. The Kansai area includes Osaka, Kyoto, Kobe, and Nara.

2. Included in this forty-five thousand children, around thirteen hundred children were placed in specialized facilities because of disability or the need for medical care.

3. In many cases, babies might be placed in institutional care shortly after birth and live there until age two or three before they are moved to a child welfare institution, placed in foster care or adoption, or reunited with biological family members. Child-development and neuroscience literature have illustrated the potential for developmental harm resulting

from early institutionalization (for instance, Browne 2009; Johnson, Browne, and Hamilton-Giachritsis 2006; Rutter and ERA 1998; Zeanah et al. 2003; for analysis, Goldfarb 2015). The prevalence of infant institutionalization in Japan has drawn criticism from Human Rights Watch (2014), after years of censure from the UN Convention on the Rights of the Child, to which Japan became a signatory in 1994 (UNCRC 2010), the Japan Federation of Bar Associations (2009), and local Japanese activists. See Goldfarb (2013) for further details.

4. The Japanese government is also facing increased international attention owing to a critical report on Japanese child welfare practices by the Tokyo office of Human Rights Watch (2014).

5. We can understand the *ie* as a type of extended family, but it is more accurately a corporate group connected to enterprise and religious responsibilities for graves and ancestral spirits.

6. The American abolition of the *ie* was an effort to curb Japanese imperialism; there were deep ideological connections in Japan among the *ie*, the Japanese emperor, and Japan's imperialistic initiatives. However, despite these legal transformations, the family registry system (*koseki seido*), which was not abolished during postwar Allied reform projects, continues to shape everyday sensibilities about legal family forms and bureaucratic documentation practices, what Krogness calls "*koseki* consciousness" (2010).

7. In the case of "regular adoption," the adoptee is entered into the adoptive parents' family registry along with a note listing the names of the adoptee's biological parents. The adoptee maintains rights and responsibilities for the natal family, including the right to inherit.

8. Numbers for this type of adoption have hovered between three hundred and four hundred per year for the past twenty years (Hayes and Habu 2006, 137).

9. The adoption of adults in contemporary Japan also has some connotations that some consider "unsavory": elderly people might conduct adoptions to decrease the overall amount of inheritance tax applied to an estate (inheritance tax decreases the more inheritors there are) or adopt with the promise of exchanging inheritance for elder care. Extramarital lovers can be adopted; in such a case the portion of inheritance designated for a legally married spouse and children would decrease. One member of a same-sex couple might adopt the other in order to assure inheritance rights (Bryant 1990). Finally, adult adoption maintains a reputation for being pitiable because families without sons to inherit often adopt the husband of a daughter, a process called *mukoyōshi*, in which the man leaves his natal home, enters the family registry of his spouse, and takes her name. Even though men who are adopted into their wives' families are generally not candidates as heirs in their families of origin, *mukoyōshi* is commonly considered undesirable for a man because within the generally patriarchal framework of the Japanese *ie*, women normatively take the man's name, not the reverse.

10. All personal names are pseudonyms, listed with family name first.

11. This is a perception that people who were raised in child welfare institutions sometimes keenly feel. One of my interlocutors, who had spent her entire childhood in institutions, once confessed to me that she doubted she would ever be able to get married. She felt that her past in institutional care, in addition to the fact that her younger brother was disabled, made people think that she had "bad blood" and would be an undesirable addition to a family.

12. Consistent with child abuse statistics in North America that show biological parents as the most likely perpetrators of child abuse, Japanese statistics indicate that the most common abuser is a child's biological mother and then the biological father. However, Funabashi's account exemplifies the common misperception that a lack of blood relationship indicates a lack of emotional investment and thus an increased likelihood for abuse (Goodman 2002; JaSPCAN 2010).

13. The leading reasons children are taken into state care are abuse, neglect, parental mental illness, and parental refusal to care for the child (MHLW 2017, 59).

14. Hara's mention of love triangles refers to children being born out of extramarital affairs who would then be placed in state care.

15. When a foster or adoptive parent uses the phrase *shinjitsu kokuchi*, which literally means the disclosure or notification of truth, one understands this to refer to the "confession" of adoptive or foster relationship specifically to the child in question. The phrase is often shortened to *kokuchi*, as in, "Have you told [*kokuchi shita*]?" "No, I haven't [*shitei-nai*]." Those who hope to destigmatize adoption refer to this process as "telling" (*teringu*, using Japanese pronunciation for the English word), a term intended to reference discussion rather than a morally loaded sense of confessing something scandalous or unpleasant (Kakugi 2006).

16. To a certain extent, one of my interlocutors told me, debates surrounding the "confession" of adoption in Japan are irrelevant: "Setting aside whether it's good or bad for anyone else to know, no matter what, if you look carefully at the family registry, you will be able to find out." The family registry contains different "proof" from the household registry; the former lists all unmarried children who share the family name, and special adoption is marked with reference to the constitutional bill that ratified the process (Hayes and Habu 2006; Krogness 2010).

REFERENCES

Bachnik, Jane M. 1983. "Recruitment Strategies for Household Succession: Rethinking Japanese Household Organization." *Man* 18 (1): 160–182.

Bamba, Sachiko, and Wendy L. Haight. 2011. *Child Welfare and Development: A Japanese Case Study*. Cambridge: Cambridge University Press.

Browne, Kevin. 2009. "The Risk of Harm to Young Children in Institutional Care." London: Save the Children.

Bryant, Taimie L. 1990. "Sons and Lovers: Adoption in Japan." *American Journal of Comparative Law* 38 (2): 299–336.

Carsten, Janet. 2004. *After Kinship*. Cambridge: Cambridge University Press.

Dale, Peter. 1986. *The Myth of Japanese Uniqueness*. New York: St. Martin's Press.

Goffman, Erving. 1963. *Stigma: Notes on the Management of Spoiled Identity*. Englewood Cliffs, NJ: Prentice-Hall.

Goldfarb, Kathryn E. 2012. "Fragile Kinships: Family Ideologies and Child Welfare in Japan." PhD dissertation, University of Chicago.

———. 2013. "Japan." In *Child Protection and Child Welfare: A Global Appraisal of Cultures, Policy and Practice*, edited by John Dixon and Penelope Wellbourne, 144–169. London: Jessica Kingsley Publishers.

———. 2015. "Developmental Logics: Brain Science, Child Welfare, and the Ethics of Engagement in Japan." *Social Science and Medicine* 143:271–278.

———. 2016. "'Coming to Look Alike': Materializing Affinity in Japanese Foster and Adoptive Care." *Social Analysis* 60 (2): 47–64.

Goodman, Roger. 2000. *Children of the Japanese State: The Changing Role of Child Protection Institutions in Contemporary Japan*. New York: Oxford University Press.

———. 2002. "Child Abuse in Japan: 'Discovery' and the Development of Policy." In *Family and Social Policy in Japan*, edited by Roger Goodman, 131–155. Cambridge: Cambridge University Press.

Harootunian, Harry. 1989. "Visible Discourses/Invisible Ideologies." In *Postmodernism and Japan*, edited by Masao Miyoshi and H. D. Harootunian, 63–92. Durham, NC: Duke University Press.

Hayes, Peter, and Toshie Habu. 2006. *Adoption in Japan: Comparing Policies for Children in Need*. New York: Routledge.

Hozumi, Baron Nobushige. 2004. *Ancestor-Worship and Japanese Law*. London: Kegan Paul.

Human Rights Watch. 2014. "Without Dreams: Children in Alternative Care in Japan." Tokyo: Human Rights Watch.

Japan Federation of Bar Associations. 2009. "The Japan Federation of Bar Associations' Report on the Japanese Government's Third Report on the Convention on the Rights of the Child and the Initial Reports on OPAC and OPSC." Available at www.crin.org/resources/infodetail.asp?id=22436.

JaSPCAN (Japanese Society for the Prevention of Child Abuse and Neglect). 2010. *Nihon kodomo gyakutai boshi gakkai* (Japanese Society for the Prevention of Child Abuse and Neglect). Materials distributed at sixteenth annual meeting, November 27–28.

Johnson, Rebecca, Kevin Browne, and Catherine Hamilton-Giachritsis. 2006. "Young Children in Institutional Care at Risk of Harm." *Trauma, Violence and Abuse* 7 (1): 34–60.

Krogness, Karl Jakob. 2010. "The Ideal, the Deficient, and the Illogical Family: An Initial Typology of Administrative Household Units." In *Home and Family in Japan: Continuity and Transformation*, edited by Richard Ronald and Allison Alexy, 65–90. London: Routledge.

Lie, John. 2001. *Multiethnic Japan*. Cambridge, MA: Harvard University Press.

McKinnon, Susan, and Fennella Cannell, eds. 2013. *Vital Relations: Modernity and the Persistent Life of Kinship*. Santa Fe, NM: SAR Press.

MHLW. 2010. *Kodomo kosodate bijyon* [Child and Child Rearing Vision]. January. Available at http://www.mhlw.go.jp/bunya/kodomo/pdf/vision-zenbun.pdf.

———. 2014. *Shyakaiteki yōgo no genjyō ni tsuite* [Present Conditions in Social Protective Care]. March. Available at http://www.mhlw.go.jp/bunya/kodomo/syakaiteki_yougo/dl/yougo_genjou_01.pdf.

———. 2017. *Shyakaiteki yōgo no genjyō ni tsuite* [Present Conditions in Social Protective Care]. July. Available at http://www.mhlw.go.jp/file/06-Seisakujouhou-11900000-Koyoukintoujidoukateikyoku/0000172986.pdf

Nakane, Chie. 1967. *Kinship and Economic Organization in Rural Japan*. New York: Humanities Press.

Nishida, Yoshimasa. 2011. *Jidō yōgo shisetsu to shyakaiteki haijyo* [Children's Homes and Social Exclusion]. Osaka: Kaiho shyuppannsya.

NNN News. 2010. *Ai no satooya kosodate*. March 9.

Norbeck, Edward, and Harumi Befu. 1958. "Informal Fictive Kinship in Japan." *American Anthropologist* 60 (1): 102–117.

Ochiai, Emiko. 1997. *The Japanese Family System in Transition*. Tokyo: LTCB International Library Foundation.

Oguma, Eiji. 2002. *A Genealogy of "Japanese" Self-Images*. Melbourne: Trans Pacific Press.

Omori, Hisako. 2016. "Creating Family: Tenrikyō Foster Homes in Japan." *Japanese Studies* 36 (2): 213–229.

Paulson, Joy L. 1984. "Family Law Reform in Postwar Japan: Succession and Adoption." PhD dissertation, University of Colorado at Boulder.

Rakugi, Akiko. 2006. "Kazoku: Ketsuen naki 'ketsuen kankei'" [Family: "Blood Relationship" without a Blood Tie]. In *Komyuniti no gurupu dainamikkusu* [Group Dynamics of Community], edited by T. Sugiman, 239–266. Kyoto: Kyoto University Press.

Robertson, Jennifer. 2002. "Blood Talks: Eugenic Modernity and the Creation of New Japanese." *History and Anthropology* 13 (3): 191–216.

Ronald, Richard, and Allison Alexy. 2011. "Continuity and Change in Japanese Homes and Families." In *Home and Family in Japan: Continuity and Transformation*, edited by Richard Ronald and Allison Alexy, 1–24. London: Routledge.

Rutter, Michael, and ERA (English and Romanian Adoptees study team). 1998. "Developmental Catch-Up, and Deficit, Following Adoption after Severe Global Early Privation." *Journal of Child Psychology and Psychiatry* 39 (1): 465 476.

Sand, Jordan. 2003. *House and Home in Modern Japan: Architecture, Domestic Space, and Bourgeois Culture, 1880–1930.* Cambridge, MA: Harvard University East Asia Center.

Schneider, David. 1980. *American Kinship.* Chicago: University of Chicago Press.

———. 1984. *Critique of the Study of Kinship.* Ann Arbor: University of Michigan Press.

Shirai, Chiaki. 2010. "Reproductive Technologies and Parent-Child Relationships: Japan's Past and Present Examined through the Lens of Donor Insemination." *International Journal of Japanese Sociology* 19 (1): 19–35.

———. 2013. "Funin jyosei ga motsu hiketsuenteki oyako ni taisuru senkō ni tsuite" [Concerning the Preferences of Infertile Women Regarding Non-Blood-Related Children]. *Shyakaigaku nenshi* 54:69–84.

Tsuge, Azumi. 1999. *Bunka to shite seishokugijyutsu: Funin chiryo ni tazusawaru ishi no katari.* [Reproductive Technology as Culture: Narratives of Japanese Gynecologists Regarding Infertility Treatment]. Kyoto: Shorai-sha.

Tsuzaki, Tsuzaki. 2009. *Kono kuni no kodomotachi: Yōhogo jidō shyakai-teki yōgo no Nihon-teki kōchiku; otona no kitoku keneki to kodomo no fukushi* [This Country's Children: Japanese-Style Construction of Social Care for Children in Need of Care; The Vested Interests of Adults and Children's Welfare]. Kyoto: Nihon kajyo syuppan.

UNCRC (Committee on the Rights of the Child). 2010. "Consideration of Reports Submitted by States Parties under Article 44 of the Convention: Convention on the Rights of the Child: Concluding Observations: Japan." CRC/C/JPN/CO/3, June 20. Available at http://www.unhcr.org/refworld/docid/4c32dea52.html, accessed June 4, 2011.

Vlastos, Stephen, ed. 1998. *Mirror of Modernity: Invented Traditions of Modern Japan.* Berkeley: University of California Press.

Yngvesson, Barbara. 2010. *Belonging in an Adopted World: Race, Identity, and Transnational Adoption.* Chicago: University of Chicago Press.

Zeanah, Charles H., et al. 2003. "Designing Research to Study the Effects of Institutionalization on Brain and Behavioral Development: The Bucharest Early Intervention Project." *Development and Psychopathology* 15:885–890.

CHAPTER 11

❖ ❖ ❖

Making Ordinary, If Not Ideal, Intimate Relationships

Japanese-Chinese Transnational Matchmaking

Chigusa Yamaura

"Ideally, Japanese should marry Japanese. That is the best marriage," said Mr. Tanaka. Mr. Tanaka is a marriage broker, but contrary to the ideal he articulated, his job is not to facilitate marriages between Japanese men and women. Instead he mediates marriages between Japanese men and Chinese women. Since establishing his transnational marriage agency in 1995, as of October 2010 he had brokered 242 pairings between Japanese men and women from mainland China. Although he is very proud of what he does, he did not hesitate to claim that the ideal marriage is always between co-nationals. After saying this, he continued, "But there are some Japanese men who cannot [marry Japanese women]. So I take them to China to find a Chinese bride." Mr. Tanaka's opinion was not unusual. From both other transnational marriage brokers and many of their Japanese clientele I had heard the refrain that for a Japanese man, finding a Japanese bride was the natural first choice.

The transnational marriage agencies (*kokusai kekkon shōkaijō*) on which this chapter focuses—Mr. Tanaka's is one example—offer brokerage services to facilitate marriages between Japanese men and Chinese women. Their services vary, but typically they include multi-day "matchmaking tours" (*omiai tuā*) to China. (In addition to marriage tours to China, some agencies also offer matchmaking meetings with Chinese women already residing in Japan.) During these tours, in a short space of time, Japanese men are usually introduced to several bridal candidates who have been recruited by branch offices in the area. Upon the assent of both sides, the new acquaintances become engaged, and the marriages are sealed shortly thereafter. At the time of marriage, most couples are still unable to communicate with each other. It is only after marriage that the new Chinese brides start learning basic Japanese. Such learning takes place in special classes in China while the women are waiting to receive a spousal visa that will allow them to join their husbands in Japan. The visa process generally takes three to six months but sometimes can take longer.

How is it that heterosexual marriages—intimate relationships heavily laden with normative expectations in Japan—are being created in such a seemingly unconventional way? If even a broker of such marriages himself believes that the ideal marriage is between a Japanese man and woman, how do these seemingly extraordinary ways of establishing marital relations become acceptable to participants? Studies of marriage in Japan have shown that the ideology of marriage has shifted from centering on "arranged marriages" that value familial relations and standing to more individualistic conceptions of "love" or "compassionate" marriages, with the main turning point being in the 1970s (Hashimoto and Traphagan 2008; Ronald and Alexy 2011; West 2011). How then do participants try to make sense of intimate relationships that appear to transgress the older ideology by being both arranged and "less than ideal" because they include foreign brides? By investigating transnational and domestic matchmaking practices in Japanese society, in this chapter I examine how these transnational unions are created and, more broadly, how the rhetorics of "ordinariness" and "naturalness" are constructed to include transnationally arranged relationships.

Tomoko Nakamatsu (2013) observes that whereas marriage by introduction is a long-standing practice in Japan, introduction agencies, including those facilitating transnational marriages, appeal to notions of "love" or "romance" as one of their strategies: "One outcome of the normalization of marriage based on romantic love was that it encouraged the growth of a new type of marriage introduction business: the promotion of romantic encounters" (ibid, 475). Whereas the transnational marriage agencies I researched made some references to "love" on their websites, as Nakamatsu might lead us to expect, on the whole my interactions with marriage brokers and their clientele revealed very different narratives, dynamics, and scenarios through which such transnational matchmaking came to be portrayed as a feasible option. Many brokers, as well as clientele, were aware that "love" does not initially exist in brokered relationships, not simply because the couples barely knew one another, but also because arranged relationships entail different constructions of intimacy in marriage: not the pursuit of intimacy itself, but rather a *possibility for* intimacy. Accordingly, this chapter is not about what constitutes intimacy per se. Rather, I ask how the Japanese men involved attempted to create a conceivable site for intimacy. Drawing upon the definition of intimacy discussed in this book's introduction and adding a consideration of future-oriented aspects, I posit that the intimate relationships here entail aspirations to marry someone in order to share a life, and therefore it is a someone that participants can imagine being close to physically and emotionally in the future. In other words, since at the time of marriage the two participants are virtual strangers, it is not intimacy itself but instead the possibility of intimacy after marriage that plays an important role. The practice of intimacy in this case—or more precisely the practice of imagining intimacy—requires an alternative way of understanding marital relationships.

To elaborate, in place of appeals to the notions of existing "love" or "romance," the Japanese men who participated in these marriages were encouraged to engage in these intimate relationships because of the "naturalness" or "ordinariness" attributed to the relationships. Male participants themselves attempted to understand their marriages as "ordinary" by framing their relationships as "not so different" from the domestic marital unions they had originally sought. Drawing upon Goffman's theorization of stigma—"an undesired differentness from what we had anticipated" (2009 [1963], 5)—I argue that these Japanese men and transnational marriage brokers negotiated perceptions of the "ordinary" as a means to construct intimate relationships. As Goffman claims, stigmatized individuals attempt to present themselves as ordinary persons by managing information about their failings. In the case of transnational matchmaking practices, the Japanese men tried to manage two pieces of information: their inability to find a Japanese wife and their inability to meet their future spouse "naturally." While they attempted to make sense of their private experiences, their negotiations also involved a public dimension, most prominently concerning how to tell others about their intimate relationships.

Love was not the foremost concern, and it was seen as something—within both domestic and transnational matchmaking practices—that would come after a marriage had already been brokered (should it come at all). The work that went into constructing these intimate relationships, as this chapter documents, involved rendering them as normal. It is important that the intimate relationships I discuss here are not created solely by two individuals but are imagined to be socially acknowledged as such. Some of the Japanese men were worried how their marriages would be seen by public eyes (*seken no me*). The key point is that it was neither love nor even passion that was seen as a prerequisite for intimacy but rather the ability of participants to view their relationships as socially acceptable, if not ordinary.

The materials referenced here were collected during ethnographic field-work in China and Japan from 2007 to 2010. During this period, I visited transnational marriage agencies on a regular basis and observed match-making processes, including Internet matchmaking meetings, match-making parties, and consultations between clients and brokers. I also followed matchmaking tours to northeast China and interviewed male clients, female bride candidates, and brokers in both Japan and China. As a comparison, I interviewed domestic marriage brokers. While I conducted research with and interviewed Chinese women, this chapter primarily focuses on the experiences of Japanese men.[1]

TRANSNATIONAL MATCHMAKING PRACTICES

The practice of facilitating marriages between Japanese men and non-Jap-anese Asian women has its origins in the mid-1980s in the Japanese coun-tryside (Kuwayama 1995; Shukuya 1988). Owing to a perceived shortage of women and women's unwillingness to marry into rural communities, many Japanese men who remained in rural areas had difficulty finding a bride. Local governments tried many different strategies, including recruiting women from elsewhere in Japan, yet none of these plans were seen as working. Importing "Asian brides" was then hit upon as a solu-tion for Japanese men who could not find a Japanese bride. Asahi village in Yamagata Prefecture is one example of this phenomenon. In 1985, the local government organized matchmaking tours to the Philippines that resulted in an almost 100 percent success rate for the participating men to find a bride (Shukuya 1988).

Today these matchmaking practices are not limited to the rural areas of Japan. Although there are agencies introducing women from Thailand, the Philippines, and Russia, most women introduced by the matchmaking industry are Chinese, especially since the mid-1990s.[2] Most of the Chinese women included in my fieldwork came from northeast China.[3] During my research, both professional and amateur marriage brokers were involved in commercial matchmaking practices.[4] Some transnational marriage bro-kers were registered at the Nihon Nakodo Renmei (Japanese Matchmakers Association) or the Nihon Buraidaru Renmei (Bridal Information Union). Both organizations are national brokerage business networks in which the majority of agencies mediate marriages between Japanese men and women.[5] Others conduct brokerages as a side job. The majority of men I met at transnational marriage agencies were white-collar businessmen living in urban areas.[6] Most of the men had full-time jobs, some even at globally known companies. Whereas these characteristics contradicted the

typical image of men seeking matches because they were socially and eco-
nomically "disadvantaged" (Tseng 2010; Yang and Lu 2010), for many different reasons most of these men had had a hard time finding a local wife.
Age was seen as one of the reasons for such difficulties. The average age of
male participants ranged between forty and fifty and included both those
never married and previously divorced. Individuals in this age range were
often seen as "too old" to find a suitable Japanese bride. Because many men
thought that having a child or children was an essential part of marital
life, Japanese women of a similar age were excluded from their conceptions
of "suitable brides." Some men confessed that if they were younger, they
would never think about marrying a Chinese woman.

Most transnational marriage agencies offer similar services. They provide a Japanese male clientele with Chinese women's profiles, either online
or in print. The profiles typically include pictures, age, height, weight,
hometown, family structures, hobbies, the women's willingness to live
with in-laws, and other pertinent details. After the Japanese client has
selected several candidates, the brokers contact their local staff in China.
The local staff members then ask the selected women if they are willing to
meet the interested party by showing them that man's profile. If they agree,
the Japanese client visits China with the broker, often as part of a group.
The man meets the women he has selected, talking with each for fifteen
or twenty minutes with the help of translators. After having met all potential candidates, the Japanese male client, the brokers, and local staff members discuss which woman he would like to marry. Sometimes, they also
decide on a second choice in case the first choice declines his proposal. The
local staff members then check with the woman to see if she is also willing.
Should both sides agree, the engagement is contracted, and they all move
on to an engagement dinner party at the same hotel. Some couples marry
the following day, and others marry in a month or so, when the Japanese
man returns for a second visit to meet his betrothed in China.

The brokerage fees vary depending on the services and the marriage
agencies. The fees include registration, consulting, matchmaking tours,
wedding tours, paperwork assistance, language lessons for the Chinese
women, and "after-care" services for newly married couples. Some agencies offer packages involving choices concerning the quality of the hotel
for the wedding party or the number of wedding photos taken at a photo
studio. The total cost ranges from ¥1,500,000 to ¥3,500,000 ($15,000–$35,000),
depending on the agency and services desired.[7] The fact that payments
were involved provoked social perceptions that these pairings were the
result of an unusual, even stigmatized, way of creating intimate relations.
In particular, transnational matchmaking tours were often criticized and

mocked by the national media, which characterized them not only as involving "mail order brides" (Shukuya 1988), but also as entailing "instant marriage tours" (*Yomiuri*, March 23, 2010), "bride-hunting tours" (*Shukan Bunshu*, March 2, 2006), and "buying brides under the name of matchmaking" (*Shukan Post*, March 10, 2006). The relative ease of such matching was specifically used as proof that it could not be based on truly equal relations.

Notably, Japanese-Chinese marriages brokered via these matchmaking practices are premised on multiple inequities—not just global economic inequalities, but also disparities at a personal level (Ehrenreich and Hochschild 2003; Piper 2003). It is always the women who relocate to a new place, where they often face substantial linguistic and cultural barriers. Simply taking "ordinariness" at its face value, as deployed by the brokers and participants, risks obscuring uneven transactions and relationships. Nonetheless, such asymmetrical relationships were made possible not simply by global economic and gender inequalities, but also were rendered seemingly "natural" through domestic values and norms used to create intimate relationships, including normalized commercial matchmaking activities and taken-for-granted gender differences in Japanese society.

"IDEAL MARRIAGE" IN THE DOMESTIC CONTEXT

Whereas transnational matchmaking services are often stigmatized in Japanese society owing to their commercial aspects, payments for matching services, quick matchings, and unequal relations are not absent within domestic matchmaking practices. Nonetheless, perceptions of these practices are different. As stated above, "love" has become a crucial element in contemporary Japanese marital ideology. Nonetheless, of course, loveless marriages exist, and the terms "loveless" or "sexless" have come into common parlance in recent decades. Love is seen as an ideal component of marital relations but not an indispensable element (West 2011). My ethnographic data also show that when one cannot find a partner based on love, many believe that some degree of compromise is necessary.

Seeking a marriage partner through introduction services is seen as one way to negotiate the ideal form of marriage. The first marriage agencies that utilized computerized matchmaking services or psychological tests emerged in the 1970s, and now there are at least 3,700–3,900 such institutions in Japan (West 2011).[8] Unlike online dating services, these agencies specifically target potential customers who are looking for a marriage partner. Contemporary marriage introduction agencies, both domestic and transnational, frequently use the term *omiai* (arranged meetings) to describe elements of their brokerage services. Nevertheless, their use of *omiai* is quite dissimilar from what the term described in a traditional sense: older relatives introducing young people to others from similar backgrounds for the purpose of marriage (Nakane 1967; Hendry 2013). For instance, during an interview one domestic marriage broker told me, "Families are usually not involved in *omiai* today. People came to the marriage agency because they themselves thought it was already too late to find a partner. Although some people asked their mothers' opinions, mothers rarely intervene in our matchmaking processes." Although agencies are likely to describe their services in terms that index "traditional matchmaking," in key ways contemporary practices are substantially different.

For those who visited domestic marriage agencies, the ideology of love in marriage occupied an ambiguous place. It was not exactly finding love that they sought but rather finding the possibility for intimacy. On the one hand, many of them still hoped to find some "love" or a "crush" or what Akiko Takeyama (2008) calls "romantic excitement" (*tokimeki*), as one broker put it. This broker told me that people cannot marry someone they do not like. On the other hand, participants are also aware that it is not only difficult to find such excitement, but also that "love" alone is not a sufficient reason to marry someone. Another domestic broker wrote that if people marry as a result of passionate love, their passion level will simply decrease after marriage, ruining their relationship. But in the case of arranged marriages, couples start with the feeling that "I can possibly marry this person"—that is, a measure that is just a passing score, 60–70 points (out of 100) Then, in the process of living together, they find the good characteristics of their new spouse (Yamada 2009). Therefore, according to the same broker, the ways in which couples try to generate "love" in an arranged marriage is a different form of "love marriage."

Although finding love is one element of the rhetoric, many men I met were focused on the means through which they might find a partner. In particular, Japanese men defined the ideal form of marriage as one in which they met their brides "naturally" since it was through such a "natural" encounter that intimacy was seen as having the possibility to emerge. For instance, one Japanese man at a transnational marriage agency confessed, "Encountering someone [to marry] naturally [*shizen na deai*] is the best." Similarly, as stated by another man, "If it is possible, I want to meet and marry someone naturally [*shizen ni*]." Their comments suggest that meeting someone through an agency (either domestic or transnational) was not natural and thus not an ideal way to establish marital relations.[9]

Nonetheless, within domestic matchmaking practices, such "unnatural" ways of meeting a partner were rationalized by emerging media discourses concerning "the marriage squeeze." During my research, *konkatsu* (partner hunting) was a topic receiving prevalent coverage in the media. The term was originally created by sociologist Masahiro Yamada and journalist Tōko Shirakawa in 2007. In describing what they mean by *konkatsu* activity, Yamada and Shirakawa (2008) explain that before the 1980s it was common to find a marriage partner with support from one's workplace or community. Thus encounters between males and females during this period were generated through social connections. However, with the emphasis on economic liberalism that became prominent in the 1980s, people became free to seek marriage partners wherever they chose. But this resulted in individuals facing an unequal playing field in their efforts to engage the opposite sex, for those who were more handsome or socially skilled would be at an advantage (Miles, this volume). In their view, people's values and lifestyles, particularly views concerning the division of labor based on gender, have become more diverse and thus have created more obstacles to marriage. Potential partners are more likely to now have very differing opinions about marital life. As a result, finding someone to marry now requires activities (*katsudō*) involving more personal effort. The inequalities created by these liberalizing trends reward personal ability and effort, and they have made it difficult for certain individuals to find both jobs and marriage partners. According to Yamada and Shirakawa, this is the social cause of the modern "marriage squeeze."

The concept of *konkatsu* correspondingly attracted media attention, and a number of professional and amateur brokers published how-to books and even held seminars for unmarried people. I attended one of the *"konkatsu* seminars" in the spring of 2009 in Tokyo. It was administered by an instructor who had authored a number of books on how to find a marriage partner. All together, forty people (approximately twenty men and twenty women) attended the series.[10] The instructor started the seminar with the question, "Why is *konkatsu* important?" Then he continued:

> We actually all want a "natural encounter" [*shizen na deai*]. I also think this is the best. But when we pass the age of thirty, we cannot have natural encounters. This is because after the age of thirty, it is difficult to create new human relationships. In the old days, more than 90 percent of people married by the age of thirty. But now, owing to the issue of late marriage, there are fewer opportunities for natural encounters. When natural encounters disappear, there is something that we have to do: that is *konkatsu*. Natural encounters also take time, and you might also fail. *Konkatsu* will give you the opportunity to meet someone one-on-one more quickly.

As part of the *konkatsu* activities, the instructor explained several different types of introduction services, including major domestic introduction companies and middle- and small-scale matchmaking services. While he claimed that it was up to the attendees as to which services they want to use, he also stated that by using these matchmaking services, "We can buy encounters [*deai wa kaeru*]! If we can buy them, then just buy them! If you cannot find an encounter by yourself, there is someone who can assist you, so then you buy it." Finding someone through marriage agencies appeared far from a "natural encounter" and thus not ideal. Nonetheless, the understanding that participants were the victims of social forces and not simply suffering from personal failings made commercial matchmaking appear to be a more acceptable solution for creating intimate relationships. Seeking a partner through domestic matchmaking services was portrayed as unavoidable or even a natural result of social changes and the tendencies toward late marriage (*bankonka*) in Japan. In this manner, seminar participants were led to view the non-ideal—arranged meetings—as necessary and even acceptable.

How, then, did some Japanese men decide that transnational matchmaking was a viable option? In what follows, I look at how such compromised options became acceptable. My ethnographic data show that transnational matchmaking systems helped male clientele gradually shift their perspectives and definitions so that an arranged marriage in a transnational context also came to seem natural and thus not really transgressive of the norms of domestic matchmaking.

FROM DOMESTIC AND SEMI-TRANSNATIONAL TO TRANSNATIONAL MATCHMAKING

Japanese men experienced the transition from domestic to transnational matchmaking practices by gradually shifting the boundaries of their acceptable "marriage market." Few men began their search for a marriage partner with a visit to a transnational marriage agency. Most of the Japanese men I met at the transnational marriage agencies had been enrolled at domestic marriage agencies and had already gone through the process outlined above, shifting away from placing their hopes in a "natural" encounter. As one transnational marriage broker confessed to me, "No one wants to marry a Chinese bride at first." A Japanese man said the following:

> Before I came here [a transnational marriage agency], I had a lot of arranged meetings with Japanese women. I do not know why, but nothing worked. I met around thirty or forty women. When I felt okay, the

other did not feel the same, or when a counterpart liked me, I did not have any feelings for her. Then, the domestic broker I knew introduced me to the transnational broker here. I felt that if it did not work with Japanese women, I might also turn my eyes to transnational matchmaking

At domestic marriage agencies, some men had dated Japanese women for a short time but had not moved on to marriage. Even after becoming clients at a transnational marriage agency, some men still did not completely give up their hopes of marrying a Japanese woman, so they simultaneously continued their memberships at domestic marriage agencies. Others complained that they had not even had a chance to meet a single Japanese woman because within the matchmaking system, which requires mutual consent before a meeting is set up, the women refused to meet them based on their profiles. Some had been enrolled at domestic matchmaking agencies for more than half a year and still had not had any matchmaking meetings, although they were still being charged monthly fees to access women's profiles. If men did not get the chance to meet women in person, they felt that they were paying monthly fees for nothing.

After failing to find a suitable bride at domestic marriage agencies, some men started looking at transnational marriage websites, and others simply shifted their target based on recommendations from their domestic brokers. For instance, Mr. Iguchi had been a member of a domestic marriage agency for a number of years. He was in his late thirties and a public servant in an urban city. His income was decent and stable. His father and brother were both medical doctors. The domestic marriage broker told me that "because Mr. Iguchi could not become a medical doctor, he has an inferiority complex, which makes his personality a little difficult. He is also short. He is not a bad person, but he talks too much about nothing important." After a number of unsuccessful matchmaking meetings with Japanese women, the domestic broker did not know what to do with him. Then she found the opportunity to introduce him to a transnational marriage agency she knew. After she sent him to the transnational agency, surprisingly, Mr. Iguchi found a bride from China quite quickly. The domestic broker was also astonished by how easy it was for a man like him to find a bride. Since then, whenever she encountered someone for whom she could not a find match at her own domestic agency, she sent him to the transnational agency.

Many Japanese men struggled with the decision to shift their target from a domestic to a transnational match. Many male clients were attracted to one of the transnational marriage agencies, China Love, because it also offered matchmaking parties and meetings with Chinese women who already resided in Japan on a trainee, student, work, or even permanent residency visa. Most of these women already spoke Japanese. For men who saw themselves involuntarily engaged in transnational matchmaking practices, such a middle ground—not totally domestic, not totally transnational—was an intermediate step when making up their minds whether they were ready to consider a Chinese wife. A Japanese man told me, "Actually going to China by crossing national borders does not give a good impression to others. If it is a matchmaking meeting with a Chinese woman already living in Japan, I can tell others that I met her somewhere in Japan." Presenting legitimate stories about how intimate relationships had been created was part of transforming an "unnatural" encounter into a "natural" one.

Over the course of my research, I observed thirteen matchmaking parties between Japanese men and Chinese women at China Love. Parties were held at a restaurant near the agency. At each party, there were ten to thirteen men and a similar number of women, though agencies always tried to have a few more women than men. The participation fees were ¥10,000 for men but free for women.[11] Drinks and a light lunch were served. Using a system of so-called "speed dating," every seven or eight minutes men moved from one table to the next, while the women always remained at the same tables. This system made it possible for everyone to meet everyone else. After that, participants submitted the names of their three favorite people. The staff members input those data into a computer program and made matches. Every party produced two to four couples. Those who became couples went out for coffee right after the party, and the other men went back to the office and further discussed other opportunities with the brokers. While sometimes disappointing, the matchmaking parties gave many male clients their first interaction with Chinese women at a personal level. On the way back from a party to the agency, one man commented, "They really looked like Japanese. I did not feel any incongruity interacting with them." Another man said, "Yeah, but like Japanese women, they also like young handsome men. . . . Like today, the most popular man was the youngest." The participants at the party realized that Chinese women in Japan were like Japanese women, in both positive and negative ways. In other words, they did not seem like total "foreigners," but they could be as demanding as Japanese women. If that was the case, many men might not have a chance to find a bride for the same reasons they had difficulties at the domestic agencies. Brokers also often invited those who did not find any match for dinner and drinks afterward to cheer them up. I was also invited to such dinners a number of times. Over dinner, one broker repeatedly stressed, "Let's go to China to find a bride!" The broker tried to convince the men that if they went to China, they would have more opportunities to meet younger and prettier women who were not too demanding. Some men indeed decided to visit China to find a bride.

In these ways, men's acceptance of matchmaking practices gradually expanded from the domestic to the semi-transnational and eventually to the transnational. While crossing national borders to find a bride who did not speak the same language seemed unimaginable for many men in the beginning, this step-by-step process facilitated a gradual transformation that did not require them to abruptly change their outlook. The arranged marriage system was already common practice for domestic marriages; moving from domestic marriage agencies to transnational ones reflected the extent to which men were willing to compromise or, to put it more precisely, stretch their conception of "ordinary" matching.

PAYMENTS AS AN ORDINARY PART OF CONTEMPORARY MATCHMAKING PRACTICES

The payments involved in transnational matchmaking, often stigmatized in society as "buying a bride," were also given meanings that built upon existing domestic practices. As discussed above, domestic introduction services require payments. For instance, domestic marriage agencies provide numerous services, including *"omiai* parties" and individual arranged meetings. In order to participate in these events, people have to be members of an agency and pay registration fees. Some agencies charge monthly or annual membership fees but have no fees when a couple gets married, while others charge lower membership and monthly fees but extra fees at the time of marriage. However, the fees are not seen as buying "a wife" (or husband) but rather as purchasing an "opportunity," partly because in the domestic services, men and women pay the same fees and are seen as equal in the process of matching. Both sides have equal rights to reject invitations or proposals. The service provided by brokers is simply "assistance" for creating encounters.

Payments do not simply signify a commodification of social ties. Viviana A. Zelizer analyzes the production of meaning in activities that entail payments to argue that people incessantly employ different forms of payment within their intimate relations: "It is not the money involved that determined the relationship's quality, but the relationship that defined the appropriateness of one sort of payment or another" (2000, 818). Although people use various forms of payment in intimate relations, they also regularly differentiate monetary transactions according to the definition of the relationships in which they are involved by "[adapting] symbols, rituals, practices, and physically distinguishable forms of money to mark distinct social relations (ibid., 819)." Zelizer further states, "This is serious work. It is precisely because different forms of payment signify differences in the character of the social relations currently operating (ibid., 826)." According to her, this differentiation can also work in the opposite direction—that is, different meanings of social ties distinguish the forms of payment accordingly.

Many men expressed their gratitude for paid services. For instance, Mr. Goto paid ¥3,500,000 (approximately $35,000) all together when he married a Chinese bride. This was the highest price paid by any male client that I heard of during my fieldwork. He purchased all the services available, including the matchmaking tour, wedding ceremony, the after-care services, language lessons for his Chinese bride, a gift package for the bride, and extra wedding photos. Regardless of the expense, Mr. Goto was grateful for the services of the marriage broker. On the way back to Japan after the wedding ceremony in China, I shared a four-hour car ride to the airport with him. He said, "I never thought about marrying a Chinese bride, but I also never thought about marrying such a pretty and young wife in my life. I wonder what my neighbors will say about me. They will be very surprised. But I am so grateful to the agency for introducing her to me." Mr. Goto was in his sixties. After his first wife passed away two years before, he became a client of a domestic marriage agency. He told me that he was even rejected by a woman in her forties. He did not expect this and was critical of such a woman's attitude. He said, "I wonder what a woman in her forties is going to do going forward."

Looking at cross-border marriage matchmaking practices in Taiwan, Lu (2005) observes that matchmaking practices take on very traditional forms (such as matchmakers, bride price, and gift money) while engaging multiple fixed financial actions. Yet she argues that these practices go beyond simply commercial transactions to also involve other types of localized social relations and reciprocal duties. My ethnographic work in Japan shows that commercial interactions were already rather an ordinary practice in domestic matchmaking. Domestic marriage services, which included fees, were rarely criticized for requiring monetary payments. In part, because being unmarried or marrying late was seen as a social problem, not finding anyone was seen as worse than investing in matchmaking services. As the payments at domestic marriage agencies were for buying "opportunities" and not for "marriage" itself, many men also saw their payments to transnational marriage agencies as buying transnational "introductory services," not "Chinese brides." The meanings attached to the fees at domestic agencies thus were transposed to rationalize payments made to transnational agencies as well.

MAKING DIFFERENCES "NATURAL":
"THEY ARE JUST MEN AND WOMEN"

My final ethnographic example illustrates the ways in which multiple "differences"—linguistic, cultural, or economic (among others)—have been rendered as the natural consequences of gender dissimilarities that also exist among domestic couples. Although many Japanese men tried to view their marriages to Chinese women as no different from domestic marriages, they nonetheless encountered difficulties and disparities. Particularly in the beginning, their married life was different from that of domestic couples. Transnational agency staff members frequently spent time responding to married clientele (male and female) who sought assistance in solving their problems. When I was at China Love, for instance, staff members were often on the phone. Sometimes they would spend as much as two or three hours talking with a client. The requests they received ranged from simple translations to help in settling a quarrel or even arranging a divorce. According to the chief broker at China Love, a common source of conflict was financial issues. For instance, a couple might have different expectations and wishes concerning the size of the remittance that would go to the wife's parents in China.[12] Another broker explained to me, "Of course women want to send remittances to their parents. However, they should not ask their husbands for ¥100,000 per month; that would be too much. They could ask for ¥20,000 or ¥30,000, but they would have to consult with their husbands. It is our job to tell wives about the reality of their husbands' financial situation."

One day, a China Love staff member was on the phone with a male customer whose Chinese bride had come to Japan three months before. He bought his wife cosmetics every month. His wife had started taking his gifts for granted and stopped expressing gratitude. He was dissatisfied with his wife's attitude and called for advice. He was frustrated not only because his wife did not understand what he meant, but also because her way of talking was too direct and often sounded rude to him. After hanging up, the staff member said, "Japanese people often ask me things like, 'Are all Chinese like this?' or 'Are these unique Chinese characteristics?'" Yet brokers and staff members often advised Japanese men to deemphasize nationality and national character. Moreover, when listening to men's complaints about their difficulties in communicating, the chief broker often stated, "After all, they are just men and women." He continued, "Men and women are different creatures; they will never understand each other." According to him, it was not simply a linguistic or cultural difficulty but rather a natural outcome of gender differences. Here, intimate relationships were discursively created as relations between a man and a woman. It was thus precisely the inability of couples to understand each other that made them ordinary couples wherein heterosexual intimacy was seen as possible.

Other brokers also shared the position that the male-female relationship was the central tension in cross-border marriages. In particular, many stated that male-female relationships were "irrational." For instance, Aoki, a broker at Wedding China, told me he was concerned about the correspondence between newlywed husbands and wives without the use of a proper translator. Sometimes, couples would use a dictionary or an online translation service, both of which often produced strange translations. Aoki said, "We don't know what can happen in a relationship between men and women. Anything can happen, and a small thing might damage their relationship. They might even break up before their marital life in Japan." A possible breakup before a woman arrived in Japan might occur, according to him, not because they did not speak the same language or did not know each other well enough, but because they were "men and women." In these ways, substantial differences shaped by culture, class, and language were minimized and naturalized as the inevitable tensions between all men and women.

The sources of conflict were thus rendered as "natural" outcomes of male-female relationships. Each couple's miscommunications and differences were portrayed as gender differences or as due to sex-based divisions of labor. Feminist scholars have questioned seemingly natural distinctions between males and females and argued that distinctions, such as public/private, production/reproduction, or political/domestic, are the products of ideology (Collier and Yanagisako 1987; Martin 1991; Yanagisako and Delaney 1995). However, these differentiated categories are still widely employed and treated as natural in society. These seemingly natural differences are employed not only to separate the sexes, but also to ease communication between them and, perhaps, sell services that aid that process (such as *Men Are from Mars, Women Are from Venus*; Gray 1992).[13] These "differences" were deployed and even rationalized in order to make sense of or conceal any difficulties the participants faced.

The broker Tanaka also used this gender-dichotomous image in order to explain household finances. Some men were concerned that they might have made the wrong decision by marrying a person who had high financial demands. Nonetheless, the broker's strategy was to show that Chinese women's financial demands were not the undesired consequence of their having married someone from a developing country or that their marital relationships were based on financial ties. Rather, he sought to reframe financial demands as the product of natural gender differences. According to him, in any marriage, the role of the man is to provide, while women are to accept what they are told. His favorite sexual joke was also to connect this dichotomous image with the idea that men penetrate (*ireru*) while women accept (*ukeru*); he said this meant that men "naturally" should initiate their desires and women should never reject. This discourse was employed to console or persuade male clients, justifying and explaining conflicts between Japanese husbands and their Chinese wives. Part of the marketing strategy of Mr. Tanaka's agency was to avoid divorces as much as possible. The broker and the other staff members at the agency often claimed that very few of their brokered marriages ended in divorce, in contrast to other agencies that introduced women who then became "runaway brides."

Acknowledging the conflicts in these marriages as something other than the result of gender differences would further stigmatize the married couples and provide evidence that the marriages were brokered based on convenience. The last thing participants wanted was to have their marriages perceived as involving two strangers who sought an easy way to achieve their goals through an unnatural arranged international pairing. In order to avoid such an image, conflicts needed to be rendered as part of the ordinary struggles that any couple must face.

Japanese-Chinese matchmaking processes negotiate the limits of doxa while still relying on it. Natural or conventional social facts, or "doxa," according to Bourdieu (1977), are always negotiated by different members of society. Although Bourdieu discusses challenging doxa in terms of the relationship between the dominator and the dominated, at the transnational marriage agencies, those producing the discourses and consulting with frustrated clients wished to reaffirm taken-for-granted assumptions about marriage. By rendering a brokered Japanese-Chinese marital relationship as simply one between a man and a woman, participants could avoid the perception that they were transgressing social norms. Such masking emphasized the relationship across sexual and gender boundaries while downplaying other borders and differences. By doing so, marriage became a place where the only acceptable differences and inequities were those believed to be between the genders.

ORDINARY OR EXTRAORDINARY?

This chapter has demonstrated that in order to establish a basis for intimate transnational relationships, the work focused on framing seemingly extraordinary ways of meeting a partner as "ordinary." Domestic commercial matchmaking services have already become acceptable, if not ideal, methods of making intimate relationships through a public discourse that portrays such practices as the inevitable results of social change in Japanese society. Participants in transnational marriages have sought to appropriate meanings attached to the domestic use of matchmaking services to render acceptable transnational matchmaking practices. As outlined above, in three different contexts, Japanese men attempted to destigmatize their intimate relationships, making them out to be as natural and ordinary as those of domestic arrangements for couples. They achieved this not by rejecting but by stretching already existing meanings, practices, and discourses within Japanese society.

These efforts demonstrate how intimate relationships can be created in transnational Japan. The ability to view one's relationship as ordinary has played a more important role than love or passion in matchmaking practices. While not everyone can create an "ideal intimate relationship"—that is, meet someone naturally and decide to marry based on love, often with the support of family and friends—the production of intimate relationships remains negotiable based on available discourses concerning what is normal. In the negotiations of these discourses outlined above, the boundaries between national and transnational, and ordinary and extraordinary, become blurred. That blurring has rendered transnational matches, linking spouses who do not share a language or culture, seem like just a slight extension of marriage patterns in contemporary Japanese society and thus a permissible basis for an intimate relationship.

NOTES

1. I do not mean to undervalue women's experiences; however, as Suzuki (2003) observes, compared with women's experiences, men's experiences seldom appear publicly or academically. I have written elsewhere my analysis of women's positions and experiences (Yamaura 2015b).

2. Marriages with Filipina women occur not only via marriage agencies, but also in local clubs or bars. In these relationships, Japanese men meet and marry Filipina women who originally came to Japan on entertainment visas (Faier 2009; Suzuki 2005).

3. The two major bride-sending communities where I conducted fieldwork were located in territory that constituted part of Manchukuo, the former puppet state of imperial Japan. I have argued elsewhere that contemporary transnational brokerage linkages were made possible based on colonial legacies in this area. In particular, terms such as "familiarity"

(*shinkinkan/qinqie*) and "blood ties" (*xueyuan guanxi*)—terms that were linked to the colonial past and subsequent repatriation—were used to legitimate cross-border marriages between Japan and northeast China (Yamaura 2015a, 2015b).

4. In order to become a transnational marriage broker, no qualification was required. However, although it is not too difficult to start a brokerage business, it is difficult to maintain it. I witnessed many brokers quit owing to a lack of success.

5. Approximately 850–1,300 marriage agencies are registered in these networks. The brokers also exchange the profiles of their clientele so that they can set up their clients with each other.

6. According to the demographic survey I conducted at a transnational marriage agency, the clients were mostly white-collar businessmen (53 percent), followed by self-employed men (14.3 percent), public servants (10 percent), corporate executives (6.8 percent), specialists (5.3 percent), schoolteachers (3.7 percent), and retired men (1 percent), with 4.5 percent of respondents choosing "other." This survey was conducted with 149 Japanese men at the transnational marriage agency.

7. Chinese women also pay brokerage fees to Chinese brokers, ranging from 20,000 RMB to 130,000 RMB. This means that female clients pay between $3,200 and $21,000.

8. These institutions include so-called go-between services (86.7 percent), in which matchmakers personally mediate meetings based on each side's requests; data-matching services (8.4 percent), in which individuals input their information and requests for the computer to find suitable matches (often with the "assistance" of an agency's staff members); and Internet matching services (3.1 percent), in which no matchmakers are involved (West 2011).

9. Chizuko Ueno (1995) observes that, whereas "love marriages" (*ren'ai kekkon*) might appear to value love and discard other socioeconomic criteria, these marriages actually are based more on class and educational endogamy.

10. Although I did not do a demographic survey on the attendees, the majority of them looked to be in their mid-thirties to mid-forties.

11. Japanese men were the main targets of the brokerage business in Japan. Hence, while women attend parties for free, the parties were designed for the Japanese men to have more opportunities to meet women.

12. Chinese women's remittance to their families in China varied, yet many women shared the wish to help their parents in some way. Some women just brought nice gifts when they visited their families; others tried to help buy a house. It is important that such wishes to help were not limited to transnational marriages. Even if they married in China, children's filial piety was seen as important (see for example, Fong 2004).

13. John Gray argues that men and women speak different languages: "When misunderstandings arise, remember that we speak different languages; take the time necessary to translate what your partner really means or wants to say" (1993, 97).

REFERENCES

Bourdieu, Pierre. 1977. *Outline of a Theory of Practice*. Cambridge: Cambridge University Press.

Collier, Jane Fishburne, and Sylvia Junko Yanagisako. 1987. *Gender and Kinship: Essays toward a Unified Analysis*. Stanford: Stanford University Press.

Ehrenreich, Barbara, and Arlie Russell Hochschild, eds. 2003. *Global Woman: Nannies, Maids, and Sex Workers in the New Economy*. New York: Metropolitan Books.

Faier, Lieba. 2009. *Intimate Encounters: Filipina Women and the Remaking of Rural Japan*. Berkeley: University of California Press.

Fong, Vanessa L. 2004. *Only Hope: Coming of Age under China's One-Child Policy*. Stanford: Stanford University Press

Goffman, Erving. 2009 [1963]. *Stigma: Notes on the Management of Spoiled Identity*. New York: Simon and Schuster.

Gray, John. 1992. *Men Are from Mars, Women Are from Venus*. New York: HarperCollins.

Hashimoto, Akiko, and John W. Traphagan. 2008. *Imagined Families, Lived Families: Culture and Kinship in Contemporary Japan*. Albany: State University of New York Press.

Hendry, Joy. 2013. *Understanding Japanese Society*, 4th ed. London: Routledge

Kuwayama, Norihiko. 1995. *Kokusai kekkon to sutoresu* [International Marriage and Stress]. Tokyo: Akashi shoten.

Lu, Melody Chia-Wen. 2005. "Commercially Arranged Marriage Migration Case Studies of Cross-Border Marriages in Taiwan." *Indian Journal of Gender Studies* 12 (2–3): 275–303.

Martin, Emily. 1991. "The Egg and the Sperm: How Science Has Constructed a Romance Based on Stereotypical Male-Female Roles." *Signs* 16 (3): 485–501.

Nakamatsu, Tomoko. 2013. "Marriage Migration: Love in Brokered Marriages in Contemporary Japan." In *Proletarian and Gendered Mass Migrations*, edited by Dirk Hoerder and Amarjit Kaur, 467–483. Leiden: Brill.

Nakane, Chie. 1967. *Kinship and Economic Organization in Rural Japan*. New York: Humanities Press.

Piper, Nicola. 2003. "Wife or Worker? Worker or Wife? Marriage and Cross-Border Migration in Contemporary Japan." *International Journal of Population Geography* 9 (6): 457–469.

Ronald, Richard, and Allison Alexy. 2011. "Continuity and Change in Japanese Homes and Families." In *Home and Family in Japan: Continuity and Transformation*, edited by Richard Ronald and Allison Alexy, 1–24. New York: Routledge.

Shukuya, Kyoko. 1988. *Ajia kara kita hanayome* [Brides from Asia]. Tokyo: Akashi shoten.

Suzuki, Nobue. 2005. "Tripartite Desires: Filipina-Japanese Marriages and Fantasies of Transnational Traversal." In *Cross-Border Marriages: Gender and Mobility in Transnational Asia*, edited by Nicole Constable, 124–144. Philadelphia: University of Pennsylvania Press.

———. 2003. "Of Love and the Marriage Market: Masculinity Politics and Filipina-Japanese Marriages in Japan." In *Men and Masculinities in Contemporary Japan: Dislocating the Salaryman Doxa*, edited by James E. Roberson and Nobue Suzuki, 91–108. New York: Routledge.

Takeyama, Akiko. 2008. "The Art of Seduction and Affect Economy: Neoliberal Class Struggle and Gender Politics in a Tokyo Host Club." PhD dissertation, University of Illinois.

Tseng, Yen-feng. 2010. "Marriage Migration to East Asia: Current Issues and Propositions in Making Comparisons." In *Asian Cross-Border Marriage Migration: Demographic Patterns and Social Issues*, edited by Wen-Shan Yang and Melody Chia-Wen Lu, 31–45. Amsterdam: Amsterdam University Press

Ueno, Chizuko. 1995. "'Renai kekkon' no tanjo" [The Birth of "Love Marriage"]. In *Kekkon: Tokyo daigaku kokai koza* [Marriage: Tokyo University Public Lectures], edited by Hiroyuki Yoshikawa. Tokyo: Tokyo University Shupankai.

West, Mark D. 2011. *Lovesick Japan: Sex, Marriage, Romance, Law*. Ithaca, NY: Cornell University Press.

Yamada, Masahiro, and Tōko Shirakawa. 2008. *Konkatsu jidai*. Tokyo: Discover.

Yamada, Yumiko. 2009. *Hisshō konkatsu method: Omiai to iu konshō.* Tokyo: Gakusyū kenkyū sha.

Yamaura, Chigusa. 2015a. "From Manchukuo to Marriage: Localizing Contemporary Cross-Border Marriages between Japan and Northeast China." *Journal of Asian Studies* 74 (3): 565–588.

———. 2015b. "Marrying Transnational, Desiring Local: Making Marriageable Others in Japanese–Chinese Cross-Border Matchmaking." *Anthropological Quarterly* 88 (4): 1029–1058.

Yang, Wen-Shan, and Melody Chia-Wen Lu. 2010. *Asian Cross-Border Marriage Migration: Demographic Patterns and Social Issues.* Amsterdam: Amsterdam University Press

Yanagisako, Sylvia Junko, and Carol Lowery Delaney. 1995. *Naturalizing Power: Essays in Feminist Cultural Analysis.* New York: Routledge.

Zelizer, Viviana A. 2000. "The Purchase of Intimacy." *Law and Social Inquiry* 25 (3): 817–848.

CHAPTER 12

❖ ❖ ❖

Connections, Conflicts, and Experiences of Intimacy in Japanese-Australian Families

DIANA ADIS TAHHAN

In late 2013, when I was attending a Christmas party in Sydney, a man approached and initiated a conversation. He had learned that I had written a book on "the Japanese family," and he, an Australian man married to a Japanese woman, felt that he had found someone to explain some of the cultural misunderstandings and frustrations they were experiencing in their daily life. My response to his experiences and questions was cautious. After all, what did I know about Japanese-*Australian* marriages, let alone their very specific relational context?

An hour or so later, the man's wife found me. She sat with me for a long time and, in many ways, described the reverse side of the same misunderstandings and frustrations her husband had expressed earlier. There was a clear distinction in their parenting methods and approaches and a mutual preference for time spent with their children without the other partner there. Poor communication, undesirable sleeping arrangements, and conflicted sexual intimacy appeared to be at the top of their concerns and frustrations.

This situation was interesting because both partners knew the other was speaking to me openly about their personal relationship. They were happily confiding in me, but I felt that I wasn't really their confidante and that they could just as easily have made these complaints known to one another (not to mention other people). I felt saddened by the discussions, struck by the significant lack of communication that could have been resolved more directly. Yet, later in the evening I saw this same couple laughing and having fun together; perhaps the very issues that deeply concerned them in our discussions were not the only aspects pertaining to their happiness and experiences of intimacy in their family.

Then there was Maki, a beautiful, kind-hearted woman in her forties who had two boys, aged two and four. Maki desperately wanted another child, but her husband was reluctant because he was in his late forties. She doted on her two children and enjoyed being close with them. She explained that she usually achieved this closeness through *skinship* (intimacy through touch), such as co-sleeping (*soine*) and co-bathing. These shared behaviors were almost exclusively experienced by Maki and her boys; for Maki's husband these had been a bone of contention. Maki slept in the boys' room, and her husband, not prepared to give up a perfectly comfortable double bed, remained in "their" room. It sounded as though Maki would have been open to co-sleeping as a *family*, but her priority was to sleep with her boys. She said that co-sleeping made her feel connected and secure, and these feelings were reciprocated by the boys. Her Australian husband found it difficult to understand the cultural significance of co-sleeping and its intimate manifestations, but he accepted it as a "Japanese custom." However, this "custom" became a fundamental issue when they had to temporarily move in with her husband's family. Her mother-in-law found it extremely difficult to understand why Maki would not sleep with her husband and implored them to buy the boys bunk beds. This argument came to a head when her mother-in-law, in a moment of frustration, said, "If you don't buy the boys bunk beds, I will!"[1] Many months later, when back in their own home, the boys had bunk beds. Maki still sleeps on the floor in their room but has a bad back and goes back to their marital bed when her husband goes to work.

Literature on the modern Japanese family includes various works on marital relations and parent-child relationships, but rarely do these explore the lived experience of intimacy, particularly via body practices.[2] For some individuals, intimate connections are strengthened by body practices such as co-sleeping and co-bathing; for others, such connections are felt via warm feelings of closeness explained through terms such as heart-to-heart communication (*ishin denshin*), feelings of "togetherness" (*ittaikan*), and feelings of being one body (*ishin dōtai*).[3] Previous research reveals that these practices and "feelings" are often described as unique Japanese cultural experiences that foreigners are not able to interpret, much less feel (Tahhan 2014). The point here isn't to try to draw comparisons with the Japanese family as a cultural entity and emphasize what is or isn't possible in a Japanese-Australian family; rather, the aspects that were important in research on the Japanese family *in Japan* may help to illuminate experiences of intimacy in Japanese-Australian families.

The conceptual framework underlying my research on intimacy adopts an embodied understanding of relationships, particularly within the context of touch, feeling, and connection. I call this connection *touching at depth*. This framework relies on a complexly embodied and sensuous experience of touch that helps us attend to the importance of affect and feelings. It presumes that when people connect with other people, objects, and environments, they feel a wholeness, a potential, a connection between them that isn't finite, nor is it located in any one body, body part, or person (Tahhan 2013a). *Touching at depth* is this relational quality that relies on the ontological change from Cartesian body to wholeness. It relates to the moment of "real" intimacy, love, or meeting between people.[4] In *touching at depth*, there are no separate bodies or subjects; this form of touch has intimate manifestations and finds meaning through an embodied *felt* relation and deep sense of connection.[5] This notion of *touching at depth* was inspired by the cultural context of Japan, but it is not necessarily restricted to it. Elsewhere I have explored its wider applicability as an analytical tool (Tahhan 2013a), and in this chapter I use it to understand the meanings of intimacy in Japanese-Australian relationships.

METHODOLOGY

This chapter is based on ethnographic research conducted in Sydney, Australia, in 2013 and 2014. The main aims of the research were to explore experiences of intimacy in Japanese-Australian families, where one spouse is Japanese and the other Australian. Among almost all participants, the wife is Japanese and the husband Australian.[6] Specifically this research sought to investigate the lived experience of intimacy in two relational contexts—namely, parent-child relationships and marital relationships. In particular the research focused on intimacy in the context of body practices and feelings of closeness. I aimed to uncover the daily practices of intimacy and how these may reveal similarities with Japanese families living in Japan. In addition, I investigated the participants' feelings within these relational contexts and explored how mutual understanding and deep care underlying their relationships were developed, negotiated, and expressed, such as there was in many Japanese families living in Japan.

The research methods employed were interviews (one-on-one and group discussions) and open-ended responses in writing.[7] In all cases, the questions centered around the positive and challenging aspects of the marital relationship and the parent-child relationship, as well as specific body practices and experiences of intimacy. Participants' responses varied depending on the method—that is, many people intimated that they might not feel very comfortable discussing such personal issues, but when the interviews commenced, they became very open about their experiences. Alternatively, the written responses were often polite and guarded, giving the impression of a cohesive family unit. It was only in follow-up interviews or follow-up written questions that the "real feelings" (honne) of some participants seemed to emerge.[8]

Out of twenty participants, only one was a Japanese male. The remaining participants were Japanese women between the ages of thirty-two and forty-eight. In general the couples had been together and/or married for at least five years. There were two groups of participants; the first group included women who had studied or worked abroad (generally in Australia), where they met their respective partners, married, and moved to Australia; the second group included women who had met their partners in Japan and had either resided in Japan for some time together or had married and moved to Australia to be with their partners. While some women spoke in Japanese with their husbands, the majority communicated in English. Most women were homemakers or employed part time. Only four women from the sample were in full-time employment. Although I approached the Australian husbands of the Japanese women, many were reluctant to respond formally in interviews or writing.[9] Indeed, the male participants' voices are an important part of Japanese-Australian familial intimacy and experience. However, for the purpose of this chapter it is predominantly women's voices that will be explored or the male perspective as understood through the lens of their female counterparts.

A methodological point needs to be made here about the women participants and their responses. The two women in the above examples had informally confided in me their frustrations with their husbands and their priority for their children over their husband. When I asked them to formally participate in the research, they both readily agreed. However, in their follow-up responses they became incredibly careful and formal, and they both explained how open and loving their marital relationships were. The sense of contentment they articulated in their follow-up responses diverged from the frustrations they had expressed in our initial conversations. I had observed these women with their husbands in informal social situations, and both couples seemed to be happy and genuinely enjoy each other's company. This confused me further and made me reassess my subjectivity and positioning in the study. Perhaps these women's lived experiences of marital intimacy were actually more satisfactory and enjoyable than they had first suggested, or perhaps their "real feelings" were not easily described in formal research settings. It could also be that the information they initially gave me (presuming what they told me informally were their "real feelings") was not integral to a quality or satisfactory relationship. The husbands of both of these women had openly discussed their marital relationship with me in informal settings and had voiced frustrations about their marriage, sleeping arrangements, and lack of sexual intimacy. However, these men were not available for me (or were not willing) to formally participate in interviews.

MARITAL INTIMACY

Literature on some Japanese marriages highlights emotional and sexual dissatisfaction and disengagement in marriage (Ataka 1995; Iwao 1993; Kamayama 2004; Lebra 1984; Yoshihiro 1994). However, there is also a body of literature that appears to contradict this seeming state of separation and instability in marriages. For example, the stability of marital relationships is understood to be related to complementarity in roles, successful rearing of children, and participation in wider kin ties (Imamura 1987; Iwao 1993). Through these elements closeness and connectedness are thought to be built. Iwao (1983, 77) refers to marital couples as two people who can tacitly and effortlessly depend upon each other and be totally at ease with one another. Lebra notes that the "mutual aloofness of husband and wife . . . is not necessarily a sign of estrangement" (2004, 89). Discourses of intuition and other ways of being connected through more subtle communication make cultural sense when viewed within the context of the Japanese family and through an embodied understanding of relationships via *touching at depth*.

What does this mean for Japanese-Australian families? There are limited references to experiences of intimacy among such families. The work that has been done on Japanese-Australian relationships has explored lifestyle migration (Sato 2001), intermarriages and interactions with the local Japanese community (Denman 2009), and young migrant experiences (Kawashima 2012), rather than focusing on the experiences of intimate familial relationships. Among my participants, there were mixed attitudes toward marriage and family life. There were some similarities with Japanese familial relations, but there were also variations, particularly in the ways women interpreted, participated in, and, at times, withheld daily intimacy with their partners.

JAPANESE-AUSTRALIAN MARRIAGES

Japanese-Australian marriages were generally described by Japanese women as "open" and "honest." Some women mentioned the respectful nature of their relationship, while others noted that their Australian husbands were "free" and "relaxed." Verbal communication seemed to be a key positive factor in many relationships, and this helped with the more challenging aspects of cultural difference.

> Tomoko (thirty-four years old): We talk a lot. We don't stop talking until we both agree. It's because we come from a different background, speak a different language; we can misunderstand each other quite easily.
>
> Yumi (thirty-eight years old): We don't just use words; we read each other's body language. We discuss face to face; we take as long as we need. We try really hard to understand and accept each other. It is challenging because words can hurt the other's feelings. Also, sometimes I can't find the right words to explain how I'm feeling, and we then get frustrated. But it is better this way because we are more careful and make sure that we are both on the same page.

Both these women seem to recognize and manage their cultural and linguistic differences through careful communication in English. Tomoko and her husband ensure they constantly talk to resolve differences; Yumi recognizes the importance of body language and non-verbal as well as verbal communication. She and her husband seem to carefully work through issues or misunderstandings to ensure they don't keep happening. Both these women spoke quite openly and lovingly about their partners and the life they share with their children in Australia. For example, Tomoko told me in English: "What we do to keep family life happy is we respect each other, care about each other, and show 'big love.'" For these women there seemed to be a deep care and mutual respect enabled through communication. There does not appear to be a compartmentalization of husband and wife; these women speak of a respect for and acceptance of differences in their marital relations. Their family life extends to and includes one another and their children.

Other women were less interested in their relationships with their partners or resolving any cultural differences. The following women noted that once they had children, there was less communication with their partners, and the emphasis shifted to the children.[10] For example:

> Emi (thirty-two years old): My husband and I used to talk all the time. But since we have had our children [ages three, six, and eight], I don't know. ... It's like I don't have the energy any more. He's at work; he barely

does anything to help with the kids [*ikuji*], but it's okay. I'm happy because I have the kids.

HANA (thirty-four years old): I am so busy all day long, with the kids [ages four and seven] and the housework and doing all the cooking. . . . He can't really expect me to be the same with him, can he [compared to before we had kids]? I mean, he's not really involved, and I'm so tired by the end of the day, . . . I find myself going to bed first before he can try and wake me up [laughs],[11] or I wait until he's asleep before going to bed. I don't really know what's changed. I don't really care to be honest. But the feeling has definitely changed. I just can't be bothered.

These two women, who are both at home with their children, have noticed a shift in their relationships with their husbands, though neither can articulate why this shift has occurred. Emi voices a preference and satisfaction with her relationship with her children; Hana appears resentful because of the workload of the home and children and in some ways seems to be avoiding and alienating her husband (that is, at bedtime). Hana's indifference reminded me of some women with whom I did research in Japan who alienated themselves from their husbands. However, there is a significant difference from the Japanese context. My Japanese participants in Japan often used the cultural practice of co-sleeping as an excuse to use their child's body to separate themselves from their husbands. The separation that existed for Hana and her husband was not about alienating the husband vis-à-vis the children and co-sleeping. That is, she wasn't using the body of her child/children to separate herself from her husband. Hana was not apologizing for this separation, nor was she making any excuses vis-à-vis her children. She was, however, still separate and alienated from her husband, even though they slept in a separate room from the children. She purposefully goes to bed earlier or later and uses her body in a way that alienates her husband. There is no physical intimate relational experience in this context, as the body of the subject (Hana) and the body of the object (husband) appear to be located within alienated, finite, identified entities. She uses her body as a tool to overcome her husband, and there is no space or depth for intimacy or connection in this particular context as she resists his desire.

Hana's experience leads me to an important aspect that seemed to underlie most of my discussions with participants: sleep arrangements. In my informal discussions with Australian men married to Japanese women, their sexual dissatisfaction and deep concern with sleeping arrangements emerged. Although I didn't formally interview Australian men about these aspects, I asked the women about their experience and their understanding of their husbands' feelings about this practice.

THE MARITAL BED AND SLEEP

Sleep in a Japanese context is often associated with co-sleeping and pro-longed physical proximity. Scholarship on Japanese co-sleeping is usually associated with functional reasons, such as house size and lack of space (Caudill and Plath 1986; Lebra 2004); a purposive reduction of sleep dis-turbances in infancy (Kawasaki et al. 1994; Latz, Wolf, and Lozoff 1999); and certain relational states from close proximity, touch, and intimacy, specifically skinship (Ben-Ari 1996, 1997; Lebra 2004; Tahhan 2008, 2013b, 2014). In many cases children sleep in the middle, between both parents.[12] I found two types of experiences in terms of sleep in the Japanese family: exclusive and inclusive sleeping arrangements (Tahhan 2014). The term "exclusive" refers to the alienation that can emerge between marital cou-ples where the child is the focus and where one parent often uses that child's body and identity to reinstate his or her own identity (as a sepa-rate bounded identity). Within inclusive relations, however, there is an all-encompassing space between the whole family, not as separate entities trying to achieve oneness and exclusivity but as relational beings that are connected. People are not just located in their own subjectivity and body. The boundaries in the relationship cannot be controlled or defined. There is an embodied connection that enables the father to still be included and participate in the life of the family even if he sleeps in a different room.

The Japanese-Australian experience of co-sleeping revealed some similarities with Japanese sleeping patterns in Japan. For example, some women noted the functional benefits of co-sleeping (for example, being able to watch over one's child, feeling secure, and helping everyone get a good night's sleep). However, there were some significant differences or variations that require attention. In Japan, there was often a mutual deci-sion or at least mutual acknowledgement that co-sleeping was a common cultural practice for the above-mentioned reasons. Rarely did participants sleep away from their children; in fact, I rarely found couples who were conscious of co-sleeping as a "practice"; it was seen as something normal or commonplace. Across all my participants in Japan I never came across a woman who voiced a preference to sleep with her husband over her child, and for many there was not a distinction. Although some participants in Japan complained of low sexual intimacy, they didn't attribute it to co-sleeping.[13] In Australia, however, there was not the same acceptance or understanding by the husband. Informal discussions with Australian men focused on the lack of sexual intimacy and closeness because their wives preferred to sleep with their children. Discussions with Japanese women married to Australian men revealed that many Japanese women found the lack of intimacy amusing and/or didn't seem bothered (for example, Hana, mentioned above), while others seemed to experience co-sleeping as a means to exclude or alienate their husbands from the room/sleep experience. For example:

NOBUKO (forty-one years old): I love sleeping with my kids. My husband doesn't get it. That's okay; if he wants to, he can join us; otherwise we see him in the morning [laughs].

AKIKO (thirty-seven years old): My husband doesn't understand why co-sleeping is necessary. He doesn't understand. He just thinks it's a "Japanese custom" and accepts that. I sleep with my two kids, and it is so nice. I find it peaceful.

KYOKO (thirty-eight years old): I sleep with my children, in between them, between two single beds. I sleep on the edge [laughs]. . . . I don't really mind. My youngest sleeps on my shoulder; it's so peaceful.

MAKI (forty-five years old): I love sleeping with my boys. My husband doesn't really understand. He finds it difficult to understand why the boys need me [or] rely on me [amaeru] and why I find it so much nicer sleeping with the boys than with him. . . . I guess it would be different if I had a girl. . . . Maybe it wouldn't feel the same. I don't know really, but with my youngest, it is so nice to sleep with him. He is like my little boyfriend [koibito].[14]

Some women seem to experience a peacefulness in co-sleeping with their children. However, this form of intimacy seemed to be at the exclusion of the husband. In some cases, sleeping with the children seemed to *replace* the husband. Maki, for example, voiced a preference for her children over her partner ("[It is] so much nicer sleeping with the boys than with him"). While Maki may feel that this is a "real" experience of intimacy with her boys, ontologically there is a disjuncture: she is a separate body/subject from the body/bodies of her child/children (her "boys"), with whom she attempts to merge at the exclusion of her husband. While this preference appears to connect Maki with her boys in an intimate experience of co-sleeping, it is less about intimacy and more about exclusion. Maki has a particular bounded idea of bodies, subjects, and objects: she is sleeping in the same room as her boys, but it is at the exclusion of her husband. Maki's husband's presence seems to be inconsequential or burdensome via-à-vis Maki's strong desire to be close with her children. Although there seems to be a meaningful relationship between Maki and her boys, I argue that such attempts to become one and merge or unite with a child or children are not reflections of intimacy. Instead, as long as the relation is an attempt to exclude a third party, there is an emptiness where issues such as objectification, control, and separation come into play. There seem to be larger issues within their relationship, and this sleeping arrangement is one manifestation of them.

Couples sleeping separately was not uncommon in Japan, but there was a possibility for *touching at depth* in some Japanese relationships that revealed an embodied felt relation and deep sense of connection so that Japanese couples felt connected even if sleeping in separate rooms. That is, even if a Japanese husband slept in a separate room, there could still exist a depth in the family connecting them in an all-encompassing thick space.[15] Japanese futons—padded mats on the floor with no bed frame—enable more inclusive, encompassing forms of co-sleeping, common to my Japanese participants' sleep experience in Japan, breaking down the binaries of parent and child and husband and wife. There is a warmth and sense of connection that softens the borders and blurs the boundaries between the family (Tahhan 2013b, 71). The practice of sleeping in beds in a Japanese-Australian context may impact the experience of co-sleeping and intimacy. Elsewhere I have discussed the identity and subjectivity of a room and a bed (Tahhan 2013b). A bed has a permanent place and space that is confined by the boundaries of a room and the physical boundaries of the mattress. Some of my participants in Australia would sleep with their children on their bed, and the husband would be relegated to a separate bedroom or sofa bed. The impermanence of the futon and the ability to place futons next to each other can help facilitate feelings of closeness and warmth that the "Western" bed may not necessarily allow.

Some of my participants would have preferred to co-sleep with children but felt they needed to adhere to their husbands' or society's expectations. One woman's husband wanted them to practice "control crying" and help their child sleep "independently."[16] Other women were conscious of the Australian health advice about co-sleeping and risks of Sudden Infant Death Syndrome (SIDS). Others simply noted the socially appropriate or expected practice to sleep with their husbands and in their marital beds, even though their "real feeling" or preference was to sleep with their children.

Women also often expressed an apologetic undertone I never heard in Japan. For example, one woman (Fumi, thirty-six years old) stated: "I know I *should* sleep with my husband, but this way the kids get more sleep, and my husband gets more sleep, and actually it's really nice sleeping with the kids, even though I know I *shouldn't*." (emphasis added). Other participants were less apologetic and simply misrepresented their experience of co-sleeping. In interviews, various women told me that they slept in their marital beds, but later on in discussions they would reveal that "sometimes" they would co-sleep with their children (for example, when a child was sick or the husband had to wake early and needed a good night's sleep). Most of these women, I found as our discussions progressed, co-slept daily and were in no rush to stop. That is, they began co-sleeping to meet a need (for example, to help soothe a sick child) and ended up enjoying it so that it was now the "practice."

Co-sleeping was the greatest concern for Japanese women married to Australian men and a significant area of miscommunication for Australian husbands. Overall, however, and aside from the concerns about co-sleeping, women claimed they felt supported by their Australian husbands and that they had autonomy to bring up their children the way they liked. The following section addresses some underlying issues that arose in interviews and discussions; while not deemed central to feelings of closeness in an intimate relationship, they seemed to underlie most discussions.

IDEOLOGICAL REPRESENTATIONS
OF JAPANESE MARRIAGES

My conversations with Japanese women married to Australian men opened up discussions about how much these women missed Japan and their families. Although they recognized that they enjoyed their lifestyles in Australia, it became clear that over time feelings of nostalgia had permeated a deeper sadness for some and resulted in a tendency to elevate what a Japanese marriage could represent. Overall, Japanese participants described their relationships with their Australian partners as open, respectful, and communicative. Upon further clarification in interviews and discussions, participants began to draw on common ideological representations of Japanese marriages.[17] There seemed to be a general feeling among my participants that their husbands could not understand them because of cultural differences. Most significant was their husbands' inability to understand them without verbalization. Specifically, these women had to use verbal communication to always express to their husbands how they were feeling:

> MAMI (thirty-three years old): Even though I am perfectly bilingual, he drives me crazy sometimes by the way he just doesn't "get it." In a Japanese husband/wife situation *aun no kokyū* [two people in natural harmony with each other] is expected. As you know, it means that we just "get" each other without saying much. Well, I have to explain everything to him repeatedly, and it drives me crazy.

SACHIKO (thirty-five years old): I do miss that part of a relationship that I could have had [*aun no kokyū*]. But we agree on one thing, and that is parenting style.

MAYUMI (thirty-two years old): In the Japanese culture, we have *iwana kutemo wakaru darou*; it means not clearly telling your partner things so that he or she has to figure out what you are thinking, what you want him or her to understand. So your partner has to sense or guess why you are upset. In my relationship, I don't think this works because we have so many different aspects. In the past, I used to hide my feelings from my partner or not tell him what I was thinking as I had this belief. But now I don't hide anything; I tell everything because nothing is *atarimae* [natural, easy, normal] between us. I learned how to communicate with my partner *because of* the language gap and cultural gap.

KUMIKO (thirty-six years old): I can imagine other Japanese wives having even more issues with communication when it comes to deep, serious conversation. That may be partly why they miss being in Japan and bathing in cultural understanding bliss!?

There seems to be an underlying longing for what a relationship could be like—that is, the "naturalness" of Japanese communication, that which is *atarimae*. These women found it tiring and frustrating to have to constantly articulate how they were feeling; Kumiko even went so far as to describe Japanese marriages as "bathing in cultural bliss." These women upheld discourses of Japanese uniqueness; not only did they appreciate the subtle forms of communication they anticipated in Japanese relationships, but they also rendered verbal and direct communication unnecessary. Mayumi viewed this difference in a positive vein, saying she communicated better now; Sachiko recognized that although she missed what a Japanese relationship could represent, she was content with the complimentary parenting style. Often the same women who mentioned their appreciation for the openness and communication possible with their Australian husbands also mentioned the "ideal" forms of communication possible with a Japanese partner. For these women the experience of an intercultural marriage, while enjoyable, did not entirely eliminate the desire for subtle forms of communication that they felt would be possible in a Japanese marriage. These issues also brought up a general feeling of sadness or longing for life in Japan.[18]

This chapter has revealed patterns of similarities across Japanese-Australian marriages and Japanese experiences of intimacy in terms of body practices and wives' attitudes toward their husbands once they had children. However, there are also some interesting variations in daily practices of intimacy. I noticed that respondents shifted their answers when I employed different research methods, moving between interviews and written responses; in more formal situations, women often articulated contentment with everyday experiences of intimacy, but in informal discussions they described deeper frustrations and dissatisfactions. As described above, it is important to note that while the Australian men married to Japanese women were comfortable engaging in informal discussions about intimacy, I was not able to conduct formal interviews with any Australian male participants. However, this would also illuminate an important, and different, "face" to the experience of intimacy in Japanese-Australian marriages.

Some women were conflicted over what it meant to be a Japanese woman in an Australian setting. Specifically, these women felt they needed to meet the expectations of their husbands and the wider Australian community. This was particularly evident in terms of sleeping patterns. Many women voiced a preference for co-sleeping and often emphasized the importance of a child's needs over a husband's needs. At the same time, their explanations had an apologetic undertone that suggested some of them felt they "should" fulfill wider societal expectations and sleep with their husbands more, even if it wasn't their preference. Conversely, in Maki's case, she eventually responded to her extended family's expectations and purchased bunk beds for her boys. However, she still sleeps with them in their room, but on a mattress on the floor.

This chapter has shown that Japanese-Australian experiences of intimacy are fundamentally complex and that this complexity reflects a different understanding and interpretation of touch, the body, and intimate connection. It is not possible to say whether Japanese women married to Australian men are all happy or feel close and connected with their husbands. As Japanese relationships in Japan reveal, there are experiences of inclusion and exclusion, but it is important that these may vary and adjust in each context.

NOTES

1. Here we can see cross-cultural value systems and hierarchies at play. There is a clear distinction between what Maki's mother-in-law feels is socially and culturally appropriate for her son and his sleeping arrangements with his wife versus Maki's own desire to co-sleep with her children. That is, Maki's mother-in-law has a clear idea of the normative physical intimacy characteristic of marital relationships in Australia, to which Maki doesn't seem to adhere.

2. For literature on marital relations, see Blood (1967), Hendry (1981), Iwao (1993), Kelsky (2001a, 2001b), and Lebra (1976, 1984). For parent-child relationships, see Caudill and Plath

(1986), Goldstein-Gidoni (2005), Lebra (1984), Nakatani (2006), Niwa (1993), Notter (2002), Sasagawa (2006), and Tahhan (2010).

3. For more on these topics, see Alexy (this volume).

4. Elsewhere I have explored different forms of touch (i.e., stroke, caress, hold) and have argued that the nature and feel of each form requires a relational understanding of what is happening between the person who is touching and the person experiencing the touch. For example, a grip might be vicious or aggressive in some cases, while in others it might be the extra holding-on grip that makes a hug more profound. Depending on the state of relationality, the touch will have a different feel. Though beyond the scope of this chapter, touch as a manifestation of intimacy requires a recognition of the type of relationship and how the body exists and changes in that relationship.

5. The potential of feeling and connection in *touching at depth* cannot be viewed via touch as a bodily sense. Theorists Merleau-Ponty (1968) and Ichikawa (1993) introduce us to the concepts of flesh and *mi* respectively, which help us become more aware of a non-finite logic of the world. Specifically *mi* refers to the body as a potential whole and moves beyond the fixed idea of the body as finite and physical and "enclosed in the skin" (Ozawa de-Silva 2002). This is the underlying theoretical framework to *touching at depth* and this chapter more broadly (see also Tahhan 2014). While Merleau-Ponty and Ichikawa help to draw out the embodied nature of intimacy vis-à-vis flesh and *mi*, they are not the focus of this chapter.

6. This is not a new phenomenon. Although there is a lack of statistical information, Denman (2009), Kawashima (2012), and Sato (2001) all refer to the tendency for Japanese women to marry Australian men more than the other way around.

7. I am in contact with the facilitator of a Japanese play group in Sydney. I emailed a letter of introduction to this facilitator, with some questions about Japanese-Australian families, and she asked for any interested participants on my behalf. From these people and through snowballing, I was able to make contact with prospective interviewees and contacts living in Australia.

8. Participants could respond in either Japanese or English (in whichever language they felt more comfortable), and aside from one participant, interviews were all conducted in Japanese.

9. While some Australian men were comfortable discussing their relationships openly with me in informal conversations, they were unwilling to formalize their responses and develop their feedback further via interviews. This stance could have been so that they could protect their families and their own anonymity, or in some cases, they may have found the conversations to be too confronting.

10. This is not dissimilar to Japanese marriages, and there is an emic notion, *kodomo chūshin* (child-centeredness), to highlight this shift. However, this did not always mean that Japanese husbands were "left out" of the relationship, nor that this shift happened in all marital relationships after children were born. For families who experience this shift, the emphasis may be on the child, but the Japanese husband and Japanese wife may still be connected and close vis-à-vis the child and the *kazoku* (family) in general (Tahhan 2014).

11. The implication in this conversation was that the husband would wake her up for sex.

12. This is referred to as *kawa no ji*, where the parents sleep on either side of the children. See Tahhan (2008) for more examples.

13. Some participants mentioned that their sex lives "fit in" with co-sleeping. For example, some would roll over to their partner's futon when their children were or seemed to be asleep, and some mentioned going to "love hotels" (Tahhan 2014).

14. It is important to note that the English translation of *koibito* (boyfriend or lover) does not necessarily accurately explain what this woman was trying to say. She was at no time implying that the relationship went beyond a mother-son relationship but simply tried to

explain that the child made her feel so content that her husband was now rendered unnecessary, even at sleep time.

15. The experience of co-sleeping in Japanese-Australian families seemed to pose an issue primarily because the Australian husband generally expected his wife to still sleep with him in their room and bed. Although children sleeping in the marital bed was quite a common experience for some participants, it seemed to be the women who chose to sleep with (and go to sleep at the same time as) the children, an action that seemed to upset husbands more, presumably because this was a direct attempt to move away from and exclude them.

16. In the course of my research, I noticed substantial cultural differences between definitions of "independence." A common concern from Australian husbands was that their children were too *dependent* on their Japanese mothers, and the husbands wanted to instill a sense of independence. The English term "independence" suggests a rational and conscious attempt to be a certain way that does not rely on others. The Japanese notion, *jiritsu*, however, is usually the term used to describe Japanese relationships as *interdependent*. This means that there is still a connectedness with others, thus helping children cope with certain experiences in different ways. In this thinking, children are able to cope with these experiences *because of* their connectedness with others. That is, they still receive support but they are not "dependent." As they reach a certain level of maturity, they do not become mutually exclusive or separated but find meaning through the relationship with self and others (see Lebra 1976; Tahhan 2014).

17. In my fieldwork in Japan, I was often informed that as a Westerner I was not in tune with the more subtle forms of communication that render Japanese communication indirect and intuitive. At first I felt these were simply ideological notions of Japanese uniqueness. However, as my research developed I became aware of a filled space (*aidagara*) that was more tangible and *felt* (and thus connected to *touching at depth*). Conversely, in this fieldwork, I found my own marital relationship questioned by some participants, as well as the sleeping patterns of Australian women in general. For example, I was asked why Australian women still felt like they needed to "please" their husbands at bedtime.

18. Although these women enjoyed certain aspects of their lives in Australia, many stated they didn't realize how much they would miss Japan until they had children. The differences that appear to emerge in Japanese-Australian marriages once there are children seem to point women toward idealizing/elevating Japanese marriages and the associated forms of communication.

REFERENCES

Ataka, S. 1995. *Sekkusuresu: Shitakunai tsuma, dekinai otto* [Sexless: Wives Who Don't Want to Do It, Men Who Can't Do It]. Tokyo: Shufu no tomosha.

Bachnik, Jane. 1992. "*Kejime*: Defining a Shifting Self in Multiple Organizational Modes." In *Japanese Sense of Self*, edited by Nancy Rosenberger, 152–172. Cambridge: Cambridge University Press.

Ben-Ari, Eyal. 1996. "From Mothering to Othering: Organisation, Culture, and Nap Time in a Japanese Day-Care Centre." *Ethos* 24 (1): 136–164.

———. 1997. *Body Projects in Japanese Culture: Culture, Organization and Emotions in a Preschool*. Richmond, Surrey: Curzon Press.

Blood, Robert. 1967. *Love Match and Arranged Marriage: A Tokyo-Detroit Comparison*. New York: Free Press.

Caudill, William, and David Plath. 1986. "Who Sleeps by Whom? Parent-Child Involvement in Urban Japanese Families." In *Japanese Culture and Behaviour: Selected Readings*, edited by Takie Lebra and William Lebra, 247–279. Honolulu: University of Hawai'i Press.

Denman, Jared. 2009. "Japanese Wives in Japanese-Australian Intermarriages." *New Voices* 3:66–69.

Goldstein-Gidoni, Ofra. 2005. "Fashioning Cultural Identity: Body and Dress." In *A Companion to the Anthropology of Japan*, edited by Jennifer Robertson, 153–166. Malden, MA: Blackwell Publishing.

Hamabata, Matthew Masayuki. 1990. *Crested Kimono: Power and Love in the Japanese Business Family*. Ithaca, NY: Cornell University Press.

Hendry, Joy. 1981. *Marriage in Changing Japan: Community and Society*. London: Croom Helm.

Ichikawa, Hiroshi. 1993. *Mi no kōzō: Shintairon wo koete* [Structure of *Mi*: Overcoming the Theory of the Body]. Tokyo: Kodansha gakujutsu bunko.

Imamura, Anne. 1987. *Urban Japanese Housewives: At Home and in the Community*. Honolulu: University of Hawai'i Press.

Iwao, Sumiko. 1993. *The Japanese Woman: Traditional Image and Changing Reality*. New York: Maxwell Macmillan International.

Kamayama, S. 2004. *Shinai onna* [Women Who Don't Do It]. Tokyo: Daiwashobo.

Kawasaki, Chisato, J. Kevin Nugent, Hiroko Miyashita, Miyashi M. Harumi, and T. B. Brazelton. 1994. "The Cultural Organization of Infants' Sleep." *Children's Environments* 11 (2): 85–96.

Kawashima, Kumiko. 2012. "Becoming Asian in Australia: Migration and a Shift in Gender Relations among Young Japanese." *Intersections* 31.

Kelsky, Karen. 2001a. "Who Sleeps with Whom, or How (Not) to Want the West in Japan." *Qualitative Inquiry* 7 (4): 418–435.

———. 2001b. *Women on the Verge: Japanese Women, Western Dreams*. Durham, NC: Duke University Press.

Latz, Sara, Abraham Wolf, and Betsy Lozoff. 1999. "Co-Sleeping in Context: Sleep Practices and Problems in Young Children in Japan and the United States." *Archives of Pediatrics and Adolescent Medicine* 153:339–346.

Lebra, Takie. 1976. *Japanese Patterns of Behavior*. Honolulu: University of Hawai'i Press.

———. 1984. *Japanese Women: Constraint and Fulfillment*. Honolulu: University of Hawai'i Press.

———. 2004. *The Japanese Self in Cultural Logic*. Honolulu: University of Hawai'i Press.

Merleau-Ponty, Maurice. 1968. *The Visible and the Invisible: Followed by Working Notes*. Evanston, IL: Northwestern University Press.

Nakatani, Ayumi. 2006. "The Emergence of 'Nurturing Fathers': Discourses and Practices of Fatherhood in Contemporary Japan." In *The Changing Japanese Family*, edited by Marcus Rebick and Ayumi Takenaka, 94–108. New York: Routledge.

Niwa, Akiko. 1993. "The Formation of the Myth of Motherhood in Japan." *U.S. Japan Women's Journal* 4:70–82.

Notter, David. 2002. "Towards a Cultural Analysis of the Modern Family: Beyond the Revisionist Paradigm in Japanese Family Studies." *International Journal of Japanese Sociology* 11:88–101.

Ozawa-de Silva, Chikako. 2002. "Beyond the Body/Mind? Japanese Contemporary Thinkers on Alternative Sociologies of the Body." *Body and Society* 8 (2): 21–38.

Sasagawa, Ayumi. 2006. "Mother-Rearing: The Social World of Mothers in a Japanese Suburb." In *The Changing Japanese Family*, edited by Marcus Rebick and Ayumi Takenaka, 129–146. New York: Routledge.

Sato, Machiko. 2001. *Farewell to Nippon: Japanese Lifestyle Migrants in Australia*. Melbourne: Trans Pacific Press.

Tahhan, Diana Adis. 2008. "Depth and Space in Sleep: Intimacy, Touch and the Body in Japanese Co-Sleeping Rituals." *Body and Society* (Special Issue on Sleep) 14 (4): 37–56

———. 2010. "Blurring the Boundaries between Bodies: Skinship and Bodily Intimacy in Japan." *Japanese Studies* 30 (2): 215–230.

———. 2013a. "Touching at Depth: The Potential of Feeling and Connection." *Emotion, Space and Society* 7:45–53

———. 2013b. "Sensuous Connections in Sleep: Feelings of Security and Interdependency in Japanese Sleep Rituals." In *Sleep around the World: Anthropological Perspectives*, edited by Katie Glaskin and Richard Chenhall. New York: Palgrave Macmillan.

———. 2014. *The Japanese Family: Touch, Intimacy and Feeling*. London: Routledge.

Yoshihiro, K. 1994. *Sekkusuresu kappuru* [Sexless Couples] Tokyo: NHK Books.

CHAPTER 13

Reflections on Fieldwork

Exploring Intimacy

ALLISON ALEXY AND EMMA E. COOK

All ethnographic research fundamentally involves "intimacy" in the broadest sense. The choices central to the ethnographic method—living with people, sharing everyday lives, building relationships—fundamentally require closeness and empathy, if not trust. Indeed, ethnography is a methodology premised on building intimacies and then leveraging such intimacies into analysis.

Relying both on the ethnographer's abilities to build connections with people in a fieldsite and those people's willingness to share stories, opinions, and experiences, long-term fieldwork comes to be "a site of social intimacy in the fullest sense" (Herzfeld 1997, 20). Behar (1997, 3) argues that contemporary anthropologists create ethnography by, in part, making themselves vulnerable and working hard not to observe "too coldly," and Aretxaga suggests that ethnography requires a researcher to place him- or herself within social structures in "situations of profound intimacy" (2005, 163). David Plath offers the descriptive term "deep hanging out" to describe the anthropological project (cited in Kelly 2013, xix). At the same time, these methods raise myriad ethical and political questions, particularly for researchers who also want to address injustices. Armbruster suggests that contemporary ethnographic methods are built on principals of empathy that can, in practice, conflict with "real experiences of closeness and distance" between researchers and interlocutors (2008, 13). Many scholars trace the ways that friendships and other intimacies both assist and complicate their projects (Abelmann 2009; Grindal and Salamone 2006; Hume and Mulcock 2004; Leonard, Reddy, and Gold 2010; Lewin and Leap 1996; Mookherjee 2008; Shryock 2004; Walker 2013; Wolcott 2002). Although some fieldworkers argue that romantic or sexual relationships occur regularly and can facilitate analysis (Golde 1986; Kulick and Willson 1995; Markowitz and Ashkenazi 1999; Newton 1993; Rubenstein 2014), others enact the principle that friendship is the most basic building block of any fieldwork project (Killick and Desai 2010, 4).

All anthropologists, no matter their research topics or questions, must consequently negotiate the social, personal, and emotional dimensions of intimacy in the course of fieldwork. For generations, anthropological monographs have narrated ethnographers' efforts to become close enough to potential research interlocutors (so-called "informants") to build the trust and relationships necessary to gather data and build analysis. We do not have to go back as far as Malinowski's (1967) salacious diary to find anthropologists reflecting on the complex challenges prompted by fieldwork's intimacies, the effort and skills it takes to get close with people, as well as the conflicts and confusions such closeness can cause (Behar 1993; Kondo 1990; Rabinow 1977).

But scholars exploring research topics that are actually centered on intimacy face an additional set of challenges. Doing ethnographic research about what we'll call "intimate topics"—from birth control practices to marital decisions to domestic violence to sexual desire—presents particular challenges to methodological norms. At the most basic level, participant observation, the axiomatic ethnographic method, is at least partially foreclosed around these topics.[1] With a few exceptions, ethnographers are neither able to participate in nor observe intimate acts, and the ethics of erotic relationships during fieldwork remain a contested, if underdiscussed, topic.[2] As a methodology, a researcher cannot participate in sexual relationships as he might participate in an annual harvest.[3] In contrast to researchers in other disciplines who might, say, create robust surveys to gather data on "intimate topics," ethnographers face particular challenges stemming from the private, personal, or stigmatized character of these topics.

Taking these challenges seriously, this chapter offers reflections from each of the volume's contributors about how they designed, engaged in, and completed research about intimate topics. The range of successful methodologies reflects the researchers' diversity: we are native and foreign anthropologists, of varying nationalities, characteristics, ages, and sexualities. However, we are all female, a truth that has prompted much discussion within our group. Although we invited a number of male colleagues to contribute to this volume, none were ultimately able to, and we understand this gender skew to reflect both the discipline's recent gender imbalance and the high likelihood that in the current moment projects framed around "intimacy" are more likely to be created by female researchers.[4] We look forward to future research from different perspectives and hope our reflections might facilitate greater diversity in the field.

These methodological reflections are written in response to a question we all regularly encounter: How were you able to do fieldwork on your chosen topic? Although we employed many different methods, these reflections, partial though they may be, make clear that we ultimately came to share helpful patterns. For instance, many of us found that some balance of distance and connection enabled people to feel comfortable sharing deeply personal narratives. We describe our research methods here in the hope that they will further understanding of the topics we analyze, as well as assist other scholars as they plan fieldwork.

OVERCOMING INSTITUTIONAL RELUCTANCE AND GAINING ACCESS: Yukari Kawahara

In this research project, I conducted ethnographic fieldwork at one junior high school and three high schools in the Tokyo metropolitan region. To compare curricula among schools and to get some sense of how social class mattered, I located myself in schools with different social and economic positions: two public schools designated as "model" schools, a commercial high school where students were almost entirely working class, and an elite private school for girls.

Negotiating with schools for access was a difficult and time-consuming task. Almost one year before I entered the field, I began by contacting an educator who had dedicated himself to sex education and was a former member of a board of education in the Tokyo region. With his introduction, I began to negotiate with the two "model" schools. I found access to the commercial high school when I met a committed health education teacher at a national sex education conference and asked to observe his class. Yet I was allowed into the schools only after particular teachers negotiated with other teachers and brought my research up in teachers' meetings, a process that suggests the relatively high autonomy of high school teachers.

Entry into a private high school was still more difficult. I was rejected by two private girls' high schools before I was accepted in a third. The first two schools didn't give me a reason for their rejection, but I noticed during my preliminary interviews with teachers that they were very concerned with "school reputation." Despite my promises of anonymity, I suspect that they probably feared that any scandals about the students' sexual behavior and sex education instruction would become public. In fact, any sexual scandals could be the ruin of a private girls' high school because parents are as concerned about girls' sexual reputations as their academic achievements.

Overall, once I got into the schools, I was not particularly welcomed by the teachers. Instead, teachers frequently tried to keep their distance from me, especially in the beginning. Time helped. I was gradually invited to drinking parties and school trips. Teachers began to open up and discuss their opinions and points of view about sex education. I had to be patient, however, and wait at least six months before they began to share such disclosures.

In contrast to the teachers, I did not have to wait so long for the students to open up. Students were very responsive partly because they were always looking for something new in their lives, and I represented that newness. Some of them were interested in my experiences living in the United States, and eventually I was invited to give talks about my American university life at three of the schools.

Before the interviews, I worried about whether boys especially would speak frankly about their sexual feelings and activities to a female interviewer. To be sure, it took longer to elicit responses from boys than girls. However, boys were generally more responsive and cooperative than I had expected. There was a generation's difference between me and the boys (in Japanese terms, *hitomawari chigai*, or twelve years' difference), and I came to believe that the age difference helped moderate the boys' hesitation and shyness.

I entered the fieldsites as a native anthropologist. Native anthropologists must consider the problem of "detachment" between themselves and their own cultures (Ohnuki-Tierney 1984, 16). Native researchers tend to take people's practices for granted and have difficulty discerning the implications of practices in their own cultures. Ohnuki-Tierney (1984) suggests that one way to accomplish sufficient distance is to research another culture before beginning the study of one's own. To address this problem of distance, I studied sex education in two schools in and around New Haven, Connecticut, before beginning my research in Japan. Because the New Haven area had high rates of teenage pregnancy and HIV, I was quickly exposed to heated debates among teachers and school nurses. This comparative observational experience helped me frame and structure my work in Japan.[5]

PERSONAL CONVERSATIONS ABOUT "ILLEGITIMATE" TOPICS: Shana Fruehan Sandberg

In her now classic ethnography of a Japanese hostess club, anthropologist Anne Allison recounts that it was difficult for others in Japan to understand how she could treat *mizu shobai* (the "water trade," or hostessing and prostitution) as a legitimate area of serious scholarship. "To look at the tea ceremony or marriage practices would be far more sensible, respect-ful, and healthy, they implied" (1994, 146). Yet her work demonstrates that there is much to be learned about normative family and corporate rela-tionships by closely examining what two male researchers mockingly called, in reference to her research, the "dirty [*kitanai*] side of Japan" (ibid.).

Similar encounters surfaced as I conducted research on young wom-en's changing understandings of romantic relationships and contraception in Tokyo a decade later; these led to questions about the legitimacy of the topic. One researcher remarked that the Japanese women I interviewed must feel great discomfort having to talk about such personal issues with an American. And yet in practice, I found that there was quite a range of responses; some women were quite comfortable speaking directly about their experiences, while others were politely vague. I took cues from each woman individually and adapted my questions accordingly. Many women pointed out that it was much easier to speak with someone who (they imag-ined) came from a place that valued frank and open discussions and that it would be more difficult to speak with someone from Japan in the same way. Moreover, all the topics we covered were regularly examined in great detail through text and illustrations in pull-out booklets from popular women's magazines and in other media.

At the end of every interview, there was always a chance for the inter-viewee to ask me any questions she had about my own experiences or the research project and in turn to say anything she had not had a chance to express earlier. Sometimes this prompted interesting discussions about the similarities or differences in our experiences, and I revealed a great deal about my own feelings and experiences in past relationships. These interviews felt much more like reciprocal conversations, with both parties sharing their experiences and perspectives. Many women said that they wished they had more opportunities to speak openly about such issues, which were important to them.

One additional note may be useful for researchers who conduct inter-views on similar topics. At first I assumed that the best method for identify-ing potential interviewees was to approach them about an interview after we had known each other socially for some time and had become closer. I tried this approach a few times, and it seemed to work well enough. It was not until after a friend recommended that I interview one of her friends that I began to realize that an acquaintance with one degree of separation typically led to a much richer interview. Reflecting on this, I realized that being recommended signaled that I was someone whom the friend could trust, and yet I was not part of the same social circle, meaning that I did not know her boyfriend, classmates, parents, or anyone else that she might mention during the interview. In this way, I became a "trusted outsider" in relation to the interviewee.

RELATING TO "UNCONVENTIONAL" WOMEN:
Laura Dales and Beverly Anne Yamamoto

We met our "unconventional women" in cafes, restaurants, workplaces, and on two occasions, in our own homes. While interviews are inevitably bounded opportunities, our discussions created a space for closeness and self-revelation for both interviewees and researchers. The scene-setting for the interview involved not only an explanation of the project, but also some autobiographical storytelling on the part of the researchers; one of us is a British-born long-time resident of Japan, married to a Japanese man, and has two children; the other is Australian, single, and without children. By offering something of ourselves through storytelling, we created trust and a space for reciprocity. The relative ease with which the women shared their own experiences and perceptions of romantic intimacy reflected this, as well as their individual personalities and propensities to self-revelation.

The effect of this relationship was particularly evident in the joint interview of Matsuda and Motohashi, held in Dales's apartment. Because they were childhood friends, the two women's conversation was studded with comfortable overlaps, casual silences, and shared laughter. In this interview there was an additional connection: Motohashi is Dales's friend from university. The established friendship of the interviewees and of one of the interviewees with one of the researchers meant that the topics of romance and intimacy were not unfamiliar or uncomfortable territory. Motohashi's knowledge of the researcher, gleaned from socializing, late-night chats, and occasional digital communications over a decade, enabled an ease of conversation that is evident in the casual register and flow of the discussion. Dales had originally met Motohashi through the latter's university boyfriend, and Motohashi had spent time with one of Dales's previous romantic partners. Relative to other interviews, this was a conversation in which Dales was likely to interrupt, to offer her own perspective, and to push the interviewee (Motohashi) for further details. It felt, to the researcher, like one of any number of chats she had shared with female friends over afternoon tea.

The gender and ethnic background of the researchers was clearly pertinent. In the Japanese context, it would have been highly problematic for male researchers to carry out such a study even if they were of the same ages and backgrounds. While not universal or uniform, the commonality of certain experiences of womanhood arguably laid a foundation for discussion of romantic and sexual intimacy. Furthermore, the researchers' non-Japaneseness may have made it easier for these women to break the taboo of silence around the issues we discussed. Some interviewees noted that they would not have felt comfortable sharing certain stories with us had we been Japanese. Our interviewees felt correctly that we would not judge them. Ironically, if our women are "unconventional," then perhaps a shared sense of being different opened possibilities for sharing stories that may not have been there otherwise. Our difference produced a sense of similarity, or at least familiarity, with our interviewees. Thus "unconventionality" shaped our research in another, unintended way: producing an intimacy based on the shared experiences of women who do not quite fit in, be it for reasons of ethnicity, age, marital status, or sexuality.

FACING STIGMA AND SUPPORT: Allison Alexy

Because divorce is such a personal, private, and potentially stigmatizing experience, many people in and outside of Japan were initially incredulous that any anthropological research could be done about it. Almost everyone who asked about my project was curious about how I was planning to do any research at all. "Do people really want to talk to you?" is one typical question I continue to hear, followed quickly by, "How do you meet people?" Outside of Japan, these questions often seem to reflect stereotypes about Japanese people as reticent; inside Japan, the questions instead seemed to assume that divorce is so stigmatizing or shameful that no one would want to talk about it. Neither is correct.

Throughout my research, the *how* of my project was intimately wrapped with being asked to explain myself. Because of how I look, most people correctly assume that I am not Japanese. When I walked into a party with friends, struck up a conversation with someone at a bar, or sat down in a support group, it was extremely natural and obvious for other people to ask me, "Why are you here?" My obviousness—which often felt like awkwardness, both physical and linguistic—not only made me an object of curiosity for some people, but also enabled me to start talking about my research in conversations in which it might not have otherwise come up. I am convinced that the structure of my literal face (I have a big, round face with lots of freckles) and my being raised in the American South (which has a culture of chatting, even with people one has just met) make me approachable, and I rarely have trouble talking with strangers. I was there, I told anyone who asked, to learn about divorce and families in contemporary Japan, and this unusual and unexpected topic was often enough to get people talking. I met a lot of people who were willing to talk with me about their own experiences and/or introduce me to other people they knew. Because people knew why I was in Japan, they were more likely to bring up divorce-related topics in casual conversation, and this meant that I was much more likely to hear about divorce. Commenting on the unusual focus of my life, a few different people labeled me a "divorce geek" (*rikon otaku*), using a word that suggests a person obsessively, and probably unhealthily, consumed by one thing. People's identification of me with divorce became so strong that they would literally gesture toward me when they said the word "divorce" in conversation, in a motion similar to what they might use to link me with "American."

Through these motions of identification, I encountered what I came to call "ambient divorce stories." Knowing what I studied, or hearing it for the first time, led people to tell me long stories about divorces they had heard about or watched happen. In these, in addition to the first-person accounts I was gathering, I would hear about their friend's divorce, their bartender's divorce, or their co-worker's divorce. As I very usefully became known as "the divorce girl," these ambient divorce stories followed me like a cloud. Through them, I was able to gather more general opinions about divorce from people who had not experienced it firsthand. During the course of my fieldwork, I was worried that by focusing specifically on divorce, I might inadvertently overdetermine the results of my research; asking directly about divorce might lead people to think and talk more about it than they would otherwise, and I would end up with a skewed sense of what was going on. For these reasons, I tried very hard to put myself not only in situations where divorce was the topic drawing all participants in (for instance, support groups), but also in others where people came together for more common reasons (like co-workers going out for a drink after work).

In Japan, as elsewhere, some divorce stories are ultimately happy narrations of freedom or self-discovery, but there were many days during this research that left me very sad. It is emotionally exhausting to hear about deeply difficult marriages punctuated by serious violence, neglect, or the gradual withering of dreams, and I began developing parallel mechanisms to respond to my interlocutors with genuine empathy and to keep myself sane. In support groups, I often found myself sitting next to a relative stranger who was sobbing, and I struggled to figure out culturally appropriate responses. (My American urge to give enormous hugs doesn't quite translate in Japan.) I finally figured out that carrying packs of tissues in my bag and offering them to anyone crying was a way to demonstrate empathy with someone who likely wouldn't appreciate being touched. During this fieldwork, my self-care often consisted of a lot of physical exercise and retreats into dumb or easy television. It remains the case that the more emotionally difficult my research is, the more light and easy I need my entertainment to be. More broadly, like any anthropologist, I work hard to be good friends with people—staying in touch, getting together whenever possible—and such contact helps me remember to contextualize the more difficult moments within a longer life.

COMPROMISING BETWEEN SAFETY AND CONTROL: Kaoru Kawajima

It was when I was working at a women's organization that I first really learned about domestic violence, although I knew that in Japanese society hitting a wife or child has been condoned in the name of "discipline." Due to the limited amount of research about and public attention to this issue, I decided to look into the support system for domestic violence victims in Japan. Because such support systems are a junction point that includes the victims as well as both non-governmental and governmental support agencies, working with the organizations seemed the most feasible way to conduct my fieldwork. I conducted "subway ethnography" (Clifford 1997, 217), consisting of short repeat visits where an ethnographer dips into and out of fieldsites, simply because I had to balance research and care of my children, who were five and nine at the time. Obtaining contacts was not particularly difficult because of my background working at a women's center for ten years. Through that position, I had met or heard the names of famous activists, professionals, and leaders involved in supporting domestic violence victims.

My fieldwork included several shelters run by both local and national government agencies in charge of gender equality policy and social welfare for women and children. I worked as a volunteer at three different shelters at varying times between 2005 and 2009. Before I began my fieldwork, I was afraid that the amount of violence experienced by people in these shelters would be overwhelming and emotionally exhausting. However, especially at longer-term shelters where I could build relationships with residents, it turned out that I found talking with women interesting and even encouraging, and every week I was anxious to go back and spend time with them. Some women gave me various tips—about cooking and money saving, for example—while also sharing stories about their partners. Of course I heard only the woman's side of the story, but many women described how much their male partners wanted to control their lives to extraordinary degrees.

They stayed at the shelter in fear of being found by a person whom they had once cared about and loved. It felt as if even after they were physically away from the perpetrators, they were surrounded by the unseen power of "intimacy," which chased after them and tried to pull them back to the perpetrators.

As safe places, shelters were very strict about safety measures. As I reflect on it now, I was rather preoccupied by their strict rules and ways of "controlling" the lives of women in order to protect them. Every time staff said "safe" or "dangerous" or "protect," which they said on a regular basis to explain the shelter activities, I was unsure what it was they were trying to protect or be protected from. Was it the lives of women and children? Was it other women and staff staying at the shelter? Was it the support system for the victims of domestic violence in Japan? It was not clear to me, and asking those questions seemed rude.

One day at an emergency shelter, I was having a conversation with a shelter director, and I started to say, "A shelter can't protect against. . . . " She interrupted and shut me up without letting me finish my sentence. She stared at me and said in an angry tone, "It is arrogant to even start a sentence about what a shelter can't protect against." She must have thought I was criticizing the shelter. Or maybe I sounded judgmental.

What I meant to say in that moment was that the shelter was one of many resources to protect or save victims of domestic violence, but it was available only to women who came to the shelter. The women who did not or could not escape their homes obviously were in no place to be "protected." I was wondering what it was that kept women in a violent relationship and how the shelter wouldn't be able to offer them any protection. The director explained, "Women enter the shelter with an understanding of our rules and conditions. We make sure again and again that they understand them. Otherwise, it would be a violation of their human rights. Their safety is maintained through our surveillance. That is what their situation requires. That is domestic violence. We protect them by controlling them." She said it all in one breath.

I was frustrated because the director did not understand my viewpoint. But then I did not agree about what she believed in, either. This episode left some bitterness between us for quite some time. I wished that I were there not as a fieldworker but just a regular staff member. It was even harder for me, as I have known the director for some time, and it changed the nature of our relationship. This tension and nervousness followed me during my fieldwork much more than the depressing, horrible stories women shared with me.

EXPLORING MASCULINITIES AND LABOR
THROUGH INTIMACY: Emma E. Cook

Although my chapter in this volume is based primarily on a documentary film, analysis and contextualization of the film's themes are critically embedded within the extended ethnographic fieldwork I conducted with men and women about masculinities and irregular labor. It is this fieldwork that my short reflection concerns.

Talking and asking directly about masculinities can be tricky. Ask someone about that person's masculinity sometime, and you'll see what I mean! What is masculinity and how is it lived, produced, and reproduced? How are masculinities and labor interlinked? These can be difficult research questions to answer, in part because they are so difficult to ask people about. However, it was through intimacy—the intimacy developed through rapport; through the sharing of stories about our lives and our intimacies (for example, about relationships with parents, peers, and romantic partners); and through a mutual vulnerability and openness—that I was able to explore the links between labor and masculinities in Japan. I found that to get men and women comfortable enough to talk about such topics, my personal openness, willingness to share stories, and the ability to be empathetic to their experiences were critical.

Being female, foreign, white, and living with a male Japanese partner were also elements that factored into the development of rapport, trust, and intimacy, though of course these also shaped and limited the possibilities of fieldwork in particular ways. The deep listening of informal ethnographic interviewing can be heady and flattering for interlocutors, and I was always conscious of this when talking with men about their lives and intimate relationships. It was an ever-present balance that I was aware of and subconsciously monitoring. In situations where it felt that people were starting to misunderstand my interest, I was careful to remind them of the existence of my partner by sharing stories that included our relationship in an attempt to maintain boundaries and prevent misunderstandings. In rare cases, however, such strategies did not work and led to a desire for more intimacy than I was willing or able to provide. Indeed, in one case, one man so misinterpreted the deep listening that anthropology entails that he suddenly became insistent about his romantic feelings. Although I was saying "no" about any romantic interest in him (initially gently and later with more vehemence), he believed I really had—or would develop—feelings for him and declared that he would keep trying until I said yes. After being bombarded by text messages (often sent in the small hours of the night) that vacillated between apologetically insisting I would come around to his love and aggressively doing so, he finally stopped when I threatened to call the police. While this experience was personally distressing and led to the loss of not only his friendship, but also that of a group of musicians and artists for whom he was the gatekeeper, it was also highly informative—providing insights about power, gender, and masculinities—and it led to revealing conversations with both women and men about their dating experiences and the gendered dynamics they experienced in relationships.

While my living with a partner typically marked me as an off-limits but safe interlocutor, it also limited the possibilities of research methods. For example, I initially anticipated that much of my research with young men would take place over drinks after work, engendering an intimate camaraderie and lessening conversational inhibitions, but this didn't happen. Although some unmarried people live together in Japan, it was relatively rare where I undertook research. Most people therefore assumed I was married and consequently unavailable for after-hours socializing. Even after knowing my unmarried status, co-workers at the cinema where I conducted much of my fieldwork were hesitant to ask me out to drinking parties. Reasons became clear when at one party a young man turned to me and said, in all seriousness, "Emma, it's past 10 p.m. Don't you need to go home to run the bath for your husband?" I assured him that my partner was perfectly capable of running it for himself, and I added that he also did most of the cooking and therefore was able to fend for himself. With a grin I then ordered myself another drink. This information elicited a chorus of shocked exclamations as both men and women at the table enthusiastically told me that typically in Japan the household division of labor—and expectations of labor—were gendered in ways that my household obviously was not. In their understanding women cooked, looked after the household, and ran baths for men. Although my "married in the minds of others" positionality limited the number of invitations I received to evening get-togethers, it also allowed men and women to talk with me more deeply about both the dominant discourses of gender and gendered roles, as well as their own desires within intimate relationships and for future households.

These reflections are just small components of building and managing intimacy in the field. Of course, all fieldwork is intimate, and indeed anthropology hinges on the successful development of intimate relationships based on trust, rapport, and shared conviviality. Nurturing and managing these relationships from our own particular positionalities makes research on intimacy not only possible, but also makes intimacy always present, even if it is not our explicit focus.

CREATING INTIMACY THROUGH
EMPATHY: Elizabeth Miles

Heart-pounding excitement, heart-rending disappointment. One feels overwhelmed by a tidal wave of conflicting feelings in the process of trying to build relationships. Disappointment leaves one bereft and grasping. Yet this feeling can quickly give way to extreme emotional buoyancy, the end result of joy and the passion of the undertaking. Nervous excitement can give way to pure terror or be transformed into sheer pleasure. Whether or not one has experienced these varying emotional states, anyone with even a passing familiarity with mass media (whether Japanese or Euro-American) can identify such passions with that of love and the building of intimate relations. Yet for this fieldworker, such a dizzying array of emotions is not the exclusive province of love but is reflective of the field research process itself. While the multiple emotions evoked by the "doing" of love may, for many, mimic those of fieldwork, the similarities extend beyond the affective. I claim that fieldwork, akin to love and intimacy-building in contemporary Japan, as discussed in my chapter, is burdensome. Requiring the cultivation of deep interpersonal skills, fieldwork forces one to confront the ways in which "failure"—being rejected by a stranger one would like to get to know—translates into professional difficulties when those relationships are at the heart of your work. Moreover, the fear of rejection, or actual repudiation, is inherent in the process.

Like dating, ethnographic research can be a series of struggles, not only to find and connect with potential informants and fieldsites, but also to be recognized. Sociologist Miyadai Shinji (2013, 65), in his most recent work, compares the act of *nanpa* with fieldwork, claiming that both necessitate the building of rapport and have the potential for catharsis.[6] In many cases, my interviews have felt more like a series of blind dates or one-night stands than any attempts at long-term relationship building. For instance, on one memorable occasion I felt a connection with a young man, and when our formal discussion ended, we moved onto casual conversation about hobbies while smoking cigarettes together at a local cafe. Unfortunately, when I emailed him the following day to thank him for his time and the nice evening, going so far as to suggest we get together for karaoke in the not-too-distant future, I received no response. Like someone following up after a first date, I found myself wondering what I had done wrong or what signs I may have misread. Reflecting on my various fieldwork experiences, I find that they often read like an article in *Cosmo* (or *An-An*) on the pitfalls of contemporary dating. I understand that such rejections may reflect the particularities of the amorphous group with whom I was attempting to engage, but I am convinced that feelings of rejection, as well as elation, resonate with other fieldworkers.

Like dating, fieldwork necessitates a certain amount of self-confidence that must be built and maintained throughout the research period. I empathize with the young postal worker at the Ebisu *machikon* that I described in my chapter; we had both come alone and, in different ways, were potentially unprepared for the evening ahead. No amount of training prepares one for the rejections that can occur in the field, just as in the dating world. Fieldwork is a minefield of possible rejections, of rebuffs for no clearly discernible reason. At the "Smash Christmas" demonstration I attended in December 2013 I had one young man silently though rather violently (to my fragile sense of self) turn his back on me as I approached. I have thought of taking the advice of *nanpa* sensei Fujita-san: "Look in the mirror every morning and tell yourself that you are desirable," though in this case "I am a researcher worthy of respect" would be more appropriate. My efforts to "polish the self" in order to be more "attractive" to potential interviewees came to include a beauty routine that would make Patrick Bateman from *American Psycho* proud. Yet unlike with the game LovePlus I described in my chapter, there is no preset formula to increase my "anthropologist power" (*jinruigakusha no chikara*).

Despite the challenges I faced in both "attracting" potential interviewees and creating long-term bonds, there have been moments of intimacy, mediated through my own feelings of empathy with these men. When one young salaryman expressed concern regarding his age of losing his virginity, especially compared to Americans, I easily quelled his fears by confessing my own "late" age. This revelation and the joking manner in which it was delivered prompted him to both trust me—that is, he felt that I would not pity him—and allowed for candidness in our following conversation. Overall, despite what I often feel to be a lack of deep rapport, I feel a certain intimacy with the men of Kakuhidō and those who struggle to find a partner, such as the young postal worker mentioned above. This is not an intimacy born out of a deep relationship but one mediated by empathy.

MOVING ON AND OFFLINE: S. P. F. Dale

Given the lack of printed materials about x-gender, my initial research and information gathering about the topic were conducted on the Internet. I myself found out about the term online, and at the time there was a growing online community of x-gender individuals.[7] My fieldwork came to consist of three stages: forging an online presence, creating a community, and in-depth interviews.

Most of the discussion about x-gender seemed to be occurring online, and in order to engage in it I needed to have a visible online presence. I created accounts on social networking sites (SNS) where there were x-gender communities, such as Mixi, Twitter, and Ameblo. I started discussions with individuals who identified as x-gender and also conducted preliminary interviews via email and online messaging. I also started a blog where I wrote about my research, as well as about myself and my personal research motivations.[8] I would refer potential informants to my blog so that they would know about me prior to our meeting.

There did not seem to be many "physical"/offline spaces for x-gender individuals to meet. I decided to create a discussion group about x-gender issues, hoping that such a group would not only help me to find out more about x-gender, but also that it could provide a safe space for x-gender individuals to meet with each other. This discussion group (initially monthly but then bimonthly) ran from April 2011 until mid-2014, when I stopped running it because of time constraints. Some of the members of the group still continue to meet individually with each other.

Creating a group is certainly an unusual step for an ethnographer, and it is also questionable as it would seem that one is creating the community one is supposed to be studying! I should emphasize that this group does not figure prominently in my analysis of x-gender community and was not an object of my study. It rather served as a forum for me to gain a broad understanding of some of the issues x-gender individuals experience. Running this group became not so much a research project for me but rather a community/activist one; I myself am queer, and my partner would also participate in this group on occasion. Participants in this group (as well as informants in general) came to know and understand me as such—as a non-Japanese, female-assigned individual in a relationship with another female-assigned individual. Participants in the group had various gender identities and sexual orientations, and the group was a means for us to discuss issues pertaining to gender and sexuality. I, in this broad sense, was one of them—not as x-gender but as a queer person.

I found informants for in-depth interviews through posting calls for research participants on Twitter, my blog, and Mixi message boards. I was also introduced to some informants through snowball references, and in total spoke with twenty-five individuals. Interviews were conducted in a variety of places, depending on the preference of each person. We met in karaoke boxes, noisy cafes, quiet cafes, and homes. I had a prepared set of questions that I wanted to ask each individual and passed each a copy at the start of each interview. However, I also emphasized that as far as possible, I would like our conversation to flow naturally, and the questions were referred to only when there was a lull in the conversation. I wanted to find out about how the individuals understood x-gender and how their every-day experiences may be entangled or defined through their gender iden-tity. The questions reflected these issues and encompassed themes such as sexuality, language, appearance, coming out, and relationships with friends and family. Interviews lasted between an hour and four hours, and I also met with most of the informants a year to two years later for follow-up interviews.

It is difficult for me to reflect on the role my self—non-Japanese (but "Asian-looking," being of Chinese/white European descent), non-x-gen-der (but queer)—had on my interactions with individuals. To an extent I very much identified with many of them, and it was indeed my own grap-pling with gender categories that made me embark on this project. I didn't experience any difficulties in gleaning information, but this was also per-haps because most of the individuals with whom I spoke were people who wanted to speak with me—they had read my blog and in most cases had initiated contact. As such, they desired to speak about their experiences.

I made it a point to be as open with my informants as they were being with me. They were free to ask me questions about my sexuality and gender, and this mutual openness allowed us to engage in candid discus-sions about very intimate issues.

UNSPOKEN AND UNWRITTEN INTIMACIES: Kathryn E. Goldfarb

Sometimes the most intimate conversations happen with total strangers. In my contribution for this volume, I describe my interview with a woman I call Hamabata Toshiko, an adoptive parent of a teenage boy to whom she had not yet "confessed" his adoption. While she knew that he somehow knew about his past, she could not bring herself to tell him straightfor-wardly that he was not her biological son. These words remained unspo-ken between them during the span of my doctoral research in Japan, from 2009 to 2010. One might remark on the oddness of a person making this "confession" to a foreign woman she barely knew when she could not tell her own son the truth. And yet as my research progressed, I came to realize that Hamabata would not have spoken to me so frankly if I had *not* been a near stranger. A good friend of hers, a foster parent whom I had recently met in the course of my research, had introduced me to Hamabata, but at the time I was not yet embedded within their social circle. Hamabata's failure to tell her son about his own past flew in the face of the foster and adoptive parent community's understanding of best practices, and her awkwardness around this topic was palpable. Once I knew this community well, I attempted a few times to suggest a follow-up interview with Hamabata, but she always gently demurred. My research topics were certainly intimate, focusing on family practices stigmatized in contemporary Japan: foster care, adoption, infertility treatment, and life within Japanese child welfare institutions. I had initially imagined that I would seek a comfortable rapport with research interlocutors before delving into their most intimate family stories. But after several intensely intimate interviews with people I had met for the first time and upon realizing that my own situatedness *within* a social circle might make me a *less* desirable conversation partner, I embraced the possibility of interviewing people I did not know and might not see again. Of course I had to interpret these interviews with a grain of salt; my deep relationships with other interlocutors and my participant-observation research helped put these one-off stories into context.

And then there were the people whom I came to know intimately and yet felt I could not write about. The people who influenced me most and appear the least in my writing are the children I met, and came to know well, at the child welfare institution where I conducted fieldwork. I spent several days a week with these children, who ranged in age from three to twelve. I was present during paroxysms of laughter and of tears; I carried them on my back and helped them in the toilet; they showed me their photo albums from before they came to the institution; and we ate snacks and watched television together. Before going to the field, I had received research clearance to interview children and had prepared a "child-friendly" oral informed-consent form. However, upon becoming acquainted with the children themselves, I realized that "informed consent" for a ward of the state seemed both meaningless and misleading. These children were already documented and traced in so many ways they could not control; how could I ethically participate in bringing their words to pages they would never read in a language they did not know? At a pragmatic level, how could I guarantee that my questions would not trigger traumatic flashbacks or waves of sadness that I could tell hung sometimes just beyond the surface? As these children grow up—I have now known them for almost ten years—some may be interested in participating in an interview or becoming more formal "research subjects." Until then, these intimacies will continue to inform my ethics as an "engaged anthropologist," as I work to produce research that will be relevant to anthropologists but will also contribute to child welfare policy and practice. These intimacies will also continue to indelibly shape my writing.

ASKING "SOCIALLY INAPPROPRIATE"
QUESTIONS: Chigusa Yamaura

"Why do you want to marry a Chinese woman?" This seemed to be a simple, straightforward question, and it was the question I needed to be asking for my project. And yet I had a hard time asking this question of the Japanese men I met. This difficulty was possibly because I felt that the question sounded rude, especially as it appeared to entail some type of normative judgment. Somehow I felt this question was almost like asking, "Why aren't you married?" or worse. This question delved into the questionee's intimate life and, more particularly, the "problems" with that intimate life. Marrying a Chinese woman through a commercial transnational marriage agency was not seen socially as a neutral practice; it transgressed the social and cultural norms of "what normal marriage should look like" in Japan. Indeed, as a Japanese woman who grew up in Japan, I was never outside of such social norms and probably unconsciously shared such a view. And by sharing these norms (or at least feeling that I did), I was conflicted between being a "culturally competent Japanese" and an ethnographer who should be able to ask any question.

In order not to appear voyeuristic or sound offensive, whenever I met Japanese men for the first time, I tried to be as pleasant, polite, and friendly as possible. I met almost all the men I interviewed through transnational marriage agencies, usually at agency offices in Japan or during matchmaking tours in China. After introducing my research topic and myself, I usually sat next to them, observed what they were doing and talking about with the brokers and staff members, and occasionally engaged in ordinary conversation. Sometimes, the Japanese men asked about my research before I asked them about their experiences. Usually my first encounters with the Japanese male clientele occurred when they participated in a matchmaking meeting or party with Chinese women who already lived in Japan. I witnessed how they gradually shifted their focus to Chinese women in China. During matchmaking tours in China, I also sat in on their meetings, joined their engagement parties, and eventually went to some of their wedding parties. After the Japanese men left for Japan, I joined in Japanese language lessons with Chinese brides and often hung out with them afterward. When I did not accompany the matchmaking tours to China, I met the Japanese male participants when they returned to Japan and visited the agency.

After we had met multiple times, many of the Japanese men—and also I myself—came to feel more comfortable talking about their experiences and feelings. When we had the opportunity to meet in both Japan and China, we were able to get to know each other better, making it easier to ask more personal questions. This was partly owing to the fact that we shared transnational experiences, including the joys and discomforts of traveling in China, and partly because the men felt safe, knowing that I would not criticize them for their practices. I also visited a number of couples once the Chinese wives arrived in Japan. My visits with couples I had already met before their marriage were relatively easy, and I felt welcomed. I was one of the few people who knew what they had gone through without judging them.

After spending some time with the Japanese men, asking "Why do you want to marry a Chinese woman?" was really not necessary. The men answered this question in many different ways. Sometimes, we assume that our informants have their answers and we have to find a good question to tease these answers out. Actually, our informants might also be asking the same question of themselves. Many Japanese men I met did not know if they really wanted to marry a Chinese woman and kept asking themselves if they were making the right decision. Thus during our casual conversations, they gradually shared with me their complex, and sometimes contradictory, feelings—not simply to provide me with information, but also to try to make sense of their own marriages.

TALKING, AND NOT TALKING, ABOUT INTIMACY: Diana Tahhan

When I was conducting my research in Japan and people found I was researching intimacy in the Japanese family, I was often met with bewildered responses and humorous remarks: what was possibly important to ask about intimacy in Japan, and why would I be doing this for my PhD research? A beloved host father used to take great enjoyment in laughing at my keen interest, and he would dismiss any questions initially and blame my lack of Japaneseness as the reason for my ignorance.

One day, he sat on his armchair after a late night working in the family's soba shop and asked me how my interviews were going. The concept of deeply depending on loved ones (*amaereu*) came up, and he sat back thoughtfully and reflected on it in the context of his relationship with his wife. He explained that he didn't need to tell her or show her how he feels because she could feel it. And besides, he couldn't run the shop without her.

I remember my host mother's shocked reaction; he had *verbalized his need for her*. She reminded me of a schoolgirl finding out that the boy she has a crush on wants to ask her to a dance. It illuminated something major to me: even though their subtle forms of communication obviated a need to communicate their deepest feelings, she still felt happy hearing his words.

Years later, I was settled back in Australia with my husband and children, and my main Japanese social network had become the Japanese playgroup my children attended. Through friendships I would often hear of the different dynamics in family relationships, particularly in the context of Japanese women's cross-cultural marriages to Australian men. While these women had adapted well to Australian society and seemed to genuinely enjoy the lifestyle and bringing up their children here, there were patterns in their concerns or complaints about their husbands—namely, their husbands just "didn't get it." That is, they just couldn't understand what the women wanted and how they wanted to do things, and there was constantly a need to verbalize feelings and issues. There seemed to be a yearning for the more subtle forms of communication about which my contacts in Japan spoke so readily or, like my host father, simply took for granted. The openness through which these women communicated their frustrations with me, and then the eagerness through which their husbands divulged their own frustrations when I would see them at social gatherings, inspired the chapter in this volume and my research. I was genuinely surprised when I began "formal" research that many of these women held back and that the men barely responded to my requests to talk about the very same topics they had discussed so eagerly in other situations.

This paradox revealed to me that while my Japanese contacts in Japan had initially found my research topic humorous, over time they understood the deep significance of intimacy in their lives. My Japanese-Australian contacts, on the other hand, reacted differently. It was as though the topic touched them a little too deeply and, for some, brought to the fore some cultural differences and concerns that they weren't yet ready to tackle.

The above reflections remind us that there is never any one-size-fits-all answer to how to do research on intimacies within Japan (and elsewhere). Much depends on positionality, personality, empathy, openness, and mutual trust. The process of doing fieldwork can require that ethnographers leverage the characteristics or skills they already have, but it can also push them to transgress social norms by broaching difficult topics. It is typically assumed that to generate trust takes time, effort, and mutual empathy—and indeed we see such dynamics working well in many of the reflections written above. Yet we can also see that being so situated can limit the possibilities of sharing intimate stories. Being unsituated in social settings—being a relative stranger outside of existing social circles —can generate deep intimate confessions because this status provides a space apart from existing social bonds and the demands such bonds entail. While it is therefore often claimed that spending time deep-listening and building empathetic friendships with our interlocutors is the only way to engage in intimate research, these reflections remind us that closeness can also be, at times, an impediment to the intimate sharing of personal experiences. The politics and potential repercussions of closeness are also relevant when considering the ethics of both asking people about their experiences and representing those experiences to a broader audience.

NOTES

1. Bestor (2003) has convincingly argued that despite popular terminology, few ethnographers are able to both fully participate and observe—the two actions are often diametrically opposed—and instead he offers "inquisitive observation" as a more honest description of ethnographic methods. Given the sensitive and private nature of many "intimate topics," inquisitive observation poses challenges similar to those associated with participant observation.

2. As Kulick and Willson (1995) describe in their framing of a volume about the erotics of ethnographic fieldwork, substantial lacunae, silences, and hypocrisies exist around this topic. Although many fieldworkers might indeed have sexual relationships during the course of fieldwork, acknowledging these relationships or analyzing them as elements of the production of knowledge is sometimes met with hostility.

3. By this we mean that although many fieldworkers apparently participate in sexual relationships during the course of fieldwork, few describe such relationships as a research methodology per se. Hermanowicz (2002), for instance, suggests that although it might be helpful to metaphorically imagine a great research interview as a date or a sexual relationship—presumably precisely because of the intimacy those activities prompt—ethical standards forbid such relationships in the course of fieldwork. An exception that proves this norm comes from Lunsing, who states, "I did not endeavor to avoid having love and sex relationships in the field" because "resistance" to "men who would want to have sex with me and with whom I would want to have sex" would "only complicate matters" (1999, 178, 180). Explaining his eventual conclusions with both rare honesty and self-serving fatalism, he says, "Increasingly, therefore, I took a lighthearted view of the ethical matters relating to love relationships in the field and gradually abandoned the idea that a researcher's ethics prescribe avoiding hurting informants. Pain is part of life, and relationships may produce pain" (ibid., 183). We ask: "lighthearted" for whom? Although such assertions are far from common in anthropological writing, they give a sense of the edges of the debate over fieldwork erotics.

4. By most calculations, anthropology as a discipline is substantially more female than it used to be. There are many possible measures by which to judge how gender correlates with an interest in anthropology—for instance, the number of undergraduate majors, students in MA or doctoral programs, students who complete a PhD in anthropology, adjunct or tenure-track faculty, or authors of publications. Focusing on just one possible measure, the number of PhDs completed in the United States, the NSF "Survey of Earned Doctorates" tracks a substantial shift in gender ratios in the field. For instance,

in 1966, the earliest year of data available, 23 percent of anthropology PhDs were issued to women, a number that climbed to 47 percent in 1980 and 63.6 percent in 2012 (National Science Foundation 2012; Thorkelson 2009). Scholars have examined these gendered patterns in the United Kingdom (Mills 2003) and the United States (Philips 2010), as well as by subdiscipline (Bardolph 2014).

5. This reflection was compiled from Kawahara's doctoral dissertation (Kawahara 1996, 12–18).

6. While in common speech *nanpa* (literally, "soft faction," referencing early and late Meiji/early Taishō era distinctions among men; see Ambaras 2006) refers to "flirting" with or "hitting on" women, Miyadai (2013, 12) uses a much broader definition, claiming that it can be ascribed to any activity that attempts to build a relationship with another person (*tasha to kankei o kizuku*).

7. Some of my preliminary online findings about x-gender and the Internet have been written about in Dale (2012).

8. http://d.hatena.ne.jp/sonja23/; accessed May 9, 2016. The blog is not active at the moment.

REFERENCES

Abelmann, Nancy. 2009. *The Intimate University: Korean American Students and the Problems of Segregation*. Durham, NC: Duke University Press.

Allison, Anne. 1994. *Nightwork: Sexuality, Pleasure, and Corporate Masculinity in a Tokyo Hostess Club*. Chicago: University of Chicago Press.

Ambaras, David Richard. 2006. *Bad Youth: Juvenile Delinquency and the Politics of Everyday Life in Modern Japan*. Berkeley: University of California Press.

Aretxaga, Begoña. 2005. *States of Terror: Begoña Aretxaga's Essays*. Reno: Center for Basque Studies.

Armbruster, Heidi. 2008. "Introduction: The Ethics of Taking Sides." In *Taking Sides: Ethics, Politics and Fieldwork in Anthropology*, edited by Heidi Armbruster and Anna Laerke, 1–22. New York: Berghahn Books.

Bardolph, Dana. 2014. "A Critical Evaluation of Recent Gendered Publishing Trends in American Archaeology." *American Antiquity* 3 (19): 522–540.

Behar, Ruth. 1993. *Translated Woman: Crossing the Border with Esperanza's Story*. Boston: Beacon Press.

———. 1997. *The Vulnerable Observer: Anthropology That Breaks Your Heart*. Boston: Beacon Press.

Bestor, Theodore. C. 2003. "Inquisitive Observation: Following Networks in Urban Fieldwork." In *Doing Fieldwork in Japan*, edited by Theodore C. Bestor, Patricia Steinhoff, and Victoria Lyon Bestor, 315–334. Honolulu: University of Hawai'i Press.

Clifford, James. 1997. "Spatial Practices: Fieldwork, Travel, and the Disciplining of Anthropology." In *Anthropological Locations: Boundaries and Grounds of a Field Science*, edited by Akhil Gupta and James Ferguson, 185–222. Berkeley: University of California Press.

Dale, S. P. F. 2012. "An Introduction to X-Jendā." *Intersections: Gender and Sexuality in Asia and the Pacific* 31. URL: http://intersections.anu.edu.au/issue31/dale.htm.

Golde, Peggy, ed. 1986. *Women in the Field: Anthropological Experiences*. Berkeley : University of California Press.

Grindal, Bruce T., and Frank A. Salamone, eds. 2006. *Bridges to Humanity: Narratives on Fieldwork and Friendship*. Long Grove, IL: Waveland Press.

Hermanowicz, Joseph C. 2002. "The Great Interview: 25 Strategies for Studying People in Bed." *Journal of Qualitative Sociology* 25 (4): 479–499.

Herzfeld, Michael. 1997. *Cultural Intimacy: Social Poetics in the Nation-State.* London: Routledge.

Humo, Lynne, and June Mulcock, eds. 2004. *Anthropologists in the Field: Cases in Participant Observation.* New York: Columbia University Press.

Kawahara, Yukari. 1996. "Politics, Pedagogy, Sexuality: Sex Education in Japanese Secondary Schools." PhD dissertation, Yale University.

Killick, Evan, and Amit Desai. 2010. "Introduction: Valuing Friendship." In *The Ways of Friendship: Anthropological Perspectives,* edited by Amit Desai and Evan Killick, 1–19. New York: Berghahn Books.

Kelly, William W. 2013. "Forward: Looking Backward at a Book That Looked Forward." In Ezra Vogel, *Japan's New Middle Class,* 3rd ed., xiii–xxii. Lanham, MD: Rowman and Littlefield.

Kondo, Dorinne. 1990. *Crafting Selves: Power, Gender, and Discourses of Identity in a Japanese Workplace.* Chicago: University of Chicago Press.

Kulick, Don, and Margaret Willson, eds. 1995. *Taboo: Sex, Identity and Erotic Subjectivity in Anthropological Fieldwork.* London: Routledge.

Leonard, Karen Isaksen, Gayatri Reddy, and Ann Grodzins Gold, eds. 2010. *Histories of Intimacy and Situated Ethnography.* New Delhi: Manohar Publishers.

Lewin, Ellen, and William L. Leap. 1996. *Out in the Field: Reflections of Lesbian and Gay Anthropologists.* Urbana: University of Illinois Press.

Lunsing, Wim. 1999. "Life on Mars: Love and Sex in Fieldwork on Sexuality and Gender in Urban Japan." In *Sex, Sexuality, and the Anthropologist,* edited by Fran Markowitz and Michael Ashkenazi, 175–196. Urbana: University of Illinois Press.

Malinowski, Bronislaw. 1967. *A Diary in the Strict Sense of the Term.* London: Routledge and Kegan Paul.

Markowitz, Fran, and Michael Ashkenazi, eds. 1999. *Sex, Sexuality, and the Anthropologist.* Urbana: University of Illinois Press.

Mills, David. 2003. "Quantifying the Discipline: Some Anthropological Statistics from the UK." *Anthropology Today* 19 (3): 19–22.

Miyadai, Shinji. 2013. *"Zetsubō no gendai" no kibō no renaigaku* [A Study of the Hope of Love in a "Hopeless Age"]. Tokyo: Chūkei shuppan.

Mookherjee, Nayanika. 2008. "Friendships and Encounters on the Political Left of Bangladesh." In *Taking Sides: Ethics, Politics, and Fieldwork in Anthropology,* edited by Heidi Armbruster and Anna Laerke, 65–88. New York: Berghahn Books.

National Science Foundation. 2012. "Survey of Earned Doctorates." Data available at https://ncsesdata.nsf.gov/webcaspar/TableBuilderIndex.

Newton, Esther. 1993. "My Best Informant's Dress: The Erotic Equation in Fieldwork." *Cultural Anthropology* 8 (1): 3–23.

Ohnuki-Tierney, Emiko. 1984. *Illness and Culture in Contemporary Japan: An Anthropological View.* New York: Cambridge University Press.

Philips, Susan U. 2010. "The Feminization of Anthropology: Moving Private Discourses into the Public Sphere." *Michigan Discussions in Anthropology* 18:283–323.

Rabinow, Paul. 1977. *Reflections on Fieldwork in Morocco.* Berkeley: University of California Press.

Rubenstein, Steven L. 2014. "Fieldwork and the Erotic Economy on the Colonial Frontier." *Signs* 40 (1): 1041–1071.

Shryock, Andrew, ed. 2004. *Off Stage/On Display: Intimacy and Ethnography in the Age of Public Culture*. Stanford: Stanford University Press.

Thorkelson, Eli. 2009. "Gender Imbalance in Anthropology." Decasia.org. Available online at https://decasia.org/academic_culture/2009/09/12/gender-imbalance-in-anthropology/

Walker, Harry. 2013. *Under a Watchful Eye: Self, Power, and Intimacy in Amazonia*. Berkeley: University of California Press.

Wolcott, Harry F. 2002. *Sneaky Kid and Its Aftermath: Ethics and Intimacy in Fieldwork*. Lanham, MD: Rowman Altamira.

Contributors

❖ ❖ ❖

Allison Alexy is assistant professor in the Department of Women's Studies and the Department of Asian Languages and Cultures at the University of Michigan. She holds a BA from the University of Chicago and a PhD from Yale University. With Richard Ronald, she co-edited *Home and Family in Contemporary Japan: Continuity and Transformation* (Routledge, 2011) and is currently completing a monograph that examines divorce in contemporary Japan. Her research has been funded by the Fulbright IIE, the Japan Foundation, and the Abe Fellowship.

Emma E. Cook is associate professor in the Modern Japanese Studies Program at Hokkaido University. She holds a BSc from the University of Liverpool, an MSc from the University of Edinburgh, and a PhD in Social Anthropology from SOAS, University of London. Her book, *Reconstructing Adult Masculinities: Part-Time Work in Contemporary Japan*, was published by Routledge in 2016. Currently she is working cross-culturally on the social experiences of food allergies in Japan and the United Kingdom. Her research has been funded by the Japan Foundation and the Japanese Society for the Promotion of Science.

S. P. F. Dale is adjunct assistant professor at Hitotsubashi University. Dale holds a BA from Warwick University, an MA from Aarhus University, and a PhD from Sophia University in Global Studies. Dale's work has been published in *Intersections*.

Laura Dales is assistant professor of Asian Studies at the University of Western Australia. She holds a BA and PhD in Asian Studies from the

University of Western Australia. Her book, *Feminist Movements in Contemporary Japan*, was published by Routledge in 2009. With Romit Dasgupta and Tomoko Aoyama, she co-edited *Configurations of Family in Contemporary Japan*, published by Routledge in 2015. Her research has been funded by the Japan Society for the Promotion of Science, and the Australia Research Council.

Kathryn E. Goldfarb is assistant professor of Anthropology at the University of Colorado at Boulder. She holds a BA from Rice University and a PhD in Anthropology from the University of Chicago. Her work has been published in *Social Science and Medicine, Social Analysis*, and *Japanese Studies*.

Yukari Kawahara was a cultural anthropologist and professor at Waseda University. She held a BA from Keio University, an MA from Cornell University, and a PhD in Anthropology from Yale University. Her work has been published in *Japanese Studies*.

Kaoru Kuwajima is associate professor of the Faculty of Business Management at Meijo University in Nagoya. She holds a BA from International Christian University, MAs from the University of Chicago and Hitotsubashi University, and a PhD in Cultural Anthropology from the University of Tokyo. Her current research centers on women's lives in protection facilities and the social roles and sociocultural meanings that such facilities hold. Her work has been published in *Interdisciplinary Cultural Studies* and *Protection Facilities for Women and Prostitution-Poverty-Domestic Violence Issues*.

Elizabeth Miles is assistant professor of Asian Studies and Gender and Women's Studies in the Interdisciplinary Studies Department at Kennesaw State University. She holds a BA from the University of California at Berkeley and a PhD in Anthropology from Yale University. Her doctoral dissertation, "Men of No Value: Contemporary Japanese Manhood and the Economies of Intimacy," is an ethnographic examination of how young Japanese men are negotiating the effects of postindustrial shifts on the production, consumption, and performance of heterosexual male desire within the "economies of intimacy" of sex, love, and marriage.

Shana Fruehan Sandberg is research scientist at the National Committee for Quality Assurance, where she works on projects related to improving the quality of health care in the United States. She holds a BA in

Anthropology from the University of California at San Diego and a PhD in Comparative Human Development from the University of Chicago. Her current work is funded by the U.S. Centers for Medicare and Medicaid Services, the John A. Hartford Foundation, and the SCAN Foundation.

Diana Adis Tahhan is visiting fellow in the School of Social Sciences at the University of New South Wales. She holds a BA and a PhD in Japanese Studies from the University of New South Wales. Her book, *The Japanese Family: Touch, Intimacy and Feeling*, was published by Routledge in 2014.

Beverley Anne Yamamoto is professor of Human Sciences at Osaka University. She holds a BA from the University of London and a PhD in East Asian Studies from the University of Sheffield.

Chigusa Yamaura is junior research fellow at Wolfson College and research associate at the Nissan Institute of Japanese Studies at the University of Oxford. She holds a BA from Komazawa University, an MA in Social Sciences from the University of Chicago, and a PhD in Anthropology from Rutgers University. Her work has been published in the *Journal of Asian Studies* and *Anthropological Quarterly*.

Index

Printed in the United States
By Bookmasters